SMALL TOWN AMERICA IN WORLD WAR II

SMALL TOWN AMERICA IN WORLD WAR II

WAR STORIES FROM WRIGHTSVILLE, PENNSYLVANIA

RONALD E. MARCELLO

UNT PRESS
Denton, Texas

Printed in the United States of America.

10 9 8 7 6 5 4 3 2 1

Permissions:
University of North Texas Press
1155 Union Circle #311336
Denton, TX 76203-5017

The paper used in this book meets the minimum requirements of the American National Standard for Permanence of Paper for Printed Library Materials, z39.48.1984. Binding materials have been chosen for durability.

Library of Congress Cataloging-in-Publication Data

Marcello, Ronald E.
Small town America in World War II : war stories from Wrightsville, Pennsylvania / by Ronald E. Marcello. -- Edition: first.

pages cm

Includes bibliographical references and index.
ISBN 978-1-57441-551-3 (cloth : alk. paper) –
978-1-57441-561-2 (ebook)
1. World War, 1939-1945--Pennsylvania--Wrightsville (York County). 2. World War, 1939-1945--Social aspects--Pennsylvania--Wrightsville (York County). 3. World War, 1939-1945--Personal narratives, American. 4. Oral history--Pennsylvania--Wrightsville (York County). 5. Soldiers--Pennsylvania--Wrightsville (York County)--Interviews. 6. Interviews--Pennsylvania--Wrightsville (York County). 7. Wrightsville (York County, Pa.)--Biography. 8. Wrightsville (York County, Pa.)--History, Military--20th century. I. Title.

D769.85.P4M37 2014

940.53'74841--dc23

2014004810

The electronic edition of this book was made possible by the support of the Vick Family Foundation.

Table of Contents

List of Figures

ACKNOWLEDGMENTS

I owe debts of gratitude to several people who aided me during the time I researched and wrote this book. Christopher N. Koontz and the late Richard W. Byrd transcribed all the tape-recorded interviews to produce hundreds of pages of typescript. Their first-rate work was invaluable in enabling me to sift through the transcripts to extract pertinent information and facilitate citing. Thanks to the efforts of archivist Richard Himmel, all the transcripts and tapes have been processed and are now housed in the University Archives at the University of North Texas, where they are available for further use by researchers. I would certainly be remiss if I did not recognize the contributions Ruth and Dean ("Whitie") Harrison, who welcomed me into their home and hosted me during my frequent visits to Wrightsville to conduct the interviews. They took a keen interest in my project. Most importantly, they served as my gatekeepers by reintroducing me to persons I had known in years past and encouraging them to be interviewed. After the deaths of Ruth and "Whitie," their daughter Kathy was most helpful in finding photos and addition information about the veterans' families. Being computer-challenged, I leaned heavily on the technical expertise of staff in the Department of History: Donna Morgan Hauptmann, Devan Gerlach, and Stephanie Friday. They made my work easier and less time-consuming.

Longtime colleagues Donald Chipman and Randolph Campbell read parts of the manuscript and offered pertinent suggestions to improve it. I am most grateful for their comments. Finally, I am indebted to all the individuals, veterans and civilians, who gave their time to be interviewed and to review the drafts of the transcripts for accuracy. Since war is a deadly serious and brutal business, the veterans in particular often were asked to recount experiences that they had for so long deliberately repressed. Nevertheless, they did their very best to answer all my questions forthrightly and honestly. They are my heroes.

Ronald E. Marcello

University of North Texas

Wrightsville, Pennsylvania

Figure 1. Susquehanna Bridges

Aerial view of the fourth and fifth bridges built across the Susquehanna River between Wrightsville and Columbia. The Pennsylvania Railroad's steel bridge was completed in twenty-one working days in 1897. During its sixty-year existence, it handled, in addition to railroad traffic, horse-drawn wagons, pedestrians, and droves of cattle. After World War I, it also accommodated automobile traffic. As the use of automobiles steadily grew throughout the 1920s, it became apparent that a new bridge strictly for motor vehicle traffic was needed. Between 1929 and 1930, the fifth bridge, at that time named the York- Lancaster Inter-County Bridge, was built just south of the railroad bridge and was part of the old US Route 30 (Lincoln Highway). Approximately 7,500 feet long with a pedestrian sidewalk, it was believed to be the longest multiple-arch reinforced concrete bridge in the world for that period. It remained a toll bridge until 1943. The last train crossed the railroad bridge in March 1958, and it was dismantled for scrap in 1963–1964. Now renamed the Veterans Memorial Bridge, the fifth bridge is still used today by both motor vehicles and pedestrians.

Figure 2. Remains of Wrightsville's limekilns.

During the late 19th century, several limestone quarries opened in the town, initially processing rock for construction purposes. Eventually, the quarry owners built kilns and burned limestone to produce lime, which was used mainly for plastering and mortar. By 1894 five different sets of kilns operated in the community. All except one operator was forced out of business when the quarrying activity struck underground springs and lacked the technology for disposing the water.

Figure 3. The Pennsylvania Railroad Station located at the entry to the railroad bridge.

The station accommodated the shipment of freight and passenger service. It remained in operation until 1958 when the last train crossed the bridge.

SMALL TOWN AMERICA IN WORLD WAR II

INTRODUCTION

This book is an account of the experiences of select individuals from my hometown, Wrightsville, Pennsylvania, who lived through World War II. My primary aim was to determine how that war affected the lives of the town's inhabitants as well as the effects of the conflict on the town itself. War, by its very nature, has always been a catalyst for change, and the Second World War was no exception. The war put an end to the Great Depression of the 1930s and brought on a newfound prosperity as America became, in President Franklin D. Roosevelt's words, "the Arsenal of Democracy." According to one authority, World War II was the "closest thing to a real social revolution in the United States in this century."[1] The war touched every man, woman, and child in the United States. There was a shared sacrifice by nearly every person. Scarcely any community of any size was spared. Virtually every family had a father, son, daughter, or close relative serving in the military. Never before or since have so many people been displaced in such a short period of time. The military mobilized 16 million men and women, and the Bureau of the Census reported that in 1945 some 15.3 million civilians had moved to a different county from the one in which they lived in 1941.[2] The rapid and sudden migration of civilian workers toward war production centers often taxed or overwhelmed existing local educational facilities and community services and created housing shortages. Particularly for women and African Americans, the war created a vehicle for social and employment gains. The need for labor, as the draft drew workers into the military, opened new opportunities for groups outside the mainstream of American life.[3]

For the millions of men and women who served in the armed forces, the war took them to places they had only read about or heard of before entering the military. Those who saw combat and experienced firsthand the horrors of war returned home with different attitudes and outlooks. Often they returned to communities they no longer recognized. They came back to hometowns that were, in many ways, alien terrain after their years of military service. Having helped win the war, the veterans also returned with a newfound confidence and sense of achievement after having lived previously through the economic hopelessness of the Depression years. Millions of GIs, while contemplating their discharge from the service, saw in the future an opportunity for upward mobility for both themselves and their children. Nowhere is this better understood than in the Servicemen's Readjustment Act of 1944 (better known as the GI Bill of Rights), arguably the most successful social welfare program in US history. In short, it underscored the commitment to security and prosperity that was so much a part of the American Dream.[4]

But what about my hometown of Wrightsville? Did it experience these changes? Did defense contracts swell the town's population, thus over-burdening its schools, housing, and community services? Did the war lift the local economy from the depths of the Depression? Did large numbers of its people move elsewhere in search of better jobs? How did the war affect the women and minorities who lived there? How many men and women from the town served in the military? What did the servicemen and women experience overseas that had a profound effect on them? How had the war changed the returning veterans? To answer these questions and to determine if World War Two did, in fact, change the town and its inhabitants in significant ways, I conducted a series of oral history interviews with Wrightsville residents who experienced the war first hand at home and abroad. Before going into the interviews and the answers they provided, however, a brief history of the river town called Wrightsville is necessary.

The Susquehanna River was Wrightsville's reason for being and was the determining factor in the town's economic history. From its beginning, Wrightsville served as a transit point across the Susquehanna. In 1733 John Wright, one of the original settlers on the east bank of the river, established a crude ferry to carry people and livestock across to the west bank as they moved into the interior seeking land. As a result of Wright's business venture, the community established on the west bank assumed the name of Wright's Ferry, later to be named Wrightsville in his honor.[5]

A series of bridges eventually replaced Wright's ferry as the need for speedier and more efficient transportation became apparent and as technology changed. Six bridges at various times spanned the Susquehanna at Wrightsville. The first, completed in 1814, was 5,690 feet long and thirty feet wide and became famous as the longest covered bridge in the world at that time. It served as the east-west link until 1823 when a huge ice flow thirty to forty feet high caused water to back up until the bridge began floating away span by span until the entire structure was carried downriver.[6]

Two years later, at a location south of the first bridge, a second covered wooden bridge was built to a length of 5,620. In 1840, during the era of canal building, two tow paths for canal boats were added on the south side of the bridge, and then in 1846 rails were laid to accommodate trains. This bridge remained in operation until 28 June 1863, prior to the Battle of Gettysburg, when the Pennsylvania militia set it afire to prevent marauding Confederate troops from crossing the Susquehanna and threatening the state capital of Harrisburg or possibly moving eastward to Philadelphia.[7] It should be noted that prior to the Civil War, Wrightsville was a way station on the Underground Railroad. Spies, informers, and slave catchers closely watched this bridge since it was the only one across the Susquehanna for twenty-five miles to the north or south of Wrightsville. As a result, creative means, including boats, railway freight cars, and horse-driven carts, were employed to help fugitive slaves cross this last barrier to freedom.[8]

The third bridge, financed by the Pennsylvania Railroad Company with construction starting in 1868, was 5,390 feet long and built on the piers of its predecessor. It, too, was covered. This bridge remained in use until 30 September 1896, when a raging storm accompanied by very high winds lifted the structure and carried it away.[9] Following the destruction of the third bridge, the Pennsylvania Railroad completed the construction of a steel bridge in 1897. In addition to railroad traffic, this bridge was made available to pedestrians, horse-drawn wagons, and even herds of cattle.[10]

With the ever-increasing use of motor vehicles after World War I, it became apparent that a new bridge had become necessary. As a result, the Pennsylvania Legislature authorized York and Lancaster Counties to issue bonds in the amount of $3 million to finance the construction of the fifth bridge across the Susquehanna as part of the Lincoln Highway. Completed in 1930 at a length of 7,500 feet, this multiple-arched, steel and concrete structure operated as a toll bridge until January 1943 when the bond issue was retired. In addition to serving vehicles, it also had a pedestrian sidewalk.[11] A sixth bridge, 5,634 feet long and part of the Interstate Highway System, was completed in November 1972 at a cost of $12 million. At present both the fifth and sixth bridges are still in operation.[12]

Canals also figured prominently in Wrightsville's history. During the age of canal building, Wrightsville became a transit station for the Susquehanna and Tidewater Canal, which opened for traffic in 1840. The canal started on the east bank at the town of Columbia, crossed the river at Wrightsville, and extended along the river to Havre de Grace, Maryland, near Baltimore, for forty-five miles. A double-decked tow path platform was attached to the bridge along the downstream side. This arrangement permitted mule teams to proceed both east and west on the bridge without interfering with one another. The third bridge, which replaced the one burned in 1863, did not have a tow path. Instead, the canal company turned to steamboats to pull the canal boats across the river. Trade on the canal consisted mainly of iron ore, coal, grain, and lumber, with maximum toll revenues reached in 1870. In 1894 a flood destroyed the locks and dams on the canal, and it was never rebuilt. By that time, though, traffic had diminished to the extent that the canal could no longer compete with railroads. During the operation of the canal, Wrightsville was truly a river town. This was the most colorful and exciting period in its history, with passing boats, canal men, saloons, and hotels.[13]

In addition to ferries, bridges, and canals, Wrightsville also became a transit point for several railroads that passed through the town. In 1840, a corporation called the Wrightsville, York, and Gettysburg Railroad was formed, and for a number of years it operated in connection with the Baltimore and Susquehanna Railway, thus connecting the town with York and several towns in Maryland. There was a continuous line from Baltimore to Philadelphia by way of York and Wrightsville to Columbia, joining the Philadelphia and Columbia Railway at Columbia. As the folly of building so many short line railroads became more obviously financially unsound, consolidation occurred. In time the Pennsylvania Railroad Company absorbed its smaller competitors and in 1897 built the fourth bridge across the Susquehanna. This bridge served the railroad for sixty years, after which the link through Wrightsville became unprofitable due to the steady growth of motor vehicles for carrying passengers and freight. In 1958 the last train crossed the river. In 1963 the Pennsylvania Railroad awarded a contract for the dismantling of the steel bridge. By December 1964 all the steel had been converted to scrap iron, and only the stone piers remained.[14]

With the end of the Civil War, the people of Wrightsville turned their attention to industrial and business development thanks to the availability of land and water transportation. During the late nineteenth century, several limestone quarries opened, initially processing rock for construction purposes. The firms transported their product to different states via the Susquehanna and Tidewater Canal. Other entrepreneurs soon entered the limestone business and built kilns that burned the limestone to produce lime. At that time both the quarrying and kiln operations became the largest employers of Wrightsville's African-American population.[15]

Wrightsville was also a participant in the post Civil War industrial revolution. By the turn of the twentieth century, iron foundries were the mainstays of the local economy. Pennsylvania produced an incredible variety of iron and steel products. Numerous towns in the state had at least one iron foundry, and many, like Wrightsville, had two or three. In Wrightsville the proprietors built their foundries along the railroad tracks where they would have easy access to the necessary raw materials. The first foundry to come on line was the Wrightsville Hardware Company in 1880. The Susquehanna Casting Company began production in 1892, and in 1906 the Riverside Foundry Company started business.[16]

During the "Prosperity Decade" of the 1920s, other businesses flourished, too. Second in importance to the foundries were the cigar factories. Tobacco was a principal cash crop for many farmers in York and Lancaster Counties, and this crop was used for making cigars and chewing tobacco. During the 1920s the town had nine cigar manufacturers employing both men and women producing handmade cigars. Wrightsville's third largest employers were two garment factories that also employed both sexes.[17]

Job creation and the ensuing prosperity led to a gradual increase in Wrightsville's population following the Civil War. The town grew from 1,544 inhabitants in 1870 to 2,247 (including sixty-four African Americans) by 1930. In addition to the three main employers, Wrightsville could claim a national bank, a building and loan association, a small brass foundry, two blacksmith shops, three colliers, two lumberyards, stone quarries, a department store, five restaurants, seven grocers, three hotels, a movie theater, a local newspaper, and a hardware store as well as butchers, ice dealers, garages, contractors and builders, clothiers, plasterers, paperhangers, and plumbers. The town also had its own water and power companies.[18]

The "Prosperity Decade" came crashing down with the collapse of the national economy and the onslaught of the Great Depression that affected Wrightsville as it did every industrial town in Pennsylvania. The foundries were particularly hard hit. Wrightsville Hardware temporarily went out of business while Susquehanna Casting and Riverside Foundry reduced their workforce while cut wages and hours for remaining workers. One of the few businesses that continued to do fairly well were the cigar factories, for the so-called "vice" industries seemed to prosper even in hard times.

As the war clouds gathered over Europe and Asia, the town's economy started to improve. Employment began to pick up as the federal government began to award contracts for the production of military equipment. In addition, the reinstitution of conscription helped alleviate the unemployment situation as single young men left for Army training camps. On the other hand, the Great Depression had forced significant numbers of the African-American community to move away. For some, hard times hit before the coming of the Great Depression. When the stone quarries struck underground springs after blasting the rock, technology was not available to pump away the water, so they were abandoned. Unemployed African Americans were unable to secure work in the foundries because all skilled positions, molders specifically, were considered the exclusive sphere of white males, and during the Depression, when all jobs were scarce, even the unskilled jobs went to whites. When Japanese forces struck Pearl Harbor on 7 December 1941, Wrightsville was essentially a self-contained town inhabited predominantly by white Anglo-Saxon Protestants. With the coming of war, as for almost all Americans, the citizens of Wrightsville pitched in either by serving in the military or contributing to the war effort at home.

The story of Wrightsville's citizens during the war is best told by the people themselves. I conducted these interviews in settings where the interviewees felt most comfortable, usually in their homes, and they were one-on-one sessions with no one else present. Most took the interviews seriously. They prepared notes for topics they very much wished to include and brought out photographs to help give a clearer understanding about the events being discussed. My office staff then prepared verbatim transcripts of the interviews and each person had an opportunity to read the preliminary draft and make corrections or further clarifications. At the end of the process, each participant received a complimentary hardbound copy of his or her interview.

Oral histories are not necessarily infallible sources of information. Time dims and distorts memories. The interviews in this book were primarily conducted during the late 1990s, almost sixty years after the events discussed by the participants. In some cases the interviewees' memories for hard facts and chronological sequence had deteriorated. This often resulted in their recounting personal impressions or perceptions of events in which they had participated. The best means of getting as close to accuracy as possible was to do extensive background research beforehand and going into the interview armed with an outline of the topics to be discussed.

No interviews with African Americans appear in this book. The records of the local American Legion post indicate that no African American living in Wrightsville at that time served in the military during World War II, and the town's African-American cemetery has no World War II markers to indicate the grave site of a black serviceman from that conflict. The few African Americans still residing there during the war were older persons whose children had all moved away during the Great Depression to seek employment elsewhere. The last black student graduated from Wrightsville High School in 1929. During its earlier history, Wrightsville had separate churches for blacks, a segregated school system, and a "colored" cemetery. The town's major industries—cigar factories, garment and sewing plants, and the three iron foundries—employed only whites. At one time local limestone quarries were the main employers of black laborers, but by 1930 all but one quarry had gone out of business. During the war, the foundries employed just two or three older African-American men as unskilled laborers. By the time of America's entry into World War II, Wrightsville's African Americans were almost an invisible minority for all intents and purposes. Thus, no African Americans were available for interviews.[19]

So, did World War II have a profound and lasting effect on the Wrightsville and its citizens? It did change individuals. Certainly, the veterans returned as changed men and women. They entered the military as immature boys and girls for the most part, but they came home as mature men and women after events on the battlefield and life away from home in the stateside military. Their experiences during the war gave them a new sense of self worth after being beaten down by the Great Depression. For most of the interviewees, service during World War II was an unpleasant interruption, and afterwards they were eager to return to civilian life, get a steady job, marry, purchase a home, and raise a family. For civilians on the home front, the war for them meant full employment, a return to prosperity after ten years of economic depression, and for the first time some women took jobs that before 1941 had never been open to them. Women now looked for employment beyond their traditional work in the garment and cigar factories.

On the other hand, unlike many other towns of the World War II era, Wrightsville did not change physically. There was, for example, no influx of outside workers looking jobs in the foundries because the skilled molders there were older men with families. In turn the local schools were not overburdened with new students, nor did the town's infrastructure come under stress in any way. There was no need for new housing or expanded city services. As was true before the war, Wrightsville continued as a white, Anglo-Saxon, Protestant village with a population that was about the same as it had been in 1940. Even today the town's population remains steady at about 2,200 people. Both veterans and civilians agreed that postwar Wrightsville was the same self-contained town it had been prior to 1941. Just like the Susquehanna River, Wrightsville had not changed.[20]

Notes

1. Geoffrey Perrett, *Days of Sadness, Years of Triumph: The American People, 1939-1945* (New York: Coward, McCann, Geoghegan, Inc., 1973), 10.
2. US Department of Commerce, Bureau of the Census, *Total Population of Ten Congested Population Areas: 1944*, Series CA-1, No. 11 (Washington, DC: US Government Printing Office, 1944.)
3. Allan M. Winkler, *Home Front USA: America during World War II* (Arlington Heights, IL: Harlan Davidson, Inc., 1986), 43-47.
4. The GI Bill of Rights provided liberal unemployment benefits, gave veterans preference in finding jobs, offered them substantial educational assistance in the form of tuition payments and living supplements, and guaranteed loans for the purchase of a small business, farm, or home. See Winkler, 89.
5. Donald Lehman, *Wrightsville, 1736-1976: Gateway to the West* (Wrightsville: Historic Wrightsville Association, 1976), 9.
6. Ibid., 9-10.
7. Ibid., 10.
8. Ibid., 14; Fergus M. Bordewich, *Bound for Canaan: The Underground Railroad and the War for the Soul of America* (New York: HarperCollins Publishers, 2008), 137, 146, 137-138.
9. Lehman, 14.
10. Ibid.
11. Ibid., 11.
12. Ibid.
13. Ibid., 11-12: William H. Shank, *The Amazing Pennsylvania Canals* (York, PA: The Historical Society of York County, 1965), 4-5, 46, 53-55; and Ronald E. Shaw, *Canals for a Nation: The Canal Era in the United States, 1790-1860* (Lexington: The Univ. of Kentucky Press, 1990), 55-56.
14. Lehman, 61; Henry V. Poor, *History of the Railroads and Canals of the USA* (New York: John H. Schultz & Co., 1860), 516-519; Roger B. Saylor, *The Railroads of Pennsylvania* (University Park, PA: the Pennsylvania State Univ. Press, 1964), 123.
15. Lehman, 41, 49; Historic Wrightsville, Inc., *Historic Limekilns of Wrightsville, PA*, Pamphlet, n.d.; The Historical Committee, *Wrightsville's Book of Facts* (York: H. O. Birnstock, Trimmer Printing Company, 1923), 34-35.

16. Ibid., 41-44; Philip S. Klein and Ari Hoogenboom, *A History of Pennsylvania* (University Park, PA: The Pennsylvania State Univ. Press, 1980), 345.
17. Historical Committee, 85, 89, 92.
18. Ibid., 84-93; US Department of Commerce, Bureau of the Census, *15th Census of the US, 1930* (Washington, DC: Government Printing Office, 1932), 1:958 and 3 (pt. 2): 748.
19. Wrightsville High School Alumni 100th Anniversary, booklet, n.p.
20. By contrast, for studies of towns dramatically transformed by World War II, see: Louis Fairchild, *They Called It the War Effort: Oral Histories from World War II Orange, Texas* (Austin: Eakin Press, 1993; rev. ed. Denton, TX: Texas State Historical Association, 2012); Marc Miller, *The Irony of Victory: World War II and Lowell, Massachusetts* (Champaign: Univ. of Illinois Press, 1988); and Robert G. Spinney, *World War II in Nashville: Transformation of the Homefront* (Knoxville: Univ. of Tennessee Press, 1998). For an account of a large city transformed by World War II, see J'Nell Pate, *Arsenal of Defense: Fort Worth's Military Legacy* (Denton, TX: Texas State Historical Association, 2011).

PART I

WRIGHTSVILLE: THE HOME FRONT

According to historian Geoffrey Perrett, World War II was the "closest thing to a real social revolution the United States has known in this century."[1] Other prominent historians agree with his assessment. They argue that participation in the war brought economic, political, and social change to an unprecedented degree. Scarcely any community of any size was spared.[2] In short, as one historian emphasized, "World War II affected every man, woman, and child in America."[3] How about the river town of Wrightsville? Did these far-reaching changes apply to this small town with a 1940 population of 2,200?

Wrightsville's leading citizens wasted little time in contributing to the war effort. On 19 March 1942, not long after the Pearl Harbor attack, the Borough Council established a Council of National Defense. Members of the Council included the town's leading citizens: the town's Chief Burgess John Redman as presiding officer; Prof. Preston E. Ziegler, principal of the Wrightsville public schools; Rev. Jacob Spangler, pastor of Trinity Lutheran Church; Dr. B. A. Hoover, physician and founder of the Wrightsville Building and Loan Association; Marlin Etzweiler, mortician and furniture store proprietor; foundry superintendant Hiram E. Nauss; Clyde Thompson, Borough Council President and manager of the Huntzburger Department Store; clothier Lehman Weitzel; Scoutmaster William Frey; and businessmen Joseph Lyle, Charles Hammer, and Alfred Williams. These men enrolled citizens for civil defense activities. The Council organized a system of air raid drills and blackouts, as well as appointing a network of air raid wardens to enforce these measures on a block by block basis. It also engaged citizens as first aid personnel and auxiliary police. Enlisting the help of the Boy Scout and Girl Scout troops, the Council organized scrap and salvage drives and on one occasion showed its appreciation for the services performed by the Scouts by voting a contribution of $5.00 to each troop. At the county level, the Council of National Defense appointed Reuben Strickler, business manager for the Riverside Foundry, as Wrightsville's representative on the York County Draft Board and the York County Ration Board. Because the two bridges across the Susquehanna River were considered important to the war effort, the Council obtained sentries from the National Guard to protect it.[4]

Individual citizens contributed in other ways. To help finance the war effort, they bought war bonds and stamps. With more than three hundred men in the armed forces, women took over some of the traditional male positions in the foundries while others sought employment in the defense industries of York and Lancaster. With rubber tires and gasoline on the rationed materials list, some townfolk simply put their automobiles on blocks and retired them for the duration of the war. Those who worked outside town organized carpools to transport fellow workers to job sites. As in other towns throughout the country, housewives saved fats and grease, which could be turned in for red ration points at the local butcher shop and then recycled and used for the production of glycerol, an ingredient in dynamite and lubricants. For the scrap drives, they donated flattened tin cans, rubber items such as hot-water bottles and galoshes, and aluminum pots and pans. Men saved the tin foil that lined their cigarette packages. Wives and sisters organized social groups where they made gloves and socks for men serving overseas. In addition to participating in the scrap metal drives, the local Boy Scout troop collected old newspapers for recycling, and they took to the fields and meadows outside town to gather milkweed pods because the fibers made excellent fillers for life jackets. To supplement scarce food supplies, many citizens participated in the cultivation of both individual and community victory gardens. In a town that had endured the Depression years, Wrightsville's citizens found no difficulty in being thrifty. They took quite literally the admonition: "Use it up, wear it out, make do, or do without."[5]

By the end of the war, more than 330 of Wrightsville's men and women served in the armed forces. Ten died while on duty and two others were taken as prisoners of war. Numerous families had several sons in the service. Mr. and Mrs. Samuel Hake had seven sons in the military, while Mr. and Mrs. Warner Morrison had six sons serving. Mr. and Mrs. John Wallick contributed four sons, while the four sons of Mr. and Mrs. William Crumbling also served. Eleven members of the Wrightsville High School basketball team, winners of the York County championship for the 1940-41 season, were all in the military by 1944, as was their coach, Joseph Wolfe. The high school graduating class of 1943 had just four males; the Class of 1944, four; and the Class of 1945, just one. Historian Stephen Ambrose was correct when he aptly referred to the US Army racing across Europe in 1944-45 as the "Children's Crusade" with hundreds of thousands of eighteen-to-twenty-one-year-old soldiers.[6]

With the exception of the return of prosperity and hope for a better future, however, World War II did not change Wrightsville or its citizens very much. Since the foundries had a workforce made up primarily of older married men with children, there was no influx of new workers seeking to replace the young men who entered military. It was true, however, that a few women took on foundry employment and paved the way for a larger influx of women into the foundries after the war. Unlike many other communities, Wrightsville's population did not swell with new residents, so there was no strain on the school system, housing, infrastructure, or social services. With male teachers being drafted or volunteering for military duty, local citizens with college educations took over classroom functions, and with so many young men entering the military before graduation, the high school athletic teams were disbanded for the duration. The population in 1950 was about the same as it had been in 1940 despite the return of the veterans and the beginning of the baby boom generation.

The following excerpts from interviews corroborate, nevertheless, the comment of Americans of the World War II generation that "we were all in it together." This response certainly applied to the residents of Wrightsville. Through their own words, a local businessman, women defense workers, a State Department employee, a teenager, and even a man rejected for military service demonstrate how the community contributed to the war effort.

Notes

1. Geoffrey Perrett, *Days of Sadness, Years of Triumph: The American People, 1939-1945* (New York: Coward, McCann and Geoghegan, Inc., 1973), 10.

2. See Allan M. Winkler, *Home Front USA: America during World War II* (Arlington Heights, IL: Harlan Davidson, Inc., 1986); Richard Polenberg, *War and Society: The United States, 1941-1945* (Philadelphia: J. B. Lippincott Company, 1972); John M. Blum, *V Was for Victory: Politics and American Culture during World War II* (New York: Harcourt-Brace, 1976); and James MacGregor Burns, *Roosevelt: The Soldier of Freedom* (New York: Harcourt-Brace, 1970).

3. Louis Fairchild, *They Called It the War Effort: Oral Histories from Orange, Texas* (Austin: Eakin Press, 1993), xix.

4. Wrightsville Borough Council, Minutes, 1 May 1942 and 3 July 1944, Wrightsville Borough Municipal Authority, Wrightsville, PA.

5. Richard R. Lingeman, *Don't You Know There's a War Going On: The American Home Front, 1941-1945* (New York: G. P. Putnam's Sons, 1970), 259. See also William L. O'Neill, *A Democracy at War: America's Fight at Home and Abroad in World War II* (New York: the Free Press, 1993), 201-266; Richard Overy, *Why the Allies Won* (New York: W. W. Norton & Co., 1996), 180-208; and David Kennedy, *Freedom from Fear: The American People in Depression and War, 1929-1945* (New York: Oxford Univ. Press, 1999), 615-668.

6. Stephen Ambrose, *Citizen Soldiers: The US Army from the Beaches of Normandy to the Bulge and the Surrender of Germany* (New York: Simon & Shuster, 1997), 285-286; personal clipping file of Mrs. Alfred Forry taken from the York, PA, newspapers during World War II; Wrightsville High School Alumni 100th Anniversary, 1895-1895, booklet, n.p.

Figure 4. Donald Smith on left with his father

Chapter 1

Donald "Red" Smith

Riverside Foundry Executive

Born on 28 September 1912, Donald "Red" Smith was the son of the founder of Riverside Foundry, Harry K. Smith. After a very short collegiate career, Donald returned to the foundry and never left. In his interview he sheds light on the attitude of his father and other small businessmen toward Franklin D. Roosevelt and the New Deal, the effects of the Great Depression on the foundry business, organized labor, and the return to prosperity as the country entered World War II. Federal spending for the war effort, not the New Deal programs, lifted the economy from the depths of economic hard times during the 1930s. During the war, Riverside prospered due to government subcontracts for the production of cast iron hand grenade and rifle grenade casings, fuse wells for bombs, and cast iron collars for parachute flares. The contracts meant steady wages for foundry workers while labor shortages due to men going into the military services led to the employment of women in the foundry for the first time, a trend that continued during the postwar years. Profits resulting from the government contracts enabled Riverside Foundry to modernize and expand. Because of wartime shortages and rationing, workers who now had income had nowhere to spend it. As a result of this pent-up demand, Riverside was able to make a smooth transition from military to civilian production after the war. Donald Smith raised his family in Wrightsville, and he continued to play an active role in the management of Riverside Foundry right up to his death on 7 October 2004.[1]

Never a very serious college student, Donald Smith left the University of Delaware in 1933 after attending for two years and went to work in his father's foundry. He remained active in the operations of Riverside Foundry for the rest of his life:

"I didn't like school, and I was not a very good student. So, I think my father was glad that I dropped out. There were three of us going to college at that time, so my father said it was getting to be too much of a financial load for him to send my sister, brother, and me to college. It was right at the depth of the Depression, so I came home and worked at the foundry, the days that the foundry worked. At that time we were working two, maybe three, days a week. I helped out wherever they needed someone to fill in. I really did a little bit of everything. I did some drilling and tapping; I shifted weights in the afternoons; and I helped with the cupola. I even tried my hand at molding a little bit. That way I got a pretty well-rounded experience after learning all facets of foundry work. I never left the foundry again. Then, for some reason or another, foundry work just got into my blood, and I liked it.

"My father never encouraged me to get interested because he thought the foundry business was not going to be a good business. A lot of foundries closed altogether during the Depression. In fact, the Wrightsville Hardware Company temporarily closed down altogether, and Susquehanna Casting just limped along. Our workforce went from thirty down to twenty-two or twenty-three men. If we got two or three days a week, it was good. Our old ledger book from which I'm reading indicates that in 1934 we worked a total of 104 days. The total wages paid to molders was $6,843, while day laborers received $4,003. Including salaried employees and the office force, we paid out a total of $13,707 in 1934. Sales in that year amounted to $22,641, and we shipped just 345,343 pounds of castings. But the men seemed to survive because everybody had their own gardens, or they'd go out and help farmers and get things. When we had work, we worked full days. There's one thing about a foundry that's different from other industries—you needed a full day to perform all the processes. The molders started at 7:00 in the morning and molded until 2:00 in the afternoon. Then at 2:00 they would 'pour off' for about an hour-and-a-half. Then everybody from other departments of the foundry had to come in after they poured the iron, and they would shift weights and knock off the castings.[2]

The travails of the Great Depression led to the election of Franklin D. Roosevelt and the coming of the New Deal. Like many small businessmen, Smith's father, Harry K. Smith, reacted angrily to new federal regulations, labor legislation, wages and hours legislation, unions, and Social Security:

"My father was a solid Republican, and he was solidly for Herbert Hoover. All you had to do was come into his office and say, 'Did you see what Roosevelt is doing?' and that would set him off. Of course, unions became very strong during that time, and in 1936 they organized all the foundries in this area. My father went into the foundry and told the workers that if they joined a union, he was closing the doors: 'That's all there is to it! I'm not going to have a union!' We had a group of older men, and they were pretty sensible. They said they wouldn't go along with it. The workers at Susquehanna Casting and Wrightsville Hardware joined the union, but we never had any. So, for some reason or another, they never bothered us after that. But they organized all the foundries in the York and Lancaster county area.

"There is no question that Roosevelt was a very controversial figure, and my father, with every election that would come up, was hoping that he would be defeated. Like most small business people, he had a *laissez-faire* attitude. I don't think you would have found a Democrat among them because the Democrats started to tell them how to run their business. They would tell them how many hours the workers could work, and they set minimum wages. Of course, then we had to pay them time-and-half for overtime, and they now had paid holidays—all those things that were new. In the foundry, they used to work a ten-hour day. That was the standard day. My father said, 'We just can't do those things. That's going to wreck everything.' At that time they also had Social Security, and that was another thing that my father did not like. That was quite an innovation. They were radical changes, and for someone in his sixties, he thought it was awful that he had to make all those changes. He didn't like Mrs. Roosevelt either because she was kind of radical for that age. Women just didn't do those things, I mean, go around and talk and stir up people. But I think, however, that history is going to record that Franklin Roosevelt did a good job.

With war clouds gathering in Europe and Asia during the late 1930s, the foundry business began to show signs of improvement. This, in turn, led to labor shortages:

"It was really in 1937 that there seemed to be a little more business, and then in 1938 we were getting orders. We started getting in five days a week, and we were getting backlogs on orders. People now had more money to spend. But then the labor market started getting short because everybody was busy. The federal government built the Naval Ordnance Plant in York, and they needed six or seven hundred people. That plant paid wages that were 10 to 20 percent higher than what we paid, and the foundry was never the first choice of most young boys to work in. Then it wasn't too long that they started drafting kids, and that took another bite out of the labor market. It was tough, but we were fortunate that our men were older. Of course, the new companies that needed workers kind of overlooked these older people, and they didn't try to hire them. So, we had a lot of older people, and they stayed with us. Also, very few of the older working people had automobiles, so they had no transportation to get to the Naval Ordnance Plant. Plus, there was the matter of education. A lot of them couldn't read or write, so they couldn't fill out an application.

Once the United States got into the war, dislike for Roosevelt and the New Deal receded into the background as patriotism and profits received top priority at Riverside Foundry. In 1941 the foundry received a very lucrative government sub-contract from a larger foundry in Littlestown, Pennsylvania.[3]

"At the Littlestown foundry, there were two men from Wrightsville who started that foundry. They went up there in 1915, a little before World War I. Their name was Snyder. My father had always been good to them; he helped them when they wanted to get started. They had a hand grenade contract, and then they got a rifle grenade contract. They also made a thing that you screwed into the end of a bomb [called the fuse well]. It was more or less a plug where the fuse would go in. They had so much work that they couldn't handle it all themselves, so they asked if we would help them out by making the castings. They did the machining and the painting. They said, 'Hey! We won't be able to make this many castings. Will you help us out?' And we said, 'Yes, we'll help you out.' Then we got together on a price. It was a very informal agreement. I don't think there was any legal document, but I think they sent us one of their order forms, ordering so many grenades. The Snyders did not have a cost-plus contract with the government.[4] They had to submit a bid every year because all the foundries wanted to get that hand grenade contract, so they had to bid them tight. Littlestown was not the only foundry making hand grenades. There were a lot of foundries that were making many, many more. That work lasted for two years for us.

"After they got the hand grenade contract, they got the rifle grenade contract. Then they got this big contract for making the fuse wells for bombs. They also made a lot of other little things. For instance, we were making a ring for when they put out these flares from an airplane. It was another government contract. It was like a collar and was made of cast iron. It had a little parachute attached to it, and it would come down slowly. On this contract, the guy came in and said he needed to have more of these rings. He said, 'I've got to have more of those. What can

I do to get more of them?' I said, 'We can't give you any more than one molder to increase the number.' He then said, 'You get me more, and I'll give you twenty-five cents for every one you make over the original order.' I thought, 'Oh, my goodness!' He didn't know that I was the owner's son. I did make him more. So, between the two foundries, it was good business.

"We made more than half their hand grenades. During the war the two foundries made 100,000 hand grenades a month, and we made about 60,000 of them and sent them up to Littlestown. We also made about the same number of rifle grenades each month. We also got priority to buy material when we were making those grenades. The Snyders had to deliver the grenades to the Picatinny Arsenal in New Jersey—100,000 castings a month. They had to get this shipment ready and put it in a certain space. Then the inspectors would come up and pick boxes and check them. The Snyders always worried that the inspector would pick out a couple boxes and find that they weren't what they were supposed to be.

"We had at that time a good group of molders. For instance, there was Karl Stroppel, Jim Townsley, Harry Fahringer, and 'Nutcher' [Clyde] Siltzer. 'Nutcher' was our biggest producer of hand grenades. He used to run 200-220 molds a day, which is a lot. The only problem with him was that now and then he'd take a day off, and he wouldn't show up. But he was a good molder, and fast.

"We were one of the last foundries to make hand grenades. In fact, the last year, Littlestown didn't want to bid on them. The war was over, so this was a much smaller contract. We then bid that directly to the Picatinny Arsenal. We got much more for that contract because the war was over and everyone was converting to peacetime work.

These government contracts returned Riverside Foundry to profitability and led to the modernization and expansion of the company:

"Those were two good jobs for us. By this time, I was pretty much in sole command of the company, so I was able to get some things that we wanted to improve the efficiency of our business. We bought our first core machine. Before that, cores were always made by hand. Then we bought a second core machine and a third one to keep up with production. We also had to enlarge our cupola so that we could melt more metal. By doing these things we were growing. And, through all this, we seemed to be able to pick up enough people. I'd say that by that time we were probably up to around ninety workers.

For the first time in its history, Riverside Foundry began hiring women to meet production demands:

"We did start to use some women in the machine shop. Some were used in the core room, like, filing the fins off the cores. That was the first time we used women laborers. We had no bathroom facilities for women. I don't know what they did. My father wasn't very much in favor of hiring women, but at the time he didn't say too much. I think the male workers on the foundry floor accepted our use of women.

"As a rule at that time, there was some discrimination against women here in that they didn't get paid quite as much. They didn't make quite as much as men. They were hired at a lesser starting wage, because they used to say, 'Well, they can't lift heavy boxes and move them here and there.' Some of the men around that area had to do that. But when it came to the machine shop, the women could do the work better than men.

"Work like this was something new for women, a new opportunity for them, and they worked hard. Women were more conscientious than men because women were glad to have the opportunity. Most women in Wrightsville worked in silk mills or garment factories or cigar factories, and foundry wages were much better than that type of work. As I remember, the first women we hired were young and single.

Even with a priority for obtaining raw materials, at times Donald Smith had to use ingenuity in obtaining what was needed to produce the grenades:

"We had our normal suppliers that we used before the war, one like Bethlehem Steel. We used to buy pig iron from them. With the coming of war, however, they just simply quit supplying us; they cut us off. They wouldn't sell us anything because they said they needed it themselves. That's the way Bethlehem Steel operated. They needed the pig iron to make their own steel, so they weren't going to give up any of their pig iron. Then there were a couple independent furnaces that made only pig iron, but their pig iron was so much in demand by everybody. So, we really had a difficult time in scurrying around to meet the demand.

"One time my cousin, Mike Smith, who had a coal truck, and I went all over town hunting iron, wherever we found a piece, to get enough to charge the cupola for one day. On another occasion we took up railroad tracks and searched anyplace we could to find a piece of steel. It was part of the patriotic spirit that we worked to keep the fighting going.

"I was responsible for obtaining the necessary pig iron. That was my job. There was a fellow by the name of Boots, who came into the office one day, a pig iron broker. He said, 'Did you ever try Spanish iron?' Of course, we were always concerned about quality, for instance, that the analysis would be off. We had used pig iron from South America before, but whether or not this was made in South America, I can't say. But this was one of those times that I took a chance, and I bought eight carloads. That was a lot for us. I went up to the bank to get a draft. We had to send a letter of credit to get the eight carloads. We had money in the bank for a letter of credit, but the local cashier at First National Bank didn't know how to handle a letter of credit, so he got help from somebody in York.

"That was one of the best things I ever did because it was good iron. As it turned out, it was just as good as the American iron, and we bought it for about a third less. Plus, at that period of time, pig iron in this country doubled in price. We used about a car a month of the Spanish iron. I can remember that they all came in at the same time, and I thought, 'What are we going to do with it?' We had so much Spanish pig iron that the Farquhar Company, a big farm machinery company in York, wanted to buy a carload of this pig iron that I had. We had made a lot of castings for Farquhar, so we had a good relationship with them. So, to keep in good standing, I agreed to sell them a carload of this pig iron. I'll never forget. I sold them a carload of pig iron, but I charged them the going rate at the time. The buyer up there said, 'I thought you said you bought that pig iron on sale.' I said, 'I did. But now you'll have to pay the going rate.' Well, I didn't change the price because it was my good fortune that I looked ahead and bought it. Why should I sell to him cheaply? They took the pig iron, but he never forgave me for that deal.

Organized labor made its most important gains in union membership during World War II. Management was hesitant to oppose unionization because of the threat of strikes, which would cut into the profits to be had through government contracts after the long drought of the 1930s. Even during the war, however, Smith continued to resist the organization of his foundry by the International Molders Union:

"That was always a threat, always in the back of my mind, but for some reason, probably good fortune, maybe with the war and all, they didn't really put on a good drive at that time. What we did do was watch what the other foundries were paying their people. We monitored Susquehanna Castings and Wrightsville Hardware, both of which had unions, and we tried to match their wages and benefits. I also had a good relationship with 'Bud' [Ralph] Wilton, who owned Susquehanna Castings. Also, it was the big shops that the unions wanted, and that's one of the reasons, I think, that they never bothered us too much. The union was more of a nuisance than a threat.

"I, myself, felt that I had a lot of responsibility. I always thought that the people of Wrightsville treated me well, and I always wanted to show that respect and treat them well. I think we had good people here. If you are fair, your workers have no need for unions. I always tried to be fair. I could see the advantage of a union at General Motors, where you have tens of thousands of people working, but where you've got a hundred people, you have to be more flexible. So, unions just don't work in small shops. It's so much easier to operate without a union in a small shop.

In mid-1945, with the war winding down, Smith and Riverside Foundry prepared for the conversion to the production of civilian goods:

"We saw the war winding down, but, of course, there was so much pent-up demand that we were pretty sure that we weren't going to have any problem. Everybody else was waiting to take advantage of the pent-up demand, and there were people coming here and wanting to know if we'd make castings for them, for things like ice cream freezers and food choppers. Those kinds of civilian goods were cut off during the war. One of the things that we made a lot of were pumps, pumps like you'd use out on a farm or for water systems. To this day, that's still a big business for us. So, I would say that for the first couple years after the war, we had no trouble getting work. There were people knocking on our door to give us work.

"We also started to get more secondary work—machining, painting, and some assembly. As a result we had no problems absorbing the returning veterans who needed jobs. And we were hiring more women all the time. We put in better bathroom facilities. When we started John Wright Company, women made up about 80 percent of the workforce. John Wright Company assembles and paints finished cast iron and aluminum products made in the foundry for households."

In the years since World War II, the foundry continued to prosper and expand. Eventually, the company was reorganized as Donsco with foundries and other operations beyond Wrightsville. Although he passed on the supervision of Donsco to his son-in-law, Donald Smith continued to play an active role in the business up to his death on 7 October 2004.

Notes

1. Donald M. Smith, interview by the author, 12 August 1996, transcript, OH1147, Oral History Collection, University Archives, University of North Texas, Denton, TX.

2. Note: "Pouring off" was the process by which molten iron released from the cupola was caught in long-handled ladles and poured into the molds on the floor by each molder's work bench.

3. For an account of how wartime contracts to big business filtered down to smaller enterprises like Riverside Foundry, see Arthur Herman, *Freedom's Forge: How American Business Produced Victory in World War II* (New York: Random House, 2012). Herman reveals how two extraordinary businessman—automobile magnate William Knudsen and shipbuilder Henry J. Kaiser—helped cajole and inspire business leaders across the country to mobilize the "Arsenal of Democracy" that propelled the Allies to victory in World War II.

4. Note: Cost-plus allowed the war goods producer to overextend himself in expanding production, knowing that his increased costs would be met by the government. He had a guaranteed customer who generously assured him of both his costs and a nice profit. Further, in many cases his plant expansion would be underwritten by either a low-interest loan from the Reconstruction Finance Corporation or by direct government handout to build new production capacity in return for paying a reasonable rent on the facilities as long as he used them and a further option to buy the facility at the war's end for a relatively low price. See Richard R. Lingeman, *Don't You Know There's a War Going On: The American Home Front, 1941-1945* (New York: G. P. Putnam's Sons, 1970), 107-134.

Figure 5. Pauline “Sis” Leber

Chapter 2

Pauline "Sis" Leber

"Swing Girl"
York Safe & Lock Company

Pauline (née Haugh) Leber was born on 28 June 1914, on a small subsistence farm just outside Wrightsville in Hellam Township. Known by the nickname of "Sis" all her life, she graduated from Wrightsville High School in 1934 just before her seventeenth birthday. Shortly before World War II started, in 1940, she married Stewart "Whis" Leber, who went into the Navy in 1943. In her interview "Sis" describes the transition from farm work to industrial work. She ultimately decided to take a job with York Safe & Lock Company, which, after the war started, converted from making civilian products to manufacturing gun tubes for various caliber antiaircraft weapons. As the interview unfolds, it is clear that her decision to work at York Safe & Lock was based on both patriotic and economic considerations. She was also motivated by the fact that three of her brothers, in addition to her husband, were serving in the military during the war. "Sis" Leber's interview is an example of how World War II influenced the widespread entry of women into the industrial workforce to assume jobs that had been previously unavailable to them. After the war, she and her husband eventually moved into Wrightsville where they raised their family. A widow, Pauline Leber died on 26 June 2005.[1]

Pauline Haugh grew up in a large family on a small subsistence farm just outside Wrightsville:

"I had five brothers: James, Thomas, Edwin, Mervin, and Bill. I was the twin sister of Mervin ('Bo'). They all called me 'Little Sister.' But 'Bo' couldn't say 'Sister,' so it boiled down to 'Sis.' He got the name 'Bo' because I couldn't say 'Brother.' I would say 'Bo' instead of 'Brother,' so that is how we got our nicknames.

"The farm had fifty-six acres—farmland and woodland. We had a cattle —a lot of cattle—hogs, chickens, geese, turkeys, everything. We raised food for them—wheat, corn. We had fruit orchards—peach, apple. We raised all kinds of vegetables, fruits, and berries. It was a nice farm. In fact, it was our livelihood. My father worked on the railroad as a salaried man at the ticket office in Wrightsville, but for three years of his life he was very sick and couldn't work. Of course, he still had his salary. But when he worked for the railroad, he came home and worked until dark on the farm. But the farm was really our livelihood. The milk was taken to Wrightsville, and my mother made butter and sold that in town. We also sold a lot of fruit and berries, and people would come out to the farm to buy them. We had our own meat; we had our own eggs, our own milk, everything. We even took the wheat to the mill to be ground into flour. It wasn't the greatest income, but we managed to have a good home, good roof over our heads, good clothing on our backs, and food on the table. It wasn't a big, prosperous thing; it was just 'get along.'"

After graduation from Wrightsville High in 1934, "Sis" aspired to further her education for a position in office work:

"I was sixteen when I graduated from Wrightsville High in 1934. Of course, I didn't have any money to go any further, but I did take a course from the International Correspondence School and passed with flying colors. It would have been background for office work. I was supposed to have a job with the Prudential Insurance Company. See, the International Correspondence School guaranteed you a job if you got a diploma.

I would have gone to Philadelphia for three months for a course, a preparation thing, but my dad wouldn't let me go. He said, 'You're too young to go into the city.' I was eighteen when I finished that course. I don't regret that because I was young and only a country girl. I wasn't a city girl."

Since going to Philadelphia was out of the question, "Sis" decided to try her hand working at a sewing factory in Wrightsville:

"I started working at Standard Garment Company as a side seamer, which meant I was sewing sides, from top to bottom, for dresses. There were all women employed there. Even during the Depression, we put in a forty-hour week, and sometimes we maybe worked a few hours on Saturday morning. But we had a flat rate, and I made $7.00 a week. To tell you the truth, money was so scarce then that we were glad to earn that $7.00 a week. I was so pleased to earn my own money. I kept a dollar a week and gave the rest to my mother and daddy. A dollar a week was a lot of money during the Depression. I would work in that factory, and then I would work on the farm in the evenings until dark.

"I worked for Standard Garment until 1939. When Standard moved to Columbia, I moved with them because otherwise I would not have had a job. When Hollis Manufacturing opened a garment factory at the bottom of Hellam Street, I went there because I was living on the farm and commuting to Columbia. Hollis's was more convenient, so I came back to Wrightsville. They opened up in 1939, and I started to work for them the second day they were open. I wound up as a hemmer on a sewing machine, and I hemmed for years! The minimum wage had started by then, but that only applied pretty much to the men working there—mechanics, machinists, cutters, whatever. All the women sewers were on piecework. Hollis was smart enough to keep that piecework price low enough so that you struggled to make more than what they would allow you to make. So, when I went to work at York Safe & Lock, I was probably making $22 a week at Hollis's. That wasn't too bad back at that time. The Hollis's were good people and marvelous to work for—no problem—and when I left there, I was really doing good.[2]

"I was still living on the farm, and I got back and forth to work in a used Model-T Ford. It was reliable transportation, except for the tires. The tires were bad, and I had a lot of flat tires. And when it rained, the road from the farm had ruts a foot deep.

"Then I married 'Whis' [Leber] in 1940, before the war started. Everybody then called us 'Sis' and 'Whis.' He worked as a mechanic at 'Babe' [Harris] Martin's garage and filling station. We fixed up three rooms in my parents' house and lived there on the farm. That was a big house."

"Sis" Leber's career changed drastically with the coming of World War II. She left a traditionally woman's job to accept a new challenge as a defense worker at a company that had previously hired only males on the production floor. She was motivated by patriotism, economics, and the fact that three brothers and her husband ultimately served in the military at various times during the war. As a result, "Sis" was inadvertently in the vanguard of women entering the defense industry and helped pave the way for the women's movement of the postwar years:

"I was probably in church when we heard about Pearl Harbor, because I never missed too much church. I can remember it very well when the news came over the radio.

"Then I felt that since three of my brothers were gone into the service, I had to do something to help out, too. I just didn't feel right sewing children's dresses when they needed help in the defense plants. I think 'Bo' went into the Army in February of 1941, and Tom went in early, too. Bill was very late going in [1944], and 'Whis' went in 1943. I just explained to Bill Hollis that I felt I should be doing something more toward helping in the defense effort. I had no problems down there at Hollis's because when I came back after the war, right away they took me back.

"I knew they were hiring at York Safe & Lock. It wasn't like a newspaper advertisement; it must have been by word-of-mouth. I had no idea about what they were paying at that time. Sometime in 1942, I put in my application, and they hired me almost right away. You had to be eighteen, and you had to have a high school diploma. They gave me a pretty stiff interview, you know, wanting to know about your background, and then I had to take some sort of a test, which wasn't too hard. They also wanted to know about your health. A lot of women were not hired because they weren't high school graduates because of the poor economic conditions, lack of money. They really didn't know where we'd work when they initially hired us because they manufactured a lot of other things besides guns.

Rubber was the first material to go to war because the Japanese conquests in Southeast Asia had cut off 97 percent of the world supply of natural rubber. The federal government quickly clamped a freeze on tires for civilians, followed by a ban on recapping tires. Only a fortunate few could get a certificate to buy a new tire or a recapped one. The rationing of gasoline soon followed. Not only was it imposed because of a gasoline shortage, but it was also a means saving the wear on tires. Gasoline rationing went into effect in December 1942. The basis for rationing was the A, B, and C system. The B sticker holder had essential driving to do, such as a defense worker who drove his/her car in a car pool, and received a supplementary allowance above the four, and later three, gallons per week allotted to the A sticker holders.[3] Because of the nature of her work, therefore, "Sis" received a B sticker and participated in car pooling:

"Getting back and forth to York Safe & Lock was something! In the meantime, I got a 1936 Chevy because the Ford had become unreliable. I hauled five other people who didn't work at my plant. Indeed, I did not charge them a cent! I didn't take anything from them. Getting gasoline was a problem, and for each ration stamp you got three gallons. I lived out in the country, and it was two-and-a-half miles to get into Wrightsville before I got to the highway [Route 30, Lincoln Highway] to

York. If you were really low, they'd maybe issue you two more stamps, which gave you six gallons of gas. They issued the ration stamps at work. They tried to figure about how much mileage you should get on a gallon of gas equal to your mileage to and from work. Now, I will say this. My oldest brother farmed, and he got gas for tractors and such, and occasionally he would put a few gallons in my car.[4] I had to do this in order to get to work, so that's what I did. But my gas allotment held out real well because I used the car only for transportation to and from work. I didn't run around. I made that trip to York seven days a week, don't forget. I was off the eighth day, and whenever you hit a Saturday, you got Sunday off. On my day off, I helped out on the farm all the time because my brothers and husband were in the service.

"Tires were a big problem, too. My tires were retreads, and they were not good. They were bad; they were bad. I was running with four tires for nearly a year before they would give me a stamp to get a spare.

"Food rationing, however, was not a problem for us on the farm. We didn't have too much to worry about. They rationed butter, but we didn't have to worry about that. Sugar was rationed, but we were never big sugar users, anyway, so we managed. I figured that if our boys could live out of a little knapsack over there, we could live without a little sugar. But we didn't have too many problems that way.

Perhaps because of her farm background and being around machinery, "Sis" Leber made a smooth transition from Hollis Manufacturing to York Safe & Lock. Nevertheless, she performed well on all the large pieces of machinery to which she was assigned, thus disproving the argument that women were incapable of handling such jobs:

"I would start work at 7:00 AM, so I would leave home around 6:00 because I picked up and left off my riders. And I also had a chance of a train being in my way at Duke Street in York. If you hit a big freight train, you had to sit, and if you didn't punch your time clock at 7:00, you lost a half-hour of pay.

"I was assigned to Department 43. The funny part about it was that we had forty-three boys go out of there and into the service, and all we had left were old men and girls. I was what they called a 'swing girl.' It's a girl who is taught to operate every machine, which comes easy when you are around them for a while. In case a girl would be off or just got sick, I could take over her job. I could go on any machine and run it. My very first assignment was being a bench grinder for the breechblocks. I think that's where they started you out until they found out what you could do. The breechblocks had rough edges on them—terribly sharp edges—and you set them at a bench with files and filed them by hand. They weighed forty-five pounds. Then the government inspectors were there all the time, and they'd run their hands along it, and you better not have a nick or anything! Boy!

"I was mostly stuck on a machine called the Borematic, which bored the powder tube, powder chamber, with five cuts, for the shell. You had a little rig, and you had to set up your own tool for each cut. The powder chamber was the same size as the shell. Our Borematic was leased from the Rockview Penitentiary. We made the tubes [barrels] and breechblocks for 32-, 55-, and 80-millimeter guns. When the process hit the Borematic, it was almost at the finishing stage. That job came real easy to me, but a lot of girls had trouble with it. In fact, they couldn't put girls in there; they had trouble with it. Some of them just couldn't get the knack. Now, whether I caught on to it quite early, I don't know, but I had no problem with it.[5]

"Then I also operated milling machines, lathes, and threaders. I was also on the rifler—the rifling machine for barrel rifling. That machine was bigger than my house, about fifty-five feet long. I also worked with the Lo-Swing. The piece of raw, solid steel is first worked on by the Lo-Swing, which was like a milling machine. It consisted of diamond-bit tools. It did the first rough cut on the tubes, which looked terrible—black—when they came through, and the Lo-Swing chipped all that away and took off the rough edges. It would take off chips—hot chips—and they'd fly in every direction. When the steel piece left the Lo-Swing, it was shiny and looked real nice. The next machine shaped the gun, and it had chipping functions, too. Then the powder chambers were ground, and then came the rifling followed by the threading, which is the next to last thing done to the tube. The internal grinder was the last process that was done on the tube. When that tube came off of there, they had a 'go gauge' and a 'no go gauge.' There could only be a .0055-inch tolerance difference between each end of the gun tube. If the 'go' went, fine; if the 'no go' went, that was a bad tube that had been ground too far. That's a pretty close tolerance. And that powder chamber did not dare have a mark the depth of a hair, or it was scrapped—it was scrapped! We also had a bluing bin there, too, and that was always as long as the tube, or longer, and hot. I don't think any girl did that; only men did that. All these jobs were pretty physical; some took a lot of strength.

"We were expected on the dayshift to finish six tubes completely in our ten hours. At night they worked twelve hours, so they expected eight tubes from them. I was very messed up by the end of my shift. On the Borematic, we did not use oil as a lubricant. Instead, we had this white solution, and that kept the machine bit cooled all the time as it ran through. Believe you me, that really messed up my clothes because it splashed sometimes!

"My least favorite job was working on the rifler. You had thirty-one cuts to make, and you walked from end of the floor to the other, and then back and forth and back and forth. It seemed like such a slow process. But it did a beautiful job. I wasn't crazy about working on the machines using lubricating oil, either, but you worked on them because the job was there to do, and they needed someone to do it.

"I had my own tools, and I kept them locked up along with my apron and hat in a metal closet. Anything personal I locked in my tool box. I had to furnish most of my own tools except for the huge, huge open-mouth wrench that the company supplied. But I had my own Allen wrenches in all sizes, three or four screwdrivers, sandpaper, and crocus cloth to polish the metal. I'm sure I had to buy most of these things myself, because I still have them now.

Contrary to what occurred in many defense industries, sexual harassment at York Safe & Lock, according to "Sis," was not a problem in Department 43:

"There was no sexual harassment. Besides the government people, we had almost all older men, and we had wonderful bosses. It was really a good place to work, I would say. And there wasn't a lot of 'hanky-panky' that went on, that I could see.

"I would say that they were pretty patriotic. There weren't too many people in there who really seriously weren't involved in the war effort and war-related production. There was very little absenteeism.

She did experience one incident, however, that would be considered either a form of harassment or a practical joke:

"It was a real cold, frosty morning, and at that time I was wearing my hair a little bit below my shoulders. Anyway, I had done the boring, and then the next guy on this internal grinder did the finishing touches on the powder chamber. It was just a practical joke. I hadn't started to work yet, so I got my toolbox, and then he hollered down to me that I had scrapped one. He shined his flashlight in this tube, and I leaned over. When I did, this spindle was going a thousand times a minute, and with the static, my hair went right in with it. It pulled my scalp away from the side of my face. I had ridges the whole way down my head. It was *BUMP! BUMP! BUMP!* He was thoughtful enough to turn off the machine, and the minute you turn it off, that spindle stops immediately. But it just pulled my scalp away. He was apologetic, but, boy, did he ever get called on the carpet!

On the other hand, there was discrimination in terms of the wages paid to men and women:

"The money wasn't that great there. I think I made $1.20 an hour, around that much, when the war ended. The men's wages were much better. I would say they at least doubled our hourly wage or maybe better. But I didn't resent it. A lot of these men that were there, they had worked there previously to the defense work. They weren't going to take a cut to come in to defense work. So, probably their wages were at a higher rate before the war. But if a man were hired at the same time as I, I would think he'd be paid more. But I never gave it a thought. I feel as though the men who worked there were up to $3.00, $4.00, $5.00 an hour, and they weren't going to take a cut.

As was the case in almost all defense industries, company policy required women to dress in a prescribed manner and to use the safety equipment then available for the times:

"Because of the nature of our machinery, I was required to pull my shoulder-length hair up under my hat. We did have to wear long pants; there were no shorts or anything like that. You could wear your own clothing, but nothing baggy, like a baggy shirt or something. On most of the machines, we had to wear safety glasses and a hat, and we all had aprons. Most of the girls on those machines had to wear hats. When the Lo-Swing was operating, the hot steel chips would fly far and everywhere. I walked past the Lo-Swing on one occasion and got hit on the forehead by a flying chip of hot steel. It hurt but it didn't incapacitate me in any way. But as a rule nobody ever got hit too much with them.

Having so many family members and close relatives in the armed forces remained a source of motivation all through "Sis's" experience in the defense industry:

"I kept abreast with what was happening on the battle fronts. My husband and three brothers were in the service, and I had seven cousins and lots of close friends serving, too. I wrote a lot of letters to my brothers and my husband, and I sent a lot of Christmas packages and things.

"Then 'Whis' volunteered for naval duty, and he was a gunner's mate on an ammunition supply ship. That's another reason why I wanted to do the best job possible, because he might have been using some of the antiaircraft tubes that I had made. So, I was fussy, and if I was to have a gun tube scrapped, it would have made me heartsick. The whole time I was there, I know that I never had a tube scrapped!

"We also received the Army-Navy 'E' for good work. That is an award for excellence in work. The product has to be good. And we **always** met our quotas. That Army-Navy 'E' was for excellent work and meeting production quotas, and it was awarded to the whole plant. It made me feel pretty proud to be a part of it. We each received a certificate with a stamp on it, but I can't remember whether or not if it was from the President. Maybe it was from the War Department or the Department of the Navy.

"I did buy a lot of war bonds, because we had a lot of bond drives at the plant. They really didn't pressure you to buy them, but they did ask you to do it. I'll never forget this one drive that they had out in the parking lot. Do you know who had it? Greta Garbo! She put on this drive and really was right out there among us. They cleared the parking lot, and everybody went out. She put on this drive, and they asked you to sign up. Then they passed a form around, back inside the plant. Of course, they did well on those drives. They always had some celebrity urging us to buy bonds, like, someone involved in the government or movies or someone like that to come through.

"Every month they sponsored a blood drive at the plant, and the blood mobile came in. They got good results. The workers really gave blood. I think I gave about three gallons in total. I gave a lot of blood. They say that it will replenish itself in thirty days, but lots of times we gave twice a month. It was the patriotic thing to do because at the time they needed a lot of blood. I never had any ill-effects from giving, and I thought that as long as I felt good, I could do it. I'd do anything to help the war effort. I would still do it if I had to.

Next to patriotism, family finances motivated "Sis" to seek employment at the war plant:

"I didn't go to York Safe & Lock to become a more independent woman, not really. Don't forget that when 'Whis' went into the Navy, he gave up his wages. I had everything to do that we had formerly done together. The $50 a month Navy allotment that he sent home was not much. I must say, though, that at York Safe & Lock, I was making more money than I had ever made in my life.

"Sis" had fond memories of President Franklin D. Roosevelt not only for his wartime leadership but also for his New Deal:

"I liked him, and I guess I had personal reasons to like him. The whole time I went to school, I studied under kerosene lamps—nothing but kerosene lamps—maybe up until 2:00 in the morning. I can't remember when it was, but we got a generator to provide electricity in our house, but we couldn't use it for some things like toasters and irons because the generator's output was insufficient to generate enough power to sustain the demands of those kinds of appliances. That was well into the 1930s because I was still using kerosene lamps when I got married. Well, Franklin Roosevelt came along, and he said, 'Every rural home and farm will have electricity [through the Rural Electrification Administration].' And we got electricity.[6]

"He also came along with the rip-rap roads built by the WPA [Works Progress Administration]. The WPA and the PWA [Public Works Administration] created a lot of jobs. Of course, when the war came along, that created a lot of jobs, too.

"Well, I'll tell you, I was sad when I learned about his death. I guess maybe we shouldn't have been sad because that man lived with a handicap [polio] almost all his life. I liked him, and it was just a shock when he died. I remember that well.

As soon as Japan formally surrendered on 2 September 1945, the federal government abruptly cancelled existing defense contracts. "Sis" remembered the end of the war and how it affected her job at York Safe & Lock:

"It was business as usual right up to the minute they announced that the war was over. And when they announced it, everything shut down. The plant was closed up. On the spur of the moment, our job was over and done. I never saw any of those people again.

"Everybody was more than happy that the war was over, but, you know, I think some people felt as though their life was almost over on account of losing their jobs. I think they almost felt that way, especially among the men, because I know some of those men made really good money. As far as the plant being shut down, of course, that was sad because you met a lot of nice people, people that you liked. But, for the war to be over, there was not anything in my mind that was better because I had three brothers in there, and I had a husband in there. I also had all these relatives, friends, and to see them come home outdid everything.

"My brother Ed was still farming, so he didn't go into the service. He had contracted to grow three or four acres of tomatoes for Campbell's Soup. I guess they used a lot of soup or ketchup in the service. I don't know. But they wouldn't let him enlist. They told him he was more valuable where he was on the farm. A couple colored people from downtown helped him pick his tomatoes, and would you believe that all kinds of people from town also came out to pitch in and help! All that stuff he raised on the farm went for the patriotic cause, too.

In looking back, "Sis" reflected on her lasting memories about her experiences in the war plant:

"I'll tell you, that was quite an experience. I wouldn't want to see another world war or anything like that, but my work there was something that was really a nice lesson to learn. It really changed me, I mean, connecting the war with the job. It made me think that there are more important things in life than just the everyday routine. You know that you are doing something that is helping out and something that is **really** needed. I don't know how much our work contributed toward winning the war, but I certainly know that we tried. I had a different outlook on a lot of things.

"Really, I came to appreciate and value the little things in life. To begin with, you're so lucky for what didn't happen. Your family is there at home again, and everybody is getting back to a normal life again. Things are going well. I think that I almost turned into a country girl again. It was such relief that the war was over and everybody was okay. It was such a relief—such a relief.

Immediately after the close of the defense plant, "Sis" resumed her job in the traditionally women's position as a sewer at Hollis Manufacturing:

"I went back to sewing—immediately. They welcomed me with open arms. I definitely did have trouble adjusting at first because I was making less money. When I went back there, I would get, like, what they called 'a cost of living raise' once a year. So, it was an adjustment. But after 'Whis' came back, then we had a second income. None of our incomes were really large at that time, but it was still a second income, so that covered what went on. The second time I started, I retired from there in 1983 or 1984, I guess, so that was from 1945 until 1984. I sewed for almost fifty years, I guess.

"I lived on the farm for forty-seven years before I moved to town. In the meantime, 'Whis' had died, and then for the last five years that my brother Ed lived, I went back and took care of him."

After the war, "Sis" and "Whis" lived on the family farm for a while and then bought a home in Wrightsville where they raised their family. A widow, Pauline Leber died on 26 June 2005.

Notes

1. Pauline (née Haugh) Leber, Interview with author, 9 October 1998, transcript, OH1266, Oral History Collection, University Archives, University of North Texas, Denton, TX.

2. Note: In 1938, Congress passed the Fair Labor Standards Act for all workers engaged in interstate commerce or in the production of goods for interstate commerce. The act prohibited child labor, and it set maximum hours of work and a minimum wage for other employees. In general, it provided for a maximum workweek of 44 hours during the first year, 42 hours during the second year, and 40 hours after October 1940, with time-and-a-half pay for overtime work. Minimum wage rates were initially set at 25 cents an hour and scheduled to increase to 40 cents after seven years. See Lester V. Chandler, *America's Greatest Depression, 1929-1941* (New York: Harper & Row, Publishers, 1970), 237; and Ronald Edsforth, *The New Deal: America's Response to the Great Depression* (Malden, MA: Blackwell Publishers, 2000), 272.

3. See Richard R. Lingeman, *Don't You Know There's a War Going On: The American Home Front, 1941-1945* (New York: G. P. Putnam's Sons, 1970), 244, 249.

4. Farmers received the C sticker, which meant that they had access to unlimited amounts of gasoline.

5. Note: The Borematic is a very large horizontal or vertical machine often used to bore cylinders in automotive air conditioning compressors. Producing a precisely positioned, sized, and finished hole for a gun tube, for instance, usually requires a boring operation.

6. In May 1935 the Roosevelt administration established the Rural Electrification Administration (REA). The REA encouraged farmers and rural residents to form electric cooperatives to become eligible for forty-year

loans to bring electricity to their members. The cooperatives either built power lines to distribute electricity from their own hydro-stations or they purchased power at wholesale rates from private power companies. See Edsforth, 220-221.

Figure 6. Mary Jane Dellinger

Chapter 3

Mary Jane Dellinger

Riveter and Driller
Armstrong Cork and Rubber Company

Born on 14 February 1922, Mary Jane Dellinger lived in Wrightsville all her life. After quitting school during her sophomore year at Wrightsville High School, she found employment in a nearby silk mill before taking jobs in the defense plants during World War II, first at Hamilton Watch Company and then at Armstrong Cork and Rubber Company, both in Lancaster, Pennsylvania. Mary Jane married Clair "Poss" Dellinger in 1942, shortly before he was sent overseas. As was the case with other women throughout the country, Mary Jane decided to take employment in the defense plants for economic and patriotic reasons. Also, like many other women, she enjoyed working in the industry and decided to continue such work after the war. Mary Jane also observed that, with the exception of a new found prosperity, World War II changed Wrightsville very little. She and her husband bought a home in Wrightsville and raised their family there. After "Poss's" death in January 2000, she continued to live there. Mary Jane died on 29 December 2008.[1]

Like other young men and women in Wrightsville, Mary Jane Essig left school before graduating due to the economic stresses of the Great Depression:

"I went to Wrightsville High School, but I didn't graduate. I quit in 1938 when I was sixteen, and then I went to work at the silk mill in Columbia.

"The Depression, I know very well. That was the main reason why all of my classmates left school. Almost none of us graduated because we quit school and went to work. My daddy worked at the Keeley Stove Company in Columbia, but he didn't have steady work during the Depression. They would work for a while, and then when things got bad, he was laid off for a while. After the war started, there were economic improvements, but before then, no.

Mary Jane's employment in the silk mill was a place that was traditionally a niche for women during that time:

"I went to work for United Throwing Company in Columbia, Pennsylvania. When I first started, I got ten cents an hour. Then when they passed a law—I don't know what year it was—we got twenty-five cents an hour. We thought we were rich! I was winding thread onto spools. We'd start at 6:00 AM and quit at 2:30 PM.[2]

After American entry into World War II, Mary Jane found a higher paying job at the Hamilton Watch Company in Lancaster. As was the case with many American businesses, Hamilton transitioned from the production of civilian products to the making military goods:

"I took a job at the Hamilton Watch Company in Lancaster in 1942, and I worked there for a year or so. They were making time fuses for bombs. I took the job because it paid more money than I made at the silk mill.

"I was doing electrical work. I was putting little screws in the fuses on this assembly line, which was made up mostly of women. Our supervisors were all older men. All the younger men were in the service, so they hired mostly women; and I guess, for little, delicate work like that, women could do it better than men. I had some adjustments to make when working on an assembly line because we didn't have anything like that at the silk mill where you worked at your own pace. At Hamilton we still got paid an hourly wage, and we put in eight-hour days, five days a week; but there were no fringe benefits, nothing like that.

"I got to work by bus. I'd get the York bus in Wrightsville and go to Columbia. There I'd pick up the Conestoga bus to Lancaster, and it would let us off in front of the company, which was located right along Route 30.

Mary Jane saw an immediate improvement in her economic situation after she made the move to Hamilton:

"We could get more things than we got when we were only making twenty-five cents an hour. I lived at home when my husband was in the Army, and I think I paid my parents $3.00 a week for room and board. Of course, even though I was making more money than before, I really couldn't spend it because of rationing during the war.

Due to a personal conflict with her boss, Mary Jane quit her job at Hamilton in 1943:

"I married 'Poss' [Clair Dellinger] in 1942. When I met him in 1938, I was really young. He went into the service in May, 1942, and we got married in August 1942 when he finished Army basic training and was home on leave. Marriages right before men went overseas were pretty common at that time. I was working at Hamilton when we got married.

"Anyway, 'Poss' was coming home on furlough because his unit was on alert to move out very shortly, and I asked my boss to let me off for a holiday to spend time with my husband. My boss said, 'No, you're working now to make things for defense,' and he wouldn't let me off. It made me mad because I didn't know when I'd see 'Poss' again, so I said, 'Well, I'm just quitting!' So, I quit. I had worked at Hamilton for about a year by that time.

Again, by word-of-mouth, Mary Jane learned that Armstrong Cork and Rubber Company in Lancaster was also hiring women for defense work:

"At that time 'Hen' [Henry] Weisser, my future brother-in-law, worked at Armstrong, and he told me they were hiring people to work in the Bomb Department. So, Corenna Young, Dorothy Myers and I went down there and got jobs. It wasn't hard to get hired. We went and filled out the applications, and they hired us right away.

"After we were hired, I rode the bus again. I had to go to Lancaster by bus, and then I had to get a bus from the square to the Armstrong plant.

Most of Mary Jane's tenure at Armstrong was spent in the Aircraft Department assembling the fuselage for the Chance-Vought F4U Corsair, a sturdy single-engine fighter-bomber used extensively by Marine and Navy aviators flying off carriers and land bases in the Pacific. She took the job mainly for financial reasons, but she also believed it was the patriotic thing to do since she would be supporting her husband, who was serving with the US Army in the Southwestern Pacific:

"I worked on the Corsairs at the Armstrong plant until 1945. When 'Poss' came home from the service, I quit. I took that job at Armstrong mainly for financial reasons. They were better paying jobs because it was 'defense work,' as they called it then. As far as pay, though, we didn't make a whole lot of money there, but it was more than I had made at Hamilton and certainly much more than I made at the silk mill. We got paid every two weeks. I can't say whether or not the men made more than we did. I just don't know.

"Of course, patriotism also played a part in my decision to take the job. My husband was fighting in the service, and I wanted to do something at home. I also had a brother and brother-in-law in the service. So, it wasn't just for the money; it was to do my part for the war effort. It seemed like everybody was working to make these things for the men who were in the war.

Mary Jane then offered a vivid description of the processes involved in fabricating the Corsair fuselage:

"I was working on the fuselages. They would have the men put them together. We worked in groups up on a platform where the fuselages were located. Cranes would pick up the fuselages and move them to the platforms. Other people in another part of the plant put them together. Then they were brought over to us to do this part.

"We'd go up the platform steps and work there, drilling holes. In this group, each person had a job. I think there were four or five of us in a group. To drill holes, they would have it already marked, and we would drill the holes. Then one person would follow us and countersink the holes for when you put in the aluminum rivets so that they'd be flush. The rivets that we put in there, the round part, would go down in that counter-sunk part. Instead of just having the round hole where you drilled, you'd counter-sink around that to make, like, a little edge. Then another person in the group would put the rivets in. There was also another person inside the fuselage when they riveted it. He or she was inside, and they'd hold a heavy metal block, something flat, to flatten out the rivet when it was driven in. That's how we did it. You didn't have just one job, because one day you were drilling holes and the next day you were putting in rivets. When we finished a fuselage, we went to another platform and started all over with a new fuselage. Another group was working ahead of us to get the fuselage ready for us. I liked the drilling better than putting in the rivets. I didn't like to be flattening out the rivets because I was afraid that I couldn't get it right. You had to be inside the fuselage, and most of the times they had the men do that rather than the women. They had to use a metal block or something, and you had to hold it against the inner side of the fuselage. The women would usually put in the rivets from the outside.

"We did not finish one fuselage in a shift. There were a lot of holes and lot of rivets to be put in. It was a whole side that you worked on, and another group would be on the other side. Since we worked as a group, then our group would try to outdo the other group. I've forgotten what we got, but we did get an award if we put out the most work. It was the company's way of trying to get us to produce more or better fuselages, I guess. We were not on piecework, but I think we got a reward of some sort if you got done in the time you were supposed to or beat out the other groups. The three shifts were competing against one another. We did have one girl, though, that they had to get after sometimes. She would take a lot of time off, and then that would sort of mess things up. Our foreman had to keep after her. On one occasion, we got an 'E' pin. The 'E' was for Excellence, and I think it was for the quality of the work that we did.

"I really didn't think this work was physically taxing. The only thing I didn't like is when we worked the third shift. You went from 7:00 AM to 3:00 PM; 3:00 PM to 11:00 PM; and 11:00 PM to 7:00 AM. That was the only thing I didn't care for. I didn't care for it because you had to sleep during the day, and I wasn't used to that. We changed shifts every week, and we did work on Saturdays. You'd get home at 11:00 on Saturday from the second shift, and then on Sunday night you'd start your week at 11:00 and work to 7:00 in the morning. You didn't get much time off between that one like you did on the other shifts. When we finished that shift on Saturday morning at 7:00, then we were off until Monday, when we'd go to work at 7:00 AM. I didn't mind the other shifts.

"I liked the job, and I liked what we did. Like I said, we worked together. If you had somebody who was slow, then he or she held up the other ones. But we all got along well. There was no bickering or anything like I saw in later years. The ones I worked with were really nice people, and everybody got along well. I never saw any 'hanky-panky,' either. If it did go on, I didn't know anything about it. Most of the women who worked in the Aircraft Department had no children. In fact, most of them were not married.

"This job was a change for me, although I had no problems in learning how to do it. It was different, but with every job I had, except at Hamilton, where you had to sit down to work, I had to stand. They told us what to do, and you picked it up easily. It just came naturally to me, I guess.

Her job as a riveter/driller required Mary Jane to dress to a certain standard:

"We had to wear slacks, and we had to wear a hair net over our heads. But we wore regular blouses and all. A woman had to wear slacks because of the type of work we were doing. It was required as a safety measure as much as anything.

Armstrong used various means to promote patriotism and war consciousness among its work force:

"They would have people come and talk to us because they wanted us to buy war bonds. There was really no direct pressure put on us, but I think that most of us voluntarily bought bonds. I know I did. I think I bought a bond every month. I know that Linda Darnell came to the Hamilton plant, but I don't remember any celebrities coming to Armstrong to encourage us to buy bonds.

"I got so much of an allotment from the government through my being married and with 'Poss' in the service. I would save that, and 'Poss' would buy bonds in the service and send them home. Besides, because of rationing, we had little choice but to save money or buy bonds or both. We couldn't spend too much on ourselves for personal items. I know that Daddy had to get rationing coupons to buy gasoline. Sugar was another thing that was rationed, and butter. Women couldn't get silk stockings because I guess they used the silk for parachutes.

"I also remember that they started deducting federal income taxes from our checks that we received every two weeks. In later years that made me mad, but right then I thought that it was great that they took it off right away.[3]

Throughout the period of their separation, Mary Jane and 'Poss' kept in contact as much as possible even though both were heavily involved in the war effort:

"He insisted that I write to him every day, and I did. He looked for a letter from me every day. Most times, though, I didn't get a letter from him every day. He was over in New Guinea and then later moved up into the Philippines when those islands were invaded.

As the war was winding down, Mary Jane was able to see that her days in the Aircraft Department were numbered:

"I saw a gradual tapering off of work on the production line, and the pressure to maximize production also diminished. However, we still continued to work six days a week.

"Then I just quit. The war was over, so I just quit. After they declared peace with Japan, 'Poss' came home in October 1945, and he was discharged in November.

"Then we had children, and I didn't work until later. After our children were in school, I went to work at Grinnell, which had bought the old Columbia Malleable, and I think I started at $1.75 an hour. When I retired, I was up to $10 an hour, and that was the first place where I really had benefits. We had no benefits at all at Armstrong. I worked there at Grinnell for thirty-two years.

Mary Jane could detect few changes in Wrightsville due to the war:

"I didn't see any changes in the town, not really. But I know that when my husband came home, he couldn't get work for a while. He finally got a job molding at Susquehanna Casting, and then he transferred over to Wilton Products [a subsidiary of Susquehanna Casting, also known by the local folks at the 'Paint Shop'] where he became the foreman. He then worked there until 1988, when he finally retired.

In looking back at her years at Armstrong, Mary Jane was proud of what she had done for her country.

"It made me feel as though I was helping my country, the same as my husband was. I liked the job and everything, but I felt that I was doing my duty, too. 'Poss' was doing his duty, and I was doing mine."

Mary Jane and "Poss" had two daughters, bought a home, and continued to live in Wrightsville. After an extended illness, "Poss" died 13 January 2000. Mary Jane passed away on 29 December 2008.

Notes

1. Mary Jane Dellinger, interview by the author, 26 May 2000, transcript, OH1345, Oral History Collection, University Archives, University of North Texas, Denton, TX.

2. Note: On 25 June 1938, President Franklin D. Roosevelt signed into law the Fair Labor Standards Act that initially provided for a minimum wage of twenty-five cents an hour, a maximum workweek of forty-four hours, and the abolition of child labor.

3. Note: The Revenue Act of 1942 , hailed by President Roosevelt as "the greatest tax bill in American history," called for a 5 percent "Victory Tax" on all individual incomes over $624, and it reduced the personal exemption amount from $1,500 to $1,200 for married couples. The Current Tax Payment Act of 1943 required employers to withhold taxes from employees' wages and remit them quarterly to the IRS. David M. Kennedy, *Freedom from Fear: The American People in Depression and War, 1929-1945* (New York: Oxford University Press, 1999), 624.

Figure 7. Evelyn "Ebs" Myers

Chapter 4

Evelyn "Ebs" Myers

"Government Girl"
US Department of State
Cadet Nurse Corps
Hines Veterans Hospital

Born on 27 February 1918, in Wrightsville, Evelyn "Ebs" Myers was the daughter of foundry molder Guy Myers and his wife Caroline. Evelyn had two younger brothers and a younger sister. Refusing to accept dead-end jobs, she decided to seek employment as a clerk/typist with the US Department of State in Washington, DC. With the country appearing to be headed toward war, the federal government was hiring large numbers of men and women to fill a variety of positions. Sensing the opportunity this presented, "Ebs" and thousands of other career-minded young women headed to the nation's capital to take jobs as "Government Girls." For "Ebs" there were financial opportunities in Washington that were unavailable in Wrightsville, and in addition the big city offered a chance to expand her horizons beyond this small town and experience new things. After three years with the State Department, she came to the conclusion that anyone could do her job and that she was not really doing her part for the war effort. As a result she left Washington and decided to enter the Cadet Nurse Corps, eventually becoming a registered nurse. She returned to Wrightsville a changed woman, but she found that Wrightsville had changed very little. Following the war, she married Richard McCune of Columbia, Pennsylvania. The couple built their home in Columbia and raised an adopted son there. Evelyn died on 13 November 2002.[1]

After graduating from Wrightsville High School in 1936, Evelyn's future prospects did not look promising in the midst of the Great Depression. Wrightsville High offered only an academic curriculum at that time:

"I graduated from Wrightsville High School in 1936. Then I went to night school at Thompson's Business College in York. It was a secretarial course, really—typing and clerking and things like that. During my high school years and even when I was going to Thompson's, I worked for Etzweiler's—the undertaker family in Wrightsville. That consisted of babysitting, running their errands, cleaning their house, and just generally helping out. Well, I was, like, at a dead end because I wasn't getting anyplace with the night school bit.

"I thought that if I took a civil service test, it might lead to something worthwhile. It was kind of vague to me, but it sounded good, so I thought, 'I'll try it.' I had nothing to lose, and I had everything to gain. So, I took the test at the York Post Office, and that is how I got my foot in the door. It took me forever to get the results. But then my first inkling that I was supposed to maybe end up in Washington was the fact that I got a telegram from the State Department in August 1941 saying that they had a clerk/typist position available.

"I had never been very far away from home except maybe to go to the New Jersey shore. But the news from overseas was getting so grim that I just felt a need to do something—I'll call it important—because the draft had already started, and the young men were starting to leave town. I think they had to serve for a year, and then they could come home. So, I felt that I wasn't doing anything important, and this job with the State

Department would be something important. Besides, it would get me out of this small town, and it would broaden my vision and interests. It was getting rather boring to be in that little town and never learning anything new, really. I was at a standstill, and this was an opening for me. And I also knew that my pay would be far greater than what I was making as a domestic in Wrightsville.

"But in hindsight, I have often thought, 'If I had thought about it too much, I'd have probably not done it.' It would have been frightening, because Washington to me was the capital of the world at that time. I didn't feel like I was that great a typist or clerk or whatever. I didn't think that I was that experienced, but I thought, 'They must think I am qualified, or they would have never sent for me.' So, I went.

"My parents said the decision was up to me, although in looking back I suspect that they saw this as one less mouth to feed. It was never said that way because my parents were too loving to say this directly, but I put two and two together. I had two younger brothers and a younger sister at that time. Also, I knew that Washington wasn't that far away, and I knew that I could come home on weekends. So, I just packed about a week's worth of clothing in a fairly small suitcase, but before I accepted I had taken the precaution of sending the State Department a telegram and saying, 'I'll come down if you find me a place to live.' They then said, 'You come down, and we'll find you a place to live.' Mind you, the State Department said that!

"My mode of transportation to Washington was kind of different. Etzweiler's—these undertakers—also had an ambulance service. Would you believe that they took me by ambulance to the train station in York, and then I went the rest of the way by train?

Washington, DC, had become a boom town. With the approach of war, thousands of civilian federal employees and military personnel descended upon the city. Beginning in 1940, government employment had more than doubled. More than 70,000 people arrived in the first year after Pearl Harbor *alone. They came on every train and bus, nearly all of them women. Formal civil service exams had been dropped for the duration of the war because the government could not wait months for the forms to be mailed, graded, and classified. If one could type and possessed a high school diploma, the person was hired at $1,440 a year. The rapid influx of job seekers strained the city's antiquated transportation system, and made finding housing in the overcrowded city an adventure. Even typewriters were in short supply.*[2] *After arrival in Washington, "Ebs's" first priority, as was the case with almost all "Government Girls," was to find housing, and this search led to her first new experience in the big city:*

"There was a representative from the State Department at the Washington train station, and he directed me to a small hotel very close to the State Department itself. At that time the State Department was right beside the White House. I was only a block away, so it was very easy for me to get back and forth to work that first week. I was there for approximately a week.

"In the meantime, whoever took care of all this in the State Department saw to it that I was informed about the possibility of an apartment here or an apartment there with other girls. Finally, I selected one of them that had an opening. The apartment was located at 1631 S Street Northwest. There were three girls already living there, and there was an opening for another girl. They were from all over the United States. One girl was from Texas, and that was Bernice; there was a girl from Boston, and her first name was 'Bea'; the third one was from Muncy, Pennsylvania, and her name was Pearl Baumgartner. They more or less interviewed me, and I more or less interviewed them. Of course, they didn't know me, and I naturally didn't know them. My first impression was that they were very congenial, very friendly, very helpful.

"We had one bedroom that had twin beds in it. In the living room, there were two beds that you could pull out. They were like davenports that you could pull out and make larger. Then in the entrance hall, which was good-sized, there was another bed there—just one of those single beds.

We had one bedroom, bathroom, living room, entrance hall, and kitchen. We had just one closet for all of us, and pretty soon it was overflowing. So, you just didn't have room to put in six months' or a year's worth of clothing in it. Of course, we did our own laundry. There were no facilities to do laundry, so we'd just use the bathroom. I had been used to a house with two stories, so all of this took some getting used to on my part. We all got along fine.

"There was a turnover in roommates. Bernice eventually went with another group, and then I got her bed. Sleeping accommodations were based on seniority, very much so. That's the way it went until, finally, I got into the bedroom, which was better.

"I made $50 a week, which was big money in Depression times, so I just knew I was rich. Our rent was $80 a month, and we divided that out. I thought that $80 a month for rent was awfully high. I'd **never** heard of such rent. In Wrightsville, you could rent a triple-story house for $12 a month. Of course, we all pitched in and paid the utility bills and things like that.

"At, first, I used to walk to work because I enjoyed walking. Then I met this one girl at the State Department, and, believe it or not, she had a car. Then two of us in the apartment found out that we could ride with this girl to the State Department each day.

"Then I decided to move. One of the girls from New England and I decided to try to get out of there and find cheaper quarters. So, we found a place still in the Northwest, and we found out in the State Department that a lady whose husband was in the service had an extra room and that she could accommodate two girls. So, we went there, Barbara King and me. She came after 'Bea' had left. To this day I keep in contact with Barbara. We were like sisters; we were that close. We got along very well.

"Our new landlady--her name was Lela--and her husband were both from Kansas, and he was overseas somewhere. She had this apartment, so she decided to rent this one room to us. She was very pleasant and kind of took us girls under her wing, almost mother-like. She had one bedroom, but in her living room she had one of these pull-out beds again. This was a davenport, and at night you could open it up to be a double bed. Of course we had more closet space, and everything was bigger—the living room, the kitchen, the bathroom, and the bedroom. Our bedroom was actually in the living room, of course. We had to pay our rent weekly. Some months had five weeks in them, and that kind of stunned me. I don't remember what we paid each week.

"Now we had to use the bus to get to work. Most of the streetcars were in the downtown area, but we did have bus facilities in our area. This new area was more an outlying area of Washington. The buses were always crowded. I always stood up—always. It would have been a rare occasion to get a seat.

With her living accommodations eventually settled, "Ebs" got down to work at the State Department. From time to time she temporarily worked in the Code Room where she was dealing with encoded material:

"I was assigned to the Communications Department where we did a lot of typing and filing. Then when we weren't too busy, they'd select a couple of us to go into the Code Room, which was overwhelmed with work. The Code Room was in the same building and down the hall from us. There were bars all over that place; I mean, it was like a jail. When I was assigned over there, I had to take my pocketbook with me, and, of course, they went through your pocketbook, I guess to see if you were a spy or whatever. In the Code Room, there were long, long tables, and you would have, like, dictionaries, I'd say, five inches thick and about ten inches wide. Every word there, you went over, and then you wrote what it meant. It was like looking up a word in a dictionary. The information on the paper was encoded, and then we would use these dictionaries to decode it. I'd have to write it out in longhand and then pass in my paper, and then I'd get another piece of paper and start all over again. They would be numbered according to what the subject was. Anyway, you'd do a whole paper's worth, but you never knew what the next page would be because the person who was doing the second part would be at another end of the table. So, eventually, whoever was in charge there would put them all together, and then that was decoded. I would never see the whole thing, the whole picture—never! I didn't do that every day. It was just when they were overwhelmed that they took some of the girls from our department and set them over there. I was mostly working in my own office in the Communications Department, but when they were overwhelmed in the Code Room, they'd send a group of us there for a day at a time, and then maybe a week or two would go by, and then we'd be sent over there again.

"As time went on, and as the international situation was really getting out of hand, this work was very, very interesting. Once we left the Code Room, they would say things, like, 'Now, you know it's just understood that when you go home or whatever, you do not talk about what you read here and what you know here.' I don't think that it was ever earth-shaking things that we were working with, but it was enough that, if the enemy got hold of it, they could have put things together and figured out something.

"Mostly, though, I was working in my own office in the Communications Department. We received all the telegrams that came back from the ambassadors overseas—all of them—and we could tell things were getting out of hand. I don't know how to describe it other than to say that it was very interesting in that respect, and **scary** in that respect. We took care of **all** the telegrams. Now, if a telegram came for Secretary of State Cordell Hull, even though we had to type up a copy, that telegram was immediately rushed to him. I'm sure he kept a copy of it in his office.

"There was one funny thing that happened around this time, although some people didn't think it was very funny. Ralph, my youngest brother, would have been about nine years old at this time, and he collected stamps. Well, here I am, with all these stamps from all over the world, so I started to take them off, because, to me, they were going to be thrown into the waste can. One day, after I would have been removing the stamps from the envelopes for some months, here comes this message across my desk: 'Whoever is taking the stamps will cease and desist because President Roosevelt is a stamp collector and the stamps are for his use.' That was the end of the stamp collecting. Isn't that terrible? They said they knew that there was somebody in our area who was taking those stamps.[3]

"We were first working eight hours a day, five days a week. Then it went up to ten hours, almost twelve hours, because we would go to work, and then we'd be allowed to go home for supper, and then we'd come back for, like, four more hours. Then after a while, everybody started to come down with illnesses because we were so tired. It was just pressure, pressure, pressure all the time. So, then they had to cut that out, but they did have us working Saturday mornings until 12:00 noon. This took place before the Pearl Harbor attack. We were all fatigued.

Despite the tiring work schedule, "Ebs" and the other "Government Girls" found time in the evenings for socializing:

"There were many organizations down in Washington that took care of the 'Government Girls.' They would see to it that we would be taken to the forts around the city to the big dances and the big parties. And we were **very** well-chaperoned. It was very, very nice, and we enjoyed it. But after a while, you were so tired that you just didn't go. We could have gone seven nights a week to any of these affairs, but after a while you had to just stop going. So, I would say that once a week, especially the girls in my area, we would go to these big parties and these big dances, which were very well-run and extremely well-chaperoned. We'd be transported in special buses. We had to meet at a central area, and our names were on a big list. As you got off or you got on, they checked you in, and they checked you out. There was no 'hanky-panky' whatsoever. The people who, I would say, were our chaperons would have been members of society. You could tell by the way they dressed and the way they talked that they were educated. They were all very pleasant.

These were our major forms of recreation, and they were mainly military functions.

From time to time, "Ebs" was able to observe members of the diplomatic corps when they passed through the State Department. These were big moments for the young woman from Wrightsville:

"I recall my 'introduction' to Ambassador Joseph Grew. I guess they had recalled him from Japan, and he would be more or less around our area. One day he was down in our snack shop. We had these huge marble stairways, and I'm flying down this set of steps to get a sandwich that was going to be my lunch that day. He came around the corner, and he and I **crashed** into each other. It's a wonder I didn't knock him down. He was startled! His eyes were [this] big. Of course, mine were bigger because here was a very important man. I didn't know it at that moment, but then I found out later that that was Ambassador Grew that I had run into. But that was my introduction to Ambassador Grew. He was a big guy—nice-looking—and very nice, very pleasant. [4]

"We had to go down for our pay in the subterranean area of the State Department. Previously, I had noticed by way of the newspapers that the Japanese peace envoys, Nomura [Kichisaburō] and Kurusu [Saburō] were in Washington. When I was standing in line to get my pay—the diplomatic elevator was very, very close to where we were being paid—I could have reached out and touched them. That's how close they were. They looked very intelligent; they looked very pleasant. One was taller than the other. The one was heftier. The shorter one was heftier than the other one. Anyway, they walked past me with whoever was in attendance with them, and I thought later, 'I could have touched them.' The feeling among us was: 'How wonderful this is; there won't be war.' It was a relief to know that they were negotiating.[5]

With the nation turning to national defense before actually getting into the war, Americans saw their incomes increase markedly over what had been the case during the Great Depression. Thanks in part to "Ebs's" income, her parents were able to afford things that had been previously beyond their reach:

"I wrote my parents once a week, and I was aware that Dad's working hours weren't the greatest. So, I would send $5.00 home once a week, like, $25 a month because, we got paid once a week. Mom saved it, and then she bought nice things for the house. One time I came home, and I was amazed to see that Mom had gotten new gas stove. Would you believe—a new gas stove! So, I knew that it was my money that was doing it. Then, would you believe she got a refrigerator! So, in that respect, it gave me great satisfaction. I'm not sure if this occurred before Pearl Harbor or shortly after the war had started and before things had become highly rationed.

Like most Americans of that generation, "Ebs" remembered where she was and what she was doing when she heard the news of the Japanese attack at Pearl Harbor on 7 December 1941. She also had some vivid memories from observing Secretary of State Cordell Hull on that day as well as watching activities taking place at the Japanese embassy:

"Of, course, we weren't working that day. When we heard about Pearl Harbor that Sunday, the radio was on, and music was playing. All of a sudden, it was interrupted, and they reported about Pearl Harbor. Everybody looked at each other, and we decided **instantly** to go down to the State Department. Three of us were working for the State Department at that time. We didn't even use the public transportation system. It was, like, eight blocks from our apartment to the State Department building, and I remember us running down there.

"As we got there, here came this huge limousine, and Cordell Hull was being chauffeured around in it. Where he was being taken, I don't know, but he had this grim look on his face, very scary, like he was going to take care of the whole situation. I can still see him to this day, the way he looked. He was staring straight ahead; he didn't look right or left at us or anybody else. After that, nothing seemed to be happening, but we weren't allowed to go to our offices or anything.

"Somebody suggested that we go to the Japanese embassy, so we went over there. When we arrived, we saw huge billows of smoke. They were burning their files and papers. We were standing there, and we were watching that. So, we put two and two together, and we saw what was happening. I'd say we were there for about an hour because we wanted to see what would happen next. I didn't see any Japanese employee out there burning all that material. They must have gotten the material together, then set it afire, and then went back inside the building, maybe they were scared that something would happen if they showed their person. But we didn't see anybody, certainly not peace envoys.

"The crowds were forming, but we were some of the first people there. The crowd kept growing and growing. There was not much hostility. It wasn't a riot scene or anything like that—nothing. I think that there was just puzzlement. We were puzzled, too. We just wondered what had happened—that was about the extent of it—because we were so young. We just couldn't understand why the Japanese attacked us. It was difficult for us to understand.

"We then went back to our apartment and just kind of commiserated amongst ourselves: 'What's going to happen next? This is dreadful!' But that particular day, we were stunned. We spent the rest of the day around the radio. Indeed! Indeed! We never left it.

While continuing her work at the State Department, "Ebs" supported the war effort in other ways:

"Within twenty-four hours after the attack, they started what was called a 'dim-out.' Before that, lights around the monuments had remained on all night long. But then, all of a sudden, we had these 'dim-outs.' It was not a complete blackout. And then, in nothing flat, we had to have these air raid wardens. Would you believe—it kind of scares me now when I think about it—I was selected in my particular area to be an air raid warden. My function was to see that the lights were out, curtains were drawn, and blinds were down. In other words, I was more or less to patrol the area. Would you believe that a girl patrolled that block, that whole area there? There was a central area where you were supposed to meet a supervisor periodically. Now, this was fairly frequently; this didn't happen just one night. All this was really scary, because in Wrightsville I had never heard of a blackout or air raid wardens, and here's the big city. I remained an air raid warden the whole time I was in that area. So, whenever the alarm would go off, that meant I had to leave my apartment and go down and get to my station or whatever. Mostly, it was to see about people getting off the street and getting into their apartments and then turning their lights off and what-have-you.

As with all Americans, "Ebs" and the women in her apartment had to adjust to wartime rationing:

While I was in the original apartment, I was chosen to take care of the ration books. I don't know why. I remember the rationing of certain canned vegetables, coffee for sure, canned meats, and shoes and silk stockings to a certain extent. The three things for sure that were rationed were meat, canned goods, and shoes. You stood in long lines. I'd come home from work, and I'd go to this grocery store. I'd stand there and stand there, and then you'd take turns and take turns. Of all the things that were rationed, for me personally, I'd say it was the fact that you couldn't buy shoes, because I did a lot of walking. Then so far as food, it was meat. That was difficult.

With Washington on a wartime footing, changes occurred in "Ebs's" routine in the Communications Section at the State Department:

"A lot of messages that were coming through were about getting people back from overseas. The [MS] *Gripsholm* was bringing people back, and we'd have huge lists. I remember typing up huge lists of these people from all over the United States. Of course, they were in the war zone, and we were trying to get them back. The [MS] *Gripsholm* brought these people back from Japan, and we had to take care of all that.[6]

"Security became tighter. When I first had to go down there, of course, I had to wear identification, but I didn't have to show my card. You always had a card that was like celluloid. Actually it was plastic. Then you had to have your picture taken, and then, of course, that photo would go with your card. Every once in a while, they would go through your pocketbook or your packages. It became strict in that respect.

"We were on the fourth floor, and there was up above us a floor that we called `The Attic.' Up there would be servicemen who manned machine guns. We would see them come down the steps because it was close to our office. The servicemen would never talk while they were up there, but when they came down they'd talk to us. But they'd never say what they did. Then if I would walk down the hall, here would come a Marine, who would have a chain attached to a pouch and locked around his waist. He'd have a pistol by his side. He was cool, very cool. He wasn't nearly as friendly as the servicemen from the Army.

"Then we would have air raid drills in the State Department. The entire personnel had to leave their desks about once a month. In the center of the second floor, we had to all form along the walls, because if a bomb fell, it would do the most damage at the top. We would be down there up against the center wall, which was supposed to be more reinforced than the outer walls. So, about once a month, there would be this specific signal. Thousands of us crowded in there, and then we'd have to wait until the 'all clear' signal was given.

"Eventually, I was transferred to a different area, and in this area—this was still Communications—we had a ticker, the teletype. It clicked all day long, and for eight hours a day I had to listen to this. So, in that respect, in this particular office, we heard about everything. It was just constant, the new things that were happening.

Although "Ebs" initially believed that she was doing something important by working at the State Department, as time went on she became restless and did not think she was contributing enough toward the war effort. As a result she resigned her position in Washington and applied for entrance into the Cadet Nurse Corps:

"My brother Gordon joined the Marine Corps in December 1941, not too long after the Pearl Harbor attack. Mom and Dad had to sign for him because he was under seventeen. After boot training he became part of the 1st Marine Division and saw action at Tulagi and Guadalcanal in the Solomon Islands. Mom always kept up correspondence with me, and since we didn't have a telephone, she wrote me frequently. She would always keep me abreast with information about Gordon. Well, then along came Guadalcanal, and she hadn't heard from him for months. Well, apparently Gordon had amnesia as a result of having malaria. He was quite ill with malaria and out of his head. That bothered me considerably.

"At one point, I counted my relatives who were in the military. Twenty-three of them, including my brother, were in the service, and I felt like I wasn't doing my duty. They were bleeding and dying on the line in all probability.

"For the first two years in Washington, I felt a lot of job satisfaction in working at the State Department. Then I decided that anybody could do my job. Anybody could sit there and type and file or whatever. I thought, 'I've been down here for two years, and I don't feel like I'm getting anywhere,' because, like I said, anybody could do this job. I didn't want to my parents to know that I was thinking about changing jobs, however, because it was a good job.

"I started to hear on the radio that they were forming a Cadet Nurse Corps. The reason they were forming the Cadet Nurse Corps was because the regular nurses were leaving to go to the battle front to tend to guys who were wounded, so somebody had to take over at the civilian hospitals.[7] This is why the Cadet Nurse Corps was formed. I thought that maybe I'd be contributing more to what my country needed by becoming a nurse. So, I called to get information, and they gave it to me. I then wrote to the two hospitals in Lancaster to see if they were taking Cadets, but they were not at that time. That's when I finally wrote the York Hospital, and they said that they were taking Cadets. I took the train and went straight to York to take the entrance examination, and then I went straight back to Washington. Shortly afterwards, they let me know that I had passed and that I should come back at a certain date. I tried to get into the September 1943 class, but it was already filled. As a result, I finally went in on Valentine's Day, February 14, 1944. It was almost like being in the service because we had to wear our Cadet Nurse Corps uniforms.

"I went through most of my nurse's training at the York Hospital, and then for my last six months of training, if it were so arranged, they would select somebody to go to a military hospital. So, I was selected to go to Hines Veterans Hospital, about twelve miles from downtown Chicago. At the time, it was the largest veterans hospital in the United States. We had a census of 2,400 guys, and that also meant there were almost 2,400 medical personnel. My first day there, I had ninety-six patients, and I'm a student! It was almost overwhelming! So, my last six months I went there to finish training. Altogether, I stayed approximately two years at Hines as both a student and a RN. We were the center for paraplegics or quadriplegics for the entire United States. We had hundreds and hundreds of these paralyzed guys. We also dealt with guys suffering from battle fatigue. They had an area for those guys, and they were able to recover pretty quickly. That was a little different for me, but mostly I handled guys with physical wounds. Mostly, my job was giving medication and all kinds of treatments and changing bandages or whatever. We had a lot of attendants to help us, and they were really efficient.

"Ebs" returned to Wrightsville in 1946. Due to her experiences during the war, she saw the town in a different light. Working in Washington and

Chicago had broadened her horizons, and she was a changed person upon her return to Wrightsville:

"The war broadened my IQ because I'm very historically minded. I loved history, and my work at the State Department was history in the making. I even had chances to catch glimpses of Franklin and Eleanor Roosevelt since we were right next to the White House. The first office I was in was on the fourth floor, and I could look right straight down into the yard of the White House. We could look out the window and see these things. One day I looked out, and here was this big limousine, an open-air car. There was Churchill and FDR. I mean, I could look them straight in the face. I was overwhelmed. I thought, 'I can't believe it!' Only once did I see President Roosevelt, but I saw Mrs. Roosevelt frequently because she was in the yard often with Fala, their pet dog.

"So, living in Washington broadened my horizons because little Wrightsville was so insulated that you never saw anything like that. This experience was educational in that respect. It was a liberating experience for me after growing up in this small town, even though I didn't think of it that way at the time. Then, too, it was kind of disappointing to return to Wrightsville. It was a shock. I'd come from this big city where everything was going on, and then I came back to quiet little Wrightsville. I don't know what I expected."

A few years after the war, "Ebs" married Richard McCune, a Navy veteran of World War II, and they built a home in Columbia. They adopted a son, and she continued her career as a nurse at the Columbia Hospital, retiring after many years of service. Evelyn died on 13 November 2002, not long after she and Dick had celebrated their fifty-second wedding anniversary.

Notes

1. Evelyn (née Myers) McCune, interview by the author, 4 August 1996, transcript, OH1148, Oral History Collection, University Archives, University of North Texas, Denton, TX.

2. See David Brinkley, *Washington Goes to War* (New York: Alfred A. Knopf, 1988), 105-109.

3. Note: An avid stamp collector, Roosevelt inquired of the State Department how it handled envelopes containing mail from foreign governments and was informed that most were thrown away. When he indicated that he would like some specific ones for his collection, he thereafter received a weekly packet from the State Department delivered by courier each Saturday. See H. W. Brands, *Traitor to His Class: The Privileged Life and Radical Presidency of Franklin Delano Roosevelt* (New York: Doubleday, 2008), 316.

4. Note: Joseph Grew (1880-1965) was appointed US ambassador to Japan in 1932. He was in Tokyo when the attack at Pearl Harbor occurred and was interned for a short time by the Japanese government. Grew was released and returned to the United States 25 June 1942. See Joseph C. Grew, *Turbulent Era: A Diplomatic Record of Forty Years, 1904-1945* (Boston: Houghton Mifflin, 1952).

5. Note: As tensions between the United States and the Japanese government escalated, Ambassador Nomura Kichisaburō and Special Envoy Kurusu Saburō were sent to Washington to work out an agreement to settle matters relating to China and other points of contention in South Asia. The goal of the Imperial government was to reach an agreement whereby the United States would essentially recognize Japanese hegemony in Asia. Nomura and Kurusu were carrying on negotiations in Washington when the attack at Pearl Harbor occurred. After the war, both denied that they knew before-

hand of the attack. See Robert A. Divine, *The Reluctant Belligerent: American Entry into World War II* (New York: John Wiley & Sons, 1965), 116-121.

6. Note: From 1942-1946, the US Department of State chartered the MS *Gripsholm* from the Swedish American Line as an exchange and repatriation ship, carrying Japanese and German nationals to exchange points, always neutral ports, where it picked up Americans and Canadians to bring home to American and Canada. In this service, it sailed under the auspices of the Red Cross, with a Swedish captain and crew. The ship made twelve round trips, carrying a total of 27,712 repatriates. See Greg Leck, *Captives of Empire: The Japanese Internment of Allied Civilians in China and Hong Kong, 1941-1945* (Bangor, PA: Shandy Press, 2006).

7. Note: The US Cadet Nurse Corps was a program established by the federal government in 1943. Its primary purpose was to ensure that the country had enough nurses to care for the needs of its citizens both on the home and war fronts. When the United States entered World War II, it became immediately clear that there was a pressing shortage of nurses, since more and more doctors and nurses were joining the military. The formation of the Cadet Nurse Corps resulted in a dramatic rise in the number of nursing students, a greater public recognition of nurses, and changes in the manner in which nurses were educated and trained. A student nurse who joined the Cadet Nurse Corps was eligible for a government subsidy that paid for her tuition, books, and uniforms as well as a small living stipend. In return, participants pledged to serve in essential civilian, military, or in other federal services for the duration of the war. To be eligible a woman had to be a graduate from an accredited high school with good grades, be between the ages of seventeen and thirty-five, and be in good health. See Jeanne M. Holm, *In Defense of a Nation: Servicewomen in World War II* (Arlington, VA: Military Women's Press, 1997).

Figure 8. Alfred "Skip" Marcello

Chapter 5

Alfred "Skip" Marcello, Jr.

Teenager

Born on 19 March 1932, "Skip," the older brother of the editor of this volume, gives an account from the perspective of a teenager growing up in Wrightsville during World War II. His comments indicate that the town went all-out for the war effort with almost every citizen contributing in one way or another. He describes the defensive measures taken to protect the town and the York-Lancaster Intercounty Bridge, air raid drills, scrap drives, rationing, and the participation of the school and churches in the patriotic effort. "Skip" also presents interesting observations on the town's young men who went into the service as well as their readjustments after returning from military duty. With the exception of a new found prosperity, he observed that Wrightsville changed very little as a result of World War II. The town, moreover, made a smooth transition from a wartime economy to a peacetime economy.[1]

The Great Depression affected the Marcello family as it did almost every other family in Wrightsville:

"Everybody was poor, but there were some people who were poorer than others. I don't think that we, as a family, were in that lower level of poor. In our family there were my parents, Alfred and Josephine

Marcello, my older sister, and me. You didn't come along until December 1939. We were probably in the middle somewhere or just below the middle. There were many, many families that had less than we had. I don't think that Dad really had steady work. He worked at a lace mill in Columbia. Some workweeks, he didn't work at all; other workweeks, he'd work maybe a couple days.

As war approached, "Skip" remembered that economic conditions seemed to improve gradually in the Marcello household:

"I think that during the late 1930s and into the early 1940s there was an improvement. You could see that we were coming out of the Depression. Dad seemed to have more work, and then after the country got into the war, he took a job as a molder at 'The Spark' [a local nickname for Susquehanna Casting]. Things got much better after he switched jobs.

Like most Americans of that generation, "Skip" remembered the reaction of people after receiving news about the Japanese attack at Pearl Harbor:

"I was playing down around the river with the Holtzinger brothers, and I came home about four or five o'clock in the afternoon. Our neighbor, [James] 'Hick' Siltzer was at our house, along with Mother and Dad, and they were talking about this bombing that took place at Pearl Harbor. So, that's basically how I heard about it. Of course, the whole community was—I don't want to say excited—concerned about it. But I'm not so sure that many people at that time realized how long this war was going to last or how many lives were going to be taken, not at the beginning, anyway.

With the coming of war, Wrightsville mobilized on the home front like communities all across the United States. One of the first priorities for local officials was the protection of the Lancaster-York Intercounty Bridge:

"Just after the war started, they employed a group of guards to stand watch over the bridge. I think that most of them had been either in the National Guard or in the service prior to the war. In the early stages, I believe they were not eligible for the draft, so they became bridge guards. It was a fulltime job for them. One time I saw them marching, and there must have been thirty-five to forty guards in that particular unit. When they first organized, all they had were armbands, and they also carried the old Springfield [Model 1903] rifles. Later on, they got uniforms.

"They were on each end of the bridge at the toll booths. They also had guardhouses under the bridge on each side of the river. When weather permitted, they had a motorboat and went back and forth on the river, checking out the bridge for any possible sabotage that might take place. Periodically, they would check inside vehicles.

US Route 30 (Lincoln Highway) and the Lancaster-York Intercounty Bridge throughout the war served a major conduit for the movement of troops from training bases to ports along the Atlantic Coast where they would be deployed overseas. Young "Skip" remembered the long truck convoys passing through Wrightsville and the reaction of local citizens toward the troops passing through the town:

"I recall the troop convoys coming through Wrightsville and going across the bridge heading east, we assumed, to some port of embarkation in New Jersey or New York. When these convoys would come through, it would be two or three hours of continuous trucks moving through our town. Everybody would go over to our main street, Hellam Street, when word got around that the convoys were coming through, and we would watch these soldiers. A lot of these soldiers would see the women along the street, and they would throw out paper with their addresses on them. Of course, everybody was waving to them.

One of the first all-out responses to the war effort was the organizing of scrap metal drives by Wrightsville's Council of National Defense:

"Every community would have scrap metal drives, maybe three or four drives a year. They were usually advertised. They were primarily looking for metals of all sorts. Steel, aluminum, and copper were truly items that were very much sought after for the war effort. Some local merchants had a truck, and they would go around town, and folks would put out their materials for the scrap drive. They would deposit those materials off to the side of the entrance to the bridge. There was a **huge** pile of scrap metal there. Every community would take pride on the amount of scrap that they would gather for the war effort.

"In the limestone quarry where we used to swim, the story always went that there was a lot of equipment at the bottom of that quarry. I can remember fellows going out with grappling hooks, trying to bring to the surface some of that machinery that they said was there. I'm not so sure that there ever was any machinery there, but I remember them exploring that possibility.

The Council of National Defense also mobilized the local Boy Scout troop for the war effort. As a Boy Scout at that time, "Skip" had vivid recollections of the contributions of his troop:

"Primarily, we would conduct newspaper drives. I don't know how they used the newspapers in the war effort, but we did gather newspapers. If you gathered so many pounds of newspapers, as a Boy Scout you received a medal. It was called the Eisenhower Medal.[2]

"Boy Scouts were also used as airplane spotters. We would have silhouettes of airplanes, and in case the enemy would attack or planes would fly over, we were supposed to identify these planes. We would have our little handbook, and when we would see a plane, we would try to match the silhouette of that plane with the silhouette that was in this little handbook. Then I think that we had a station that we had to report to, and maybe we would even have to report to our scoutmaster. Of course, by that time the plane was probably long gone, or it would have dropped all its bombs by then. The Boy Scouts would be stationed at some high point to act as plane spotters. They'd send us anyplace that was high or to a particular building that was high or any landform that had a higher elevation. We would go there in teams of two or three. I think that all this was an exercise that gave the Boy Scouts something to do and gave them a feeling that they were contributing to the war effort. I'm not sure how efficient it was.

"We also assisted the air raid wardens during an air raid alert or during a blackout. The Boy Scouts would serve as runners, messengers, and that type of thing within the air raid system.

"The Boy Scouts also collected milkweed. We even did that in the schools. We would go out and collect bags of milkweed pods. The milkweed itself was used in life preservers. That was a busy activity for everybody. We had bags upon bags of that. We would usually gather it in rural areas—local farms and fields. Of course, milkweed grows almost anywhere, but that is where we'd find it, mostly.

Local schools and churches also actively participated in the war effort:

"Besides, the academic subjects, everything else pointed toward the war effort or had a patriotic theme attached to it. Our songs were all patriotic. I can remember—I don't know who sponsored this—what was called 'Write a Fighter Corps.' We had little stencils that we'd put at the top of letters, and we'd write letters to servicemen to boost their morale.[3]

"We would also practice air raid drills. When the alarm sounded, we would get under our desks for protection, and, of course, everybody had to be quiet.

"Also, the schools would sell what were known as 'defense stamps.' They were either ten cents or twenty-five cents apiece, and you would put them in a booklet. When you had accumulated $18.75 worth, you could purchase a war bond, and it would pay you $25 after maturing in ten years.

"School activities were restricted because you just couldn't buy the supplies that were needed. Sports programs did continue, but since most of the male teachers were in the service, the schools received permission to hire non-teachers as coaches. For example, Jack Wilson, who was a postal carrier, coached the boy's basketball team for a couple years. There just weren't any men available who were teaching at that time.

"A number of guys left high school early, before they graduated, to join the service. Then they would either get their diploma after the war, or some dispensation was given to them so that they could get their diploma while they were in the service. I think that a number of fellows did that.

"Churches also got into the patriotic fervor of the times. In addition to the normal church music, we also had patriotic songs. Our Youth Fellowship made checkerboards for the soldiers who were in hospitals. We made other items for servicemen to spend their time on while recuperating. One of our leaders in the Youth Fellowship group early in the war was Richard Wakefield. He was drafted and unfortunately was killed on D-Day during the invasion of Normandy.

Very shortly after American entrance into the war, the local Council of National Defense organized a rationing system in compliance with federal mandates:

"I do remember some things about the rationing system in Wrightsville. Everybody—and this pertains not only to Wrightsville—had to sign up. You had to go and sign up for your rationing books. There were various stations throughout the town. For our ward it was at Bailey's garage on Hellam Street, between 4th and 5th Streets. You signed up, and you were issued ration books. The number of ration books and stamps was based on the size of your family and the age of the children. You had to use these ration stamps for purchasing various items.

"Basically, everything was rationed. Butter was a hot item. Back in those days, you couldn't get butter, so you used 'butterine,' which is better known as margarine these days. [4] Shoes were rationed. Meat was rationed. Another hot item was coffee, which was also rationed. Another hot item—no pun intended—even though they weren't rationed but were very scarce, were cigarettes. Many people started to roll their own cigarettes. They would buy the little machines and roll their own cigarettes.[5]

"The big item that was rationed, of course, was gasoline. The alternative was public transportation, believe it or not. It was during this time that bus service was initiated between Wrightsville and Columbia. Prior to that, there was no public transportation between the two towns. A lot of people would go to Columbia for work and shopping. We had a local individual who had a pretty good position with the York Bus Company. His name was Clyde Thompson [also a member of Wrightsville's Council of National Defense]. This bus was almost—but not quite—like a tractor-trailer and was painted red, white, and blue. I think it was called the 'Liberty Bus.' I can remember it coming through town. So, most people relied on public transportation, either buses or trains. We had what was called an electric railcar, like a trolley, that went from Lancaster to York, so we used either of those two.

"As I said, gasoline was rationed. Some people actually put their car on blocks for the duration of the war. One of [Brenneman] 'Bren' Kline's sons had evidently bought a new car before he was drafted into the service. His garage was right next to the old Wrightsville Elementary School, and we could look into their garage from the playground, and here was this car, setting up on blocks with the four wheels taken off to conserve the rubber. There was also a car over in our neighbor 'Nettie' Eddy's garage that belonged to Chet Scantling, and it was also up on blocks for the duration of the war.

Air raid alerts became a regular part of everyday life for Wrightsville's citizens:

"Periodically, we would have air raid alerts. Some of them would be announced, and others would not be announced. Of course, when the siren sounded, we had to pull down our shades and turn out the lights, and they specifically said that we should get under the table in case there was any falling debris. These air raid activities continued throughout the war, even after the initial excitement and panic subsided. I think that, for the most part, most people took them rather seriously, and they carried out their responsibilities. You have to remember that there were quite a few households without men, and the women of the families certainly didn't want to take any chances. They took everything rather seriously.

"Dad was an air raid warden. When we had an air raid alert, he would put on his helmet with the proper insignia on it, and he had an armband. He had a certain area that he had to patrol during these drills. He was making sure that all the lights were out, that people had heard the siren, that no one was on the streets, and that there were no moving vehicles. Basically, that was their job.

With the coming of war, the drafting of young men accelerated, and young Marcello noticed how this changed the face of Wrightsville:

"Going back a little bit to the Depression, all these fellows had lived in our neighborhood, and they didn't have jobs. For some reason, as a youngster, I became very close to them. When the war started, of course, just about every one of those fellows was drafted. It seemed like half the population had deserted the town. There was a huge gap; there was a huge hole. This being a small town and the war taking so many people out of the town, it left quite a hole in the population. You just didn't see any young men around town. There were either men in their forties or much older. Before we started this interview, I made an estimate of the number of persons in just a two-block section from up and down Walnut Street from Second Street to Fourth Street, and I counted at least thirty-five men and one woman. The Holtzingers must have had four or five in the service; the Crumblings had four; the Townsleys had two; the Bocks had two; the Yeagers had two. If you keep adding those up, it doesn't take long to get thirty-five or forty. It was almost like the robins migrating —they were gone.

"Skip" also remembered the negative attitudes of citizens toward those who received deferments for various reasons:

"Let me give you the two key terms that were used for these people. The '4-Fer' was not a positive term at that time. It had a negative connotation. Those of draft age who were classified as having essential occupations were referred to as 'draft dodgers.' That status was probably one step below the '4-Fers,'as far as not being popular in the community. There weren't too many of those, but there were a few around. I didn't see any overt hostility toward them—I don't think there was any—but there was a lot of talk. They were not looked upon very favorably. Particularly if they did not have an essential job before the war, and then when the war started and their draft number was close to coming up, and they would switch to an essential job, that's when people looked down upon them.

"I remember what occurred at [Harris B.] 'Babe' Martin's service station. 'Babe' had a defense job, and Mary Bailey pumped gasoline at the station. It was highly unusual at that time to see a woman pumping gasoline at a service station. There was no reaction at all to her doing this. It was probably complimentary because it was all toward the war effort.

As was the case in most other communities, and particularly if there were family members in the military, people closely followed news from the battle fronts and turned out for patriotic demonstrations:

"Each ward dedicated a flag that included the number of individuals from that ward who was serving in the armed services. I remember the dedication of the Second Ward's flag, which took place at Second and Walnut Streets by [Harry] 'Ikie' Woods's grocery store. The Reverend Jake Spangler, who was the minister of the Lutheran church, gave the dedicatory speech. He probably did that because he was a veteran of World War I. Our neighbor, 'Nettie' Eddy, made the flag. It was a huge thing with a big star on it, and there was a number on it that indicated the number of individuals who were serving in the military. The number would be changed periodically. I would say there were twenty-five or thirty people there. Again, remember that this was a patriotic time, and if anything patriotic went on, it pulled in a fair number of people. That's not a large crowd to some people, but for our town and our ward, that was a pretty good crowd.

As a young teenager at the time, "Skip" had mixed emotions when the news of the wounded and dead local servicemen reached town:

"I'm going to answer questions about battle casualties from my own perspective because I was only eleven, twelve, thirteen years old at the time. There were a couple of young men from our neighborhood, Bob Scantling and Warren Billet, who were both killed in plane crashes. This did not have a profound effect on me for whatever reason.

"I mentioned Richard Wakefield earlier, and that one hit close to home because I had known him quite well. He had worked with us in our Youth Fellowship at church. The other one that made an impression on me, for whatever reason, was when Harold Crumling was killed. I had known him, and consciously or subconsciously I thought about the family he had left behind. He had two children. That one, I think, hit closer to home than a lot of the other casualties that occurred.

"Most households that had men or women in the service would hang a little red, white, and blue banner in the window. The number of blue stars on the banner indicated the number for that household who were in the service. I can't recall if there was any color for being wounded, but, of course, if there was a gold star, it meant that a member of that household had been killed.

World War II returned prosperity to Wrightsville as it did for other communities, but the war brought no real physical changes to the community:

"The foundries were going full-blast. There were three of them in town. The one in particular that I can remember is Riverside Foundry, which made castings for hand grenades. There were always a couple hand grenade castings at school because some of the kids would work down there at night. Some of these grenades would be on the scrap pile, so we'd just pick them up, and that was a big deal. I'm not sure what the silk mill made during the war, but I know that they were involved in defense work, as well as the other two foundries.

"The workforce at the foundries was made up of older men, married men with children, even kids who were still in high school and worked at night for a few hours. All the other fellows were in the service. The older men had been established there for years and just continued to work there.

"The war brought no demographic changes to Wrightsville. Unlike the case of other towns, that was not true for Wrightsville. Very few new people moved in, so there were no new houses built. The people who worked in the foundries were the people who had worked there for years, or they were members of families that already lived in Wrightsville. Not too many outsiders moved in. Absolutely, it was pretty standard for the son to follow the father into the foundry. So, the economy was good, and there was plenty of work for everybody. There was no place to spend the money, however, because you couldn't buy anything. Everything was being used for the war effort. By the end of the war, those people came out of it pretty good, financially.

Even as a teenager, "Skip" also benefitted financially from World War II:

"I took a job in Columbia, working in a shoeshine parlor operated by John Bardaxe, who was a Greek immigrant. Servicemen home on leave would visit the shoeshine parlor, and they were big tippers. Money didn't seem to mean much to them. One fellow, I remember, gave me a dollar tip, which was astronomical. Believe it or not, I saved a lot of my income. By the time I finished high school in 1950, with that income and the income I made during the summers while in high school, I had enough money saved for my first two years of college. Part of the source of that money was derived from the tips that I made while shining shoes.

As was true for all communities, Wrightsville's citizens greeted the end of World War II with public celebrations:

"There was no big celebration, only minor ones, for V-E Day [Victory in Europe] because we still had a war going on in the Pacific Theater. On V-J Day [Victory over Japan], people ran out into the streets and started yelling and celebrating. Church bells rang; sirens went off. It was just a huge celebration by everybody in all of the towns. Down at Sprenkle's Hotel, [Elmer] 'Chees' Sprenkle brought his jukebox out on the pavement, and people were dancing on the sidewalks and on Hellam Street in celebration of the end of the war. That celebration was followed, of course, when the veterans came home, with parades in each of the towns honoring these men and women.

When the veterans returned to Wrightsville, most of them very quickly got down to the business of making a living, getting on with their lives, and making up for lost time:

"I think I said earlier that these were young men in their teens and twenties, who I knew during the Depression, and then they went off to war. Then, of course, after the war, these people gradually came back. In thinking back, I don't believe there was a big, radical transition from their military life back to civilian life. Most of these guys just came back to town, took off their uniforms, and went back to work where they had worked before because their jobs were protected.

"As a community, Wrightsville had a very positive feeling toward the veterans. I'm not so sure anything special was done. Again, you have to remember that this was a laid-back, small town. They did have a victory parade where they honored the veterans, and the American Legion became much more active in the community because of the World War II veterans.

In looking back through fifty-five years of hindsight, "Skip" had positive memories of Wrightsville's participation in the war effort:

"I have never witnessed in my lifetime such a uniform and serious united effort as there was during the war, as far as winning the war and the war effort. I've never seen our country so unified."

"Skip" Marcello graduated from Wrightsville High School in 1950 and then matriculated to Millersville (PA) State Teachers College, earning a

BS degree in 1954. He served two years in the US Army, and after being discharged he started his teaching career at Columbia High School. He eventually earned a master's degree in educational administration at Pennsylvania State University. Marcello finished his career in education as principal of Carlisle High School in Carlisle, Pennsylvania. "Skip" married, raised a son, and he and his wife currently live in Carlisle.

Notes

1. Alfred J. Marcello, interview by the author, 7 August 2000, transcript, OH1356, Oral History Collection, University Archives, University of North Texas, Denton, TX.

2. Note: Due to the wartime demands for lumber, there was a shortage of wood pulp. This shortage resulted in the initiation of conservation and salvage campaigns. Inspired by the General Eisenhower Waste Paper Campaign of 1945, Boy Scouts trudged from house to house collecting bundles of newspapers. Scouts who collected 1,000 pounds of paper received the General Eisenhower War Service Medal for Extraordinary Patriotic Achievement bearing the general's likeness. In lieu of the medal, however, Scouts received a paper certificate explaining that there was a metal shortage: "The necessity for rushing the manufacture of the Military Awards for Heroism delayed your General Eisenhower Medal. You will receive it just as soon as it arrives." See Richard R. Lingeman, *Don't You Know There's a War On: The American Home Front, 1941-1945* (New York: G. P. Putnam's Sons, 1970), 273.

3. This program was sponsored by the creators of the radio adventure series *Jack Armstrong: All-American Boy*. The series maintained its popularity from 1933-1951. The storylines centered on the globe-trotting adventures of Armstrong and his friends. By 1943, more than a million schoolchildren had joined the "Write a Fighter Corps," pledging to write once a month to a serviceman.

4. Note: Butterine is a substance prepared from animal fat, usually beef or mutton fat, with some other ingredients intermixed as an imitation of butter.

5. Note: Cigarettes became scarce in 1944 because of lowered production after a record high in 1943. Thirty percent of all cigarettes made went to the armed forces, though the military made up less than 10 percent of the population. See Lingeman, *Don't You Know There's a War On*, 264-265.

Figure 9. Mervin "Merv" Garver

Chapter 6

Mervin "Merv" Garver

Foundry Worker
4-F

Born on 10 April 1923, Mervin Garver, the son of Clara and Edward Garver, spent his entire life in Wrightsville. "Merv" did not serve in the military during World War II because he was classified by the Army as 4-F, meaning that he was "not acceptable for military service under established physical, mental, or moral standards." Outwardly looking physically fit, "Merv' had to endure the social stigma attached to those who were known as "4-Fers" during the war. This attitude was particularly marked in Wrightsville, a small town of 2,300 people where everybody knew one another. Many citizens considered such a person to be a coward or worse. As a result, "Merv" during the war and for many years thereafter carried with him a sense of shame and guilt for not having served. To his credit, he contributed to the war effort in other ways by working in the core room at Riverside Foundry, which had several defense contracts, and by regularly purchasing war bonds and war stamps. His feelings of guilt regularly emerged when the town celebrated Memorial Day every year. "Merv" married, bought a home, and raised two daughters in Wrightsville. A widower, he resided in Wrightsville and remained very active in the Locust Street Methodist

Church. Due to a series of illnesses brought on mainly by old age, "Merv" spent a short time at the Pleasant Acres Nursing and Rehabilitation Center in York, Pennsylvania, before his death on 23 September 2011.[1]

Unlike many Depression-era young men in Wrightsville, "Merv" graduated from high school and had some advanced education taking commercial-related courses:

"I went through school in Wrightsville and graduated from Wrightsville High School in 1941. Then I went to Thompson's Business College in York for almost two years. I worked during the daytime and went to Thompson's at night, taking regular business courses like typing, shorthand, and courses like that. When I graduated from high school, my first job was at the Hellam Furniture Factory, and I worked there for about a year. It was still very difficult to get a job at that time. I got my job at the furniture factory because my buddy's father ran the unloading department. The only way I got in was because I knew somebody. I put in forty hours a week and made thirty cents an hour. I was unloading lumber, something I was incapable of doing, because I wanted money so badly. I got $11.88 a week.

"Then I went to work at Riverside Foundry, and eventually, after several years, I was able to transfer to the business office. At the foundry we made gray iron castings and so forth. I worked in the core room, and I made cores that were inserts that went into the manufacture of castings. In other words, we made holes in the castings. At Riverside, I made fifty cents an hour. In the core room, I was apprenticing for Ralph Johns and Pete Young. Pete was a good one. He had spent fifty or sixty years making cores there.

Like most Americans of the World War II generation, "Merv" had vivid recollections when he heard about the Japanese attack at Pearl Harbor:

"I was in my grandfather's living room when I heard about it on the radio. At first nobody believed that it had happened. It couldn't have happened. Then people were angry.

As an eighteen-year-old at the time of the attack, "Merv" had already registered for the draft, and shortly afterwards he received his induction notice from the York County Draft Board. This was the beginning of his troubles:

"I had turned eighteen a month before I graduated from high school, and I received my notice to report for induction in early 1942. So, I was headed to the Indiantown Gap Military Reservation shortly afterwards. Indiantown Gap was located in Lebanon County about twenty-three miles northeast of Harrisburg. Of course, we went through the regular ropes there with physical examinations and all that sort of stuff.

"I had a problem, and I didn't know what was going to happen to me. I didn't know how to express it, so I just thought I'd keep my mouth shut and go through the ropes the way they were meant to be. When I told them about my problem, I ended up being pushed around and so forth. They were kind of a little rough with me because I don't think they believed me. But I answered their questions as truthfully as I knew how. When I was done, they told me I was 4-F. I don't think they told me why at the time, but I knew I didn't pass because I came back home. At that time, those who were qualified for the Army were being sent straight through for basic training.

"My 4-F notice said that I was psychoneurotic. It was a matter of being almost convulsive at one time. I would get so sick with a headache that I'd have to go to bed for three or four days at a time. I would get so numb. My tongue would get so numb that I couldn't talk—things like this. Of course my folks always called the doctor, and it was always the local doctor because he was the only one we could afford. His advice was always the same: 'Oh, just let him go. He'll get better.' In three or four days, I'd almost be back to normal, but still with a terrific headache. That would last for a couple days. This condition occurred about every five or six months. As far as I know, my condition was diagnosed right there at Indiantown Gap.

"I felt kind of rough about being classified as 4-F because everybody else my age was going into the service. Everybody was going, but I had to stay put. Well, then I had to face everything that was being said about me. It kind of made me miserable because everyone wanted to know why I was able to stay out of the military, and it wasn't easy for me to express why I wasn't drafted. Oh, yes, people were direct: 'Hey! Why aren't you in the service?' It was that direct. I don't want to name names, though. I used to go to Columbia occasionally with my parents when they went to the Eagles Lodge and places like that, and we'd stay there quite late. It often happened that I'd be questioned there because most of the people who hung out there were veterans, and they'd probably had a few beers by then. They didn't mind being direct because they had other veterans in back of them, so they didn't mind forcing the issue with me. I always tried to fend them off because I knew there was nothing I could do about my situation.

"I think I was sent to Indiantown Gap on three separate occasions. I guess they were thinking that my condition had changed. One time I came home, and there was only one other guy on the whole train. There were only two of us who came back on the train that was returning to York. It made me feel like I was worthless. I wasn't wanted; I wasn't needed. So, that was tough. Here I was, single and so forth. I didn't get married until 1949. There were people in Wrightsville who believed that I was a physically healthy human being, so they couldn't see what my problem was. There were those who didn't know that I had a problem. They just thought anything, I guess, that they wanted to.

Under the circumstances, "Merv" decided he could demonstrate his patriotism by contributing to the war effort at Riverside Foundry. In addition, thanks to World War II, his job in the core room offered him an opportunity to make more money than he ever had before:

"I continued to work in the core room for the next seven or eight years, so I was there throughout the war. I was just the little, lowest guy out there in the core room. I was there again because my dad had been working in the foundry and because there was an understanding as to my health and so on that, if I got to the point where I couldn't work, I could leave my job, and that was it. I couldn't work around heat, and I wasn't strong enough to shift weights. There were a lot of things that I couldn't do, but I had a good job there in the core room and an opportunity to make a good deal of money.

"On one occasion, [Donald] 'Red' Smith, the son of the owner of Riverside Foundry, came into the core room and said he needed these radar cores and hand grenade cores. Riverside had government contracts to make both the radar parts and the grenades, and he needed them produced as soon as possible. The radar apparatus was a round core about six inches in diameter and maybe three inches high. The difficulty in making them was this little protrusion that went into the side, and there was a lip that came up. Well, even if you kept the lip on in the sand and made the core and got a good one, you had trouble baking it because, if you baked it too hard, you'd burn off that lip. So, that was quite a deal making them, and they were difficult to make. Even after they were made, they had to be transported to the molder, and sometimes it would break off or get broken. Well, our facilities in the core room were also limited, so we could only make so many at a time. We only had medium-sized ovens, and all these cores had to be baked. So, 'Red' told Ralph Smuck and me that he would give us three cents apiece for every radar core we made. Well, that was a lot of money in those days. I remember the first week we got paid ninety bucks. Can you imagine ninety bucks when I was used to making twelve bucks before? So, we switched from an hourly wage to piecework.

"But, anyhow, we really worked day and night. I know we put in more than twelve hours a day, and we worked every day except Sunday. We had a little stove, so we even used to cook our meals there. We spent very little time at home since we usually worked there until midnight. We were the first ones there and the last ones to leave. Lots of times we would put in our regular day, and even though the core room closed down, we would work until midnight. We'd get about six hours of sleep and then go right back to doing the same thing. Then we had Sundays to rest because there wasn't any place to go. We didn't have cars and couldn't have found gas even if we did have a car. So, it was all work. We also didn't like the facilities in the company shower room because there was nothing in there but sweat, and neither Ralph nor I had a bathroom in our parents' houses. I had a canoe, so we'd take this canoe out and bathe in the river in the summertime.

"So, the money was important to us, but still this was our chance to do something to help the war effort. But I think everybody felt the same way. Everybody was in this to do something for your country, and you spent your money for bonds and that kind of stuff. You had money for bonds deducted from your paycheck. They were deducted right from your paycheck. That was a thing the company put into effect. You could say that you wanted so much money taken out of your paycheck, and then when the bond was paid for, they would see that you got one with your paycheck. I don't think that there was much pressure for you to buy bonds because everybody just did it. It was something that everybody thought they had to do for the war effort. If you were at home making money, and the servicemen were overseas and possibly giving their lives, it was something that you had to do. Then we also used to go to the post office and buy stamps. We'd save the stamps, and paste them in a special folder, and when the folder held enough stamps, we could take it back to the post office and buy a bond. I think each stamp was ten cents or something like that. My brother Jake, who was eighteen months younger than I, had gone into the service. Jake was sent straight to Germany. So, that was another reason for me to produce more and to buy bonds.

World War II also improved the Garver family's finances:

"The family's economic situation became much better. We were much better off because when I was growing up, my dad worked one day a week at the foundry, and he got $3.28 for that day. Can you imagine? There were five of us in the family. In addition to my parents and my brother, I also had a sister, Charlotte Mae. Things were really rough, but fortunately for me, we lived next door to my grandparents, so that's where I usually took my meals. Before the war, we bought everything 'on tick,' on time, down at the store. To supplement our income during the Depression, we paid our bills by cleaning out paper and cartons from the cellars of the Huntzberger and Benedict stores. They threw all that stuff down their cellars, and we cleaned that out. Then we took that paper home and baled it and sold it to the junk man. That's how we made our money to have Christmas. My brother Jake and I had to help. Dad had a wagon with big wheels, and that's how we carried the paper and cartons home. Then Dad would take that money and save it. He wouldn't sell the paper until it was close to the holidays. The junk man would come and get it, and that's where we got our money.

"Merv" also offered his observation about the workforce at Riverside Foundry during the war. It still remained a male bastion, but due to a shortage of men, Riverside began to employ some women:

"As I remember, the molders were usually older people who were well-established. They didn't move on. The molders had a trade that they had learned, and it took them years to learn it. Of course, most molders were married with children and were beyond the draft age. They were going to be the last ones to go into the service. Now, there were some younger people who, like me, worked there and were getting this minimum wage.

"Riverside's business manager, Reuben Strickler, also was responsible for keeping certain workers from being drafted. He was a member of the York County Draft Board, and he tried to keep out certain people. I know this for a fact, and I know the people whom he helped. If that person was needed in the foundry, then Reuben could see that that person got a deferment. For a while Reuben kept out Bill Haugh, because Bill was a wonderful mechanic who helped to keep the foundry in operation due to many of his inventions and innovations. Nevertheless, Bill did eventually get drafted. Reuben still offered to keep him out of the Army, but Bill decided to go in.

"Riverside also began to hire women, and it was pretty well accepted by the men because they didn't work in the foundry. Carrie Smuck, for instance, faced cores and so forth to get the rough edges off them. Other women also worked in the core room. They did not work out in the foundry because that was a pretty rough place back at that time. Also, there were certain older men who just thought they could do anything and say anything to a woman, but that didn't go over too well with Donald Smith. But I do know of some instances when some of the men were quite obnoxious. So, women first worked in the core room, and they were sort of separated. Usually at first, they worked part-time. These women would work just limited hours. But it was work that had to be done, and it was a way to get it done cheaply. I know for sure that in the beginning they didn't get the same hourly rates as men in the core room. The women didn't seem to resent their lower wages because it was the custom in those days. Nevertheless, they were patriotic, too, and were trying to do a job to help the war effort. They also needed the extra money like everybody else. World War II was the opening wedge for women in the plant because of the need for workers, and then more and more women came in after the war. They became grinders and sanders and things, and they worked in the core room. The war let them get into the workforce and take jobs they had never had before.

Due to wartime shortages, Riverside Foundry often had problems getting raw materials, but through the efforts of the proprietor, Donald Smith, Riverside's production did not falter:

"We always had problems getting materials that we needed, especially good scrap iron. We always had trouble getting materials in quantity. Scrap iron was a big part of the material that went into the cupola to produce the molten iron. Usually, the scrap iron came in by truck from York because York seemed to be full of scrap yards. Of course, pig iron, coke, and that sort of thing always came in by rail. In fact, the rail line came right up beside the foundry. The same people who worked in the core room also unloaded the coke cars.

"Donald Smith had a lot to do with coping with the shortages and seeing to it that we had everything we needed to produce the hand grenades and rifle grenades. I have nothing but good things to say about him in the forty-some years that I worked for him. He treated me well all my life. Donald used his wartime profits to innovate and modernize and expand the operation. He did this continually, and he received a lot of help from Bill Haugh along the way before, during, and after the war.

"Donald Smith treated his workers well, and as a result Riverside Foundry never unionized. The union leaders would come and stand on Locust Street beside the foundry and pass out organizing materials to the workers as they came out. Donald would look over the union's demands and then offer his workers the same thing the unions would have given them. It was just as simple as that. I thought it was a wonderful way to do it because it kept out the union. So, he didn't have a problem, but the union used to fight him like mad.

Like all Americans, "Merv" and his family had to deal with the inconvenience of consumer shortages and wartime rationing:

"Rationing was very rough, especially with gasoline. Of course, as I mentioned before, gasoline rationing didn't bother me because I had no car, and I didn't have to drive to work. So, that saved me from that kind of rationing. Most of the molders didn't have cars, so they walked to work. In fact, there weren't a lot of cars in Wrightsville at that time. For people who had cars, they used them whenever they had to, and if they didn't have gas, they didn't go. If we went anywhere, we had to go by bus or some other kind of public transportation. My family never had a car, and I usually bicycled everywhere I went.

"To conserve gasoline, we also had what was known as 'The Victory Bus.' It was a tractor-trailer setup, and it ran between York and Lancaster. It had a conductor on the back, and it had a side door. It had seats all around the outside compartment, and when the seats were occupied, you hung on the straps from the top. They would pack in as many people on there as they could get on, and nobody minded being packed in. It would stop at certain places. There was a rope that you yanked when you wanted to get off. That rope ran a buzzer, and then the driver up front knew when to stop. My trouble with riding 'The Victory Bus' was that everybody was sitting there looking at me and wondering why I had money enough to go anywhere and what I was doing here rather than being overseas. There was a lot of resentment as far as I was concerned.

"Getting meat was a problem, especially certain kinds. So, rationing affected us, but I can't say that we lived any differently, because we raised a lot of stuff that we ate. My dad had a garden, and my grandfather had a garden. My grandfather also raised hogs and had them butchered. I learned to be a gardener, a butcher, and everything else with it. We didn't suffer as far as eating went.

Air raid alerts and scrap metal and paper drives became a part of everyday life in Wrightsville during the war:

"I do remember the blackouts, and there were air raid wardens and that sort of thing. I was either working or sleeping, so the air raid alerts really didn't bother me. Those were the only two things I did. Now, if they occurred on a weekend, then it was different. There were wardens who went around, but I don't think they were too effective.

"The scrap drives were mainly done by the Boy Scouts here in town. I know that everybody went out of their way to put everything to be collected in front of their houses. Sometimes they put out things that were not supposed to be collected. Regardless of what the drive was, though, everybody went all-out.

"Merv," like many Americans of his generation, had warm feelings toward President Franklin D. Roosevelt:

"It was quite a shock when we learned that the President had died in April 1945. I remember that the big thing was his funeral train. Of, course, it didn't pass through Wrightsville, but I know there was a deep respect for him. He was top-notch, as far as I was concerned. If I were to select my favorite guy for the century, it would be President Roosevelt. I always have appreciated him. I know that he had his faults, but we all do. I think Mrs. Roosevelt would run a close second to him. When there's anything now on television about Roosevelt, I never miss it. What I think of most about him is that he gave us everything he had, and he didn't have to. He was a giver. He really served his country. I can't think of anybody who put himself on the line more than he did. He had everything to live for, and he had everything he wanted. You see, I grew up with him as President. He's the only President I ever really knew about up to the time he died.

At the time of Roosevelt's death, victory was inevitable, and defense work began tapering off. Riverside Foundry was no different from other defense plants in this regard. In "Merv's" case, the end of the war meant that he had to accept a diminished weekly income. He also noticed a change in attitudes toward work after the war:

"It was a big letdown when we stopped making the hand grenade castings. There was no real tapering off to my knowledge. When the war was over, we stopped making the grenade castings. I believe that Riverside had a subcontract from a foundry in Littlestown to produce them. My days of making $90 dollars a week for piecework were over. Pretty soon I was making $40 a week, and that included four hours on Saturdays. After the war we started making such things as lighting fixtures and barbells.

"I don't think the size of the workforce got smaller, though. 'Red' Smith was a go-getter, and he always had plenty of work for us. The foundry was also able to absorb many of the returning veterans, some of whom had worked there before the war. I don't think there was any problem with that. Also, I don't think a lot of them wanted to go into the foundry because there were much better jobs popping up in big plants in Lancaster and York. I know that my brother didn't go to the foundry when he came back.

"I did notice that everything became more lax at the foundry after the war. I remember people pulling tricks like punching the time clock and then going over and having lunch or leaving early. I remember people doing thing things like that, but I never remember anybody doing that during the war, like, cheating and everything. It seemed as though during the war everybody did what he thought he had to do, and he did it when he thought he had to do it. Slackers weren't present during the war.

As far as Wrightsville itself was concerned, "Merv" did not believe that World War II produced too many significant changes:

"The war didn't change the town very much because the same old people who always ran it kept on running it. And they kept running the town until they died. Certainly, Wrightsville didn't get any bigger. I think the town continued much in the same way after the war as it did before the war.

"I do think that the war educated a lot of the people, especially the veterans. I think that when they came back from the service they expected more. They thought that the country owed them something, and I think they had every right to think that.

"Maybe the biggest change was at the workplace, as I mentioned before, with the influx of women. More and more women began to work at Riverside as it expanded, and I think those few women that we had hired during the war paved the way for more women being hired after the war. Among the most common things that occurred afterwards was that women finally had their own restroom. I honestly don't know what toilet facilities they used during the war.

For years after the war, particularly on Memorial Day, the fact that he had been classified 4-F continued to haunt "Merv":

"Memorial Day was always a day that I liked to see come around, but it was a day that I despised. I used to go over to Hellam Street and stand at the top of the hill and watch the parade go by. I used to see everybody strutting and waving and having a good time because they were veterans. I wasn't a veteran, but it wasn't my fault. I just felt intimidated by the Memorial Day ceremonies. That was my feeling. It wasn't that anybody said anything to me. Nobody approached me about anything when I went to the Memorial Day parade, but even when I went to Fairview Cemetery, I would never go up front to hear the speeches and so forth. I stood back among the trees somewhere. It was just something that I thought I wanted to be part of, but I did not feel as though I belonged there. I guess that's the essence of the whole thing. I just didn't feel like I belonged. I didn't feel like I was part of the community that day."

"Merv" continued to work at Riverside Foundry for more than forty years, eventually becoming a bookkeeper due to his attendance at Thompson's Business College. He married in 1949, and he and his wife had two daughters. His wife Thera is deceased, but "Merv" continued to live in Wrightsville until the maladies associated with old age forced him to move into a local nursing home. "Merv" died on 23 September 2011.

Notes

1. Mervin Garver, interview by the author, 6 August 1999, transcript, OH1309, Oral History Collection, University Archives, University of North Texas, Denton, TX.

PART II

THE NORTH AFRICAN AND ITALIAN THEATERS

THE NORTH AFRICAN AND ITALIAN THEATERS

The invasion of North Africa beginning in November 1942 was primarily a British plan. Prime Minister Winston Churchill and his military advisors feared that Germany and Japan would gain control of India, the Middle East, North Africa, and the Suez Canal. On the other hand, President Franklin D. Roosevelt and his generals wanted to stage a cross-channel attack into northern France as soon as possible. They argued that the quickest way to defeat Germany was to drive across France and conquer the industrial heartland of the enemy. Such an undertaking was out of the question, asserted the British, because of the limited forces then available for such a complicated, ambitious operation. For two years, the British had been fighting a seesaw war against a combined Italo-German army in Egypt and Libya. Since they had done most of the fighting and had contributed the most manpower up to that time, the British strategy prevailed. Roosevelt finally gave in because he wanted to get American forces into action against Germany somewhere by 1942 because such a move would enable him to resist pressure to concentrate on the war against Japan and still permit him to maintain a Europe-first policy.

Operation Torch was launched 8 November 1942, with the landing of 90,000 Allied troops, 65,000 of them Americans, on the shores of Algeria and French Morocco. According to the Anglo-American plan, the British would launch an offensive aimed at pushing the Axis forces out of Libya, while the Americans in the west would invade the Vichy French colonies of Morocco and Algeria. Then the two Allied armies, converging from the west and east, would catch the enemy in a vise and annihilate them. Instead of a quick victory, however, the Allies were bogged down in a campaign of attrition that went on through the winter of 1942 and into 1943. Finally, Allied air and sea attacks cut Axis supply lines to Tunisia, while steady ground attacks began to take their toll. On 10 May 1943, 275,000 Italian and German soldiers surrendered, securing North Africa for the Allies.

Buoyed by success in North Africa, Churchill next insisted that the Western Allies follow up their victory by invading Sicily and then Italy. Referring to Italy as the "soft underbelly of the crocodile," he convinced Roosevelt to go along with this campaign against what was perceived to be the weakest of the Axis nations. By knocking Italy out of the war, Churchill believed, the Allies could attack Germany through the proverbial back door. Italy did surrender, but this was not the "soft underbelly" that Churchill had promoted. The Germans had anticipated this strategy, so they simply took over Italy as another occupied country. For Allied soldiers, the German occupation now meant they were fighting a large, strong, well-led enemy army instead of disinterested, war-weary Italian soldiers. During the next two years, the Allies slowly slogged their way up the Italian boot against fierce resistance, often in terrible weather and mountainous terrain, with the Germans defending the high ground while gradually retreating north. The Italian Campaign turned out to be a dead end, with the establishment of air bases to attack Germany being the only positive outcome of this struggle. The commitment of troops to a theater on the periphery of Nazi-occupied Europe delayed the timetable for the Normandy invasion while at the same time engaging only a limited number of German forces. By having to postpone the cross-channel attack, the Western Allies lost an opportunity to exert greater influence in western and northern Europe. Even if the Germans had been pushed out of Italy, the greatest natural barrier in Europe, the Alps, lay between the Anglo-American armies and the Reich.[1]

Notes

1. For the most recent books on both the North African and Italian campaigns, see Rick Atkinson, *An Army at Dawn: The War in North Africa, 1942-1943* (New York: Henry Holt & Co., 2002) and *The Day of Battle: The War in Sicily and Italy, 1943-1944* (New York: Henry Holt & Co., 2007). These are part of a projected three-volume series entitled *The Liberation Trilogy*

Figure 10. SSgt. Mervin "Bo" Haugh

Chapter 7

Staff Sgt. Mervin "Bo" Haugh

B Co., 1st Btn., 66th Armored Reg., 2nd Armored Div.

Born on 28 June 1917, on a farm just outside Wrightsville, Mervin "Bo" Haugh initially participated in the North African and Italian Theaters and later saw action in the Northwestern European Theater. After Congress passed the Selective Training and Service Act in September 1940, all males between the ages of twenty-one and thirty-five were required to register for the draft, which was initiated in October of the same year with men being selected by lottery. "Bo" was the first person from Wrightsville to be selected, receiving his notice 7 January 1941. For "Bo" what was supposed to be a one-year military obligation with duty restricted to the continental United States turned into a five-year stint mostly overseas in combat. As one of the initial draftees, "Bo" rapidly rose through the enlisted ranks and was part of the training cadre for other incoming draftees at the time the country entered World War II. "Bo" saw very little action during his time in Italy and Sicily, but the experience there proved valuable after his division was pulled from Sicily and sent to England for eventual service in Northwestern Europe. In Northwestern Europe he participated in extensive combat, was wounded, and later sent back into the fray with his old unit. After the war, "Bo" returned to Wrightsville, performed factory work, retired, and was farming part-time for his son when he died on 8 November 2003.[1]

"Bo's" early years on the Haugh farm mirror those of his twin sister, "Sis," whose interview appears earlier in this book:

"I was born on a farm in Hellam Township, right outside Wrightsville. It had fifty-seven acres, and we raised specialty crops, and, of course, with cattle we had hay and corn and other things like barley. On a specialty farm, we grew a variety of crops. Then we had about ten acres of apple and peach orchards. The people of Wrightsville liked potatoes and things, so we'd take them into town, and they would buy them from us. We sold almost everything locally, but we did haul the apples into Baltimore. We'd package them in bushel containers, and we'd take a hundred bushels down there. I think we also raised ten acres of tomatoes for Heinz, and we hauled them to Millersville, which was their receiving station. Dad worked for the Pennsylvania Railroad and took the tolls at the railroad bridge, which was the only one across the Susquehanna River at that time. I think they charged three cents apiece if you walked the bridge.

"There were five brothers and a sister in the family, but my brother James died from appendicitis when he was very young. As we got older, we all became farm laborers. In other words, the farm ended up with a lot of help. As you know, [Pauline] 'Sis' and I are twins, and she was the one who gave me my nickname. When she learned to talk, she tried to say 'Brother,' but 'Bo' was all she could get out. So, that was how I got my nickname.

"I graduated from Wrightsville High School in 1934, and then I went back to work on the farm. Later, two of my brothers, Tom and Ed, and I got jobs with the Pennsylvania Railroad when they were converting from steam power to electric power. My job was hauling engineers to these different substations. I'd go from Columbia clean down into the Baltimore area or else up into the Harrisburg area—wherever the substation was located. I think there were ten substations that distributed electricity to the overhead catenary lines.

With the initiation of hostilities in Europe and Japanese aggression in Asia, it was clear that the United States could not avoid war. Although American policy clearly left the decision for war in the hands of Germany and Japan, Congress with President Roosevelt's support passed the Selective Training and Service Act of 1940, the first peacetime conscription in US history. The act required all men between the ages of twenty-one and thirty-five to register with local draft boards. The government then selected draftees through a lottery system. The legislation also limited service to one year, and drafted soldiers were to remain in the United States or its territories located in other parts of the world. "Bo" Haugh was among the first men in Wrightsville to be drafted under the Selective Service Act:

"When I got my draft notice on January 7, 1941, I was working as an electrical helper at Sparrow's Point outside Baltimore. I wasn't expecting to be drafted that early. The way I understand it—and I don't know how to verify it—Elmer Hersch and I were the first two to be drafted from town. I had to report to a Doctor Dellinger in Red Lion for a physical examination. He was very, very cautious and wanted to make sure that I wasn't getting into the Army with something wrong with me. He was very thorough. I did pass, and I was really looking forward to going. Now, not to go where the war was going on or anything, but I thought maybe it would be something for one year that I'd really like. I thought it might be good to make acquaintances with different people, which I did —a lot of them. So, my papers were processed for a year, and then they 'burned' them and told me I was in for the duration after December 7, 1941. I was prepared to come home at that time. My one year was about up, my papers had been processed, and I was preparing to come home.

After processing "Bo" eventually began his Army career at Ft. Benning, Georgia:

"My first trip after being drafted was out of York to Harrisburg. Reuben Strickler from Wrightsville, who was a member of the York County Draft Board, accompanied Elmer Hersch and me to York. He sort of gave us a send-off because he was in charge of the draft there in Wrightsville. In Harrisburg we took our oath and whatever, and then we got on a train and went to Ft. Meade in Maryland. At Ft. Meade I was interviewed. They wanted to know what my occupation had been, and I told them that at home on the farm we had one of the first track-type tractors. He put that down on the questionnaire.

"Anyway, the tractor, I think, was what sent me down to Ft. Benning, Georgia, which was the 2d Armored Division's headquarters. I first went through basic training there. We also went through a lot of field exercises—they called them 'problems'—there at Ft. Benning. Altogether, we went through about seven weeks of basic training there, and the non-coms tried to make it pretty rough on us. They wanted to get their point across that you had to take this thing seriously, so I cooperated.

"Bo's" world changed on 7 December 1941. Having been drafted in January for a year's service, he was looking forward to getting out of the army and going home. The Japanese changed his plans, for what was to have been a one-year stint turned into military service for five years:

"When the Japanese attacked Pearl Harbor, I didn't feel too good about that because I was now in for the duration. I had been really looking forward to going home. I think the general feeling of the whole company was sort of the same as mine. Even the guys who had come in and had been in the company for maybe a couple months were disappointed. It was a letdown. I'll put it that way.

"As a result of getting into the war, we were losing a lot of our experienced cadres, who were now going to Officers Candidate School or who were training other troops. For a time the loss of these guys affected the efficiency of our outfit. I know that I was given more responsibilities since I had been in the service longer than a lot of the guys.

By the time he had finished basic training at Ft. Benning, "Bo" had already been assigned to a tank crew. He eventually trained on the tank that he used overseas. The description of his tank's capabilities offers a glimpse of the state of American armor in the North African and Italian Theaters of Operation during World War II:

"I was already assigned to a tank crew and was taking driving instructions. The tanks we had at this point were World War One tanks, but some of them didn't even have guns on them. I don't know why. Also, they were hard to operate, and they shifted gears really badly. They were beaten down to almost nothing. They'd work on them and work on them to keep them running. Of course, when we actually went into combat, we didn't have those. We then had replacements and newer tanks.

"I was designated as a tank commander, and I think they made me one was because I was taking everything seriously. I also believe I had to take some tests and got good ratings on them. Anyway, I ended up on a fifteen-ton tank [the Stuart Light Tank M3] with a five-man crew. It had a driver, assistant driver, gunner, loader, and the tank commander. The assistant driver also operated a ball-mounted machine gun. This tank didn't have much firepower. It had a 37-millimeter gun, so it did not have the firepower to penetrate tanks. In fact, the thirty-ton Sherman tanks didn't have that capacity, either. So, the German tanks were a little bit too big for us. Now, our tank was speedy, however. You could go fifty miles an hour in it, and the other tanks couldn't go that fast. I guess they figured that maybe they were better to draw fire with than the bigger ones because they were fleet-footed.

"I must say they left us with the impression that we had good tanks that were comfortable to fight the Germans in. The thinking in America was 'big.' They had automobile people building tanks, so they were used to mass production. I think they felt all along that if they built enough tanks, not worrying too much about what happened to the crews, they could overcome the difference of the better German tanks. And they definitely were better, as we were to find out. We didn't know what the

German tanks were like until we got overseas. If they hit you someplace, they usually knocked you out. We weren't schooled on the probability that we were going to be outgunned. I wouldn't say that we would be outmaneuvered, but we were going to be outgunned.

"It also got very hot inside our tanks. It got so hot that you couldn't stay down in the tanks sometimes. It fatigued the driver, so he and the assistant driver would switch off, and the other guy would drive for a while. It was terribly hot, even unbearable, or terribly cold in there, depending on the outside temperature. When we were in North Africa and Sicily, you couldn't get down inside for more than fifteen minutes. I know that you could have fried an egg back on the deck of that tank. So, the driver had a lousy job driving that thing. If we were moving in a column, even I would get down in and drive to trade off with everybody, and the rest of the crew would ride on the outside. The driver was the only person inside, and then another one would hop down in really quickly. We were all taught to drive the tank. Everybody who came in the tank could drive.

"I must say, though, that the tank rode pretty comfortably if you were going fast. If you were going faster than, I'll say, seven miles an hour, it smoothed out really well, especially on a highway. But on a highway, if you were going at a speed any less than that, the thing quivered all the time. A lot of times you didn't get to go that fast. The driver and the assistant driver also had to take care of cleaning the motor compartment of the tank.

"The ammunition handler put the projectile in the gun. What happened was that the gun was semi-automatic. It would spit out the old cartridge and leave the chamber wide-open with the breechblock down. Then he had to push a lever and swing the breechblock in position. Then it was ready again. We had different kinds of ammunition on racks. We had high-explosive and armor-piercing rounds. I've forgotten how many of each we had, but there were plenty of them. We had another type of projectile that was loaded with balls for anti-personnel purposes.

There were a couple hundred balls in each projectile, and they were like ball bearings, and it'd splash them out of there. It was my job as tank commander to determine the type of ammunition that we would use.

"Incidentally, the tank commander was always exposed from the waist up, although you could obviously drop down. There was a seat under which was a piece of spring-loaded steel tubing that ran up and down. When you pulled a lever, it shot you up or down, depending on which way you wanted to go. You had to get pretty adept at using that device —when you wanted to be outside or inside the turret. You needed to pop up quickly and go down again just as quickly. Usually, you were exposed until you thought that something was going to happen. However, I always felt safer in the tank than being an exposed infantryman. I'm pretty sure that infantrymen were exposed to more fire than we were because they could get killed by small arms fire. If small arms fire hit a tank, it'd just bounce off. I do know for a fact that infantrymen took heavier losses than we did.

"When we were overseas, we were getting an awful lot of replacements, and it was a relearning process every time we got them. I think I had maybe at least six different drivers. I think that one of the best things that happened to me, as far as the service was concerned, was that I was drafted early rather than after the war started, when they were grabbing men here and grabbing men there. I'm not down on anybody they were training, but it gave me time to get myself acclimated to the Army and to the procedures and what they did. I had confidence. I was confident that I knew what to do with a tank. I was in one company the whole time. I didn't switch companies; I was always in the same company.

Fearing the loss of Egypt and the Suez Canal to the Germans and the Italians, British Prime Minister Winston Churchill persuaded President Franklin D. Roosevelt of the strategic value of removing the Axis threat. Clearing the enemy from North Africa, Churchill argued, would open what he called the "soft underbelly of the Axis powers," providing a way for the British and the Americans an opportunity to move against the Italians and secure the Mediterranean. The Allied plan to gain control of North Africa called for offensives from both the east and the west. The British 8th Army would attack westward from Egypt, while a combined Anglo-American force would launch an amphibious operation, codenamed Torch, to occupy and control the French colonies of Morocco and Algeria. "Bo's" 2d Armored Division was one of the American divisions selected for Operation Torch because the desert terrain was ideal for tank warfare:

"We did not have any amphibious training before we left. Not a bit. We left from Norfolk, Virginia, actually from Hampton Roads. I didn't help load the tanks. The only thing that I did help load were a lot of accessories. One of them was Milky Way candy bars. I mean, we had stacks of them in boxes! We also loaded boxes and boxes of sanitary napkins. In other words, I suppose this was a fighting mission and a goodwill mission. There were other objects—a lot of candies and everything—but they weren't for the soldiers. They must have figured on us winning because they claimed that's what we needed. Those items were for civilians when we got to where we were going. I was trying to figure out where they were going to store those Milky Ways on the ship, and I did find them!

"The ship was pretty crowded because we had infantry as well as the tank crews. Conditions aboard that ship were pretty bad, and there was a lot of seasickness. A lot of the guys used their helmets for vomiting, and that made for a steamy, hot affair. Along the walls on both sides, they had canvas racks where we slept. The other thing I didn't care for was that you had to bathe in saltwater. There were so many men on that ship that there was not nearly enough fresh water for us. They served pretty good food, but one time we had a severe storm, and those plates and cups would slide across the tables.

"Somewhere off the coast of England, we met the other ships that were going to participate in the invasion. I think there were supposed to be about 830 ships altogether. Around this time we got into another very severe storm, and the water really got rough. Our darned tanks—they had chained them fast—broke loose. They all went over to one side, and that caused the ship to list. To compensate they had to shift thousands of gallons of fuel from one side to the other.

By early November the invasion task force lay off the coast of French Morocco. The landings took place on 7 November 1942, and the 2d Armored Division was part of the Western Task Force. "Bo" then described what happened from the time of the initial naval bombardment until his unit landed on shore:

"When we stopped—I'm not good at guessing, but I'll say we were about a mile-and-a-half or two miles offshore—the battleships were setting broadsided, and they were firing into shore at that time. They were really unloading their big guns. There were two invasion points—Casablanca and what they called Port Lyautey, both in French Morocco. I was scared, but then I got in one of those bunks on the ship, and I went to sleep. So, I didn't dwell on it anymore. When the naval bombardment started, I just thought, 'This is it!' That bombardment made me feel better because I figured those 14-inch guns could do a lot of damage. Then the airplanes were taking off from their carrier, so it was really an extravaganza when you were out there.

"Our ship was an old merchant ship, and it was still steam-powered. We didn't have any LSTs [Landing Ship, Tank], so the Navy came in with a flat-bottomed landing craft that could handle just one tank at a time. Our ship had these four lifting lugs, two on the front and two on the back. They hooked four cables there into one cable, and they lifted each tank out of the hold and brought them over the side of the ship. In the meantime, before the cable operator put each tank on the landing craft, the tank crew had to crawl in. He then lifted the tank out of the hold and brought them out over the side of the ship. We got in swells about this time, so the ship would roll to one side and then to the other, not up and down or front and back, but sideways. The tanks would hit the side of the ship and then bounce off and swing out. This was all quite a thrill for the tank crews.

"Of course, our tanks had been waterproofed before we left the States. Anyplace where a tank could leak, we used either Permagum or other means of sealing. We were particularly careful to do this where the turret rotated, and this meant taking care of every nut and bolt connected with it. The crews did this. The muzzle of the gun had to have a cover on it. All the hatches except the one for the tank commander—that one was rubberized—and all the periscope movements had to be sealed so we could operate in the water. Then on the back of the tank, where the air intake was, there was a huge shroud with a lanyard attached so that we could pull it and discard the shroud. That let us get into ten feet of water if we had to, and we'd still keep running.

"So, these flat-bottomed boats took us into shore, almost. When we unloaded, they would float back out. So, we went actually from there right on up to the shore. When we got on shore and assembled, things got pretty good. The tanks then went up a hard road in column formation. The only resistance came from two little French two-man tanks. We demolished them and thus eliminated them pretty quickly. The French weren't too friendly. I don't know the reason, but they were not friendly. In this brief operation, we didn't lose any tanks. We got settled at that point, and we spotted a big chateau with great vineyards and wheat fields all around it. I went up and knocked on the door and indicated to the lady of the house that I wanted some wine. They had given us a French handbook, and I had had French in high school. She slammed the door on my face, so I guess they were still pro-German.[2]

After the initial landings and the collapse of French resistance, the 2d Armored Division was finished with combat operations in North Africa. "Bo's responsibilities for the remainder of his stay there was in the role of a training cadre:

"Our main objective was Rabat, which was the capital of French Morocco, but we didn't get into anymore combat. That was the end of my battle in North Africa. My job then was to teach new American replacements coming in. We furnished replacements out of the 2d Armored

Division for the 1st Armored Division. Every day there were guys leaving from the 2d Armored and going into the 1st Armored. In Africa we also lost a good many men with malaria. So, we now had replacements coming in and going through training. That was the reason why we moved to Tunisia. At this point, I doubt if we had over five original enlisted soldiers—cadres. Since I was a tank commander, this training was turned over to me. Every tank commander was a sergeant, and I wound up as a staff sergeant. In fact, I also taught the French. We had French troops coming in. The French troops I'm talking about were the Free French. Some of them were aviators. What we would do was that we went up and over the Atlas Mountains and into Tunisia, and then we got into a support role. I taught machine-gunning again as well as aircraft identification and chemical warfare. From that point on, I was an instructor.[3]

"This was the first time that I got to see the German tanks. I think I was sick. I felt terrible when I looked at those things. If you've ever seen the muzzle on that thing—gee whiz! It was a huge thing! They could fire three shots without reloading, and they used huge shells. That 88-millimeter gun had a terrific muzzle velocity, too. They were well-built tanks, but they were not very fast. But I knew that what tanks we had would be no match for the German tanks.

"Bo" remained as part of the training cadre for the 2d Armored Division from November 1942 until July 1943. His division was preparing for Operation Husky, the invasion of Sicily. It was not until May 1943 that the Axis forces finally surrendered, at last bringing all of North Africa under Allied control. Once the region was secured, the next step was to cross the Mediterranean and attack Sicily and Italy—Churchill's "soft underbelly." Fortunately for "Bo" and his group, the Italians were friendly and put up very little resistance:

"For the invasion of Sicily, we used the LSTs [Landing Ship, Tank] for the first time, so we loaded our tanks on them. They were flat-bottomed vessels, and they'd set on the water better than the ones we had used for coming ashore in North Africa. We ran into some bad luck during the invasion of Sicily mainly because we got into some terrifically bad weather. I think they told us there was a forty-mile-per-hour gale at one point while going in. We'd go up and down in the swells, and we lost our barrage balloon because the cable attaching it to the ship snapped.

"We landed on Sicily at Gela at night on July 10. At that point we had airpower to help us, so we didn't experience much resistance except for a little bit on the beach. There were a few tanks there and a bunch of Italian prisoners. They seemed like they were relieved to be captured, though. I think what happened was that from then on the Germans used Italians as a front force or shield a lot of times.

"From Gela we circumnavigated the island. I remember some of the towns we liberated—Castronuovo, Partinico—but there were a lot of little towns we went through. We advanced rapidly and finally got to Partinico, which is about twelve miles from Palermo, but I must admit that we never fired a shot during the whole operation. We mostly encountered Italian troops, and they would sooner have been someplace else dancing and having a good time rather than being out there trying to pick off somebody. We were also getting a good reception from the Italian civilians. They were waving and throwing us flowers. Of course, there again we had hard candy and things that we'd throw out, and the kids would scramble for them. I guess we were using candy instead of bullets. I don't think the Italian people were in favor of that war, so we didn't run into any disturbances as we went through these towns. I don't think they had the heart for it. Those people were destitute down there because the Germans were taking everything. It was right in the grape season, and I believe everybody was living on grapes. So, we took a lot of food in there, too. If you keep people from being hungry, they're going to be friendly.

On one occasion, "Bo" had a brief encounter with General George Patton, who commanded the American troops during the Sicilian Campaign:

"Where we were going it was terribly dusty and bone dry, and everyplace we went it seemed like that lava dust from Mount Etna had blown down. At one point they pulled us over to the side of the road, and, by gosh, there came ol' Patton. At that time he a four-wheel drive command car. He was standing up and hanging on to the windshield, bouncing along and saluting everybody. I said to our gunner, 'I believe the war's over! There goes Patton! He's gonna go up front and out ahead!' I figured it was all settled. What he was actually doing was taking a shortcut to Palermo so he'd be there when [Gen. Bernard] Montgomery got there. They had such a personal rivalry going on that I thought they were acting like two kids.

As had been the case in North Africa, the combat experience of the 2d Armored Division was also limited in Sicily. As soon as the Sicilian Campaign had been completed, the 2d Armored Division was transferred to England for eventual deployment for the cross-channel invasion:

"My combat experience was very limited to that point. In other words, I was sliding pretty good. I wasn't trying to avoid combat. I just did whatever they told me.

"We landed in England on Christmas Eve of 1943. We left all our equipment behind; we didn't take any equipment along with us. When we got to England, we got new equipment. At this point we went into training for the invasion of France."

The 2d Armored Division landed in Normandy on D plus 3, 9 June 1944. It fought in France, Belgium, and Germany. "Bo's" story will continue in Part VI dealing with the Northwestern European Theater.

Notes

1. Mervin E. Haugh, interview by the author, 31 May 1999, transcript, OH1298, Oral History Collection, University Archives, University of North Texas, Denton, TX.
2. Note: The Allies rightly considered the French North African colonies as actively serving the interests of Germany. French administration of their colonies continued despite France's defeat in 1940 only because of the willingness of some French leaders to collaborate with Germany. The Germans had taken advantage of this situation by permitting the establishment of a French-led, pro-German government at Vichy in southern France. This "independent" government administered the southern third of the country. The Vichy government also had responsibility for the administration of France's North African colonies. When the Allied invasion of North Africa occurred, the Vichy government ordered its 120,000 troops to resist. In some places the French troops fought the British and the Americans, while at others they offered no resistance. After two days, the French command reached a cease-fire agreement with the Allies. See Gary R. Hess, *The United States at War, 1941-1945* (Arlington Heights, IL: Harlan Davidson, Inc., 2000), 42-43.
3. Note: The Free French were fighters in World War II who decided to continue fighting against the Axis forces after the surrender of France in June 1940 and the subsequent German occupation. Although Charles De Gaulle headed the Free French organization from London, some Free French forces did fight against the Axis forces in Tunisia in early 1943.

Chapter 8

Pfc. Glenn Blouse

2d Plat., D Co., 1st Btn., 135th Reg., 34th Infantry Div.

Born on April 1924, at Long Level, a small community on the Susquehanna River just south of Wrightsville, Glenn Blouse was the only child of Ora and Paul Blouse. Almost immediately after graduating from high school in June 1941, Glenn had to register for the draft as the country drifted toward war. On 23 April 1943, the Army called him to active duty. After stateside basic training, Glenn was sent to Italy where he joined the 34th Infantry Division as a replacement. He spent the rest of World War II in Italy, participating in the Naples-Foggia Campaign, the Rome-Arno Campaign, the Northern Apennines Campaign, and the Po Valley Campaign. While fighting in the Apennines, Glenn was the recipient of the Bronze Star. His story offers a graphic description of the miserable fighting conditions endured by infantrymen as they slowly struggled up the Italian Peninsula, Prime Minister Winston Churchill's "soft underbelly of Europe." After the war, Glenn married, settled in Wrightsville, and raised a son. He died on 21 July 2000, the victim of a hit-and-run driver.[1]

As the country drifted toward war, Congress passed the Selective Training and Service Act of 1940, and Glenn, like almost all eighteen-year-olds, had to register with his local draft board. With the Japanese attack at Pearl Harbor, Glenn more or less marked time because he knew that he would soon receive his induction notice:

"I graduated from high school in 1941. When I left high school, I thought that I would be eventually drafted because the government brought out a program where eighteen-year-olds had to register for the draft. I was one of the first eighteen-year-olds to sign up. Then I worked at various places because I knew that eventually I was going to be inducted. Eventually, I did get drafted, about a year-and-a-half after the war started. I guess it took awhile until they finally decided that they were going to take people as young as I was. I turned nineteen years old, and a week later I went into the service. I left on a Sunday.

"My dad never said too much about my going into the Army. He never said too much about anything. He kept his thoughts to himself, but I knew that it was awful for him, that his only son was going into the service. But my mother showed her emotions, and she was very upset; but she knew it was something that had to be done because it was for the country. I was inducted in Harrisburg, and the following Sunday they had a big dinner for me. A lot of relatives were there because it was 'kickoff' day.

After induction, Glenn went through the same Army basic training that thousands of other young men experienced. He believed that basic training taught him the fundamentals of being an infantryman and molded him into top physical shape, but it in no way prepared him for the realities of combat he was to face in Italy:

"We were first shipped to Ft. Meade, Maryland, and we were there for two days or something like that. Ft. Meade was sort of like an induction point. Then we boarded a train for Camp Wheeler, Georgia, for basic training, and I was assigned to a heavy weapons company. We did take rifle drill. We fired the rifle for effect, so to speak, to learn how to operate it. We fired the machine gun quite a bit, but I never fired the mortar, which was part of our weaponry. We had 81-millimeter mortars and .30-caliber Browning water-cooled heavy machine guns. Eventually, I was assigned as a machine-gunner, and I had no choice in that decision. Basic training lasted sixteen weeks altogether, but it did not prepare me for what I was to experience later in combat. I'm only saying this for myself, but if I had followed 'the book' [Army regulations and training manuals] in combat, I personally don't think that I'd be having this interview with you. I will say, though, that when we came out of basic training, we were tough physically.

"I did have one choice, or thought I did. Right after basic training, there were about a hundred of us who took a test to go to college. Well, four of us passed, and I was one of the lucky ones who passed. We even had our orders to go to college down in St. Petersburg, Florida, to Stetson University. We had received our orders, and we were heading for the train, but it so happened that Italy was 'hurting' for troop replacements. The Italian Campaign had bogged down, and casualties were mounting, so they needed people for infantry replacements. They then reissued my orders and sent me to Ft. Eustis, Virginia, and from there I went to North Africa. Because I had been reassigned to go to Stetson University, I didn't stay with my company from basic training when I went overseas.[2]

Glenn's ship was part of a large convoy heading for Italy by way of North Africa. Other than a few minor discomforts, his trip was uneventful:

"From Ft. Eustis, we went to Newport News and boarded a ship for North Africa on November 3, 1943. We were on the ship for twenty-one days. We were going across the North Atlantic at its roughest in terms of winter storms and weather conditions. There were about five hundred of us on that Liberty ship, and it wasn't the best trip I ever took. I didn't get seasick, but it seemed to me like 498 of the 500 men did. When I got down in that hold to sleep, the stench from vomit was miserable. As a result, some of us decided to sleep in the weapons carriers up on the main deck of the ship. We took our showers in mid-November, and they were saltwater showers. There were no freshwater showers available on that Liberty ship. But we made it over with no real problems. We finally landed at Casablanca, and then they put us in old boxcars and sent us up to Oran, Morocco, which was then controlled by the French. We probably stayed there about three weeks, and then we left there and landed at Naples, Italy.

After being engaged in continuous heavy combat for seventy-six days around the Volturno River and Mount Pantano during October and November 1943, the 34th Infantry Division was pulled out of the line and sent to the rear for rest and retraining. Casualties during this period had depleted the division's manpower, so it was sent to the area around San Angelo d'Alife to fill out its units with newly arrived replacements from the States. As one of the replacements, Glenn was assigned to D Company, 135th Regiment, for training and learning the fundamentals of teamwork. On Christmas Eve 1944, the division was notified that it was to relieve the 36th Infantry Division in the San Pietro sector. The division's objective was to drive the Germans off a chain of hills running north and south across Highway 6, which led to Monte Cassino and the Gustav Line. Glenn's account of this action offers a glimpse of the difficult life of a replacement infantryman during the Italian winter and his baptism under fire:

"They first put me in a replacement center. It was a holding place where they decided which division you were going to go to and where you were needed the most at that particular time. Normally, as I was to find out later, we rarely got replacements when we went back to the rear for rest and recuperation. Most of the time, they came up to us while we were on the front lines, because as you had a casualty, you got a replacement. Finally, they decided. They took us one night to the front lines. This was not too far outside of Naples, and I'll never forget that we went up a mountain trail. There were about ten of us, I guess, as a round figure. There was a captain there from the 34th Division. I didn't know what his job was, but I guess it was to determine where people were going to serve—what outfit, what company, everything. He sent me to the 135th Regiment of the 34th Division. First, he put me with the 60-millimeter mortars, which would have been with the rifle companies, and I wasn't too wild about that. I don't know how it happened, but at the last minute he changed his mind and put me in Company D, heavy weapons.

"When we went up there that night, they had a buddy system. When you dug foxholes, there were two guys that had the same foxhole. Well, they didn't have anybody to put me with that particular night, so my introduction into combat was to dig a hole and be in that hole all night by myself. And I was one homesick dog! Normally, a foxhole was about four feet deep and three feet wide, big enough to keep two men in it. Beginning the next day, though, the other guys in the Company D sort of 'mother-henned' me. They talked to me and introduced themselves like they had known me all their lives. They made me feel like one of the company—one of the platoon—because we were like brothers in that platoon. We depended on each other for our lives, so, I mean, we were all like brothers. I think that the first priority was for the safety of the whole company, not just the individual, because individuals could be replaced real easy. Later, when we came home and finally got out of the service, we were saddened by our separation from each other. We still think of ourselves as brothers, and we try to get together every year.

"There were six men in our machine gun crew. As far as the fighting they had experienced, they never said much about that. My training with them was on-the-job training. In that crew I did all the things connected with the machine gun. When I first started in actual combat, I was an ammunition bearer. Those boxes of belted ammunition for the Browning .30-caliber machine gun were heavy 'suckers.' I carried one in each hand, and they weighed approximately twenty-five pounds apiece. Then I became the assistant gunner, so I carried the tripod that held the machine gun. The gunner carried the weapon. I did all of this eventually; I went through the whole 'schmear.' In the wintertime we had to put anti-freeze in the water jacket of the gun, which was water-cooled, so it didn't freeze up. I also carried a Colt semi-automatic pistol and a carbine.

"When we went into combat, as machine-gunners we were never on the front lines, unless we were in a defensive mode. Now, when we were pressing forward in an attack, we were always 1,000 to 1,500 yards in back of the riflemen, so we never really had too much of an opportunity to be in contact with the German soldiers because the riflemen always did the dirty work. We backed them up. Now, later on, when we were in the defensive mode, it was entirely different because we'd be sitting out in 'no man's land' on a machine gun post. Our machine guns did not fire as rapidly as the German automatic weapons. They had what we called a 'burp gun' [Schmeisser]. If they missed you the first time, the whole string of bullets was going to miss you. That's how rapidly they fired, and the bullets weren't like those of our machine guns. That American machine gun was like a shotgun. It sprinkled bullets all over the place.[3]

"This was not 'Sunny Italy.' All we had was mud, snow, ice, and rain. That's all we ever had during the winter. The weather and terrain caused a lot of supply problems. See, we had mule trains in Italy. They had trouble getting up the trails, and what we called a 'trail' was really a goat path. For four days there, we didn't get any food because the Germans knew the trail that the pack trains were coming up, and they'd throw artillery in there. So, the pack trains didn't get up to us, and we didn't have any food for four days. We had fairly good armored support, and we had fairly good air support. By then our Air Force pretty well controlled the skies. At times German planes did come in, and they caused some problems, but not like they did in North Africa and Sicily. Our communications were lousy at times because they didn't know what they were doing. You'd ask for artillery support, and half the time they didn't know where to fire, really.

"The Germans were retreating, but it was an orderly retreat with them always holding the high ground. The Germans conducted maneuvers in Italy before the Second World War ever happened. They knew Italy like

I know Wrightsville. They knew where **everything** was located, and they had map grid coordinates for potential targets for artillery barrages registered. They knew exactly where we were coming from, so we were at their mercy. They would throw artillery at us and machine guns and rifle fire from ambush. We were literally at their mercy, but we still kept on going forward. I'll admit that I wasn't the bravest person, but I knew that I had a job to do. I knew that I was defending my country, and I think that's what kept me going, because if we lost and Germany kept getting stronger and stronger militarily, eventually they were going to come to the United States. So, I think that's what kept most of us going —a belief that they had to be taken care of right there.

After fifteen days of conducting a steady, grinding attack against stubborn German resistance, the division had finally driven the enemy back to its main winter positions. Following a brief period of rest and recuperation, the 34th Division's next assignment was to participate in the attack on the abbey at Monte Cassino, which was located on a high peak overlooking the town of Cassino. The reason for the assault was the mistaken belief that the Germans were using the abbey as an artillery post to command the valley below:[4]

"We went up there at division-strength. We went across this river, and we went up in the mountains right across from the abbey, which was about 500 yards away. When we got to the top of a mountain adjacent to the abbey, I mean, it was miserable. It was snow, rain, ice, and mud once more, and we got wet. We practically dug foxholes in shale, and it took a long time for you to dig a foxhole in that. Morale really got low. For a lot of fellows, trench foot was a big problem. Your feet would freeze, and if they remained frozen too long, you'd lose your toes or eventually your foot due to gangrene setting in. What a lot of fellows were doing— I hate to say this—they were intentionally sticking their feet out. They'd take off their socks and boots and stick their feet out so that their feet froze. They'd get trench foot, and then they'd be sent back to the rear. That's how bad conditions were on that mountain. I never got quite that far because I always felt it took a lot of guts to intentionally cause harm to yourself. There were also some fellows who shot themselves in the leg so that they wouldn't have to be in combat. I could never do that, but I held no animosity against them because I knew what they were going through, and it just got the best of them. I did think of sticking my feet out there to see if I could get trench foot, but I never did it.

"We went up on that mountain at full strength, and when we came down off that mountain—when the British relieved us—we were only at one-quarter strength. That's how many casualties we had due to the Germans or due to the weather conditions. All we did was to fight in a defensive mode there. We didn't actually assault the monastery. We were in a defensive position for—I don't know—maybe a month. Our job was to keep the Germans at bay more so than us going over and taking the monastery. In other words, we just sat there for about two months. The riflemen were up in front of us, but not too far. Then we would set up the machine gun posts, and they were there until the day we came off the mountain.[5] As I said, we were right across from the monastery, and we could see the Germans come out. We could see them bring out their small artillery pieces, but we couldn't do anything. We had strict orders not to fire on the monastery for fear of damaging it. Our Air Force couldn't bomb it, and we couldn't fire artillery shells in there.[6] So, the Germans had a field day. Most of our casualties were coming from German artillery, but sometimes their planes would come over and strafe us. They had good mortars, too, and they were mighty quiet. You didn't hear the mortar rounds coming in until they had practically hit. Then they had a weapon that we called the 'Screamin' Mimi,' and that thing had six shells. Five of them went to the target, but you never knew where the sixth one was going to land. That was the weirdest sound I have ever heard in my life. It was just like somebody screaming. It was plain, downright miserable, and they'd mainly use it at night.[7] I suspect we were losing almost as many men to trench foot and that kind of stuff, though. I and the guy I was with eventually had a foxhole dug about six or seven feet deep. It was a good foxhole, but we weren't able to cover the top of it. I don't know how we ever got through that rock. But I'll tell you what—when that German artillery was flying around you, you could do things that you never thought that you were capable of doing. All this didn't help our morale because here we were, being shot at. Oh, we could shoot at them with our rifles, but at a range of 500 yards, you had to be a fairly good marksman to hit a man at that range.

"Getting supplies was also a problem up there. There were four straight days when we didn't get any supplies at all. We had nothing to eat. We had those D-Bars, but they, in my mind, were worthless. If you read the directions on a D-Bar, you were supposed to use a half-hour to eat it because of all the vitamins and stuff that were in it. Otherwise, it would make you sick.[8] When we ate one of those, we drank water that we collected off our shelter halves. You know, we carried those little two-man shelter half tents, and we collected water from them. That didn't taste too good. But the Germans wouldn't let the supplies come up. They seemed to know whenever they were coming up with that mule train, and they'd shell it.

"Finally, after the English relieved us, Allied planes started to bomb the monastery. That, we couldn't understand because we did suffer casualties and stuff. If they could do it after we left, why couldn't we do it while we were there? People got killed, and it got to the point that if we took some prisoners, they never made it back to the POW compound. The general sent up orders to kill them—take them back over a hill or two. As a matter of fact, that was before we even got to the monastery hill. We were getting too low in reserves to provide guards to take prisoners to the rear, so he said, 'Don't take any prisoners!' Then he had to rescind that order and say 'Take prisoners!' because they were killing everything in sight. I actually heard shooting when they took them back over a hill or two. They killed them, and to me that wasn't right. The regular German soldier was in the same boat that we were in. He really didn't want to be there, but he had no choice. Now, the SS troopers, they were a bunch of lice. That's all I can say about them.[9]

After being relieved on 14 February the 34th Division returned to San Angelo d'Alife to rest and recover the strength that it had expended so freely in the Cassino hills. On 11 March the division was ordered to prepare to move by sea to the Anzio beachhead, by now a legendary place where hard-pressed Allied troops had just succeeded in holding off determined German counter-attacks.[10] *The Anzio beachhead was a small piece of land measuring less than ten miles at its widest point and no more than eight miles deep. This terrain favored the German defenders, who held the hills overlooking the beachhead and could see everything that went on in the 34th Division's sector in daylight. When the 34th arrived at the beachhead, the enemy had just failed in two concerted attempts to drive the Allies into the sea, and it appeared the Germans would try a third time. When it became apparent that the Germans were planning a third assault, Allied headquarters planned an offensive designed to drive across the Italian boot and trap the enemy troops before they could retreat further north. On 11 May the offensive started, and what follows is Glenn's perception of the combat from the standpoint of an infantryman. He views events strictly in terms of his own limited world with no thoughts concerning grand strategy or the so-called "Big Picture." As a consequence, Glenn presents his perceptions of what he experienced through unconnected events that happened to him personally:*[11]

"We went back below Naples, and we proceeded to have a rest period, plus we took training to go up and land at Anzio. That involved maybe three or four weeks at the most. It was similar to our basic training back in the States. They were just getting us ready and biding their time for us to go up and land at Anzio. We had no training as far as amphibious landings were concerned. We came into Anzio after the actual invasion. It was to sort of rejuvenate your basic training that you had had, which, as far as I was concerned, didn't amount to a tinker's damn, because if you had gone 'by-the-book,' you'd have been a dead person. You had to learn a lot of that stuff on your own. It had only taken a week for me to learn how to stay alive. You learned not to stick your nose where it didn't belong. By that, I mean, if you went into a town, you didn't go and open a door there, although you would have liked to. Maybe there would have been a German pistol in there. I know I always wanted a pair of their field glasses made by Zeiss and a Lugar, but I was smart enough to know that you didn't go and open doors. I saw on occasions where our people had opened doors, and the whole side of the building caved in because it had been rigged with booby traps. The Germans were good at setting booby traps.

"Well, they did take the division up to Anzio on landing craft, and we landed there. We got shelled while we were landing because at that time the beachhead was only a couple miles deep. Eventually, I think, the perimeter around the whole thing at the deepest point was around ten miles or something like that. But we did take a good shelling when we came off the landing barges into Anzio. We replaced one of the divisions, but I don't know which one.

"We went back in from the beachhead about ten miles deep, and we formed a defensive perimeter. We stayed up there, if I remember correctly, something like eighty days, and it was all on the defensive. Nobody was going nowhere. The Germans didn't try to attack us, and we didn't try to attack them. We were up there a long time, about eighty days. We got that filthy that my hands had sores on them. And we were lousy. In one place we slept in a small outbuilding. They had some straw in there, and it was full of lice, and we got them Those lice were a half-inch long, and, I mean, they just stuck to you! We had no water. We had nothing. We had to conserve all our water. We didn't shave. Even now I don't have a heavy beard, but—I'll tell you what—I had a heavy beard that time. Our clothes were rotten, and the odor was awful because we couldn't take the usual steps concerning hygiene. You didn't have anything to make yourself the way you should be. You know, we were in a position where we could do nothing. I'll never forget that one off my closest friends up there said, 'When I saw you guys, I couldn't believe how you looked.' We looked pathetic. I was lousy and had sore hands because I didn't have a bath for around eighty days. Finally, they took so many of us back where we could take a shower and get an issue of new clothing. I washed and washed and washed, and on the tops of my hands it was that dirty that it took off skin and everything. Then they brought us right back up. Believe you me, it was safer on the front lines than it was back behind the lines because that 'Anzio Annie' could scare the daylights out of you even if it didn't land near you. It fired a huge shell! The Germans fired it out into the bay to hit the ships out there.[12]

"You had to be careful in the daytime because the Germans had their binoculars, and they were looking down our throats. But we got used to it. We went up a hill one day, our whole battalion—D Company, riflemen, and all. We started at the bottom, and I'd say that hill might have been about 800 feet high. It was a small one; it wasn't actually a mountain. The Germans let us come up the hill. When we got up to the top, we were kind of winded. We put all our stuff on the ground, and we took a break. That's when all hell broke loose. Boy! We got clobbered! They started machine-gunning us, and they had an antitank gun up there. Hand grenades came from everywhere; machine guns fired. I saw a 'potato masher' coming through the air, and it was coming end-over-end.[13] I dropped to the ground, and fortunately the grenade, which a concussion-type weapon, landed far enough away that it didn't hurt me. If you're too close, the concussion from its explosion in a confined area was what would kill you. The 'potato mashers' had no shrapnel or anything like that in them. They were also throwing Italian hand grenades at us. They were about the size of an egg and painted black. I saw some of those come rolling down that hill. I mean, they rolled everything they had at us that day. We just got disoriented. They really had us. We didn't know what we were doing. We thought the whole German army was up there! Anyway, the Germans ran the whole battalion back down that hill. So, bit-by-bit and piece-by-piece, everybody went back down the hill. Fortunately, nobody got killed. Nobody even got hurt despite the way the Germans were shooting at us. We got behind this building, and the company commander said, 'We're going back up!' We then regrouped down there and came back up and ran them off. How many do you think there were?

Four Germans! The riflemen captured four Germans! We were taking prisoners at that time.

Finally, with the Germans in full retreat, the race began for the capture of Rome. In this operation the 34th Infantry Division and the 1st Armored Division received the mission for an all-out pursuit of the enemy north and northwest of Rome. Again, what follow are Glenn's personal experiences concerning the capture of the Italian capital:

"We rode on the tanks of the 1st Armored Division, and I was among the first troops into Rome. It was probably about forty miles from Rome when we started riding the tanks. Rome had been declared an open city, so there was hardly any damage in the city. There were still snipers in Rome, but they were quickly cleared out. Boy! The people of Rome really welcomed us as heroes! They pulled us off the tanks to kiss us and everything, gave us flowers and all that. The people were glad to see us come in. They welcomed us as liberators, which we were, because the German occupation of Italy was a tyranny for the Italians. They were going to leave us in Rome as occupation troops for a couple weeks, but too many of the guys got carried away and did things they shouldn't have done. So, they took us out again.

"At the time of the liberation of Rome, the Normandy invasion had taken place, so they had already been taking divisions out of Italy and sending them to England. The history books today say that Italy was a sideshow, but we knew nothing about it at the time. We were in the dark about that. But it sort of upsets me today. That Italian Campaign was one terrific battle. We faced everything that Hitler had to offer. I'm not taking anything away from the invasion of Normandy, but we didn't get our due, and the North African Campaign didn't, either. Everything is about the Normandy invasion, and it's not fair. If you're going to praise veterans of one battle, then you should praise everybody because facing the issues of life and death are involved in every battle. But we didn't know anything about the D-Day landings, really, until it happened.

After the liberation of Rome, the 34th Infantry Division joined other Allied units in pursuing the retreating Germans northward. For Glenn and his comrades, this meant a prolonged slog through the Northern Apennine Mountains, where the enemy had established a strong defensive line, known as the Gothic Line. The division mired down there due to rain and snow and German resistance. It went into a defensive mode from August 1944 until a breakout into the Po Valley in April 1945. During his time in the Apennines, Glenn earned the Bronze Star, and what follows are the details of that achievement:

"We sat in the Apennines for, oh, I guess, three months before we invaded the Po Valley. There we went into a defensive position, and I'll never forget this because it's where I got my Bronze Star. One night I was on outpost—a machine gun outpost. This was in the Apennines, and we had just had a terrific snowstorm. The snow was about two, three feet deep in those mountains. We had a pit there that we had our machine gun in, and then we had a covered place where you could crawl back in for shelter. I had a rifleman with me, and it was his first night in combat. I'm out there on the machine gun, and, I mean, it's clear, the moon's shining, and the wind is blowing terrifically. When you go into a defensive position, you had a four-hour watch, and I was about 500 yards in front of the rest of my unit. We were out in 'no man's land.'

"It was just my dumb luck that a German patrol came along on my watch. I happened to look a little bit to my left, and here I saw two men coming about thirty feet away from me. Well, I thought it was the 51st Division that was on our left in defensive mode, but they were out a little bit farther than we were. So, I thought that maybe they had some men out on patrol and they had gotten lost. They were very quiet. So, like a dummy, I hollered, 'Halt!' By the time I got out 'Halt,' they were within six feet. As I hollered, I saw that here was a German patrol. All of a sudden, I looked up, and there they were! It ended up that there were about twenty Germans, but I only saw two. One of the guys I saw had a 'burp' pistol. I mean, that thing goes 'BRRRRRRRRRRRRP!' He had to have missed me by just inches! He didn't know exactly where I was, but he fired over my head, and he missed. And I missed him! I swear we were only six feet apart! I had my machine gun, and I missed him. Then my machine gun quit firing after about five rounds because somebody took out a tracer bullet and forgot to put a regular bullet in. See, there were certain times when we didn't want to use tracers because they showed where you were located. Well, I grabbed my carbine, and I fired one round, and that jammed.

"Then I tried to get some hand grenades, but the hand grenades were frozen in the snow. I then took a spoon, and I was digging out the hand grenades. I pulled the arming pin, and I let them go for about three seconds. Oh, I must have thrown eight, ten hand grenades out there! Back in that day, I could lob hand grenades like a baseball. They later said I killed one, which I'm not proud of that, and I wounded a couple. But I'll say one thing. It sure got them out of there. They didn't like those hand grenades because they were like small artillery shells. I was scared stiff, but when you're scared you can still fight because the adrenalin kicks in. After it was over, I couldn't get that rifleman out on the gun. He wouldn't come out, but I can hardly blame him, though, because it was his first night in combat. To me this whole thing lasted just a matter of a minute, a minute-and-a-half at the most. The first time I shot, the only thing that German wanted to do was to get away. They didn't fire back at me after that.

"The next morning we looked down in the valley, which was down about 1,000 yards, and we saw a German ambulance come in. They took stretchers, and they carried I don't know how many men out of there. We never bothered them because by the Geneva Convention you're not supposed to, and we didn't. I guess that patrol was out there for reconnaissance or maybe to grab a prisoner or two because they didn't know really where we were. So, that was one of the close calls that I had of becoming a casualty. I thanked the Good Lord that I was alive, and that's the Gospel Truth! I knew how close to death I really was that night.

They said I killed one. Well, they can't prove that I killed one, but they can't prove that I didn't. They do know that I wounded some because the German ambulance squad came in and got them out. Like I said, if I did kill one, I'm not proud of that, but it was a thing of self-defense.

During the winter months in the Northern Apennines, with all the rain and cold and snow, an infantryman had to make a real effort to protect his equipment and stay as comfortable as the elements would allow:

"Well, first of all, you had to keep your equipment well-oiled because in that weather it would get sluggish. We used anti-freeze in the machine gun jacket because it was a water-cooled weapon just like the radiator in your car. If that sucker froze up and burst, because water expands as it nears freezing temperature, you had a problem. Now, we carried spare barrels, but after firing a burst or two that barrel would be rendered useless because the heat of firing weakened or even melted the heated barrel. So, that's why we put anti-freeze in them—so they wouldn't freeze up.

"It was cold in the Northern Apennines—very cold. All that we ever had were the olive greens [winter-weight woolen fatigue uniforms]. We wore long underwear that was not insulated. You'd try to wear a couple sets of socks. In case one pair got wet, you'd take that one off and let it dry; and then if another set got wet, you'd just keep drying them like that to keep your feet dry. We did have good field jackets. I don't remember if we carried an overcoat then or not. We were supposed to carry one, but we already had too much gear in climbing those mountains and everything. That's all we ever did, was mountain fighting, so you couldn't carry a lot of gear.

"In the Apennines you knew that every single hill or mountain was going to be contested. You'd take one hill, and the Germans had moved on to the next hill. It was just one hill after the other. It's like getting up for breakfast every morning. You get used to it. You know that you have no other choice. I think the worst thing that affected me—plus a lot of my friends—was that when they pulled you back, they'd give you all kinds of booze, especially grappa. It's distilled grape wine, almost pure alcohol, and it is nasty stuff. Is it ever! They brought it to us in five-gallon water cans. They brought it to us by the truckloads, and all that they were doing was providing a morale booster. If you got that drunk, you didn't know what you were doing—and I mean that! That's the Gospel Truth! What they did that for was to keep up your morale because, if you were half-drunk, your nerves weren't shot then. That was one of the Army's ways of keeping you sane because you knew that when you went back up to the front lines, all you were going to do was walk right into the enemy. You knew that that was coming.

"We slept in a room of a house one night when we were on the move. We were tired. When you're marching all the time, you're dead tired. So, we went into this town one night, and we thought it had been secured. The riflemen were ahead of us. We all threw our packs on the floor and lay down. We slept all night, and the next morning we got up, and one guy went over and opened the door, and here in the other room were three fully armed German soldiers. We never knew they were there, and if they had wanted to wipe us out, they could have done it very easily. But they gave up. I think they had it in their minds that they wanted to give up. But we never knew they were there.

"One of the places that the GIs liked to find was a cellar because it was low. You could rest there because there was some warmth, and it was relatively safe from artillery and mortar fire. Plus, there was the fact that there might be wine in there. One time we found a big hogshead. Now, that's a wine barrel that's real big. The farmer or whoever lived there didn't want the Germans to find it, so he had buried it, and we dug into it accidentally. Now, you talk about drinking and having a good time! Did we ever have one! This was a sweet wine, and it was delicious.

"Especially in towns, we ran into a lot of civilians. They didn't want to leave. Their homes were there; that was their home. I don't know how I would have felt if somebody had invaded my home. I probably wouldn't have wanted to leave, either. And they were starving; they had nothing. But when fruit was in season, they'd give us apricots and plums. I'll tell you, they had the best plums, I think, that I ever ate in my whole life. They'd give you the shirts off their back. I used to give all my candy to the little kids because I pitied them so much. The Italians were a loving people. They were caring. Really, they weren't a warring people. The Italians weren't fighters. We had an Italian division over there that we had to back up because you couldn't trust them to fight. They were lovers; they weren't fighters.

It was not until April 1945 that the Allies launched their spring offensive, attacking across the Po Valley. Known as the Po Valley Campaign, it began with the British 8th Army attacking on the eastern flank with the American 5th Army assaulting and capturing Bologna. The 5th Army then drove due north and crossed the Po River and pushed on toward the Alps. The Po Valley Campaign lasted only twenty-one days because the Germans were caught by surprise and could not organize a retreat or a fall-back position. The fighting was very confused and very fast-paced with the Germans surrendering by the thousands. During this push, Italian partisans launched attacks behind the lines against German troops, and Benito Mussolini was captured by partisans and executed. The Germans surrendered on 2 May 1945, thus ending the Po Valley Campaign and the war in Italy. Glenn was an eye-witness to these events, including viewing the body of Mussolini, and he again presents events from the perspective of an infantryman's small world:

"I'll tell you one thing, and that's that everything was mixed up. There wasn't anybody who knew where anybody was. How we kept getting rations is beyond me because we were continuously on the move once the Po Valley Campaign started. We never had any defensive positions set up. We just kept going. At that point the Germans were using horses because they were running out of gasoline. We were taking large numbers of prisoners, and we'd send them back to camps. They had different makeshift camps that we put them in. It only took a few guards to escort the prisoners to the rear. The Germans were glad to go because they were sick and tired of this war. The further north we went, the war damage to Italian cities wasn't too bad because the Germans were on the run. We liberated Florence and Bologna, and they were beautiful cities.

"As we got closer to the Alps, there was a lot of partisan activity, and they were strictly communists. You couldn't trust them, but we had to use them because they hated the Germans with a purple passion. Boy! Those communists were a hard-hearted group! They were cut-throats. They really were! Like I said, they were buddy-buddies of ours, even though you couldn't trust them, because they were helping us against the Germans. See, they worked behind German lines. That's where they did their damage. They'd sabotage a lot of things. They'd sneak in and blow up places and stuff like that, and that was a big help. It demoralized the Germans. It really did. They'd often give us information, but half of it you really couldn't believe.

"As the war was just about at its end, we went through a town [Giulino di Mezzagra]. They had just killed Mussolini and about fifteen of his henchmen and his mistress. I saw him hanging. I was only about forty, fifty feet from him. Do you remember how they butchered hogs years ago and had them hanging head down? We went into this town and were riding on trucks or weapons carriers, and somebody said, 'Look over there!' They had this big, long scaffold erected, and there were at least fifteen people hanging there. One of them was Benito Mussolini, and another was his mistress, and the rest of them were fascists. The communist partisans had caught up with them, and they never gave them a trial or anything. They shot them right on the spot. They were just shot—just shot. We didn't see any mutilation of any type. They just gunned them down and hanged them up. By this time, I was so battle-hardened that it didn't bother me. It was just another corpse. We didn't have time to stand around and gawk because we were on the move. I don't know where we were going, but we just happened to see them as we were going by. We knew who it was, though.[14]

"When the war started winding down and we knew the end was near, that's when I really started worrying: 'I made it this far. Will I make it the rest of the way?' You really started to worry. You're super-cautious. For the most part, when we went into the Po Valley, we didn't run into much opposition, but when we did run into it, there were hot firefights lots of times. Staying alive was in my mind the whole time.

"When the Germans surrendered [3 May 1945], we had one hell of a party. We were in San Remo when the war officially ended. This was a summer resort. Boy! We led the 'Life of Riley' there. They threw a big party for us one night, and we went over to Nice, France. We brought four truckloads of WACs over. We danced and had a big party. Nobody got out of hand, but we had a wonderful time.

"Then, after the war in Europe was officially over, we started thinking about Japan, but I don't think I would have ever gone to the Far East because I had enough points for my wartime service to get out of the Army. I only lacked two points from coming home on the points system.

Eventually, we went down to Naples and came home on a luxury liner. It took us about six days to get back to the States, and I'll never forget that we pulled into Newport News on November 3, which was the date of my mother's birthday. I was discharged on November 8. We had a good homecoming, but I was a mixed-up kid. World War II definitely changed me because of all the combat I had experienced. I didn't know what I wanted to do. I drank a little more than what I should have. Then, finally, one day I said to myself—I had done quite a bit of drinking—'The only thing you're going to do is that you're going to kill yourself.' But I was mixed up. I was still just a kid. I was only twenty-two when I came home. So, I settled down, and I met Roma [Mrs. Blouse]. I dated her for two years, and we got married, and life has been a breeze since then."

Glenn and Roma settled in Wrightsville after their marriage, and he found permanent employment in Wrightsville with a division of the Susquehanna Casting Company. They had one child, a son. On 27 July 2000, while doing lawn work beside the street outside his home, Glenn was killed by a hit-and-run driver who has never been apprehended.

Notes

1. Glenn Blouse, interview by the author, 3 August 1998, transcript, OH1262, Oral History Collection, University Archives, University of North Texas, Denton, TX.

2. Note: The ASTP [Army Specialized Training Program] was created by Secretary of War Henry Stimson. His idea was to take 150,000 of the brightest draftees and offer to put them through college. Those receiving the offer were young men whose test scores indicated they would get soft rear echelon jobs or get rapid promotions or be sent to Officers Candidate School. Men who opted for the ASTP would forego those opportunities and remain as privates. At the Army's expense, they would take regular classes at the colleges and universities, majoring in areas where the Army anticipated specialists would be needed later in the war, such as mathematics, engineering, or foreign languages. Due to manpower needs by the summer of 1944, however, the program was drastically reduced by Army Chief of Staff George Marshall, and more than half of these men got sent to rifle companies as replacements. This was undoubtedly the case with Glenn Blouse. See Stephen E. Ambrose, *Citizen Soldiers: The US Army from the Normandy Beaches to the Bulge to the Surrender of Germany, June 7, 1944 to May 7, 1945* (New York: Simon & Schuster, 1997), 274-275; and Robert E. Humphrey, *Once Upon a Time in War: The 99th Division in World War II* (Norman: Univ. of Oklahoma Press, 2008), 26-31.

3. Note: The MP40, which fired a 9-millimeter bullet, was a submachine gun developed by Germany and used extensively by paratroopers and platoon and squad leaders. It had a relatively low rate of fire and low recoil, which made it more manageable than other contemporary submachine guns. The MP40 was often called the "Schmeisser" by the Allies, after weapons designer Hugo Schmeisser. Although the name was evocative, Schmeisser did not design the MP40, but helped design the MP41, which was really a MP40 with a wooden rifle stock.

4. Note: See David Hapgood and David Richardson, *Monte Cassino* (New York: Congdon & Weed, Inc., 1984).

5. Note: Blouse has understated the action involving the 34th Division. Although the 34th Division was attacking as a diversion on the 5th Army's far right, its advance cost one casualty for every yard gained. By the end of this campaign, the 34th Division's seven-mile advance to its objective had taken six weeks at a cost of 16,000 casualties. See Rick Atkinson, *The Day of Battle: The War in Sicily and Italy, 1943-1944* (New York: Henry Holt & Company, 2007), 281, 328.

6. Note: The Allies at that point had not undertaken to fire on the abbey in view of its importance to the world as an ancient religious institution.

7. Note: Blouse is referring the *Nebelwerfer* (German for "smoke launcher"). It was a towed rocket artillery piece with six 150-millimeter barrels, and each fired a 75-pound rocket. Its range was about 4.2 miles, and a full salvo was spread over ten seconds. The loud screeching noise of the rounds led American soldiers in the Sicilian and Italian campaigns to nickname it the "Screaming Mimi" or the "Moaning Minnie." After firing, however, a long streak of smoke could be seen from far away, making it an excellent target for counter-artillery fire. Nevertheless, its dense and sustained penetration of its multiple rockets made it extraordinarily lethal against unarmored infantry.

8. Note: Manufactured by the Hershey Food Corporation, the D-Bar was to be used as an emergency ration to be eaten only when on the verge of starvation. It was high in energy value, weighed four ounces, and was purposely designed not to taste as good as regular chocolate bars so that they would not be too tempting to soldiers to eat on a regular basis.

9. Note: According to historian Gerald F. Linderman, the evidence suggests that just prior to the Normandy invasion, high-ranking American officers ordered that no German prisoners be taken. The rationale for such a policy was that every fighting man was needed on the frontlines and that no stockades were available early on. There was one instance in Italy where

a sergeant was charged after killing thirty-six POWs and a captain accused of machine-gunning forty-three others based their defense on a claim that Gen. George Patton had given a orders just prior to the invasion of the Italian mainland that all prisoners be killed. Patton denied ever giving such an order, and the men were convicted, but returned without punishment to their units. There was never an official policy with regard to killing prisoners. In most cases, as indicated above, such atrocities were individual decisions. On the other hand, as Blouse suggests, GIs placed SS troops in a special category. The SS troops were considered the epitome of Nazi ideology, so they were frequently summarily shot when captured. See Gerald F. Linderman, *The World within War: America's Combat Experience in World War II* (New York: The Free Press, 1997), 120-121, 129, 132.

10. Note: Operation Shingle, initiated 22 January 1944, was another scheme of Winston Churchill's. The idea was to launch an amphibious landing against Axis forces in the area south of Rome near Anzio and Nettuno. The Allied forces would then drive across the Italian boot to cut German communications and threaten the rear of the German XIV Panzer Corps. If successful, the operation would open the way for the conquest of Rome. The American command opposed the operation, but Churchill succeeded in persuading Roosevelt to give his backing. Poorly planned and executed, Operation Shingle almost resulted in the Allied forces being driven back into the sea. See Atkinson, *The Day of Battle,* 536-564.

11. Note: See Carlo D'Este, *Fatal Decision: Anzio and the Battle for Rome* (New York: HarperCollins Publishers, 1991).

12. Note: All supplies for the troops who had landed on the Anzio beachhead had to be brought from Naples by supply ship, and being too large to dock in the port of Anzio, they had to anchor in the bay. To disrupt the landing of these supplies, the Germans used a pair of 208-millimeter guns with seventy-foot barrels, which they nicknamed "Robert" and "Leopold" but were known widely by the Americans as "Anzio Annie" or "Whistling Pete." Each fired a 600-pound shell as far as thirty-eight miles. Near misses in the anchorage raised spouts 200 feet high; even duds landing ashore burrowed

fifty feet into the ground. The guns were mounted on railroad cars, and after firing a half-dozen shells, they would withdraw into a railway tunnel just south of Rome some thirty-five miles away. See Atkinson, *The Day of Battle*, 491.

13. Note: The "potato masher" was so-named by Allied troops because it resembled a manual potato masher in shape.

14. Note: On 27 April 1945, Mussolini and his mistress, Clara Petacci, were stopped and identified by communist partisans near the village of Dongo on Lake Como as they headed for Switzerland. The next day they were taken to the small village of Giulino di Mezzegra, and they were both shot, along with their fifteen-man train, primarily ministers and officials of Mussolini's rump government, the Italian Social Republic. On 29 April the bodies of Mussolini and Petacci were taken to the *Piazzale Loreto* in Milan and hung on meat hooks. This was done both to discourage any fascists from continuing the fight and as an act of revenge for the hanging of many partisans in the same place. The corpse of the deposed leader became the subject of ridicule and abuse. See Ivone Kirkpatrick, *Mussolini: A Study in Power* (New York: Hawthorn Books, 1964), 660-672. For a more detailed account of Mussolini's capture and execution, see Christopher Hibbert, *Il Duce: The Life of Benito Mussolini* (Boston: Little, Brown and Company, 1962), 310-334.

Figure 11. Pfc. Alfred "Bud" Forry

Chapter 9

Pfc. Alfred "Bud" Forry

C Co., 362d Reg., 91st Inf. Div.

Born on 16 May 1925, in Wrightsville, Alfred "Bud" Forry has lived in the town all his life, with the exception of his sojourn with the US Army during World War II. He was drafted 7 August 1943, shortly after turning eighteen. After basic training, "Bud" was sent to Italy as a replacement infantryman and became a BAR [Browning Automatic Rifle] man in the 91st Infantry Division. He participated with that division in the Northern Apennines Campaign of September 1944-April 1945 and the Po Valley Campaign of April-May 1945. His division had reached the foothills of the Alps when the German army in Italy surrendered in May 1945. "Bud's account of his experiences in Italy underscores the limited world as seen by a combat infantryman trying to perform his duties to the best of his ability, staying alive, and getting the war over with as soon as possible in order to come home and move on with his life. Like almost all his comrades in arms, "Bud" knew nothing about the so-called "Big Picture" and grand strategy. One Italian mountain looked like another to him, and he could not remember the names of the towns he helped liberate. Following his discharge, "Bud" married a hometown girl in 1948, and they raised two children. He performed foundry work during the postwar years, eventually becoming a plant superintendent. After retiring in 1990, he continued to work part time as a foundry consultant. His wife died a few years after they celebrated their fiftieth wedding anniversary in 1998.[1]

Like many young men in Wrightsville during the Depression era, "Bud" quit school at an early age and went to work. When he turned eighteen, he registered for the draft as required by the Selective Training and Service Act of 1940. Due to the country's desperate need for manpower, "Bud" was drafted very soon after registering:

"My education was not very much. I really didn't get through eighth grade. I didn't take too much interest in school, to tell you the truth, so I got out and went to work when I was sixteen. Quitting school was pretty standard for boys back in those days. Then I worked at a silk mill in Columbia until I was eighteen.

"Then on the day I turned eighteen, I registered for the draft in York, and I think it was maybe about two months before I was called. They were taking young men just as fast as they could grab them, and I knew that the draft would get me. I wasn't looking forward to it, but I knew it was something that I had to do. When the time came, I was a scared boy because I had never been away from home. My parents [Walter S. and Marion E. Forry] didn't want to see me go because I was their only son, but they couldn't do anything about it. I had to go. It was just one of those things, so I had to go.

"I was inducted into the service on August 7, 1943. I got on a train in York, and we went to Ft. Meade, Maryland. That was really the induction point where they were handling people who were going into the service. At Ft. Meade, I received all my shots and inoculations, and then they shipped me to Camp Hood, Texas. I took basic training there for about ten or twelve weeks, and then I trained with a tank destroyer unit. Incidentally, I had no BAR training whatsoever until they handed me one in Italy when I joined my unit. Also, I must say that basic training did not prepare me for what I experienced in combat. I was immediately put into a front line infantry company, and the training that I had did not help me one bit—not one bit—other than how to handle a rifle. That's the only thing that basic training did for me.

"Before I left Camp Hood, they transferred me to the infantry, and since I needed more infantry training, they sent a group of us out to a place in California in the mountain area. We had maybe a month or a month-and-a-half of mountain training. It was in the real wet part of the season, which was really miserable, and there I learned the more technical points of what an infantryman does. You learned how to handle your rifle and to keep your head down, which is one of the things they always stressed; you learned how to successfully assault positions, like, when you are up against a machine gun position or something like that. Plus, they got us in physical shape for mountain fighting because they must have known that we were going to Italy at that point. They just had to know that because the terrain in that part of California was similar to that in Italy. So, I think that was one of the main purposes in sending us to California. We were there in the mountains for maybe four to six weeks, and I still had absolutely no training on the BAR. I had training with the M1 but not with the BAR.

"I really didn't have a unit until I went overseas as a replacement and joined the 91st Division. When I left California, I came home for a two- or three-week furlough. Then they sent me and a group to either Newport News or Hampton Roads, Virginia. We all boarded a transport, and it was full. It was really full. Everybody was a replacement because they needed all kinds of people in Italy. When we left we were not part of a convoy although we did have Coast Guard escorts. I got seasick before we were even out of the bay, but I was one of the fortunate ones. I was sick for only about four hours, maybe five hours, or something like that. Then I got all right because I did get a chance to get up on the main deck, and that fresh air helped me a lot. But it was terrible down below decks. When people had to vomit, the only thing they had was their helmet, so that was what they used. You kept that helmet at your bunk at all times. Our trip occurred in either May or June 1944, and the voyage took about ten days.

"We landed in North Africa at Oran, Algeria. Then they put us in big pyramidal tents outside the city, and we were there, oh, for maybe a week-and-a-half or so. Then they put us back on ships, and we landed at Naples, Italy. After we debarked, they put us on LCIs [Landing Craft, Infantry], and we went up the coast. I think we went up about ninety miles, just south of Rome. It was a terrible trip because the weather was bad. The move was made at night, and these landing craft were just piled full of soldiers with all their equipment. So, it was pretty rough.

"Bud" soon joined his outfit after landing, and he quickly adjusted to combat conditions:

"When we got to a certain location, we landed, and they put us on two-and-a-half-ton personnel carrier trucks, which had seats on each side. Then they took us through Rome to somewhere north of the city. There I joined my unit: Company C, 362d Regiment, 91st Infantry Division.

"As I mentioned previously, I was put into Company C, and that's where we were issued ammunition. At that time the personnel strength of the company was way down. They had lost quite a few people. I can't remember how many replacements went into my company, but there were quite a few. Maybe it was ten or twelve. Still, it didn't bring the company up to its authorized complement of men, which the company is never up to full strength when you're in the infantry. It's never up to full strength. The veterans were very glad to see us—very glad to see us—and they didn't have too good a word to tell us. They told us about some of the rough combat they had had to go through, and, of course, losing personnel and things like that. They were all demoralized. The whole company was depressed, but they were still glad to see us there to help out. At that point the company had just experienced some of the toughest fighting that had been experienced in Italy by the time they got across the Arno River. During its drive to the Arno, the 91st Division was subjected to heavy fire from German artillery, mortars, and tanks, with the Germans always holding the high ground and being able to observe the American troop movements.

"But the guys in my company were a bunch of veterans, and they knew what to expect the next day; and they went out, and they did their job. I ran into one veteran who really helped me, an Irishman by the name of 'Red' McLaughlin, who was an older guy. He was right around forty years old, and, of course, I was around nineteen at that time and scared to death, like a replacement normally would be. 'Red' was a draftee. I got in his squad, and he kind of took me under his wing and helped me all he could. He didn't tell me much about the German soldier. He didn't give me any advice along those lines. In other words, he more or less wanted me to learn that for my self—what the Germans were like as soldiers. I appreciated what he did for me, and we became real good friends. We remained good friends even after the war because we got out of this thing together. The first thing he told me: 'Never volunteer for a thing. Don't volunteer.' Well, you're going to volunteer anyhow because I wanted to do what I could, but I was a guy who didn't want to stick out his neck, which I saw happen over there and those people didn't come home. My number one priority was to keep myself alive, and my number two priority was to contribute whatever I could to my immediate group, which would be the squad. You don't want to let down your buddies, but you still don't want to stick your neck out.

"When I first got to the company, my squad didn't have a BAR man; he had already been killed. They gave me instructions on this thing—how to shoot it, how to load it and unload it, and that kind of stuff. That was about all the instructions I got on this thing. I had another guy with me who was the assistant BAR man, and he carried the ammunition. Sometimes we had a tripod, but we got rid of it. That was more excess baggage, so we didn't carry it. The BAR was heavy, weighing around twenty-seven pounds. But they needed a BAR man, and I was a young guy, so they knew that I could carry it. So, with very few instructions, I was the BAR man.

When "Bud" joined the division, its mission was to establish a defensive line along the Arno River to protect the right flank of the 5th Army. This period was characterized by extensive reconnaissance and patrol activity, harassing artillery fire, and occasional patrol skirmishes. During the day there was very little activity except artillery duels. At night, however, both German and American patrols would cross the river to probe their enemy's lines. The mission of the 362nd Infantry Regiment was to learn as much as possible about the Germans' strength, positions, firepower, and movement, and to scout along the river and its banks for information to be used in a possible river crossing operation later. To accomplish this mission, an average of five combat patrols consisting of eight to twenty men, and fourteen reconnaissance patrols of four to eight men, with an officer leading each patrol, covered a prearranged route each night. "Bud" hated these nighttime patrols and dreaded participating in them:

"There are a lot of awful scary moments when you're out on the line. One of the scariest moments, I would say, that I had was on night patrol. They would send out four or five people on night patrol, so you would be bogged down for the night. The officers wanted to know where these Germans were out in front of us, so they would send out these night patrols to draw fire from the Germans. Nobody really wanted to go out on these night patrols. Nobody! Nobody! They would say, 'We want [so many] volunteers,' but they didn't get them. Then they would say, 'You! You! And you!' And then you went. They just didn't pick certain people. Everyone got their turn out on night patrol. To get ready to go, you don't take any more stuff with you than you actually need. You take your rifle and your canteen with you, and that's it. But you don't want to take anything that's going to make any noise. These patrols would usually start right after dark, as early in the evening as you could go out. You would blacken your face and take off all the shiny stuff you might be wearing; all your equipment is discolored, so you don't show up in the moonlight. Obviously, there would be no lit cigarettes. You would go out, and you would listen for noise. You would stay as quiet as you could, advance as far as you could, and when you would hear vehicles or the Germans in any way at all, through talking or anything else, that was as far as you would go. Then you would return and report this information because our officers wanted to know locations, where the Germans were. Then they'd set their program for the next day.

"I remember one of the scariest night patrols that I went on. We were supposed to investigate this one house, which, they said, had Germans in it. As we were getting up to this house, the sergeant in charge passed word back down to fix bayonets, and I don't think there was a guy in the outfit who had a bayonet. At that point we didn't know if we were going into hand-to-hand combat with the Germans, but it was quite scary. By the way, I never smoked a cigarette in my life until I got on the front line. Then my nerves began to get the best of me, and I started smoking. I never stopped smoking until 1978.

"It was the same way with day patrols. You always knew that the Germans were watching from the hills. You knew this, especially if they put you on the point. If you got out on point, you were obviously the first one, and you're walking twenty yards ahead of the whole group of people. You're a dummy, in other words. You're out there, and nine times out of ten, if you are going to be fired upon, the point guy is the one who usually gets wounded or killed first. He's the guy who steps on the first mine. But we really didn't have too much of a mine problem. Occasionally, we went through mine fields, but not too often.

By the time "Bud" had joined his unit, the Rome-Arno Offensive had been concluded, so his crossing of the Arno was relatively uneventful as the 91st Division joined in the northward pursuit of the retreating Germans:

"Well, we waded across the Arno River, and that was done at night. The water was about chest-high, so we had to keep our rifles above our heads. In the area where our company went across, we didn't hit any resistance at all, but farther up and down the river some companies did encounter Germans. In our case, the artillery had done a real good job by firing ahead of us before we went across, so they had backed up the Germans. A couple hours before we moved out, our troops dropped a lot of mortar shells and artillery shells on the other side of the river. We got across in the early morning hours, and then we continued on. Occasionally, we ran into a sniper or two here and there, but it wasn't too bad. We always had German stragglers, like, in a house here and there, so we had a few of them that we had to clean out. That's the kind of fighting that we had after we crossed the river. Like I said, the Germans were driven out by our artillery. Artillery to me was one of the biggest friends an infantryman has.

"I can vividly remember the first time I got into really hot-and-heavy combat. I'm not quite sure of the location, but we were supposed to take a ridge ahead of us. At that time, we didn't know it, but the Germans had some of their tanks setting up on that ridge. We had to cross a lowland that was a grass field with the grass maybe two feet high. The Germans waited until we got out into that field, and then they started shooting their machine guns. Of course, everybody hit the deck, and it happened to be just our luck that the grass was just high enough that it concealed us. You couldn't dig a hole; you couldn't lift your head off the ground. You just had to crawl into your helmet, is what you really did. It was about an hour-and-a-half that we were pinned down in this field, and then they called up a couple of our M4 tanks, and they drove the Germans out of there. At this point they couldn't use artillery because these German tanks were too close to us. The only thing they could do was to bring up some M4s and blast them out of there. Once they started firing, the Germans took off. Thank God for those tanks! We lost a lot of guys, but a lot of us survived the thing. They pretty much knew where we were, so you couldn't stick your head out. That was one of the scariest moments I had. If it hadn't been for the fact that we had a lot of grass cover as well as those tanks, they would have wiped us out. You always have somebody to be thankful for when you are on the front lines. But that was a terrible experience.

"The noise of battle is kind of interesting. You hear mostly rifle fire and artillery fire. One of the worst sounds that I can recall was the sound of the German '88' [-millimeter] artillery piece. It was like a shrill whistle that 'ZOOMS' right over the top of you. They could shoot farther, and they had more velocity than what our 75-millimeter pack howitzers had. Their machine guns had a terrific rate of fire, and they had another weapon that they carried that was one of the fastest things I ever experienced. We called it a 'burp' gun [Schmeisser], but what its actual name was, I don't know.[2]

As indicated earlier, "Bud" joined his unit at the very end of the Rome-Arno Campaign, so most of his time was spent in the Apennines during the winter of 1944-45. Late in September 1944 the Allies began gradually pushing the German forces northward before the campaign bogged down in the Apennine Mountains. Life became miserable for the soldiers on both sides. Late in September the infamous Italian rain, cold, and fog set in to be followed later by snowfall. Intermittently during October, fog blanketed the Apennines, concealing the enemy, hampering communications, and reducing the effectiveness of artillery. Then the almost constant rain drenched the infantrymen and turned the roads into rivers of mud and installations into quagmires. Under these conditions assaulting the Germans' so-called Gothic Line was considered too costly. Both sides dug in and stopped major offensive operations, instead engaging in small unit probing activities. In this section "Bud" describes the life of an infantryman during this period when his unit made slow progress as it slogged up unnamed mountains:

"The Apennines were fairly high, but they weren't real steep. At places they were more like rounded at the top. They weren't like the Alps, but they were terrible at this time of the year. The Apennines were high mountains, and they were rugged mountains. When we were going up through the Apennines, there were roads that went up through, and that was more or less the extent of our fighting—up the roads—because the Germans were backing off, and they would destroy the road. So, that was where most of our fighting occurred—along the roads, the houses, and up through the mountains. Not too often did we have to go, like, straight up over mountains because the Germans were backing off all the time as they were hunting for an escape route. It was not a rout. We were just pushing them, and they were backing off. Occasionally, they would stop on high ground and hold on for a while. Then we would have a hard time getting them out of there, so we would have to call in artillery to force them out. We would then advance again, and that is the kind of fighting we did in the Apennines. It was slow—very slow—going.

"We were up in the Apennines all during the winter months. We got as far north as to the last ridge, or the next to last ridge, in the Apennines Mountain Range, and that's where we built a fortified line for the winter. We were there for at least two months, and it was right off the crest of the backside of the mountains where we dug in at the very tops of the mountain crests. We had foxholes, big foxholes about chest-high, dug up there, and there were always two men in a foxhole. You could be comfortable standing in it. The foxhole on the top was the one used by everybody in the squad during their watch. There were two people up there all the time—looking. You would be there for a couple hours, and then somebody else would come up and relieve you in this lookout post. We always dug at night. If you dug during the day, the Germans would spot you, so we dug at night. I had a very good buddy from Kentucky by the name of Gerald Schrader. He and I were manning this foxhole on lookout one day. It was during the afternoon, and all of a sudden he was hit on the upper part of his arm. He was shot from a far mountain by a sniper, and the reason for this was the fact that we were using field glasses. With the sunlight reflecting on them, the German picked up that glare. Their snipers were very good marksmen. Gerald was taken back to the States after they took him down off the mountain.

"Then after digging the two-man foxholes, we dug big bunkers down on the back side of the crest. They brought up sandbags because they knew we were going to be there for the winter. We filled sandbags, and we dug into the hillside and built the bunkers with the sandbags. We had something for a roof, but I don't know what it was. Anyway, it was comfortable in there, and the whole squad would get in it. There were no fires made. They used to bring up a little, round thing, but I don't know what it was. But you could heat your bunker with it. We built all kinds of fortifications with sandbags, but we still couldn't keep out the cold. It was cold—very cold. But that's just the way we stayed in there for two months. We didn't advance into the Po Valley until the weather broke.

"It was rugged, and we had no way of getting food up, other than they would come up the mountain so far with pack mules, maybe eight or ten pack mule trains. They could come only so far, and then they were always hunting for details to go back down the mountains so far to put these big boxes of rations on your back. They had backboards, and they would carry them back up the mountain to where the company was located. Often we had people who would volunteer for that kind of duty because there wasn't too much danger in doing that. Even when we got the rations up there, we still never got any hot rations at all. They didn't come up with field kitchens or anything like that. It was all C-Rations or K-Rations. We also carried this powdery stuff that was to be like soup, and we could mix it with our canteen water and heat it. We used to have candy bars, but I don't remember what they were called. We always carried a couple of them because we never knew when we were going to get something substantial to eat from one point to another. But you could eat a bar of that candy, and you didn't get hungry all day because it had so much stuff [nutrients] in it. It had what you needed for a daily nutritional requirement. These things are what we had all winter long. Occasionally, they would get some sort of hot meal up to us, but not too often. We lived most of the winter on these rations.

"One time up in the Apennines, it was raining an awful lot during that period. We were up there for forty-five days without getting any kind of relief. See, what they would do with the infantry personnel, they would keep you up in the front lines for so long, and then they would pull you back for a week or a week-and-a-half. You never knew when this was going to happen. You never knew when you were going to get back. Then, all of a sudden, you would see some new people come in all dressed up in nice, clean clothes and fresh-looking rifles and things like that. Then you knew you were just about to go back. When everybody was informed about the situation, we would all drop back to a certain point where we'd join the rest of the company again. Then we all moved down out of the mountains, usually to the first road that was passable, and there would be vehicles waiting for us. We would load into these vehicles, and they would take us, oh, I would say, anywhere from seven to ten miles back from the line. It was called a 'rest area,' and they had medical facilities and showers and things all set up for you. You could get a bath and good food, and all new clothes, and people would take care of any of their physical problems and stuff like that. They would assign you a bunk in these big pyramidal tents. You did nothing there; you just laid there and relaxed for the time you were back there. You couldn't believe just what the joy of sleeping on an ordinary cot was like. It was wonderful, and there is where you thought you were in heaven. They never would even come around for roll call or anything like that —nothing. You just did your thing, what you wanted to do. It was like heaven! You couldn't believe it! Then you would go back up on the line again, and that was a sad day for everybody. But everybody knew they had to go back. You were a soldier, and you wanted to live up to what you were put there to do. Most of the men felt that way.

"Like I said, I was forty-five days on one trip to the line without a bath, and I had no other clothes. I wore those same clothes for forty-five days, and it was raining and muddy. So, you can imagine what that was like. Everybody was in the same situation, so you didn't mind the stench and body odors and things like that. Morale was definitely low during this period. The guys were tired; they were just played out. In other words, we were fed up with the whole thing. You couldn't expect anything more than that from the men. We did have some guys who got pneumonia. In fact, I was sick at one point after we got down out of there. I was in the hospital for about two weeks. I had something that was similar to pneumonia, but I don't think it was actually pneumonia. Respiratory ailments were one of the big problems during the winter months, so the hospitals were pretty full. The Apennines during the winter dispelled any notions of 'Sunny Italy.' There was a lot of mud and rain, and it was rough. We fought in our ODs [olive drab woolen fatigue uniforms], you know, regular wool ODs, and we had combat boots. That's all it was—combat boots and big, heavy jackets. It was a big, heavy field jacket that they issued. That was the extent of it; that was how we got through the winter. It was a terrible winter.

"During our time in the Apennines, a lieutenant was the highest-ranking officer that we'd run into. Normally, it was a 2d lieutenant. We hardly even saw a 1st lieutenant. We had mainly sergeants and corporals up there on the line, but there was never too much 'brass' up there—not too many.

"The Germans would stay at a place for so long, and when they saw that we were getting in close on them, they'd run. It was all delaying tactics. Once we got up into the higher parts of the Apennines, then it turned out to be a mop-up situation all the way up. When we'd come to a house or a small village, what you'd try to do is circle this thing if you could. Oftentimes you couldn't do it, and a lot of times you'd try to get as close to them as you could. If anybody had any hand grenades, we'd use them; and any kind of heavy fire support you had, you'd use it first. Artillery to me was the best friend an infantryman had. Up during our times in the mountains, when we were trying to advance from one mountain to the next, the artillery or planes would bombard that next mountain ahead of you. They just softened them up and kept the Germans moving, kept moving them back, so we were just more or less like a clean-up operation, picking up stragglers here and there. A lot of times we were lucky, and we could get them out of there in a hurry. We took a house one day, and I think there were three or four Germans in it. They didn't hold us up. They didn't put up too much resistance. In fact, they were at the time sitting down at a table and drinking wine. We ran them out of there pretty quickly. I got the wine glasses and brought them home. I stuck them in my pack and brought them home. I don't know why I did it, but I just did it. I carried them in my pack, and I didn't break them. So, we ran them out, and they took off. That was usually what happened. They'd stay at a place so long, and when they saw that we were getting close to them, they would run. It was all just delaying tactics on the part of the Germans. There was no big number of troops engaged in fighting each other; I mean, there was nothing where you have got two or three or four battalions closing in on one thing. Our purpose was to drive them out—that's what our purpose was—and it was done on a small scale. You have to remember that there weren't too many German soldiers down in Italy. At that time they had most of their troops up in the Ardennes during the Battle of the Bulge in Belgium. There were no large numbers of troops involved in Italy.[3]

"I think it only ever happened to me one time when I had the opportunity to really fire my BAR a lot. At that time we sort of surprised these Germans when they were in a house. We came up, and everybody just started firing, and we got them out of the house. We got a few, but most of them got away. You just don't stick your neck out, you know. You try to get them out of there without losing any personnel. I never experienced any hand-to-hand fighting. We never had to do that, thank God. I would use a rifle, the M1, when we went on patrol. On patrol I would never carry the BAR.

"I only ever saw one replacement that ran off during his baptism to combat. He got shell-shocked. It was in the middle of the afternoon, and there were a lot of German artillery shells coming in. He was just a young guy, and, all of a sudden, he just took off and started running. We never saw him after that. Seeing an individual do this was scary. It was scary. I didn't consider him a coward. I was there to do a job—the best job I could—and it wasn't that I was happy with the job. I was scared half to death, just like that guy, but I managed to get through it. And I believe that most people felt that way. Most of the soldiers felt the same way. They all wished that they were home in the States. All of them wished that, but they had a job to do.

By the spring of 1945, the Allies were ready to take the offensive once again as the Italian weather turned more favorable and move rapidly into the Po Valley. To improve morale the Allied command had rotated units to rear areas for rest, relaxation, and training; replacements were worked into tired units; and damaged and worn equipment was replaced or rebuilt. The immediate objective of the offensive was the heavily fortified communications center of Bologna. Preceded by a massive artillery and aerial bombardment, the 92d Division jumped off on 5 April 1945:

"We knew the offensive was coming, but we didn't know exactly when. We knew that we were going to mount an attack within about an hour or two before the actual push because the outgoing artillery fire was terrific. Our artillery was shooting so many shells over the top of us that you couldn't believe it. It was terrible! That's all you could hear up and down the line, was hundreds of artillery pieces firing. That went on —I don't know—for a couple hours before we moved out. You wouldn't believe that there was anything left alive on the other side of that mountain. Then the planes came in. We saw the planes ahead of us, so we knew that it was coming. Then we started to move out. It was around daybreak this particular morning, and we advanced on foot for about a day-and-a-half. So, the initial advance started with a lot of firepower—a lot of firepower.

"We took a few prisoners along the way. The first thing we did was search them. The second thing we did was to take the cans of sardines out of their backpacks. I'll tell you, the Germans had the best sardines in the world, and they always carried them. Honest to God, they carried four or five packs of sardines on them all the time, and we loved those things. That was the second thing we did, and then we would take them back to the rear. We weren't taking any large numbers of prisoners at a time. We were taking them scattered here and there all the way up the valley. They were not holding out or anything like that. I think they had gotten separated from their companies. The Germans were retreating as fast as they could in whatever vehicles they could scrounge, so we were capturing the stragglers. I've heard rumors about GIs executing prisoners, but that is something that I can't verify. I'm not saying that it's not possible, but I never saw it; and knowing the guys in my company, I don't think that they would do something like that. That's my impression of it. I don't think my company ever faced any SS troops. We were facing people who had been drafted and who were as tired of this war as we were. They were human beings, and they were sent there to do a job for their country, the same as we were. I didn't like them, as far as that goes, but let's face it—they had to do it. They had to do the same thing that we were doing. When they were taken prisoner by this time, they were happy. Most of them had smiles on their faces. They had had enough of this war.

"Then it got to the point that the Germans were retreating so much faster. They were trying to get out of there. To catch up to them, we started riding in Jeeps, but they didn't have enough Jeeps, so they brought up personnel carriers. We then just more or less ran around on all the roads and mopped up through the whole valley. When we crossed the last ridge going down into the Po Valley, it was right south of Bologna. We could look down and see the city from the mountain ridge, and it was a beautiful sight up through that valley. Since Bologna was a relatively important city, the Germans tried to hang on, but they were pushed out rather quickly. There was a lot of street fighting in the city for a while, but we weren't involved in it too much. I think we were on our Jeeps when we went through there. Once in a while, we would be fired on, and everybody would jump out of these Jeeps, and we would try to get the Germans out of the building one way or the other. Usually, we would shoot through the window because we knew they were in there somewhere. You couldn't do much more than that. I usually would be providing covering fire for the riflemen.

"We had very little contact with Italian civilians as we went through these towns, but all that we did meet were friendly. I do remember one time we took a small town, and we ran into some local residents. We hadn't experienced too much resistance in that town—very little—because I think the Germans saw us coming. That particular day, the residents came out, and as soon as they saw us, they were screaming and welcoming us to the town. Some of them would come up and hug you and that kind of stuff. They were so pleased to see the Americans, after being practically tortured by the Germans during the time they had occupied the town. They gave us all the wine we wanted. Their main liquor was grappa, which was made from distilled grapes, and then they had a cheap red wine that we called 'Dago Red.' They were the two most popular drinks over there at that time. I could never handle that grappa. I brought a whole bottle home to my father, and he couldn't handle it, either. Incidentally, we didn't run into too many booby traps as we went through these towns. It just seemed like the Germans were in too big a hurry to get out of there. They wanted to save their own necks.

The war in Italy ended with the surrender of the German forces on 2 May 1945. For "Bud" and his comrades, it was a time of joy and relief that the war was over. At the same time, they lived with the distasteful thought that they would be sent to the Pacific since the war against Japan was still raging:

"The thing in the back of your mind is that you want to get out of this thing alive. You want to get home, and you are going to do all you can to do that. Yet, you don't want to do anything foolish at this point, as the war is winding down. You want to get out of this thing.

"What I can remember is that we were in the foothills of the Alps, in the northern part of the valley, when we got the word. Oh, man! Everybody was really happy! At last you knew that you were going to get out of this thing alive and come home. You knew that! Of course, everybody celebrated because it was a terrific feeling. It was a great feeling; it was a great feeling! Everybody got together, and we hugged one another, and I think we shot almost all the ammunition that we had. Somehow, we got wine, and we had a party. That was the extent of our celebrating.

"Then we were pulled off the line. We pulled back after we had driven the Germans up the valley. They brought in reinforcements, so we didn't actually take part in the surrender after we got the word. They took us to a rest area in the rear, and we just stayed there and stayed there and waited for orders. I believe we were there for about a month, and we just couldn't wait to get out of there.

"I believe that we finally left on a ship out of Naples, but I'm not sure. Then when we were aboard the ship en route back the United States, they told us that we were going to get a forty-five-day furlough, and then we'd be sent to the Pacific because the war against the Japanese was still going on. The thought of going to the Pacific was terrible! Terrible! Nobody wanted any more combat. We felt that we had had enough and that we had done our part. We just wanted to come home. That's what we wanted to do, but there was nothing we could do about it. If the Army says you go, you go. That's the way the Army operates. Fortunately, Japan surrendered before we could be transferred over there.

"When we got back to the States on September 10, 1945, I was given a forty-five-day furlough, and then back at that time, everybody was on the point system. At that particular time, you had to have sixty-two or sixty-three points to get out, but I had only fifty-nine. So, what they did to me after my furlough, they sent me down to Camp Rucker, Alabama, and I laid around down there. I didn't do anything. We didn't exercise or anything. They just held me over there for a couple months. Finally, they put a group of us on these trucks, and they hauled us all night long. They took us to Ft. Benning, Georgia. After two days there, I was discharged on November 29, 1945.[4]

After returning to Wrightsville, "Bud" had no problems in adjusting to a civilian routine once again. His experiences in Italy had matured him, and he was ready to find a job and get on with his life:

"As young as I was, I didn't have a good education, but I saw this war as one between good and evil. I did know then that I had a job that had to be done. I realized that. As I look back, my experiences in combat made me a more responsible person. It matured me, and I settled down. I had no problems at all in adjusting to civilian life. I soon met my future wife, and we got married in 1948. I think that that alone made a difference, too. At that time soldiers being discharged had no problems getting a job. Employers were looking for people like us. In 1945, soon after I was discharged, I went to work for American Chain and Cable Company in York. I first hired on there as a laborer, but I wanted to make more money, so I took up the trade of molding. I molded there at York Chain and Cable for a couple years. Then I left there, and I came down to the Wrightsville Hardware Company, and I molded there for a couple years. After they closed, I went up to Susquehanna Casting and molded there for a year or so. Then they started a new foundry over in Columbia at the end of the bridge—US Lock and Hardware. That was in 1956, and we poured our first iron on January 1, 1957. I gradually worked my way up there and became a foreman, and I eventually became the plant superintendant. After thirty-three years, I retired in 1990. Of course, I was not happy doing nothing, so when they asked me to come back and work part-time, I accepted. What I'm doing now, I'm working there three mornings a week for four hours. I do a lot of consulting work with them when they are having problems.

"As far as Wrightsville as a whole, I don't think it changed much during the time I was overseas, except the people seemed more prosperous. But I don't think the town changed much otherwise. The thing I remember the most, though, was that the people in the town seemed like they were so much more appreciative of soldiers than what they had been before the war. I think they realized what the servicemen were doing, and they set up big boards in each ward with the names of all the soldiers who were in the service during the war."

"Bud" and his wife Geraldine made their home in Wrightsville and raised two children there. Geraldine passed away shortly after they celebrated their fiftieth wedding anniversary. "Bud" played an active role in the construction of a monument mounting the names of all Wrightsville servicemen who served during World War II. He still resides at the family home in Wrightsville.

Notes

1. Alfred Forry, interview by the author, 12 August 1998, transcript, OH1261, Oral History Collection, University Archives, University of North Texas, Denton, TX.
2. Note: For a description of the "burp" gun, or Schmeisser, see the interview with Glenn Blouse.
3. Note: Contrary to "Bud's" assessment of German strength, as 1945 opened the Allies still faced an organized and determined foe consisting of twenty-four German and five Italian fascist divisions. The majority of Axis troops were experienced veterans who belonged to relatively intact units. Although well-led, the Axis troops lacked vehicles, firepower, and by early 1945 increasing shortages in nearly every category of equipment. For a general overview of the campaign, see Carlo D'Este, *World War II in the Mediterranean, 1942-1945* (Chapel Hill, NC: Algonquin Books of Chapel Hill, 1990).
4. Note: The Advanced Service Rating Score was a scoring system that awarded points to a soldier and was used to determine who were to be sent home first. At the end of the war in Europe, a total of 85 points were required for a soldier to be allowed to return to the States. Otherwise, with less than 85 points, one could expect to continue to serve in the Army and most likely to be sent to fight the Japanese. When the Japanese surrendered, the point system was still used to determine who was sent home and who remained as occupation troops. Points were awarded for the following: one point for each month of service, one point for each month overseas, five points for the Bronze Star and five points for each additional award, five points for a Purple Heart, twelve points for each child under eighteen (up to a limit of three), and five points for campaign stars worn on theater ribbons. See John P. Delaney, *The Blue Devils in Italy, a History of the 88th Infantry Division* (Nashville, TN; Battery Press, 1988).

Chapter 10

Pvt. Donald W. Peters

C Co., 83d Chemical Mortar Btn.

Born 30 September 1924, Donald Peters was unique among the Wrightsville veterans of World War II in that he was on separate occasions both wounded and a prisoner of war. The son of John and Mary Barnes Peters, he was the youngest of two brothers and two sisters. Like almost every other soldier from Wrightsville, Donald was a draftee. During the war, he served in the Italian Theater and in the invasion of southern France. He was wounded by shrapnel when his landing ship hit a floating mine off the coast of Anzio. After recovery in a US Army hospital, he rejoined his unit, fought briefly in Italy, and then participated in the invasion of southern France (Operation Dragoon) in late summer 1944. Donald along with other members of C Company was captured in the Alps while helping to protect the right flank of the advancing VI Army Corps in southeastern France. He subsequently spent the remaining seven months of the war as a POW at Stalag 7-A outside Moosburg, Germany. After returning to Wrightsville, he married and lived in Columbia where he raised his family. Donald died on 10 November 2003.[1]

Like most Depression era young men in Wrightsville, Donald's education was limited as he sought employment with local industries. Having registered for Selective Service as required by law, he waited for the local draft board to send him his draft notice:

"I probably never would have enlisted, but I didn't do anything to keep out of the service. Finally, I received my draft notice on April 24, 1943. We spent a few days at Ft. Meade, Maryland, and Ft. Lee, Virginia. Then I took my basic training at Camp Wheeler, Georgia. Basic training lasted seventeen weeks. The Army got us in good physical shape. On the other hand, I don't think that basic training really prepared us for combat. Nothing does, really.

"When we left the States, we were in a convoy bound for North Africa. There were about 300-500 men on our Liberty ship, so it was very crowded. To avoid submarines, we zigzagged all the way across the Atlantic. I guess this is why it took us somewhere around thirty days to get to North Africa. Then they loaded us on some kind of ship and took us over to Naples, Italy, and put us in a replacement depot. I went overseas to a replacement depot, and I didn't know anybody there. I went to another replacement depot, and I didn't know anybody there. When I finally joined my outfit, I didn't know anybody there. I just had to make friends over and over and over. One friend that I had throughout most of my time overseas was Miles Von Decker, who was from Pittsburgh. He could understand German, and he would figure prominently in my story later on when we were captured. It was right outside Naples, at Benevento, where I was processed, and then shortly thereafter I joined my outfit as a replacement.

"So, I wasn't assigned to a permanent unit until I got overseas. Since I was a replacement troop, the Army sent me wherever I was needed. In my case, when I got to Italy, I was assigned to C Company of the 83d Chemical Mortar Battalion. Companies C and D were the ones that had seen most of the combat, so they needed replacements. C Company was made up mostly of fellows from Pennsylvania and Virginia. In fact,

Robert Yeager was a fellow from Wrightsville who was in this outfit. He was in a different company, though, so I never met him. After I got in the unit, the various companies were split up, so we were all over the place. The battalion was never entirely together as a unit. The companies just went wherever they were needed, and we were not attached to a division. Mostly, we were attached to the 1st and 3d Rangers. We were their back-up mortar outfit. They called us a 'chemical battalion,' but actually it was just a regular mortar battalion. I was an ammunition carrier. I had to supply the gunners with their ammunition. These mortar projectiles were fired by our 4.2-inch [107-millimeter] mortars, and they weighed thirty-two pounds apiece.

Donald and the rest of the replacements joined C Company just as the battle for Monte Cassino was coming to an end. Although his unit was not directly involved in combat there, he was able to observe some of the fighting:

"The unit was on the front line at Cassino. We went up there, but we didn't stay there very long. The battle was just about over by then, so we were there for only about a week. We were more or less on standby at the time. We did not come under any fire. To tell you the truth, there were not too many old veterans in the company. As I mentioned before, C and D Companies had seen a lot of action and had taken a lot of casualties, so they needed a bunch of replacements. There was still a lot of action going on, though, but most of the fighting was around the top of Monte Cassino. We were halfway down the mountain, while the Rangers were up toward the top. They'd take the top, and then they'd lose it, and then they'd take it again. That went on the whole time we were there. Then we moved outside Naples again.

"I don't know whether I should say this or not, but when we first joined the outfit up on the mountain, the Rangers used to come down to our camp. They had mules and everything to bring prisoners or dead down off the mountain. They used to say that they had orders: they had a half-hour or three-quarters of an hour to go down to the bottom of the mountain to drop off these prisoners and go back up. How far it was, I don't know. Maybe a couple miles or so. But down in back somewhere, you'd hear a couple shots, and you'd see the Rangers coming back up over the mountain. They had shot the prisoners. I saw that myself there, and that went through my mind when I was taken prisoner later.

Donald's first actual taste of combat occurred off the coast at Anzio. Operation Shingle, another amphibious assault championed by Winston Churchill, started 22 January 1944, and was designed to land forces in the area around Anzio and Nettuno in an effort to outflank German forces on the so-called Winter Line. If the operation succeeded, then Rome would be open for rapid conquest. Designated to participate in this landing, the 83d Chemical Mortar Battalion boarded LST-422 [Landing Ship Tank], which was to take them ashore. In addition to the troops, LST-422 was loaded with trucks, Jeeps, M3 halftracks, ambulances and other vehicles. Many of the trucks were loaded with very volatile white phosphorous 4.2-inch mortar shells, while the decks also held many barrels of gasoline plus a variety of ammunition. At about 1:00 on the morning of 26 January, disaster struck while the ship was at anchor awaiting its turn to unload men and cargo at the Anzio docks. An intense storm whipped up a gale wind that blew the LST into a known minefield about twelve miles offshore, and the ship hit a floating mine. The explosion ripped a fifty-foot hole in the bottom and starboard side, and the ship's fuel oil supply immediately ignited. Most of the men of the 83d Mortar Battalion were asleep in the tank deck, which was the first to flood. LST-422 finally broke up and sank at approximately 4:30 AM on 26 January.[2] *What follows is Donald's account of that event and how it affected him:*

"My first actual combat was at Anzio. After being pulled back from Cassino, we went to a training camp outside Naples. It had been a racetrack at one time, and we stayed there until such time as they were ready for the invasion. Then they put us aboard the ship. All the ships in this convoy rendezvoused, and then we moved in. They had invaded Anzio a few days before we moved in, but since we were a mortar outfit, I imagine they didn't need us until they had established a beachhead. So, we were to go in a few days after the initial landing, but we never got to the beach.

"Our ship hit a floating mine and caught on fire. It was in the middle of the night when we heard this explosion. I was down in the hold sleeping in my bunk and using my life jacket as a pillow. When it hit, the explosion threw me out of my bunk. All the lights went out, and I started smelling smoke. I immediately knew I couldn't stay down there. Then I started to hear more explosions, and I thought to myself: 'Hey! You shouldn't be down here!' Everyone down there was panicking by this time, and they were running around in every direction. I don't know where I ever got the strength or whatever you want to call it to go to a passageway. It was pitch-black; it was dark. You couldn't see a thing. I thought, 'It's [that] way.' I was still more or less stunned from being thrown from my bunk, but I started over and found this railing going up to topside. By this time it was getting hot, and you could just feel the heat building up in the sleeping quarters and this passageway. I yelled, 'We can't stay here! We've got to get out of here!'

"We came up, and we were behind a big steel hatch door. The hatch door was open, and there were five of us back there. Now, we were close to the bow of the ship, and the rest of it was on fire. There were shells exploding because we were a mortar outfit, and we had our shells and mortars on there. Jeeps were exploding, and parts were flying. But from where we were and from there up to the bow, it wasn't too bad. So, we were sitting back at this spot, and everyone who started out with us and was still there got hit by shrapnel and flying debris. The first guy would say, 'I'm hit!' I was next in line—the second one in—and I said, 'Well, I'm hit!' The one in the middle said, 'I'm hit' I think I'm done for!' I looked over, and his arm was just hanging on by the skin. His stomach and intestines and everything were almost laying out. The guy on the other side said, 'I'm hit, too!' All five of us were hit.

"I had a piece of shrapnel that went through my thigh, right above the right knee. It didn't hit any bone or anything, but you could have laid your fist in the hole there. There was also a piece of shrapnel in my instep, and there was another one here in my back. I took out the one in my back myself. There were some other little pieces as well, and they were about the size a fingernail in thickness. The one in my foot was about the size of a thumbnail in thickness, and that's the one they took out of my foot about ten years after I got discharged. Now, the piece that went through my leg must have been pretty big because it made a pretty nice-sized hole. But that's another thing. The knee wound never bled. Even as big as the hole was, it didn't bleed. I guess the metal was so hot that it, like, cauterized the wound as it went through. So, it didn't actually bleed, and I couldn't say that I really had any pain at that time.

"Then this ship came alongside to take off whatever survivors were left aboard. We had to watch ourselves because the ships would have to come together, and right quick you'd have to drop down onto the other ship. We dropped down from a LST to a LCI [Landing Craft, Infantry]. If you know the sizes of the two ships, the LST was a much bigger ship, and the LCI was much smaller. So, we had a distance of about twenty-five feet or so to jump down. Our ship was still on fire, and there were explosions while we were being taken off. The ship was sinking, and it was also snowing and raining that night. The snow and rain may have been a Godsend, too, on a burning ship. That snow was blowing in, and it kept you cold and wetted down.

"When I dropped down, I just went down on my hands and knees on the deck. I then gathered myself together, and I got up and crawled down below decks. I walked down through the hatch and crawled into a bunk. This might sound like a boast, but I laid there and never said a word to anybody that I was hit, until these sailors went around and checked everybody. They said, 'Is there anybody else?' I said, 'Well, I think I'm hit.' They came over, and they checked me out. At that point I couldn't have gotten out of that bunk if somebody would have paid me $50 million. I walked down there, but I couldn't have gotten back out of it. No way! They say that when you're scared you'll do anything because the adrenalin is flowing. Maybe that's what it was. I don't know. I certainly was scared; there is no doubt in my mind that I was scared. But I managed somehow to get down there. Boy! When I got down there, the pain really set in!

"They took us to shore and into Anzio, and they had set up field hospitals with these big tents. I guess this was a temporary aid station because I was only there about three or four days, maybe. They just more or less cleaned me up and bandaged the wounds. They were supposed to take the shrapnel out of my foot, but they didn't. Then they put me on a British hospital ship and took me to a hospital right outside Naples. That was an experience in itself. The pain started to set in again while I was aboard ship. Most of my real care came at the hospital in Naples. It was a regular hospital, and I was there for three months. It took awhile because I had to take physical therapy. The leg stiffened up, and I had to get the muscles to start moving again. They had put my leg in a splint, so I couldn't pull or bend it.

After leaving the hospital, Donald rejoined his old unit and stayed with them through the push north of Rome:

"After recuperating, I went back to the 83d Chemical Mortar Battalion, which was right outside Naples. In fact, it was at just about the same place that I had joined them the first time. As before, due to casualties they had suffered, I knew almost nobody. We went back up to Anzio then. When the infantry pushed off of Anzio, we had supporting fire constantly for twenty-four hours solid. Every piece of artillery and every mortar had a twenty-four-hour mission. We kept firing until our weapons broke down. I can't imagine what it was like for the Germans on the other side, having that kind of artillery fire coming in on them for twenty-four hours. Oh, my! That must have been horrible! The Germans weren't throwing too much back at us. When our infantry moved in on them, they said that the Germans were just sitting in their bunkers and shaking all over, just shivering from fright. A lot of them just cracked; they couldn't take it anymore.

As the German forces were being pushed back, the 83d Chemical Mortar Battalion was pulled from the line to prepare for the invasion of southern France, code-named Operation Dragoon, which was to begin 15 August 1944, between the cities of Toulon and Cannes:[3]

"We knew it was rumored that we were going into southern France. It wasn't any secret as to where we were going. We didn't like the idea, but there was nothing we could do about it. Then we got ready to ship off for the invasion of southern France. So, we loaded up, and we went somewhere between Nice and Marseilles. We anchored out there in the Mediterranean—circling, circling, circling—and then one landing craft would depart for shore, and then another landing craft would head in toward shore. We were going in on LCVPs [Landing Craft, Vehicle, Personnel]. The front end would open up, and we'd go on out. There were battleships setting out there, and they'd open up with those big cannons, and you'd see those ships rocking back from the recoil! Man! Those battleships dropped those big shells in there. Whew! Well, there weren't any Germans there, so we just walked right on in and set up our camp. By this time the American forces were moving across France from the west, so we thought, 'Well, we'll meet somewhere along the line and push right into Germany. Let's do our job and get this over with. This is a good start toward going home!' There were very few Germans there—very few. Our troops kept moving right up through France because there was no resistance. So, our company was more or less just laying low, waiting for them to stop.

On 28 August 1944, C Company relieved a battalion at Briançon and established a defensive position east of the city. Patrols indicated enemy activity in the area, and during the night, unknown to C Company, German forces infiltrated the area to the rear of the American position. The first indication of the German presence was the attempt by engineers to repair a blown bridge at dawn. C Company stopped the Germans with mortar fire, but at 8:00 a well-planned German attack in battalion strength in coordination with heavy supporting fire overran the American position. As a result, the enemy outflanked C Company's position, sending it into a rapid retreat. During the withdrawal, Donald and a large number of his comrades were captured. What follows is his version of events:

"I don't know where we were at, but they told us that we were going up into the Alps to relieve some infantry company. So, we had to go into the Alps traveling under blackout conditions. We were riding on ammunition since our trucks were loaded down with ammunition right up to the top of the boards. We finally got to this fortress [Fort de Trois Tetes] that looked like a castle. The walls must have been ten feet thick or more. It was right on the border with Italy. It was in the afternoon when we moved up there. Our mission was that if the Germans came across a bridge down in the valley—there was a bridge across a creek or river—we were to destroy the bridge.

"There was this officer—a 1st lieutenant, I think—from the infantry who was there before we came in. Some of these guys were drinking, and they got to arguing back and forth. Our officer said, 'Aw, we can blow out that bridge down there with three shells!' The other officer said, 'Aw, no!' They were half-drunk, and they went back and forth this way. So, our officer said, 'Okay, I'll prove it to you.' So, he called for a fire mission and called out a crew. I was watching all this. So, he called for a fire mission and told them where he wanted them to put the shells. They fired one round, and that one went out over the bridge. The second round was short. The third one was right in the middle of the bridge. That was all well and good, but actually the bridge had been knocked out before they started firing. But in the process of doing this, they killed some German engineers who were down there trying to repair the bridge and make it passable.

"So, that night the Germans sent an Alpine division up over the mountains. They came in on us, and at about daybreak they opened up on us. We were still in this fort with a drawbridge and everything. There was even a moat around the fort, and the one side was nothing but sheer rock. There was only one way out, and it was over the drawbridge. So, the Germans opened up on us with artillery fire. We started to return fire with our mortars. We fired all our rounds until finally we didn't have anything left. Then we blew up our mortars, so all we had were carbines and pistols. That was the extent of our firepower, and we soon used up all that ammunition. At that point we just waited for the Germans to come in. There wasn't anything else we could do but just wait for them to come in.

"So, the Germans came in and lined us up against the wall. There were two machine guns and an automatic weapon of some kind in the middle. They then started to argue back and forth about what to do next. Well, the guy on one of the machine guns and the guy with the automatic weapon wanted to shoot us, but the guy on the other machine gun said in effect, 'No, we'd better not.' All this time Miles, my buddy, was translating from German and relaying this to me. After a while, a German officer came in, and he said, 'These men are soldiers, and they're to be treated as such.' Boy! That was like a load off my shoulders! They laid their weapons down, and then they came through and searched everybody to see if we had any weapons or anything. They were also confiscating rings and wristwatches. I really didn't have anything at that time that they'd want.

"Then they lined us up, and they marched us single file down trails all around over the Alps. There were about thirty or forty of us. We wound up in Italy, and we stayed one night in a chalet. They put us in the mess hall area, and we slept there on the floor and on tables. They'd ask us questions, like, where you lived, and then they'd slip in a question about the military situation every now and then. We didn't know anything. There wasn't too much we could tell them because we didn't know what was going on most of the time.

"We stayed there just one night, and then they loaded us on trucks and took us to Torino, Italy. This city was still held by the Germans, of course. As we walked down the street when they got us off the trucks, we walked to a kind of city jail. During this march, civilians lined the street and yelled at us and spat on us and threw things at us. I honestly don't think they were Italians. They might have been German men and women who had come down there to work. Maybe their husbands were stationed there or whatever. A lot of them were blondes, which would give you the impression that they were Germans rather than Italians. We were there for several weeks, and then they loaded us on boxcars and took us up through Brenner Pass. They took us up into Germany to Stalag 7-A, which was at Moosburg. It was not too far from Munich.

Stalag 7-A was to be Donald's home for the rest of the war. What follows in various segments are his account of life for an American prisoner of war. He starts with a physical description of the camp:

"I think that there were two or three upright fences of barbed wire. There were guard towers, and there was a main entrance that was manned by two or three soldiers.

"Our living quarters were just regular wooden barracks. They had wooden floors with nothing on the floors. We had wooden bunks with, like, excelsior mattresses. The mattresses had very finely shaved wood in them. There were two sections to each barrack that met in the center, and right in the middle was a washroom. There was just a sink. There wasn't a shower or anything; you just went in there and washed up.

"There was no heat except in this center section. If you were lucky enough to have a blanket, why, you stayed warm. In fact, I think they gave us one or two blankets per person. I had on winter clothes. I had gotten an overcoat somewhere. I don't know whether it was an American coat or what it was, but I had some kind of overcoat. But it wasn't enough to keep me warm. There was this one stove in the center, and it was a wood stove. We were lucky if we got something to burn in it because there wasn't anything to burn. They didn't supply us with wood or coal. If you were lucky enough to run across some coal or something like that while on a work detail, you'd bring it along back and throw it on the fire.

"The latrine was outside in another building. It was brick, I'm pretty sure, and it had a cement floor. There might have been two or three barracks that used the same latrine. Of course, we're talking about an outdoor privy.

"There were three different sections to the camp, and they changed from time to time. The section we were in was for the enlisted men. There was another section where they had all different nationalities. They had Serbs, Greeks, Italians, and other nationalities in there. I don't know what they did with all those nationalities, but, all of a sudden, they brought in hundreds and hundreds of officers and put them in that compound. These officers were of all different nationalities, including Americans. Each compound was separated by another inside barbed wire fence.[4]

Like all prisoners of war held by the Germans, particularly during the latter days of the war, food became an obsession for Donald and his comrades at Stalag 7-A. He describes the ingenious methods used to scrounge additional rations:

"Food was the thought that was most prevalent on our minds. Any chance you got to get food, well, you took it. I mentioned that influx of those hundreds of officers into one of the other compounds. We used to take turns taking their food into them. We had to take their food into them, and there would always be extra rations for them. When you took it in, you waited. After they divvied up amongst themselves what they wanted, we got whatever was left. You might have had thirty or forty men's rations, which meant a lot to us. That way we got extra bread, potatoes. Then you'd try to share with everybody, although the extra food actually belonged to the five or six of us who had taken the food to the officers. This detail was rotated; everybody got a shot at it.

"Our typical meal consisted of loaves of hard bread with what looked like sawdust on top of it. You could have driven a nail in it. We could always tell when we were getting limburger cheese because you could smell the wagon coming from miles away. There was soup, usually. It was, like, barley soup. Of course, there was no meat in it. We did get liverwurst or some kind of bratwurst every now and then, but I couldn't eat it because I couldn't stand garlic. Another thing I can still picture in my mind was dehydrated sauerkraut. They'd heat it up, and it would be brown. It was horrible-tasting, and when it would get cold, there would be white things all through it. It was like tallow or something through it. We obviously ate it when it was hot, before it got cold. Another thing we ate, I'd swear, was just regular grass clippings. It looked like it, and it tasted like grass. It was made into a soup.

"I was one of the fortunate ones. My parents and my buddy Miles's parents used to send us cigarette parcels. Even though my dad had a small grocery store and would send me cigarettes, I never got any of the parcels he sent. Very, very few of those ever got through, but the two of us decided that if either of us got anything like that from home, we'd share it. Well, he was lucky enough to get a cigarette parcel with, I think, ten cartons of cigarettes. I believe that Miles was the only person in our barrack who ever got a cigarette parcel. Well, needless to say, he was like a millionaire, and I got my share. The Germans didn't give all of them to us at one time. They'd give us maybe one pack every so often. The Germans would distribute them to him because he was the one that they had been sent to. One of the reasons the Germans wouldn't give us all our cigarettes at once was because, if we would have had them, we could have bought our way across the Swiss border, which wasn't too far away. If they had given them to us all at once, that was ten cartons of cigarettes. Man! We could have bargained with some of those Germans to sneak us across the border.

"We used the cigarettes to buy meat from the German guards. If Miles and I wanted some meat, we'd meet the guard on the sly at night. Miles could speak German to them across the fence. Certain guards had certain things to sell every night, and since we had access to cigarettes, we were able to deal. So, we had our cigarettes to smoke, and then we had extras. In fact, we'd trade one American cigarette for maybe ten Canadian cigarettes, maybe twenty Serbian cigarettes for one American cigarette. Then we'd use all these to trade for food.

"Cigarettes were the big trading tool. You could be short on food but not on cigarettes. You could always tell when cigarettes were scarce —when everybody was at each other's throat. When cigarettes were scarce, tempers just flared. Guys would get on each other at just the snap of a finger. They maybe wouldn't fight or anything, but they go back and forth all because of cigarettes. Miles and I would sell chances. We'd sell maybe thirty or forty chances at a cigarette a chance. Whoever won got the meat that we had traded with the guards for our cigarettes. Whoever won, it was their meat. We seldom ate it because we didn't know what it was. We didn't know if it was horse meat or what it was. So, we were living pretty good. We had it a little better than the average prisoner there.

"Once in a great while, we'd get a Red Cross parcel. They didn't come too steadily. When we did get them, they were supposed to be for two people. Usually, though, there would be six people who would have to share one, so we would have to break them down. There would be a can of Spam or maybe a can of that Eagle Brand sweetened condensed milk. There wasn't too much that one person could get if six people had to share that one can of milk. Each of us would take a spoon, and we'd pass it around. That's the way it went. That Eagle Brand milk was some high-energy stuff. Oh, boy! Was it ever! You took a spoonful, the next guy took a spoonful, and the next one took a spoonful until it was all gone. There'd be a few of the little cigarette packs in it, and there would be some little candy bars from Hershey. Every once in a while, there'd be blocks of chocolate.

"Work details also provided opportunities to get extra food. We used to go into towns on work details. We'd travel back and forth in boxcars. In one town they had these bombed-out railroad cars there that had wheat in them. So, what we did was take our jackets and tie the arms shut and fill them with wheat. We took that back to camp, and we took cans and other metal objects to mash down the wheat, and then we'd sieve it through a tin can with holes in it. Then we'd have our flour and roughage, which was like a cereal. Sometimes we'd use that chocolate in the Red Cross parcels and cook it over our stove. If there were prunes or raisins in the parcel, we'd put all this in with crackers, bread, or anything else we had and let it simmer. It would get cooked down like a bread or whatever.

"Wherever we went, food was always on our mind. That was the main thing. We worked in Munich, and if we got a chance to talk to civilians, we would trade a little piece of chocolate or a cigarette for a loaf of bread —the good, regular bread instead of the hard, sour bread. Actually, by this time the civilians didn't have much food to trade with us. They were hurting for food, too. Now, if you got caught coming back into camp with that bread, they'd take it from us. If we saw them searching us that night coming back into camp, we'd throw the bread over into the medical compound, which was right over from where they searched us. We'd throw it over to them, and they'd take it to their barrack. That way, it wouldn't go to waste, and the Germans wouldn't get it back.

The prisoners experienced very little harassment at the hands of German guards or civilians:

"The camp was run by the German army. The high noncommissioned officers were in charge of the barracks. Some higher ranking German officer would tell him what to do, and then he gave his orders to our highest ranking non-com. We didn't come into contact with the guards too much except in the mornings, when we went to work. Some of them we didn't want any part of. We had one little guy there who had been a prisoner during the First World War. He was a nice guy. We were in town one time working out of that boxcar, and we saw him coming down the tracks late in the evening, He had a keg of beer, and he brought it down to us, and he stayed in the boxcar with us all night. He could speak some English, and he was a pretty nice guy.

"Most times that we worked in Munich, we were stacking bricks. We'd knock the mortar off the bricks from the bombed-out buildings and pile them up. That was one of the main things that we did in Munich. The German civilians never seemed to bother us. Most of the time, it was so darned cold that we didn't run into anybody. One time we were downstairs at the Munich railroad station, which is where we usually ate our lunch. They had vats of beer down there. I'd say they were twenty-five or thirty feet high, and round. That was full of beer down there, and they had one vat after the other. When we went in there and ate, the civilians would give us a glass of beer.

Due to the close living accommodations and an inability to take proper sanitary precautions, the prisoners suffered from an infestation of vermin:

"Oh, my! We had fleas, lice, and crabs. There were no ifs, ands, or buts about it. You could bathe as much as you wanted, but you had to put the same clothes back on. You washed your clothes, and then you had to get back into your bunk, which was loaded with them. So, we really didn't have any way of getting rid of them until after we were liberated. Then they took us through some kind of a spray thing. In the meantime, you just had to put up with it. They got into your clothes because they were in that excelsior on your bunk. That excelsior was like chopped-up wood. At Easter time they used to put that a lot of times in Easter baskets and so on. It was sort of yellowish in color, and that was what was put inside these mattresses. It used to be funny at times. You'd see guys sitting cross-legged, and another guy would be picking the lice and crabs and fleas off of him just like you'd picture a monkey picking them off another monkey. That's the way these guys used to do it. You'd have a hard time seeing them, so another guy had to do it.

As news of the Allied advance across Germany filtered down to the prisoners, they eagerly anticipated liberation:

"We found out about different things. I don't know how they ever got the information, or where, but as American troops moved, we knew just about where they were located. We knew ahead of time, within a very short while, that we were going to be liberated. A short while later, the Germans told us to stay inside the barracks and not leave. The war was still going on, but the Germans told us to stay in the barracks. There wasn't any battle or anything going on close to the camp. There wasn't any shooting or anything.

"So, after a certain amount of time, why, we decided to go outside the barracks, and we saw the American troops come in. The guards were up there by the gate, and the Americans were taking their weapons and throwing them into a big pile. Then they took the guards away. The war was just about over by that time. The Americans didn't bring us anything, to tell you the truth. They didn't provide us with any food or anything.[5]

"I guess it was about the second day when General [George S.] Patton came riding through, sitting in the back of his Jeep. He had his ol' pearl-handled revolvers flashing in the sun. Patton didn't mess with the enlisted men's section, though. He went right on back to the officers and talked to them, but he never bothered talking to us even though he had to ride right through our compound. His Jeep never stopped in the enlisted men's compound.

"The Americans eventually sent in a team, and they loaded us up on an airplane. I don't even remember how we went to the airport. Anyway, we flew from right outside Munich somewhere and then up into France. They had different camps that that they sent the prisoners to—Lucky Strike, Chesterfield, Pall Mall—but I can't remember the name of the one where they sent us. By that time we had been deloused and everything and had been issued new clothing. Wherever we were sent, we had free rein. The mess tent had all the broasted chicken you wanted to eat. They had big containers of eggnog that we could drink all the time we were there. Anytime of the day or night, we could go up to the mess tent and eat. They were trying to put weight on us. There were regular meals, too.

"Then we flew to from there, from that part of France, to another part around Cannes or more toward the coast. We flew on in and loaded on a ship there at that city [Marseilles]. It was an Italian luxury liner. I don't remember the name of the ship anymore, but they had converted it into a troop transport. It was a big thing, and it was fast. From there we came back to the States, and I think I had been a prisoner of war for seven months, almost to the very day.[6]

Donald received his honorable discharge from the Army on 26 October 1945. He had a few problems adjusting to civilian life once again:

"I was still young man twenty-one years old, and when I first came home, I said, 'Mom, tonight and tomorrow are your days, and I'll stay home.' But from then on, well, I was pretty much living off the bottle. The next thing I knew, I was an alcoholic at that time. But I turned my life style around, and I quit drinking. I gave it up. After I got married, I thought, 'This is foolish.'

"Was I going to get all my money and give it to a hotel owner and let him take vacations with my money? No way!' I just quit.

"Concerning my wartime experiences, I figured the Good Lord in some way has some kind of meaning for me. I was too close to death so many times. He must have had some kind of aim for me. I didn't know what it was, and I still don't; but in some way or another, He must have had some reason for letting me come back. I've often thought of that—that He must have had some reason because I was so close to death so many times. But why did he pick me to come back? That's entered my mind a lot. When we were on that ship off of Anzio, I'd say that less than 10 percent got off of there alive, maybe a lot less than that.[7] Robert Yeager, the other Wrightsville guy, was also on that ship, and he perished. I heard that they were trying to get away from the ship, but he couldn't go any further. That was the last they saw of him. So, that's the only thing I could tell the Yeager family. Some of them asked me about Robert, and I said, 'All I know is what information I got from some of them in Company D.' They told me he was swimming in the water, and he was trying to get ashore. I guess he had a life jacket, but he never made it to the beach."

Donald Peters married, bought a home, and raised his family in Columbia. He died 10 November 2003.

Notes

1. Donald W. Peters, interview by the author 6 August 1998, transcript, OH1273, Oral History Collection, University Archives, University of North Texas, Denton, TX.
2. Note: See Barbara B. Tomblin, *With Utmost Spirit: Allied Naval Operations in the Mediterranean, 1942-1945* (Lexington: Univ. of Kentucky Press, 2004), 334-335 and Brooks E. Kleber and Dale Birdsell, *The Chemical Warfare Service in World War II* in *The US Army in World War II* (Washington, DC: Office of the Chief of Military History, 1966), 446-447.
3. Note: For an account of Operation Dragoon, see William Breuer, *The Invasion of Southern France*(Novato, CA: Presidio Press, 1988).
4. Note: Stalag 7-A housed 110,000 POWs at the time it was liberated by the US 14th Armored Division 30 April 1945. It was Germany's largest prisoner of war camp. See Stephen E. Ambrose, *Citizen Soldiers: The US Army from the Normandy Beaches to the Bulge to the Surrender of Germany, June 7, 1944-May 7, 1945* (New York: Simon & Schuster, 1997), 457-459.
5. Note: The prisoners at Stalag 7-A were liberated by elements of the US 14th Armored Division 30 April 1945. See Ambrose, *Citizen Soldiers*, 459.
6. Note: Donald was captured 29 September 1944, and was liberated by troops of the American 14th Armored Division on 30 April 1945. See Ambrose, *Citizen Soldiers, 459.*
7. Note: According to US Navy records, 454 Americans lost their lives when LST-422 went down. See Tomblin, *With Utmost Spirit* and Kleber and Birdsell, *The Chemical Warfare Service in World War II.*

PART III

THE NORTHWESTERN EUROPEAN THEATER

THE NORTHWESTERN EUROPEAN THEATER

Even before the Japanese attack on Pearl Harbor, President Franklin D. Roosevelt had decided that in the event of having to fight a war against Germany and Japan, American resources should be concentrated against the stronger enemy—Germany. He viewed a German victory over Great Britain a possibility and a subsequent threat to the United States. The American military leaders agreed with the President's assessment as did Winston Churchill and Josef Stalin, whose countries were bearing the brunt of the Nazi onslaught. US Army Chief of Staff General George C. Marshall accepted the conventional American strategy that victory required concentrating strength against strength. He believed that an attack across the English Channel, preceded by a massive build-up of men and material in the British Isles and a round-the-clock strategic bombing campaign against German targets, was the most effective and efficient way of using American and British forces to defeat Germany. Once securely lodged on French soil, Allied forces would then advance across Northern and Western Europe to strike directly at the German industrial heartland, thus destroying the enemy's capacity to wage war.[1]

In the early morning hours of 6 June 1944, a large amphibious force successfully landed 70,000 Allied soldiers on five beaches along the Normandy coast. Fortress Europe had been successfully breached, and within just a few days the Western Allies had 130,000 men ashore for the initial thrust across France. It was not, however, an easy endeavor. At one time or another, some forty-four American infantry and fifteen armored divisions saw action, and it was not uncommon for these divisions to have a 100-200 percent turnover in men due to casualties.[2]

The interviews with Wrightsville's soldiers who served in Europe reflected the thoughts of most other troops who were in that theater. As the combat troops moved across France, they came to realize that only peace, wounds, or death would bring release from war's miseries. Some even began to talk about getting the "million dollar wound," one serious enough for evacuation to a rear area or even return to the United States. Like most American infantrymen, the Wrightsville soldiers did not have a distinct animosity for the German enemy. Most were unemotional concerning feelings toward their opponents. If they were unemotional about the Germans, however, they held sober attitudes toward their work. Without a doubt, coping with fear was the most taxing challenge soldiers had to face, and if they survived one encounter with the enemy, they worried about becoming a casualty in the next fight. They experienced various kinds of combat stress: the thought of killing or being killed; the presence of noise and confusion; depending on comrades for safety and welfare; a lack of shelter; constant wetness, cold, filth, and sleep deprivation. Few seemed to have actually fired their weapons in combat, instead waiting for artillery to deal with the Germans. Most soldiers viewed the war in terms of their immediate environment and rarely thought about broader values such as fighting for democratic principles or destroying dictatorships. They wanted to get the war over with as quickly as possible while inflicting maximum damage on the Germans and keeping their own casualties at a minimum. Wrightsville's soldiers knew that the only way to get the war over and go home was through hard fighting.[3]

Notes

1. Gary R. Hess, *The United States at War, 1941-1945* (Arlington Heights, IL: Harlan Davidson, 1986), 47-49, 64.

2. Stephen E. Ambrose, *Citizen Soldiers: The US Army from the Normandy Beaches to the Bulge to the Surrender of Germany, June 7, 1944-May 7, 1945* (New York: Simon & Schuster, 1997), 280-283; Michael D. Doubler, *Closing with the Enemy: How GIs Fought the War in Europe, 1944-1945* (Lawrence: Univ. Press of Kansas, 1994), 235-237, 239-251, 253-259, 263. Portions reprinted in Mark A. Stoler and Melanie S. Gustafson (eds.), *Major Problems in the History of World War II: Documents and Essays* (New York: Houghton Mifflin Company, 2003). Note: For the most recent overall account of the Northwestern Europe Campaign, see Rick Atkinson, *The Guns at Last Light: The War in Western Europe, 1944-1945* (New York: Henry Holt & Co., 2013).

3. Michael B. Doubler, "The Travails of the American Combat Soldier in Europe," in Stoler and Melanie S. Gustafson, *Major Problems in the History of World War II: Documents and Essays*,156-169; Gerald F. Linderman, *The World Within War: America's Combat Experience in World War II* (New York: The Free Press, 1997), 48-89; and Robert E. Humphrey, *Once Upon a Time in War: The 99th Division in World War II* (Norman: Univ. of Oklahoma Press, 2008), 194-215; and Peter S. Kindsvatter, *American Soldiers: Ground Combat the World Wars, Korea, and Vietnam* (Lawrence: The Univ. Press of Kansas, 2003), 192-232. Other general works on the world of the combat soldier include Paul Fussell, *Wartime: Understanding and Behavior in the Second World War* (New York: Oxford Univ. Press, 1989); and John C. McManus, *The Deadly Brotherhood: The American Combat Soldier in World War II* (Novato, CA: Presidio Press, 1998).

Figure 12. MSgt. Edward "Tarp" Reisinger

Chapter 11

MSgt. Edward "Tarp" Reisinger

4th Signal Co., 4th Infantry Division

Born on 1 September 1919, in Wrightsville, Edward "Tarp" Reisinger was a child of the Great Depression who found a home in the US Army. With slim economic prospects in Wrightsville, "Tarp" joined the Army on 15 July 1940, and served for twenty-seven years, retiring in 1967 at the rank of chief warrant officer. His specialty was in the field of radio communications. "Tarp" was in the Northwestern European Campaign from the beginning to the end, from the Normandy invasion on 6 June 1944, to the German surrender on 7 May 1945. He participated in the Normandy invasion, the drive through northern France, the Rhineland Campaign, the Battle of the Bulge, and the thrust through central Europe. After his retirement from the military, "Tarp" eventually settled in Wrightsville with his wife and family. He died on 21 January 2002.[1]

Growing up during the Great Depression and with poor job prospects in Wrightsville, young "Tarp" saw the US Army as an institution that offered both security and opportunity:

"There were three children in the family in addition to my mother and father. They had lost a son and a daughter before me, evidently from the flu or pneumonia. I had two sisters, and I was the oldest child. My father was a cigar maker—he rolled cigars—when there was a job available. He also worked at the lower foundry [Wrightsville Hardware Company] back in those days as a molder. That molding was a terrible job back then, and it still is, actually. But I think you could primarily classify him as a cigar maker.

"I went to Wrightsville High School and graduated in 1937 from the new building that had just been completed by the Works Progress Administration. This was still in the midst of the Great Depression although things had become a little bit better, but not really too much. So, I would take almost any work I could find.

"I lived at home until I was twenty years old, which doesn't speak too highly of me, but that was the thing to do back then until you got married. I don't know what motivated me to go into the service, but it might have been—I can't say for sure—heavy thinking about living at home and all that. But it sort of made me decide that I had to get away, so that's what I decided to do—join the Army. Besides, economic prospects and advancement in Wrightsville were pretty slim to non-existent, so the service offered a viable alternative, plus there might have been a little bit of wanting to experience something different. I can't say it was wanderlust, but I wanted to get out and to see maybe what the rest of the world was like. The Army pay was seventeen bucks a month, so it wasn't all that great.

"Tarp" officially enlisted in the Army on 15 July 1940. Very shortly after joining, he started training in radio operations, a specialty in which he would serve with distinction during his twenty-seven-year Army career.

"The draft had not yet started, but the Army had decided to expand, and they were looking for people who could enlist for a particular unit and a particular kind of job. At this time they were looking for people for the 4th Signal Company, which was part of the 4th Infantry Division. I went directly to Ft. Benning, Georgia, and that's where I took my basic training—I guess you could say infantry training—and then I also advanced to the Signal Corps, climbing poles and splicing wires and all that stuff. The 4th Signal Company serviced the 4th Infantry Division with communications, which meant radio, wire, teletype—whatever was necessary. We had to lay wire lines to the infantry regiments and to the special troops, like, the medics, the engineers, and the rest of them.

As a result of the Japanese attack at Pearl Harbor, the routine for "Tarp" and his comrades changed drastically:

"After Pearl Harbor, everything changed. For example, I had originally signed up for a three-year enlistment. Now I was in for the duration plus six months. It didn't matter to me very much because I was a career man—I had volunteered—but the draftees were the ones who didn't like it, naturally. I remember the first contingent of draftees in our company, which became a provisional training company. We had to train these guys, and, of course, they were only in for a year—so they thought. But when things changed, there was a lot of griping, and I don't blame those guys. In the end they turned out to be good soldiers, and if it hadn't been for them, we could have been in bad shape. In my case, I had already decided that the Army would be my home even before I went overseas. I liked it. I don't know exactly why, but there was the camaraderie. Another thing, I suppose, was the fact that you were pretty well taken care of. You always had your meals available, your clothing, and what-have-you. Of course, being a child of the Depression, that sort of had some effect on me, I think.

"After the Pearl Harbor attack, we moved to Camp Gordon, Georgia, and the Army decided to send me to a radio school up in Pittsburgh, Pennsylvania. This school was called the Keystone Radio School, and it was run by the Army. The instructors were primarily retired naval operators, not from the Navy itself but from merchant marine-type work, and they were good. The object was to teach all of us to be able to send and receive at least twenty-five words a minute in International Morse Code, and that was about it. I stayed there for four months and became a high-speed radio operator. Then we went back to our units and learned the rest of it—the different call signs, the military phonetic alphabet, and the rest of it. By then I was a tech sergeant as well as the assistant radio platoon sergeant.

With the war already going on and large numbers of men going overseas, hasty wartime marriages were quite common. Before he went to Europe, "Tarp" met his future wife, Margaret Lilly, whom he married before departing:

"We had moved to Camp Gordon in late December 1941, and then I met Margaret in early 1942 in Augusta, Georgia. She had originally come from Tennessee and was down there working for Liggett Drug Company. I had been out flying Piper Cubs that day, just taking flying lessons on my own, and I had been out the night before and had had a few beers. My eyes were red, and in those days you could go into a drugstore and get a couple drops of Murine put in for a quarter. She put the drops in, and our relationship went on from there. When I came back from the radio school in Pittsburgh, she was still there, so we started to see each other again, and we got married on Christmas Eve 1942.

"Marriages prior to troops going overseas were pretty common. There was a feeling back in those days among, I guess, most of the soldiers that, geez, you didn't know what was going to happen. Once you got overseas, you didn't know if you would come back or not, so I think there was a desire to get a wife and enjoy a little bit of married life before you had to ship out. Thinking back, it's hard to figure out why you did it, but it was just one of those things. There was a man and a woman who liked each other, and we decided to get married. I might mention that back in those days you had to get permission to get married from your commanding officer. The service, moreover, didn't provide any enlisted housing for married couple[s], so we had to live on the local economy. After we got married, we lived in Augusta. We had to find our own places and get into work in the mornings the best way you could. Incidentally, my only son—he's Edward L., Jr.—was born in July 1944, after I was overseas. He was almost a year old by the time I first saw him.

Since the Allied leaders had determined that the opening of a second front was the proper strategy for defeating Germany as quickly as possible, "Tarp's" 4th Infantry Division prepared for participation in that effort:

"About September 1943 we reverted to the standard infantry division and moved to Camp Gordon Johnson, Florida, and were assigned to the Amphibious Training Center at Camp Carrabelle, which was located about thirty or thirty-five miles south of Tallahassee, right on the Gulf of Mexico. Of course, none of us realized what we were getting into. This was the beginning, I think now, of when they had decided that the 4th Infantry Division was going to be used at Normandy, and we were starting the training. The object, I guess, was to familiarize the whole division on landing craft. We made practice landings on an island there, called Dog Island. We spent four months down there, so by that time we had become pretty familiar with landing craft. Of course, they also had facilities for rope ladders and all so that you could practice getting into craft. Back in those days, they had no ships available, so it had to be done on shore. They just built a big wall and then dropped netting down the side. We had to practice going both ways, going up and coming down, but there were no bobbing craft there, where you had to judge the tops of waves and jump in when they came up. But it was simulated to some degree.

"Then in December we went to Ft. Jackson, South Carolina, just to bring our shots up-to-date, make our wills, and receive our clothing. Making out the will didn't make me feel very good. This was mandatory for everybody, so you just took it as another thing that the Army required. At first, however, you did think a little bit about it. Actually, you were usually so busy that you didn't have time to brood on stuff, and you were so tired at night that you couldn't lie in bed and rehash it, either. It was preparation for the final overseas movement.

For "Tarp" and his comrades, the voyage to England was rather uneventful except for the usual GI griping about conditions aboard ship:

"We left from Brooklyn in January 1944 as part of a convoy. I think the ship was the SS *George Washington*, which had been, if I remember correctly, taken from the Germans after World War I and renamed. Naturally, it was jammed with soldiers. Billeting wasn't that great, either. The bunks were about four high, and you always tried to make sure you got the top one because seasickness was rampant. The latrines were always a mess due to vomiting. It was terrible! You really sympathized with those guys. They'd be lying on the floor of the latrine, and everything is stopped up. I swear the vomit and water was a foot deep and sloshing back and forth. It would go into your fatigue jacket and fill up things. Some guys were praying for the ship to sink. Then there were a few who had to be taken to sickbay and fed intravenously. I got lucky when they asked for volunteers who could communicate by radio. German submarines were no problem because we had pretty much taken control of the Atlantic by that time. We had also been able to get those long-range patrol planes to cover us all the way across.[2]

Upon arrival in England, the 4th Infantry Division spent another four months of training and practicing more amphibious landings as part of the rehearsal for the cross-channel invasion:

"We landed in Liverpool in January, and this was the first real indication that we knew there was a war going on. The docks were still smoking from an air raid, and everything looked terrible. Everything was devastated—at least to us. We then got on trains and went down through southern England to the little town of Tiverton, and we were billeted there until we actually embarked for France.

"There was a beach close by, called Slapton Sands, which, I didn't know then, resembled Utah Beach at Normandy. Slapton Sands was part of an area in southern England that had been completely cleared of all civilians. Everybody had been moved out. We would practice landing there, backed up by ships actually firing. This was all live ammunition. By then we did have enough landing craft, so we'd get aboard them and go ashore. Once ashore we'd fire our weapons, and the artillery would also fire. These were pretty realistic exercises that would occur maybe once a month.

"All our vehicles had to be waterproofed because the waterproofing had not been done before they came out of the factories. We used a compound that was in five-gallon cans, and I think it was called Asbestos Waterproofing Compound—AWC—and, of course, that had to be put on behind the dashboards and all the instruments, all the electrical equipment. In our case, the 4th Signal Company was responsible for all the motorized radio equipment. We did not deal with back-mounted radios. Back in those days, they had a vehicle called a command car, and a lot of our radios were mounted in them. Each command car had a four-man crew. We furnished each regiment with a crew because we were responsible for getting communications back to us. We also furnished one to the division commander, Major General Raymond Barton. I also had to send out a radio crew to the 8th Infantry, one to the 12th Infantry, and one to the 22d Infantry. That was all part of my job—radio communications.

"As far as security precautions at Tiverton, we had the usual guards. Although we knew we were training for the invasion, we had no idea about the precise time until we moved into the secure areas along the coast. Suddenly, we left our billeting area with all our equipment and went into these areas where we were completely locked in. You could never, ever get out. Then the next morning after we had been in there and locked up, they brought out the maps and put them on the wall. They ripped off the covering, and there was the coast of France. That was a shock. Of course, we had known the cross-channel invasion was coming, but we didn't know exactly where. Everything up to that time had been top-secret, naturally. In addition to showing us the map, they gave us some idea of what to expect when we attempted to make the landing, as far as the information that they had. There were two German divisions, I think, on maneuvers in that area that we had no word of, so that was the joker in the whole pack. We were briefed. First of all, in the Utah Beach area, there were three causeways. The area behind the beach had been flooded by the Germans, so we had to depart or leave the beach over one of those. All the areas were picked, and all the landing craft and the loading had been set up, so everybody knew which craft they were going to be on.

"The thing that raised the hair on my head, and probably the hair of a lot more guys, was the fact that, all of a sudden, we started doubling personnel and doubling equipment because they figured that we would take 50 percent casualties. That, you know, you don't like to hear. Luckily, it didn't turn out that way. By then I was a platoon sergeant—a master sergeant—and I had the responsibility for all of these people. They doubled everybody in the radio platoon to about eighty people—can you imagine that—plus all the equipment.

Loading for the assault began on 31 May. Finally, weather conditions were such that General Eisenhower made the decision for the attack on Fortress Europe to begin on 6 June. For "Tarp" and his comrades, there was a sense of anticipation to get on with the task for which they had trained so hard and so long as well as a realization that death could be waiting. In most cases, however, anticipation overrode fear, but there was no joking or pranks. Any humor was infrequent or forced:[3]

"Well, we went down to what was called "the hards"—that's the British word—and they had the ships and the LSTs and the LCPs [Landing Ship, Personnel] pulled up with their ramps down, and we got on. Of course, there were loading plans for each ship—who would go on, what equipment would go on. They would load them in reverse because the last on were to be the first off. [4]

"We got on the thing in either Dartmouth or Torquay or Exmouth, I think—I'm not sure—and we sailed off into the blue, you might say. Then that storm came up, and we were sort of torn between returning and calling the thing off. But, of course, 'Ike' [Eisenhower] decided to do it after his weatherman told him that the next day would be a fine day—not completely fine, but pretty nice. So, we had been on the ship, and we never got off until we got to the beach.

"By this time, we had different emotions. First of all, when we knew it was about to happen, everybody said, 'Hey! Finally! Let's get this thing over with!' Then the invasion was postponed, and I think that was a disappointment, as far as I could see, to a degree. I certainly couldn't say it was a carnival atmosphere. There was some apprehension, sure, but to us young guys it was maybe an adventure. We didn't know what we were due to get into, and nobody else did, except for the guys who had been in the Pacific or North Africa. But North Africa had been relatively easy. Also, they tried to keep us busy, too—maybe doing calisthenics and checking equipment and all the other stuff—so maybe your mind wasn't completely thinking about the invasion. Sometimes you got a little bit miffed about all this make-work, as they called it. So, sure, there was apprehension, but in a way we were sort of looking forward to it because these preparations had gone on and on and on. We had been training from 1940 on, which was pretty long. So, I think everybody wanted to get it over with. You never—at least I never did—thought of getting hit. It's like an automobile accident. It happens to everybody else but you. Naturally, there was apprehension, sure, because we didn't know what we were about to get into.

"Prior to the actual landing, there was a tremendous naval bombardment and also wave after wave of airplanes coming overhead. I can remember that we stood on the upper deck because it was connected to the lower deck by an elevator. It was almost like an aircraft carrier. Anyway, we stood on the deck. This was somewhere maybe around just a little after midnight when the airborne troops started to come in. That was a show that I guess you'll never see again—all those tracers of different colors, searchlights, and almost anything. We couldn't hear very much noise because we were still out pretty far, but that was quite a show. Then as morning came on, they started the bombardment with the battleships. The first landings were at 6:30 [am] or somewhere around there, so it was before then that they started to lob the big ones in. You know, they had to use psychology on us, which is normal. In the prior briefings, they'd say, 'Hey! We're gonna cover this thing so well that there probably won't be a German left!' Of course, everybody knows Utah Beach was fairly easy. We did lose some people, but at Omaha Beach those guys suffered.

"There was now quite a lot of noise, and then, of course, there was the return fire from the Germans. We were a little bit too far out, but you could see when it got lighter. You could see the geysers come up where the German shells hit. Then you began to think that something really serious was in progress. But I think the thing that made the biggest impression on me, and what made me realize that this was for real—because we had been through so many practices that were practically the same—was when they started to bring the dead and wounded over the sides of the LST to bring them back on. Then you began to realize that really it was a serious business. No more practices. This was the real thing.

Upon reaching the shore, "Tarp" experienced the usual confusion and fog of war as he tried with some effort to find the 4th Division command post:

"I was not on the first wave, or the second wave, or even the third or the fourth. I think I went in maybe around 11:00 that morning, and I landed with the assistant division signal officer, who was a major. We had gotten ashore without even a wet shoe. Well, in the English Channel we had been on an LST, but they brought around an LCT and married it. We transferred some equipment and everything to that, and that's what went ashore. The guy went right on in and dropped that ramp right on dry sand.

"Then we had to find the CP [command post]. Everything by then had been marked with what they called 'engineer's tape'—minefields and every entrance were marked—so we went up through the causeway. Of course, we could see the evidence of what had happened. We saw dead GIs—not many because we didn't lose that many. But there were some who were dead, and we could see parachutes. Some paratroopers had landed in the water. We saw equipment, weapons, and tanks—almost everything you could name. It was the carnage of war with leftovers and abandoned equipment. It was all shot up and burned. Like I say, I was a long way from being in the first wave, but it was still an adventure.

With the beachhead secured, the 4th Infantry Division began its advance across France, beginning with the push through the hedgerow country. As a radio communications specialist, "Tarp" was not on the front lines with the infantry. Instead, he was positioned at the division command post to the rear. What he now describes is mainly his observations from battles already fought:

"I stayed with the division's CP, which was then located, I think, outside St. Mère Eglise. At that time our 8th Infantry was assisting elements of the 81st Airborne Division while the other regiments were enlarging the beachhead. Of course, every day ran into the next one because it was nothing more than just gaining ground. I didn't have to fight for it, and my company didn't, but the division had a tough time, especially in those hedgerows. The French called it the *bocage* country. These hedgerows were used to separate fields. Over the many years they had been built up to where they were often eight or ten feet high. They had allowed trees and other vegetation to grow over them, and with all these roots and everything in the hedgerows, it was hard to break through. It wasn't just a mound of dirt; it was a barrier. The roads that went through these areas were sunken roads, more or less. These hedgerows were on each side and maybe the trees had grown over to form a canopy. So, it was pretty difficult country. Then the Germans usually had foxholes in one corner, which meant they could cover the whole field, or maybe they'd have one on each corner so they could cover the area with two machine guns using interdiction fire. Our infantry had a terrible time.

"Movement was slow, very slow, until some sergeant devised a method for putting some of those pieces of railroad tracks that had been taken from the beach and rigging it to tanks so they could break through those hedgerows. They were the tetrahedrons that Rommel had out on the beaches for obstacles.[5] Before that, as soon as the tanks got to the top, they were exposed, and the belly of the tank, of course, was the real vulnerable spot. So, it was slow going. If they took one field a day there for a while, it was good. Our mission even before we left England was to land on Utah Beach, turn right and then north into the Cotentin Peninsula, and then capture the port of Cherbourg by June 15. We didn't meet that schedule, for sure. I think it had to be June 26 or whatever date before we got to Cherbourg. The things I remember about Cherbourg were the fortifications up around the perimeter of the harbor. There was nothing but great, big concrete pillboxes. They were massive things, and I think they could have held out for a long time.

For nearly a month, the Americans had been bogged down in the hedgerow country. To break the stalemate and open a decisive gap in the German defenses, General Omar Bradley, commanding the 1st Army, planned a massive air-ground assault named Operation Cobra. On 25 July 1944, 1,800 B-17 and B-24 bombers pummeled enemy targets for three hours. The heavy bombers were supported by medium bombers and fighter planes dropping napalm. The German defenders were decimated. What had been a war of attrition now became a war of rapid movement. The American armored and infantry divisions then swept through the gap but still met fierce resistance as they pursued the retreating Germans southward and westward.[6] What follows is "Tarp's" description of the scene during and after the American assault:

"We got ready for the breakout from Normandy. The thing I remember very vividly about the breakthrough was the aerial bombardment. It was terrible! When I say 'terrible,' I am thinking about how bad it was for the Germans. There were thousands of aircraft. Initially, the B-17s came over. Then there was antiaircraft fire. Every once in a while you'd see a bomber drop out of formation and sort of slide over and go into a spin. You could see every once in a while parachutes opening up. Then you'd see some planes come down all afire. In fact, there were a couple of planes that just blew up completely, and there was no evidence of anything. But the bombers just kept coming, and there was a steady rumble of noise. The ground actually shook and vibrated from all these bombers, and it just went on and on. You would hear that rumble, and you'd think, 'Well, that's the end of the planes." Well, geez! Here came some more!

"The 4th Division's mission was to take off then and go through with, I think, the 2d Armored Division. It was one of them, anyway, that accompanied us. We started through there, and everybody thought it looked like the surface of the moon because there was nothing but craters on craters. The surprising thing was the fact that our infantry ran into resistance. Then there were a lot of Germans who were completely dazed. They had no helmets; they had no weapons. They were bleeding out of their noses and ears and were completely disoriented. But the surprising thing was how the Germans could fight back after this saturation because it was limited to a certain area in width. I was with the division command post. Between us and the front, you had the regimental command posts, and then you had the battalion command posts, and then the company command posts.

The pursuing Allied forces finally caught the disorganized German forces in the so-called Falaise Pocket. What followed from 12-20 August was a massacre similar to what occurred during Operation Cobra. Almost completely surrounded, the Germans were again pummeled by a combined aerial and artillery bombardment before the Allied infantry and armored divisions move in the close the pocket. Again, "Tarp" describes the aftermath of this slaughter:

"That was carnage that, I guess, nobody will ever see again. I hope they don't. It was just total destruction. It was just terrible, really, and I don't hope that any army would really have to suffer that much again because it must have cost the Germans thousands of men. Luckily, some got out—or unluckily for us—you might say. The Germans used a lot of horses in their army, and, of course, dead horses were all over the place. The roads were blocked, and they had to take bulldozers to get weapons, food, trucks, men, animals—all kinds of mess—cleared away. This went on for several miles. You thought it would never end. It wasn't pretty, and, of course, the big thing by then was the stench. It was in August, and it was hot. If you've ever smelled a dead body, there's something that's distinctive about it. There's no other smell like it. For some reason a German corpse would turn yellow or bluish-yellow. It might have been because of their diet or whatever. As I said, it wasn't a pretty picture, but warfare is warfare, and you either win or you lose. And we were there to win, right? That's about what it boiled down to. After a while, though, you get to the point where you take this carnage for granted.

"At first, I think, you wanted to kill all Germans because it was either you or them. But then, as it progressed, especially after the slaughter at the Falaise Pocket, I think you started to feel sorry for the individual, and for the German people, because they were misled by Hitler. As the war went on, everybody knew they were going to lose it—there was no question about it—but Hitler decided to just keep on and on. You had to pity the people, especially when you saw what they had—nothing. There were refugees and other people on the roads. Young children were one of the things that you felt badly about because they didn't know what was going on. It wasn't their fault. But at first, all you wanted to do was kill Germans, and I think everybody had that same outlook. But then it changed a little. We were glad when the thing was over.

With the German forces now seemingly on the run, "Tarp" and his comrades had visions of being home for Christmas 1944, especially after the liberation of Paris, which turned out to be a rollicking affair for the Americans:

"We were moving so fast across France that the kitchen couldn't keep up with us, so we ate cold rations. Back in those days, they had one they called '10-in-1' rations, which were ten meals for one man or one meal for ten men. It was pretty good if you could find a place to cook it. They had some good Canadian bacon and powdered eggs. The food had improved an awful lot, even the C-rations. At first all we had were three selections: meat and beans, hash, and stew. Then later during the war, they came up with spaghetti and meatballs.

"Again, here in France we were moving so fast that we had no living quarters as such. Some of our people operated our big radios that were mounted on a two-and-a-half-ton truck. It was a regular house-type affair that was manufactured as a radio station. They could maybe sleep in there because it was warm and dry. But since it was still relatively warm, the majority of us would find a place under a truck or other vehicle. Sometimes in France we could maybe go into an abandoned farmhouse, but most were so miserable and dirty that we didn't like to do it. The barn was usually connected right to the house, so the smell of manure permeated everything.

"Since we were on the move, we'd go for days and days and days without bathing. You'd maybe be able to wash your feet and maybe take a shave. Sometimes you'd maybe bathe out of your helmet, but that was about it. You wore the same clothes all the time. Maybe you could wash out a pair of socks. We usually carried those in our helmets, so you could have a dry pair. There were a few times that they set up a showerhead, when they could. You had to go back from our positions. You would undress and leave everything on a pile, except your shoes because they had to fit. Then you went through the shower, and there was somebody there with a whistle who said, 'Okay! Soap up!' You'd turn on the water, get wet, and then soap up. Then they'd give you another minute or so to rinse off. They'd then blow the whistle again, and that was it. At the other end they had bales of new clothing, and you tried to get a set that would fit you. The sizes were marked on the outside—the trousers and shirts—and sometimes you got lucky. But at least it was new clothing, and who the hell cares if the cuff was an inch above the shoe or whatever. That was it, and it was like heaven to get into that hot water with soap. That was really a treat.

"We were sort of thinking that we'd be home by Christmas. You heard the word every once in a while. We had broken out, of course, and started across France. Our progress was so fast that we couldn't lay any wire. We depended completely on radio communications because sometimes we'd move forty miles a day—the division CP—and we were supposed to cross the Seine River south of Paris. For political reasons, the French 2d Armored Division was sent into Paris because they were French. Evidently, they couldn't hack it because, all of a sudden, we were diverted into Paris, too.

"Paris was one place I'll never forget because it was crazy there—actually 'nuts.' I can remember how it happened. The night before we got into Paris, the Army Air Force radio crew said, `Hey, Reisinger! We're gonna go into Paris!' I said, 'We haven't captured it yet.' They said, 'Oh, yes, we have!' So, we took off and went into Paris. It was crazy. The whole town just went berserk—completely berserk. Maybe you'd be on the street, and the people would be coming out with cognac and champagne and all this other stuff, but on one street over you'd have a tank battle going on, or there'd be a battle between the Free French Forces and the Germans going on. That first night we went into a French bistro where they had the Apache [pronounced *ah-pahsh*] dancers and the smoke-filled room and all.[7] I think we could have had anything we wanted because we were the object of all the attention and everything. One guy who was a member of the Free French Forces said, 'Do you need some cognac?' I said, 'Yes.' He took me out, and we went up the street and went to the top of an apartment house. That thing was jammed full of weapons, cognac, and champagne. The place was full of champagne, and he grabbed a case and gave it to me. So, that was the night that Paris went crazy, and then the next day the division went in, and it was still crazy.

"The other thing that I remember about Paris was the black market. In my experience I remember what happened in Paris later. As I said, our division moved into Paris and stayed the night, and the next day we were on our way out. As we progressed, say, into Germany and as things sort of settled down, every once in a while they'd pick somebody to go on leave to Paris for 'R&R' [rest and recuperation], as they called it. So, everybody would get together and give him all our extra cigarettes. Sometimes they'd leave for Paris with a barrack bag full of cigarettes, and that's all they needed because cigarettes were, you might say, the currency back then. That's all they needed.

After the liberation of Paris, the 4th Infantry Division headed north toward the Belgian town of St. Vith. In early November the division moved to the Hürtgen Forest region where it participated in the VII Corps's effort to penetrate German defenses in that formidable natural barrier. Here the division experienced some of the fiercest and costliest fighting of the war. The American strategy was based strictly on getting to the Roer River, Rur River in German, as quickly as possible, and the commanders believed the Hürtgen Forest lay in the way. Within the forest were several massive dams that managed the flow of the Roer and its tributaries. These dams were of far more strategic value than the useless forest, which could have been bypassed to the south with the dams as the objective. The American planners chose to ignore them. Historian Stephen Ambrose described the Hürtgen Forest as "forbidding." It had fir trees twenty or thirty meters high with interlocking branches that grew close to the ground and required a man to stoop to get through them. They blocked the sun, so the forest floor was dark, and damp. Ambrose added: "It was like a green cave, always dripping water." The rugged terrain consisted of a series of ridges, deep gorges, many streams, and several rivers. By the time the fighting for the forest had ended, the 4th Infantry Division had lost over 7,000 men.[8] "Tarp's" dream of getting home by Christmas began to disappear:

"Our unit spent a month or so in the Hürtgen Forest, and it was terrible —really terrible. I don't understand why we couldn't go around it instead of going through it. There was not anything that should have been an objective. There was no military reason to bother with that place. We could have gone around it and isolated it like we did with some of the Japanese-held islands in the Pacific. It was just a forest, period, although I guess the Hürtgen Forest opened up on the Cologne plain eventually. But Cologne was not an objective right at that time. I don't know why—and I don't think anybody else knows why—we were in there. It was a miserable, dirty place. When I say 'dirty,' I mean from the standpoint of the GIs. It was wet and rainy and cold and foggy.

"And the Germans had everything registered in because if they heard a little noise at night—they knew where the road was, and they knew that it had to be somebody on the road, like a vehicle—they would unload a deadly artillery barrage. Then there were minefields, and you couldn't see because of the trees and the fog. We couldn't use our armor in that forest. I remember one time we were trying to use armor, but because of the mines on the road and everything, they decided to call in one of those threshing tanks or whatever they called them. Boy! When they sent that up everybody was happy. This was really going to do the job. But the next thing you know, this thing is missing a couple tracks, and that was it. It was just a miserable place. We lost a lot of men in the Hürtgen Forest, and, I guess, for no good reason.[9]

"After Hürtgen we moved down to Luxembourg City for integrating replacements, cleaning our equipment, refurbishing, or whatever you want to call it. We had our mess with us, and we moved into a schoolhouse. Things were just fine, and we were doing well. Then, all of a sudden, the word came down that the Germans had attacked, and the Battle of the Bulge started.

On 16 December 1945, the Germans launched a massive counteroffensive with infantry and masses of heavy armor through the Ardennes. The objective was to cross the Meuse River and drive on to the Belgian port of Antwerp. Hitler argued that the surprise onslaught would split the Amer-

ican and British forces, and when the Germans had taken Antwerp, the British would have to pull another Dunkirk evacuation.

"I believe we knew that we were under attack, that the Germans had attacked, but I think everybody thought that it was just diversionary or something not that serious. But then the word came down that they wanted everybody who could be spared to be on the front line because we had to hold that bulge. We were on the southern shoulder of the bulge. So, they needed all the riflemen who were available. They sent up spare cooks, they sent in ordnance people—anybody who could be spared. Then it started to snow there, and we had a lot of snow.

"We left Luxembourg and started to move the CP—after they stabilized the area around the bulge—and moved on through. We got to the town of St. Vith again. In September when we had been there, it was intact. There was little damage to the railroad yards. When we went back through there, not to get to Bastogne, but to get up into that area, St. Vith was nothing. It had been completely obliterated. It was a communications area where maybe as many as five roads came together. It was terrible.

"The other thing I can remember was that all of the German equipment had previously been our equipment. It was actually a lot of our captured stuff and was now marked with the German swastika—maybe an American tank or a truck or whatever. And it was so cold!

Northwestern Europe at the time of the Battle of the Bulge was a terrible place. That year Europe experienced one of the coldest winters on record. A mixture of sleet, snow, rain, fog, and cold combined to make life miserable for the GIs. To make matters worse, the rivers were at flood stage, and the already poor road system had been turned into muddy quagmires. In this section "Tarp" describes the life of a soldier like himself, who was not on the front line:

"The snow was on the ground. It was cold and sometimes foggy. You had no place to hunker down to avoid the elements. If you wanted to sleep—if you could sleep—you would just sweep away some snow somewhere and try to lie down, stay warm, and get some sleep. For clothing we had our field jackets, woolen shirts, and woolen trousers. We didn't get rubber overshoes until later because the front echelons had them first. It was really a mess. The cold, as I remember, was so bad that you got to the point where you didn't mind it anymore. That's pretty close to freezing to death, isn't it? That's what they tell me. We had sleeping bags and a couple blankets, but I don't remember a ground cover. Regardless, you couldn't stay warm. It was a continuous chill, and there was no way you could get rid of it. There was nowhere to get warm. You couldn't build fires, of course. Every once in a while, I would maybe get into one of those trucks with our radio equipment, but not always because I had to be out in a Jeep—an open Jeep, really, with the top down and even the windshield down. The people who really suffered were the ones who were in the foxholes and had to sit there hour after hour. They got frostbite, and they lost toes and even legs and feet, I guess. Of course, the Germans suffered as much as we did. It was just a terrible winter.

"We had to dig our foxholes long enough to lie in and deep enough so you could get all of your body below ground. The width was just enough so that it was comfortable, depending on your size. The big thing was to make sure you covered it, so you looked around for limbs and other stuff and cover it. Then you'd put ground on top of it because the Germans would use what they called timed artillery—time-on-target. The rounds were made to explode above the ground and throw down shrapnel, so you had to have protection over you. A lot of times you'd find a nice place to snuggle down, and the next thing you know, the artillery fire starts to come in, and you have to find a hole. At first you get so scared, and each shell that you hear makes you think it's yours, and it has your name on it. When we'd get some heavy artillery rounds, you'd get in that foxhole and just hope the shells are going to go over or under you, but not on top. That was all you could do. When the shells go off, the concussion sort of lifts you up, and then you hit the ground again. I was never very religious, but sometimes you'd talk to somebody. It's an experience, I guess, that you have to go through in order to get the feeling. Everybody takes it a little bit differently, I suppose. But after a while, you get to the point where you just sort of say to yourself: 'Well, what the hell! If it happens, it happens!' I believe that's the attitude that most of the people had because there wasn't a thing you could do about it. That was it, so you would bear with it. If you were lucky, you made it. It's a terrifying experience. It's sort of like Russian roulette—you never will know when a shell will take you out. I was lucky because, being in a signal company, we weren't exposed to the front lines all that much—just once in a while. So, what it did, I guess, was make men out of boys, and really quickly.

"During the Battle of the Bulge, I saw what happened to replacement troops. Our type of replacement system was to bring in a troop for a troop who had been a casualty. If a guy got killed, they sent in a replacement for him. In the Ardennes, I saw troops come up who still had the chalk marks on their helmets to signify troop movements and troopships or replacement depots. They were sent to the front one day, and the next day the truckloads were coming back with mattress covers over the dead guys. So, replacements often had very little chance of surviving. The 1st sergeants never knew a lot of those people. They'd say 'Okay, your name is [So-and-So].' They'd put his name in a book, send him up to a foxhole, and the next day he's gone. You would see these dead GIs along the roads. They were dead and were laying in the cold and snow. You'd think of what kind of a family they had—whether they were married or single, their mother, their father, their brothers and sisters, and all that. I don't know why, but that went through my mind, and I got to thinking about it. It was sort of pitiful to know that these guys would never get home.

"Then the weather finally cleared, and here came the Air Force. That was a beautiful time to see those contrails. Everybody was glad to see that because those planes just shot up everything. Of course, the Germans then had to more or less run for their lives because our planes were on them like a pack of wild dogs.

The German Ardennes Offensive having been broken, Allied troops resumed the rapid advance into Germany similar to the one across France in the summer and fall:

"Then we could continue with our regular offensive and getting across the Rhine River. So, we went across the Rhine at Worms on a bridge built by the engineers. Once we got across the Rhine, we could almost see the beginning of the end, more or less. That's the way maybe that I looked at it. Of course, there was still some hard fighting to go, but we just kept on and on and on. We went through Munich and were heading for the Brenner Pass when we were relieved and sent west to Nuremberg. The 101st Airborne came in and relieved us.

"As we passed through these German towns, there were always white sheets, white flags, and what-have-you flying from the upper floors. They resented us, for sure, and I don't blame them. We weren't allowed to carry on too much of a conversation or fraternize with the civilians. We'd just rap on the door and say, 'Hey! You gotta get out of here! You got ten minutes because we're taking over!' This was warfare, and you didn't give it a second thought, really, back then. Now that I look back on it, it was too bad. Then we would round up civilians and have them work for us. They would work like crazy for a couple cigarettes, plus the fact that we had our .45s on them.

Like all GI's, "Tarp" welcomed the German surrender and looked forward to coming home. He had served continuously from D-Day on 6 June 1944, to the German surrender on 7 May 1945:

"When the word came down that the Germans had surrendered, there was a lot of shooting in the air for one thing. Everybody was relieved. Then the big worry started: 'When will I get home?' Of course, it was all back on the point system back then, and those with just a few points went into another unit, say, scheduled for the Pacific and the war against Japan. In fact, out unit was scheduled to go to the Pacific, and it did return to the States and was retraining to go to the Far East.

"The radio officer came down and said, 'Hey! That's it!' I said, 'What do you mean—'That's it?' He said, 'I'm sending you home. You're going home.' So, I think I was gone seven days after the war was over. I was with the first contingent of our division to come back. I came back on the SS *Marine Devil.* It was more of a pleasure trip because I was going back to something that was familiar rather than to something that was completely unfamiliar. In looking back, I can remember being on that train from Liverpool down to Tiverton. You sat there and looked out at the countryside, and I began to think: 'Will I ever get back to the States?' It was sort of a funny feeling. Here I was, in a foreign country, and I had no control over my life because I was part of the whole entity, I guess. It was sort of tough there for a while. Homesickness had set in, and I hadn't been homesick in a long time, except for the first day or so in the Army. It made me realize that this was serious business, and all the fun and other stuff was gone.

"The training that we got, I think, paid off. The training we got in England at Slapton Sands was very realistic. I guess you can never get enough training to expect or know what's going to happen. No training will ever get you to the point where it will completely get you ready for combat. I was about twenty-three when all this took place, and I think combat makes a man out of you really quickly. It changes your philosophy of life because up to that time it was sort of a good time. You could drink some beer and do all this other stuff, but then it got to be serious business. It makes you sort of wonder, first of all, about whether you would make it or not. I guess I'm like the guy in the song about Custer: 'Hey, Mr. Custer! I don't wanna go!' But World War II was just a thing that had to be done, and that's it. I was forced into it, even though I was a volunteer; and even the draftees were forced into it, but they made the best of it, and they did a good job. If it hadn't have been for the draftees, why, we might have lost the war.

"We went into Boston Harbor and then proceeded to Camp Miles Standish. The next morning at, I think, 9:00, we were on a train to Ft. Dix, and on June 17, 1945, I became a civilian, and that was about it.

"Tarp" returned to Wrightsville after being discharged, but he soon became restless in civilian life and yearned to get back into the Army. Although he could see that Wrightsville held no future for him, he had already unwittingly decided to follow through on an earlier decision to make the Army his career:

"There was nobody in Wrightsville when I returned after receiving my discharge. Most of the guys were still in the service. So, Wrightsville had changed, I suppose, only because I had been away for so long. After I came back, I carried mail for a while, but that didn't pay very much. It paid forty cents an hour, and I carried it six days a week.

"One day I came home, and I told Margaret, 'I've got to go back into the Army!' She said, 'Well, it's up to you.' I figured that I might be able to go back because I'd already gone over their ninety-day limit for going back at your old rank. I thought I might get back in as a corporal or, if I got lucky, as maybe a sergeant. I had been discharged as a master sergeant. So, I went to York and talked to the recruiter, and he told me that he had just gotten directive that said I could go back in at my old rank no matter how long I had been out. Well, a permanent rank of master sergeant wasn't too bad because it affected getting quarters and other priorities. I reported back in 1946 and spent the next three years at the Signal Corps School at Ft. Monmouth, New Jersey. My working specialty was cryptographics and counterintelligence. The next thing I was put in for was warrant officer. I waited and waited and waited, and finally one day I got a letter from the Army Security Agency addressed to 'Warrant Officer Edward L. Reisinger.' I had made it!"

From that point, "Tarp" went on to a distinguished career in the US Army. He eventually became responsible for White House communications during the presidency of Dwight D. Eisenhower and had forty men under his supervision. "Tarp" accompanied the president on trips to Camp David, the Eisenhower farm at Gettysburg, and several European summit conferences. On occasions he carried "The Football," which contained the information necessary for the President to authorize the launching of nuclear weapons. "Tarp," Margaret (whom the locals nicknamed "Rebel"), and their two children eventually retired to Wrightsville after his twenty-seven years of military service. He then worked for another ten years for a local telephone company in Columbia. "Tarp" died on 21 January 2002.

Notes

1. Edward L. Reisinger, interview by the author 5 August 1999, transcript, OH1312, Oral History Collection, University Archives, University of North Texas, Denton, TX.

2. Note: For a graphic description of the overseas voyage to Europe, see Robert E. Humphrey, *Once Upon a Time in War: The 99th Division in World War II* (Norman: Univ. of Oklahoma Press, 2008), 50-54.

3. For a detailed account of the entire Normandy invasion from the planning stages to the push inland from the beaches, see Carlo D'Este, *Decision in Normandy* (New York: Harper Perrenial, 1994).

4. Note: "The hards" refer to long stretches of harbor beach paved with foot-thick blocks of solid stone or concrete to move tanks and troops down the slope to landing craft. There were LST "hards" for Landing Ship, Tank, and LCT "hards" for Landing Craft, Troop. Each type had a concrete or stone apron above high water with a flexible matting below. These were the places from which 850,000 men embarked for the Normandy invasion.

5. Note: According to Stephen Ambrose, Lt. Charles Green, a tanker in the 29th Division, devised a bumper salvaged from railroad tracks that German Field Marshal Erwin Rommel had used as beach obstacles at Normandy. It was very strong and enabled the Sherman tanks to bull their way through the thickest hedgerows. See Stephen E. Ambrose, *Citizen Soldiers: The US Army from the Normandy Beaches to the Bulge to the Surrender of Germany, June 7, 1944-May 7, 1945* (New York: Simon & Schuster, 1997), 66-67. Ambrose's version, is, however, disputed by historians Michael Doubler and Peter R. Mansoor. They argue that the "Rhinoceros" was the handiwork of Sgt. Curtis G. Culin, 102d Reconnaissance Squadron. Lt. Green saw an earlier hedgerow device made of pipes and improved on it by making one from salvaged railroad tracks. But it was Culin's invention that was nicknamed the "Rhino." See Michael Doubler, *Closing with the Enemy: How GIs Fought in*

Europe, 1944-1945 (Lawrence: Univ. Press of Kansas, 1994), 44-45; and Peter R. Mansoor, *The GI Offensive in Europe: The Triumph of American Infantry Divisions, 1941-1945* (Lawrence: Univ. Press of Kansas, 1999), 165.

6. See Ambrose, *Citizen Soldiers*, 77-84.

7. Note: *Apache* had a reputation for being rough with female dancers. Violence and speed were characteristic of *Apache.* Dancers had to be fit to survive the abuse because elements of the dance involve a lot of pushing, dragging, hitting, and throwing the female dancer about with occasional slaps. The women then normally crawl back to the male dancer for more abuse and to beg forgiveness. Often the dance was meant to reflect a relationship between a pimp and a prostitute. A combination of French *mime* and vaudeville, it has a similarity with the tango and is still performed by Broadway shows and nightclubs.

8. Ambrose, *Citizen Soldiers*, 167-183.

9. Note: Reisinger is referring to the so-called "flail" tank. The flails consisted of heavy chain dangling from a boom-type device extended in front of a standard tank chassis. The links dragging across the ground before the tank would detonate pressure-sensitive mines thus clearing the area for both infantry and armor to advance.

Figure 13. Pfc. Lloyd "Lem" Crumbling

Chapter 12

Pfc. Lloyd "Lem" Crumbling

1st Btn., 134th Reg., 35th Infantry Division

Born on 9 January 1918 in Wrightsville, Lloyd "Lem" Crumbling lived in the town all his life with the exception of two stints in the US Army. His parents, William and Grace Crumbling, raised seven children, six boys and one girl. "Lem" was the fifth child. Another child of the Great Depression, he found various part-time jobs until he decided that his future lay with the military. He joined the Army for a three-year enlistment in 1935. After his discharge in 1938, "Lem" worked in local foundries, married and divorced, and then volunteered again in 1942. He went overseas with the 35th Infantry Division in 1944 and landed on Omaha Beach in early July of the same year. "Lem" fought with his division through the French hedgerow country but received a severe wound from mortar shrapnel during the battle for St. Lô. For "Lem" the fighting was over, since he had received the so-called "million dollar wound," which rendered him physically unfit for further combat. After recuperation he spent the rest of the war behind the front lines with an ordnance unit. He returned to Wrightsville after the war, remarried and raised a family, and worked as a molder in various local foundries for thirty-five years. "Lem" died on 28 December 2005.[1]

Like most youths in Wrightsville during the 1930s, "Lem" experienced the hard times when jobs were scarce. Due to the limited economic prospects, he decided that the Army offered more opportunities for him:

"I made it to the eleventh grade in high school, and then I quit when I was sixteen. Boy! I'll tell you! It was rough! I did what I could to make a dollar. I helped my dad dig cesspools, and we cut wood up in the woods outside of town. The town had foundries and cigar factories, and there were sewing factories for women. That's all we had around here. You couldn't get a full-time job. I really do believe that a molder had to die before you could get a job at one of the foundries, and even then they were going to hire a man who had a family rather than a single guy. That's why I went into the Army the first time—for the money.

"I was only seventeen years old when I went and joined in 1935. I went in in September, and I wasn't eighteen until January 1936. I had to have a baptismal certificate or something, so I went to the Methodist preacher back on Locust Street and told him what I needed. He put on it that I was born in 1917—a year earlier than I really was. I was accepted, so I went down to Ft. Meade, Maryland, for my basic training. They had a lot of old guys there, and I guess they were career men. 'Lifers,' we called them. They were hard drinkers and everything. Some didn't like it when I made private first class because some of them had been in the Army for fifteen years and were still privates. I guess I made PFC because I made a good score on the rifle range and was an expert marksman. For three years we did the same things over and over again. You know: 'Left face! Right face!' Marching and parades and things like that. I stayed at Ft. Meade the whole time. I wanted to enlist for Hawaii, but there were no openings over there at the time, so I had to settle for Ft. Meade for three years. During my first enlistment, I had no specialty. I was just an infantry rifleman in Company A, 24th Infantry, 8th Division.

After three years in the Army, "Lem" decided to take his discharge and return to Wrightsville, thinking that the economy had improved and that he would find steady employment:

"My three-year hitch was up, so I got out and right away joined the Army Reserve. I was in the Reserve from 1938 until 1940, and I got $24 a year, $8.00 every four months. Believe it or not, I joined the Reserve for the money. Well, anyway, I guess they knew that something was coming in 1940, so they discharged us from the Reserve. But then right after that they activated the National Guard into the federal service.

"After my discharge from the Army, I went down to the upper foundry [Susquehanna Casting], and I was molding there by 1941. A couple guys died, so I finally got into molding. Even at that time, the Depression was still having an effect, so we were putting in a lot of three- or four-day weeks. I soon got tired of molding because it was hard and boring work. I didn't think that being in the Army would be that hard, so I decided to reenlist. In the meantime I had gotten married in 1940, but that marriage only lasted about six months.

The combination of a bad marriage and a dislike for molding led "Lem" to reenlist in the Army in 1942:

"I went to Harrisburg to reenlist, but they turned me down because I had a hernia. Back in those days almost every molder had a hernia or even a double hernia. After coming back to Wrightsville, I made an appointment with one of the town's doctors, Sydney Levy, and he sent me to the York Hospital to have the hernia repaired. The operation happened in July, and I was in the hospital for eleven days—just lying in bed. Well, I finally got back into the Army again in September 1942 because I guess they needed manpower by that time. Then I tried to get into the paratroopers, but during the physical examination they saw that scar from the hernia operation, and they wouldn't take me. Now, I'm glad they didn't, believe me!

"The Army sent me to Camp Croft, South Carolina, where I had to take basic training all over again. Everybody had to take basic training, no matter how much previous time you had had in the Army. I was down there for three months. Most of the guys in my basic training company were eighteen- and nineteen-year-old kids, and I was twenty-four. I was the 'old man,' and I was already starting to get gray, so they called me 'Pop.'

"After basic training I moved all around. In December 1942 we took a train out to California to a place up in the mountains called Ojai. We pitched our tents there and stayed until about the beginning of January 1943. Then they moved us halfway between San Francisco and Los Angeles to a place called San Luis Obispo. We stayed in little four-man cabins there until March. Most of the time there, it rained. We drilled when we could, and we trained out on the rifle range. We also did a lot of hiking to get us in physical shape.

"It was at San Luis Obispo that they formed the 35th Infantry Division. Then we took a train to Camp Rucker, Alabama, and we went on maneuvers there. Then we went to Camp Butner, North Carolina, for additional training. From there we went to Camp Kilmer, New Jersey, for shipment overseas. Although I didn't have a choice, I would much rather have gone to the ETO [European Theater of Operations] than to the Pacific because there was much more civilization over there than down in those jungles. We left in May 1944 from Brooklyn as part of a convoy. The food was lousy, and the ship was crowded. I didn't get seasick, but I stayed in my bunk most of the time. The only time I got up was to eat.

Upon arrival in England, the division resumed training before being sent into France after the Normandy beachhead had been established:

"After landing in England, we got on a troop train and went to a place called St. Ives, which was right on the coast there. We were billeted in hotels there, and by coincidence I stayed at the York Hotel, which was pretty small. Our training there consisted mostly of hiking. There wasn't much we could do because that area was overrun with Army divisions. This was all taking place down in the Cornwall area. Believe it or not, the countryside there kind of resembled the French hedgerows that we would encounter later. However, nobody ever told us that we would be fighting in these same things in France, so we had no training in how to breech them. To tell you the truth, I didn't know what I was getting into. I knew that there was a war going on over there, but I didn't know much beyond that. Maybe I didn't want to think about it. I don't know.

Between 5 and 7 July 1944, the 34th Infantry Division moved across the English Channel and was immediately thrown into the Battle of the Hedgerows in the Norman countryside. The hedgerow, developed by farmers to serve as borders for their fields, was a growth of hedges and small trees typical of the Norman countryside. The thick vegetation grows in an earthen embankment three to five feet tall with small lanes and roads running alongside. No terrain was better suited for defensive action than the hedgerows. Typically, there was only one entry into a small field thus enclosed. This terrain caused the Allied soldiers deadly problems during the fight for Normandy. Tanks could not climb the embankments without exposing their vulnerable undersides to anti-tank fire, and tanks moving down the narrow, tree-covered lanes could be ambushed by German armor, assault guns, and anti-tank weapons. Disabled tanks would block the lane for the other tanks in the column. Moreover, a small German unit with a few machine guns supported by anti-tank weapons could prevent an entire battalion from advancing. As a result, undertaking an offensive through the hedgerows was costly, time consuming, and frustrating. It was closely akin to fighting in a maze, for platoons often became lost and squads got separated.[2] *In the following selection, "Lem" described the travails of an infantryman fighting in the hedgerows:*

"We left England around July 6 or something like that, and we landed at Omaha Beach. Oh, brother! What a sight! There were no dead troops still there, but there were all kinds of damaged and destroyed trucks and equipment scattered everywhere on the beach. That's what made you think. After you got there and saw that mess, it definitely made you think a little bit.

"We infantrymen never had any hint about grand strategy. I never knew much of anything. They'd say, 'Go up [there]! There're Germans up [there]. And we'd go. You know, the company commander would say, 'We're going [here]' and things like that. They'd tell the platoon leader, and he'd tell the sergeant: 'We're going to do [this].'If you saw a dead American soldier, you'd think, 'I'm glad it's not me.' You were sorry for the other guy, you know, your friends and the guys you knew when you were in training. The guys that you went to town with and things like that, when they ended up wounded or dead, you were saddened.

"We went into the line almost immediately after landing in France and got our baptism to combat in the hedgerow country. These hedgerows had big trees growing out the top of them, and they were covered by brush and everything like that. Some were kind of low, and some were real high, about as high as a kitchen ceiling, maybe eight feet high. They might have been fifteen feet thick; I mean, they were huge, a lot of them. The German artillery had those hedgerows pretty well zeroed in by grid coordinates and everything. We'd dig in if we could. Sometimes when you'd take over one of these hedgerows, where the Germans had already dug in and everything, we'd use their foxholes. When we tried to advance, we'd go up the sides of each hedgerow. I remember one time when we could hear the Germans talking real low on the other side. We threw hand grenades over, and everything got quiet. I don't know if we hit them or if they took off or what. We hoped we had hit them. Mostly, it was the German artillery that was doing the damage to us in the hedgerows. Very seldom was anybody shot with a rifle except when you got out in the open or if a German was on kind of high ground and had a good shot at a GI. But it was mostly artillery that hurt us. I had a BAR [Browning Automatic Rifle], so if we'd get to the top of a hedgerow, I'd just look over and spray the area down below. You'd never know if you hit anything. Then I finally did get a rifle. They gave that BAR to another guy, and I was a rifleman from then on.

"Anyway, I remember the first day in the hedgerow country. There weren't any German foxholes there, so we just stayed up underneath the hedgerows. We pulled up to this hedgerow, and the German artillery was coming over—the '88s' [88-millimeter] and mortars. We were all lying there, and the company commander, a captain, yelled, 'Get up! Get up! Get up! Be like me! Stand up! Stand up!' He was walking around there when there came a 'BOOM!' from an '88' or a mortar. It blew him up. Two medics then put him on a stretcher, and they were taking him back through the field, and here a shell hit them and blew up all three of them. Our sergeant crawled up to me and said, 'So, we'll never see combat, huh? **Never** see combat?' I used to tell him back in the States: 'This outfit will never see combat.' I could only now say to him, 'Yeah, I think we will.' He was blown up later, too. We took heavy casualties, especially among the junior officers and the non-commissioned officers. While we were in the hedgerow country, I remember we had a second lieutenant named Gurren. The lieutenant and another guy and I were standing there talking to him one day, and the next thing you know, a sniper shot Gurren right through the neck and killed him instantly.

"Most of our junior officers and non-coms were knocked off because they were out in front, so before we even got to St. Lô, they wanted to make me a staff sergeant—a leader. I said, 'I don't want it. I don't want to be a non-commissioned officer.' Then the platoon leader said, 'Well, just take it for this one time. We got to reconnoiter and see if there're any Germans around [that] farmhouse. Just do it this one time, and then I'll get somebody from another squad.' So, I said, 'Well, okay.' He assigned four or five guys to go with me, and he instructed me to proceed on one side of this hedgerow, and the others were to go up the other side. Well, they were all killed or wounded, and I was over on the other side and didn't even get shot at. One of those killed in this action was Jim Bird from New Jersey. Right before we went overseas, he got a new watch. When we went up there the next morning to retrieve his body, the watch wasn't on his wrist. It was gone. The Germans had stolen his watch. They always stripped a GI if he had a watch or ring or some other valuable item on him. So, Bird was killed, and I was still alive, so I said, 'No, I don't want to be any non-com.'

"Tanks—I always hated those things because they always drew fire. Every time we were close to American tanks, those '88s' would open fire. The German artillerymen seemed to know where the tanks were. The Germans must have had observers somewhere on high ground where they could see those tanks. Man! Would that fire ever come in then! I do realize that the tanks did their job, but Jesus! The Germans would usually wait until our tanks got to the top of one of those hedgerows to where they had exposed their vulnerable undersides, and then the '88s' would just tear them apart. They finally invented something to put on the front of the tanks that would just chop right through those hedgerows rather than try to go up over the tops, so that helped us quite a bit in getting through.[3] Now, I must say that the American artillery support that we received was very good, although not in the beginning. That's probably helped win the war—the artillery and planes.

"I had mixed thoughts about the Germans while we were in hedgerow country. The first one I shot, I thought, 'I hope I just wounded him.' Then it began to get more personal. When you'd see your buddies getting killed or wounded, you'd just shoot them, period. Your attitude was: 'What the hell! I killed him!' That's the way it went for me at least. I don't know about anybody else. I think all the men in my squad were good soldiers, but they didn't last very long, even me. A couple of them were wounded the first day on the line by artillery fire. With but a few exceptions, we lost most of our men from artillery or mortar rounds. That Lt. Gurren that I mentioned a moment ago, at the time he was shot and killed, he had received a telegram about a week before that his wife had had a baby. So, he never had seen his baby, and that made me hate the Germans. I remember another time when this soldier was about twelve feet away from me. A mortar round came in where we were. 'BOOM!' I looked over there, and I was going to ask him if he was all right. But he was all gone. His head and his arms and everything were blown off, and the rest of him was just laying there. I didn't even know the guy since he was a replacement who had just recently come into the squad. On another occasion, a replacement troop and I captured a German down in the hedgerows. He came walking toward us, and his hands were shaking. So, this other guy saw him coming toward me, and he shot and killed him. I said, 'Why did you shoot him? He wasn't even armed!' He said, 'The way he had his hands down, he might have had a knife.' Army intelligence was always telling us to take prisoners if we could. Some of the guys took prisoners, and some didn't. They shot them all. And I know that they shot them. They didn't even bother taking them back to the rear.

After finally breaking out of the hedgerow country, the men of the 35th Infantry Division were ordered to take Hill 122, a German-held high point that dominated approaches to the transportation center of St. Lô. Hill 122 took its name from its height in meters and consisted of a series of plateaus with the usual hedgerows and sunken roads across its gently-sloping face. Defending the hill was the German 352d Infantry Division, a unit that had been organized in 1943 for the defense of western France. The nature of the elevation gave the Germans an extraordinary observation point, and as usual they had constructed well-coordinated defensive firing positions as well as a belt of minefields. On the morning of 15 July, "Lem's" 1st Battalion, 134th Infantry, began the initial attack with a frontal assault. The Germans met the attackers with a barrage of artillery, mortars, and small arms fire. So well-entrenched were the Germans that only direct hits from American artillery had any effect. In the face of this resistance, the Americans had to crawl forward and throw hand grenades into the hedgerows. Casualties were heavy on the American side, and it was not until 18 July that the hill was completely in American hands. "Lem" was not around for the victory, however, for he suffered a leg wound on the first day of the assault. For him, all combat was over. He never rejoined his unit again. After convalescence he was assigned to a replacement depot and was placed in an ordnance outfit behind the front:[4]

"To tell you the truth, I knew nothing about Hill 122. As always, your platoon leader told you to do something, and you did it. In fact, I didn't even know anything about Hill 122 until several years after the war, when one of my buddies came through Wrightsville and stopped to see me. He said something about us being on Hill 122, and I said, 'Was that it?' He seemed to know more about it than I did. As an infantryman, I was only concerned with what was happening in my particular area.

"Well, we started out at about 0600 in the midst of an American artillery barrage. The 134th Infantry was selected to lead the assault with the other two regiments on our flanks. The Germans had the high ground. Almost immediately, those '88' shells and mortar rounds started coming in, and guys were getting killed. Rifle fire was coming in, too. I happened to feel something hit my knee. I looked down, and the blood was running out. I didn't know what had hit me, but I have to think it must have been a piece of mortar shrapnel. I don't think it was from an '88' round. I didn't feel any pain at first. It was just numb. The guys continued to crawl up the hill, but I knew right away that I wasn't going up that hill anymore. One of the soldiers looked at me and said, 'A million-dollar wound!' And I said, 'I hope so.'[5]

"After I was hit, I went back down the hill, hopping on one foot. Then I started to feel the pain about five minutes later. It was now real painful, and my pants were soaked with blood. There was a building there, but the place was roped off. I put the rope down and continued hopping toward this building. An engineer hollered at me: 'Hey! You just crossed over a mine field!' I said, 'What!' He said, 'Yeah, there's a mine field there!' He had it roped off. My God! I didn't know whether to believe it or not! Well, I got around the corner of the building, and there was a medic there. He cut off my pant leg and bandaged the wound, and then he put a compress on it. They put me on a stretcher and took me back to a field hospital.

"The next day they put me on an airplane that took me back to Bath, England, to a hospital there. When I was in the hospital, they presented me with the Purple Heart, and they gave me a paper [citation], but I lost it. At Bath the doctor took a probe and pushed it right through my knee. Brother! Did that ever hurt! The shrapnel had gone right through [my] knee, and that's why he put that probe in there. He put some stuff on cotton and cleaned out the wound. Then he bandaged me up and gave me some medicine for the pain. I was there, I guess, almost up to September or the latter part of August. Boy! Was military medicine ever crude at that time! They didn't give me any therapy or anything like that. I got out and did some limping. I never made it back to combat again.

After his recuperation, the Army intended to send "Lem" back to his old unit, engaged in combat near Nancy, France, at that time. When debarking from a landing craft returning him to France, however, he reinjured his knee, and he was declared unfit for combat. The Army then assigned him to a replacement depot, and he wound up in an ordnance unit repairing weapons behind the front lines:

"I just took what they gave me in terms of an assignment. I was sent back across the English Channel to France on a landing craft. We were still on the water, so I jumped off and hit the beach, trying not to get wet. When I landed on the shore, I twisted my knee, and that thing swelled up very quickly. They took me to a field hospital, and they did this, that, and everything. Then they finally took me to a regular hospital close to Nancy, about fifty miles from there or something like that. By this time my knee was so swollen that I couldn't walk on it at all. I thought I had water on my knee, but the doctor took a big hunk of blood out of it with a hypodermic needle. After I had been at that hospital for a week, the doctor noticed that the swelling had not gone down, so he took out another vial of blood. He finally said, 'Your leg is not getting any better, so I'll designate you as a noncombatant.'

"I was then put to work in an ordnance detachment—cleaning rifles, fixing rifles and machine guns, and things like that. We'd move up toward the front, but we'd still be fifty or a hundred miles behind the line all the time. Sometimes we'd bring prisoners back—loads of prisoners—and we'd put them in a POW stockade. We'd be in Jeeps, and the prisoners would be in trucks. We'd then put them behind barbed wire and guard them. Some of the regular German troops were so arrogant that you'd have thought they were winning the war. They used to sneer at you and things like that—like they were better soldiers than we were. But they were prisoners, so they weren't so hot after all. Some of the POWs were of mixed nationalities, like, Poles, Czechs, and even one Russian that they'd picked up. That's about all I did for the rest of the war. But I'd finally made it to ordnance.

After the war, "Lem" returned to Wrightsville and had no serious problems adjusting to civilian life once again. His wounded knee still continued to give him problems on occasion:

"I was mustered out in November 1945, and when I got back I found that Wrightsville had not really changed at all. My knee would swell up easily after the war. When I got home, I ran into [Clarence] 'Patty' Reisinger, who had also been wounded. He said that we should apply for a pension, so we both went up to Harrisburg for a physical examination. My leg was still swollen a bit, and it was weak. The doctor thought we were eligible for a pension, so we both applied for one. About three months later, we got it. At first I was getting $11 a month, and now I'm up to $94 a month—after fifty years. Ten percent disability is what we got. Otherwise, I had no problems. My experiences never bothered me when I got out of the service.

"As part of the GI Bill of Rights, after you got out of the service, you could join the '52-20 Club.' You could draw an unemployment check of $22 a week for fifty-two weeks. I put in for it, and I got it for two weeks.[6] Then I started to work in various foundries as a molder. I molded for thirty-five years all together, and that was a hard way to make a living, I'll tell you. I now get a pension from the AFL-CIO for working all those years."

"Lem" remarried shortly after the war, bought a home, and raised his family in Wrightsville. He died on 28 December 2005.

Notes

1. Lloyd Crumbling, interview by the author, 9 August 1997, transcript, OH1187, Oral History Collection, University Archives, University of North Texas, Denton, TX.

2. See Stephen E. Ambrose, *Citizen Soldiers: The US Army from the Beaches of Normandy to the Bulge to the Surrender of Germany. June 7, 1944-May 7, 1945* (New York: Simon & Schuster, 1997), 34-35 and Peter R. Mansoor, *The GI Offensive in Europe: The Triumph of American Infantry Divisions, 1941-1945* (Lawrence: Univ. Press of Kansas, 1999), 133-159.

3. Note: See the previous selection with "Tarp" Reisinger (footnote number 4) for an explanation of the so-called "Rhino" tanks that were used to tear through the hedgerows.

4. See John C. McManus, *The Americans at Normandy: The Summer of 1944-The American War from the Normandy Beaches to Falaise* (New York: Forge Books, 2004), 259-266.

5. Note: The term "million-dollar wound" referred to a wound that necessitated a soldier being returned to a rear area or even the United States for treatment. Upon completion of the treatment, the soldier was not to be returned to combat duty.

6. Note: The Servicemen's Readjustment Act, better known as the GI Bill of Rights, provided liberal unemployment benefits, gave veterans preference in finding jobs, offered them substantial educational assistance, and guaranteed loans for the purchase of a home, farm, or business. It underscored Franklin Roosevelt's continued commitment to provide security and prosperity that was so much a part of the American Dream.

Figure 14. SSgt. Mervin "Bo" Haugh

Chapter 13

SSgt. Mervin "Bo" Haugh

B Co., 1st Btn., 66th Armored Reg., 2d Armored Div.

When the Sicilian Campaign ended, "Bo's" 2d Armored Division was transferred to England, where it trained for the Normandy invasion and the drive across France. The division entered France on D+3, 9 June 1944, and went into action in the vicinity of Carentan. It then raced across France in July and August and drove through Belgium in September. On 3 October, the 2d Armored Division launched an attack on the Siegfried Line and later helped push back the Germans during the Battle of the Bulge in January. Having been wounded prior to the Battle of the Bulge, "Bo" did not participate in that action. After recuperation from his wounds, he rejoined his division in February 1945 as it drove across the Rhine River and became the first American division to reach the Elbe. Perhaps because of the rapidity of most of his unit's advance throughout the Northwestern European Campaign, "Bo" had very little knowledge of either geography or grand strategy. His account of the period is one of various personal experiences and specific incidents. Like many soldiers, "Bo" was mainly conscious of what was happening in his immediate surroundings.[1]

At the conclusion of the Sicilian Campaign, the 2d Armored Division was sent to England as preparations for the Normandy invasion were under way:

"When we left to go to England, all our equipment, including the tanks, stayed behind. I imagine they needed it somewhere else. In England we got all new equipment, and then we were very busy there. We went to various firing ranges with our new tanks, but mainly we were up in northern England. We did a heck of a lot of firing—a heck of a lot. I don't care what roads you went on in England, there was either an ammunition dump or a fuel dump. When we got the new tanks, we had to go back over that whole waterproofing thing again, and that took about a month until we got it done. It was cold at that time, so we had to heat up the Permagum and use it quickly in order to get everything sealed.

"These new tanks were sixteen-ton models [Stewart M5VI] with four-man crews including a driver and assistant driver. They were powered completely differently from the older ones that we had used in Sicily. They had two water-cooled Cadillac engines in them, and this meant that we would no longer have to warm up the engines for twenty-five minutes as was the case with the diesel-powered engines that we had in our old tanks. Now, this new tank was also very maneuverable. You could be going forty miles an hour and quickly make a sharp forty-five-degree left or right turn or even do a fast U-turn. The tank had a 37-millimeter gun on it, and the projectiles weighed about two pounds each, so the gunner could take care of loading and firing it himself. The cannon could fire bursting shells or high-explosive shells or ball-loaded shells or white phosphorus shells. The new tank had three machine guns—one .30-caliber coaxially mounted with the 37-millimeter gun; one ball-mounted .30-caliber in front so that the assistant driver could sweep it; and one .50-caliber on top. As tank commander, I handled the one on top, and in my travels I figure I probably shot 20,000 rounds. One of the worst features of our tanks was that too many of them burned because of that gasoline engine. They lit up quickly, and we called them 'Ronsons,' named for the cigarette lighter. When one burned, all that was left was a pile of bones. B Company had seventeen of these new tanks.

"Since these new tanks were fast and maneuverable, their purpose was to draw fire, which didn't make us feel too good. In other words, they would be used for reconnoitering and escorting infantry. If the infantry called for support, then we would split off maybe two or three tanks from the column to help them. Most of the German tanks we were to face were the Panthers [PZKpf V], which weighed forty-five tons and had a 75-millimeter gun. Moreover, all its armor was slanted from the tracks right on up. The front had a terrific slant, and so did the sides. The turret was big, and it was also slanted. You could hear and see our little shells ricochet off those monsters. Now, the best thing you could do was to try to get behind them because the motor compartment had just inch-and-a-half steel doors. If you could shoot into there, you could stop it by catching that motor on fire.

As the time for the invasion approached, the troops became tense even though they did not know the exact date for the landing:

"It got jumpy because we knew that this was 'The Big One.' It just got you a little bit more jittery. I tried to stay calm, though. I smoked. I guess I chain-smoked because cigarettes were six cents a pack. At that time, in 1944, I was twenty-seven years old, which made me much older than the average GI. There were others who were pretty old, though.

"I was married at that time. We married about a month before I went overseas. My wife had come to Georgia, and then she went back to Wrightsville when I went overseas. Then I guess she figured that after two-and-a-half years of not seeing me got to be a long time. I guess she had met somebody else, so she asked for a divorce. I don't know. But, really, I wasn't hurt by all this. I was just soldier-minded at the time, and I figured there wasn't much of anything that was going to shock me.

The 2d Armored Division did not go ashore on D-Day. Rather, it landed in France on D+3, 9 June 1944:

"We went in through Omaha Beach, but the beach didn't look too bad where we were. There had been German bunkers there, and they were blown up, probably with Bangalore torpedoes. Our first assignment was to relieve the paratroopers at the town of Carentan, which was sort of a railroad center. The paratroopers were scattered so badly, so we would catch up to them here and there to help them out and reinforce them. On one occasion here, the infantry called for help, so our commander sent my tank and another one to relieve them. We saw these Americans pinned down behind an embankment, and there were three or four dead soldiers lying there. Behind another embankment were a bunch of German soldiers. So, I pulled up with the other tank beside me and got within twenty feet of the Germans. The other tank commander pulled out his pistol and shot two Germans. Then a German machine gun round killed the commander, who fell back into his tank. I didn't shoot, but I got out of the tank and walked toward the Germans, and they surrendered without firing another shot, I guess because they thought they couldn't take out two tanks. So, that was my first contact with the enemy.

"My next encounter was with a German tank. I heard a noise coming down over this hill, and it was a big German tank, probably a Panther. This Panther was going at least thirty miles an hour, when he spotted one of our tanks at an intersection. He knocked out that tank and evidently didn't see us because he went right on by. I told my gunner, 'Wait until he gets down the road a way and shoot for the back-end of him!' He fired a shot and stuck it in the backside. I was about to say, 'The son-of-a-bitch is getting away,' but about that time the German tank burst into flames. As I said before, even with our little 37-millimenter gun you had a chance to take out a Panther if you could get behind him. Then a little later, I saw a German truck coming up, and I thought, 'Boy! That looks like a fuel truck!' I never said anything to my gunner, but he fired and blew up that truck. One German soldier got out, and we captured him.

Like the infantrymen and other tankers, "Bo" and his crew had a tough time in the hedgerows of Normandy:

"We had to help one another to get through the hedgerows. What happened was that we went back to the beaches and cut up the steel obstacles that the Germans had erected to stop the invasion. Then we made hedgerow-diggers to put on the front of the tanks. We called these contraptions 'Rhinos' because they kind of resembled the horns of a rhinoceros. There was a sergeant who came up with that idea.[2] Right out in daylight, they fastened them on as fast as they could. These long prongs were huge steel things, and they fastened them onto the lifting lugs and the towing lugs. I'd say these prongs were maybe seven or eight feet long. The tanks that had them put on worked day and night right out in the fields. What they liked about our small tanks was that you could get them up to forty miles an hour going across a little field and let it fly into the hedgerow. They'd take out a chunk and then back up and charge again. These hedgerows were at least ten feet high, and they had trees growing on top of them. A lot of times there was a little ditch in front of them. The hedgerows served as fences for the fields because there were no fences as we think of fences. At one corner there'd usually be an opening, and they figured that the Germans would block that opening to keep us from getting through. But these forks worked. They were really successful. Once we had knocked a hole in the hedgerow, then we'd stick our cannon through there and fire a white phosphorus round into the corners of the opposite hedgerow to try to knock out the dug-in German machine gun pits. Then we'd take our .50-caliber machine gun and rake the entire base of the hedgerow where the Germans were holed up. We tankers loved the white phosphorus shells because, if you fired a couple rounds into a machine gun position, in most cases you no longer had to worry about those Germans.

After completing the Battle of the Hedgerows, the American forces were poised to break out into the open fertile, rolling countryside lying beyond. There were numerous tarred and even some paved roads, and the major objective was to seize control of the transportation hub of St. Lô. The front line ran on or close to the St. Lô-Periers road, which was straight paved east-west highway. Standing in the way of the Allied advance was the

German Panzer Lehr Division, which had to be eliminated. For this purpose, the commander of the American 1st Army, Gen. Omar Bradley, planned Operation Cobra, which consisted of a massive bombing campaign to be followed by an artillery barrage and a rapid thrust by combined tank-infantry assault. Cobra began on 24 July 1944:[3]

"I've heard it said that 3,800 bombers hit the German positions so that we could break out. Just hundreds and hundreds of bombers flew over. It would be maybe fifty planes at a time, and they were way up, at a high altitude. Once they started, the bombs just kept coming. That aerial bombardment just came in waves. There were bomb craters everywhere. In the aftermath, due to the bomb craters, we had to pick our way through because they were so tightly packed. In some places, we had to go in different directions to get through them because they were so tight.

"As we went on through afterwards, we came to a farmhouse, and since we had lost our drinking water somewhere along the line, I thought we'd fill our water tank here. There was a pump there, an old wooden-handled pump, so I thought, 'Well, I'll take the canteens and get some water. There was a German halftrack setting there burning. We stopped and I got out but couldn't get to the pump because this vehicle was burning. So, I circled down around the barn, and I noticed that the door was open. When I got to the door, I just looked in, and there were three Germans sitting back there. They seemed to be in a daze, but when I said, '*Achtung*!' they jumped up and threw down their weapons. I had heard that the terrific aerial bombardment had driven some of the German troops nearly berserk, and some of these guys appeared to be in shock. In addition, it must have gotten hot for them because they had taken off their shirts and coats. They had on their underwear and trousers. Anyway, these guys were happy to give up because they didn't make one iota of a struggle.

Once the breakout had occurred, the 2d Armored Division raced across France in July and August and drove into Belgium in the vicinity of the

Albert Canal by September 1944. From there the advance continued to the Siegfried Line:

"From St. Lô we started heading north. We were on the move, and then we really moved. On the Siegfried Line, we went into the lowlands. I remember the 'dragon's teeth' at the Siegfried Line. They were these triangular antitank obstacles made out of concrete that were laid out in vast, deep rows. I'd say they were maybe five feet high. They were stout, but all we ever did was to come in while our equipment made a roadway right over top of them. They just made a roadway. Our Army had every kind of equipment there was. I don't care what it was, the engineers had it. It was the same way when they were building bridges. It was the most fantastic thing that I saw, those bridges. They were just pontoons with railings on them. Those guys knew what they were doing; they were trained.

"During this time we got involved in the most ferocious tank battle that I can remember. This particular day, we were setting up in a wooded area, and we had our camouflage nets over the tanks. We finally got the word to move out, but we didn't get very far until the third tank ahead of me got hit. I saw the commander of that tank—a lieutenant from my outfit—fly up in the air. When he came down, the next tank ran over him. There was a wheat field there, so I turned off and went into it because I knew that we were about to come in for a heavy bombardment. The rest of our tanks followed me. We didn't see any German tanks around, but we did run into a couple hundred German soldiers in this wheat field. We quickly obliterated them. Out ahead of me, I saw this German tank come up behind one of our tanks and was getting ready to fire. But my tank fired first, and we got him.

"Then we finally got going again, but the next thing we knew, the German tanks attacked us from across the road. They knocked out five of our tanks quite quickly, and they all burned up in flames. I think the Germans also damaged at least that many. But we didn't get hit. This battle only lasted about ten minutes. We got one of theirs, but we lost at least ten of ours either destroyed or damaged before we retreated. Now maybe that doesn't sound like we lost too many, but losing ten tanks out of fifty-seven cuts a hole in your armored strength. Other than at the Battle of the Bulge, the Germans rarely attacked with more than five tanks, but they had more this time. But five of theirs was about equal to about twenty of our light tanks. In a battle with tank-against-tank, their tank was going to win. We would lose.

"We also had to be on the lookout for German small arms fire, especially from their *Panzerfaust,* their version of our bazooka. On pretty near every road we took, the Germans had taken French labor and forced them to dig a series of trenches in the configuration of a series of 'V' formations. In other words, they see-sawed them as protection against our airplanes because if you got caught in there, you could get against a side that protected you. But the Germans also used these ditches to fire their *Panzerfausts,* and at that short range they could blast you right to pieces. So, what I always did, when I got to where I could locate them, I just kept firing sporadically. I'd just take the machine on the top of the turret and rake them. I thought that worked pretty well. I did the same thing when we encountered houses. A lot of houses were vacated, but when we encountered a house with windows up above us, all the Germans had to do was drop a grenade in on us. So, again I'd throw up a wall of protective fire. We had ammunition galore, and it was nothing for me to use a couple boxes a day. I didn't have to see a moving target before I'd fire.

"One of the worst assignments that I had during this time was to examine tanks that had been hit in order to see what was left or if anybody was alive. I don't know why I had to be the one, but I was to crawl in the tanks to see if I could count the bodies because they needed to keep personnel records. The first sergeant usually didn't go into combat, but he kept all the records. The worst thing that could happen in a tank was that, if it caught fire and went up in a blaze, you were going to lose the crew. Usually, if that tank got hit, all that you had in there were burnt corpses. What I tried to do was locate dog tags for name recognition. I hated this job. I tried to harden myself, but it didn't do any good. You must keep in mind, though, that the infantrymen suffered more casualties than the tankers because they had almost nothing to protect themselves.

"Another thing that happened was that we started missing morphine syrettes in the first aid kits. That got to be quite a problem. I don't know if we had people with drug problems or if the morphine was simply given liberally to the wounded troops. I remember one time when we were in Holland someplace where we came across this German soldier who had a pretty nasty wound, and he was crying because he had so much pain. I took out a syrette of morphine and injected him with it.

In October 1944, "Bo" was wounded and evacuated for medical attention. As he describes this action, one is reminded of the fog of battle, for "Bo's" perceptions are vague at times. Because of his wound, he missed both the Hürtgen Forest Campaign and the Battle of the Bulge. Like many soldiers who found themselves in the same situation, upon recovery he wanted to get back to the security of his old unit and be with familiar comrades:

"We were in another tank battle. One morning we were going in the direction where we were supposed to go, going to our objective. Our first tank that moved out was knocked out by a German tank, so I went further down the road from where the tank had been hit, and then I shot across the hard road. About that time I heard a German tank coming down the road toward us. I then joined up with some of our bigger tanks. We came around to this building where there was a crossroads, and as I looked through a hole in the building, I saw a German tank setting right on the other side. I told my gunner, 'Fire two shots into him down at his tracks. Maybe we can hit a bogey [track guidance and tension wheel] and bend it,' because I knew we couldn't pierce the German's armor. If we knocked out a bogey, we could at least disable the enemy tank so that it couldn't move. I then told my driver, 'When you hear the second shot being fired, back up to the left.' He did this.

"In the meantime the company commander came up near us. This wasn't a normal procedure because of the danger of having their tank knocked out and then being unable to direct the battle. When I saw him, I jumped out of the tank and ran over to him as fast as I could because I needed some more information. I had looked up to the top of a hill there and saw something that I couldn't identify. My binoculars were next to useless since I had previously bumped them against my tank and had broken a lens. As a result, I didn't know whether what I had seen was friend or foe because of the distance from us. I wanted the commander to take a look, so I went down to have a conference with him. Since it was now late afternoon, we decided to stand by and hold our ground and not pull out until dark.

"So, as I went back to my tank—and I don't know where it came from —I was hit by an exploding mortar round that sent shrapnel through my arm and leg. But I still kept running. For some reason I figured that speed would help. I got back to my tank, and the crew put a tourniquet on my arm because I was bleeding pretty profusely. For the leg I just wrapped a bandage up and around it. No bones were broken, but the shell that went through my arm was pretty close to a bone. Well, these wounds sort of knocked me out of the war for a while. That ended my career until they got me to a hospital and back out again. I lost a couple weeks as a result.

"What's so strange is that I really don't know how all this happened. But, boy! The next morning I was hurting! At that time the Germans had us surrounded, but somehow the medics got through and took me out in a tank, which was the only way they could do it. I guess they figured they could at least fight their way out. They had a first aid hospital somewhere close by. My wounds by this time were burning badly, and the arm and leg were stiff and sore. It hurt but I could walk. They got me to the hospital, put me on some kind of a stretcher or wheeled affair, and took me into the operating room. They put me under anesthesia, and when I came out it appeared that they had opened up the arm wound and put in cotton and something else, which looked like Vaseline to me.

For my leg, I guess they cleaned it out or something. After recuperating, I never had any trouble with either wound.

"When I came home after the war, someone told me that I should put in for a pension. I said, 'If I got a pension and my dad saw me walking, he'd disown me.' He wasn't a believer in that kind of thing. I saw a guy with his face blown off and another one with his leg missing, so in good conscience I couldn't apply for a pension on the basis of my wounds. There were so many guys who were wounded much worse than I was. I never counted all the guys in the outfit who died, but there were a good many, especially among our infantry. We really worked well with our infantry, but they had one valid complaint, and that was that was that the tanks drew German artillery fire. You know, as I look back, I really didn't think too much about being killed or wounded. It seemed to me that as long as you used good sense, you were going to make it all right. There's no question about it that being in combat for a long time hardens you as far as not being afraid. In the first couple weeks, though, the fear did hang with you.

"What bothered me more than anything, even more than getting wounded, was being worn down for so long. Most times we started out at 2:00 in the morning, and we'd continue until midnight. Even then there was no way you could sleep, so this just wore you down. When you were on the tail-end of a tank column instead of up front, you always had to be alert because sometimes there was more action back there than there was up front. The Germans loved to let you bypass them and then get you in a pincers and squeeze you. That was one of their favorite tactics, and it wore you down to be at the back of the column.

"Anyway, after a couple months of recuperation—it wasn't too brief—I was sent back into action again. Well, I wasn't too happy about that, but that's the way it was. At least they sent me back to my old outfit where I saw familiar faces. That amazed me. I certainly didn't want to be sent back to a 'Repple-Depple' [replacement depot] and then assigned to a new unit. I did, however, change platoons and was assigned to a different light tank. In addition, I was promoted to platoon sergeant and then later to staff sergeant.

By the spring of 1945, the 2d Armored Division advanced rapidly into Germany as enemy opposition began to diminish:

"This was the spring offensive, and we had to contend with muddy roads due to the winter snow and rain. Our tanks had all kinds of trouble moving, so what the engineers did was cut down the reforested trees lining the roads and rip-rapped them down that whole stretch, which was about four miles in length. Even then, our tanks sunk the trees below the mud, and I wondered if all the tanks following us got through.

"The higher-ups had our tanks out in front as we raced across Germany. Nevertheless, these German troops, although on the verge of defeat, seemed to be defending every crossroads, every bridge, every city block—whatever. I didn't hate the Germans or anything. I highly respected them for their training. They knew every trick in the book, so you had to be prepared at all times. I think what really whipped them was our air forces. When we or the infantry got in trouble, we'd call in airstrikes from our P-47 Thunderbolts. Those planes carried a lot of firepower, everything from rockets to bombs to cannons to eight machine guns. My understanding is that the Germans hated and feared those rascals. I also heard that the Germans couldn't stand to see their cities being obliterated by our big bombers. As we neared the end of the war, they had obviously been whipped, so we began taking thousands of prisoners at a time. I remember one column of POWs that were four abreast coming down this dusty road, and there must have been at least 30,000 of them.

As the war was winding down, "Bo" was among one of the first groups of GIs to be sent home due to the amount of combat time that he had accumulated in North Africa, Sicily, and Northwestern Europe. Under the point system then in effect, he had top priority for rotation back to the States:

"That was a happy time for me after having two-and-a-half years—thirty months—in combat. They were sending people into Paris for rest and recuperation, but they said to me, 'How would you like to go home instead?' So, I came home and was mustered out at Ft Dix, New Jersey, and was sent to Harrisburg from there.

"When I came out of the service, I didn't know exactly what I was going to do. At my age, and with a high school diploma, I guess I could have gone to college, but I really didn't want to forfeit another four years just to further my education. Another thing is that I was interested in the welfare of my mother and dad. They seemed to have aged so much during the time that I was away, considering that my brothers Tom and Bill were also in the service at the same time as I was. I think that my parents went through more mental stress than I did.

"So, what I did was to go back to the farm again, and I got myself sort of rehabilitated. I think I did really well on that. There was a lot of work to be done on the farm. I didn't have any flashbacks or anything like that, like, going to bed and thinking about something that had happened in combat and jumping out. I did, though, have one nightmare that I was in a tank, and a big shell was coming through the turret, and I was trying to get out. That shell seemed to be coming straight at me, but by the time it got to me I woke up. I don't remember anything else like that.

"Finally, I went to work in the auto body shop owned by [Harris] 'Babe' Martin for about seven or eight years, I believe. Then at age thirty-five I went to work at the York Corporation, now York International, and eventually went into their research and development branch. That turned out to be highly successful, and it was an interesting job. I worked there for twenty-nine years and retired at age sixty-five. Now I do some farming on the side for my son, but it has gotten to be almost full-time. He farms 800 acres, and I drive the tractors and combines along with his wife.

"As I look back at my military experiences, I still think that the best thing that happened to me was that I was caught so early in the draft. I did really learn. I really learned. I learned under the professionals, and if you weren't top-flight with them, you weren't anything."

As he indicated, "Bo" readjusted to civilian life rather quickly. He remarried the same woman from whom he was divorced, raised a family in Wrightsville, and remained active all his life. "Bo" died on 8 November 2003, in Wrightsville.

Notes

1. Mervin E. Haugh, interview by the author, 31 May 1999, transcript, OH1298, Oral History Collection, University Archives, University of North Texas, Denton, TX. His account of the North African-Italian Campaign appears earlier in this book.

2. Note: There are disagreements concerning the inventor of "Rhino." For the origins of "Rhino," see the accounts of historians Stephen Ambrose, Michael Doubler, and Peter R. Mansoor as presented in Edward Reisinger's story (see footnote 4).

3. For an account of Operation Cobra, see Ambrose, *Citizen Soldiers: The US Army from the Normandy Beaches to the Surrender of Germany, June 7, 1944-May 7, 1945* (New York: Simon & Schuster, 1997), 77-106.

Figure 15. Sgt. Charles Kervin "Kirvey" Hake

Chapter 14

Sgt. Charles Kervin "Kirvey" Hake

A Bty., 386th Field Arty. Btn., 104th Inf. Div.

Born on 18 March 1922, in Wrightsville, Charles "Kirvey" Hake was one of thirteen children of Samuel and Sarah Diehl Hake. He was inducted into the US Army in December 1942 and served in Northwestern Europe as an artificer with an artillery battery. As an artificer, "Kirvey" was qualified to maintain any part of the 105-millimeter howitzers and function at any position necessary for the firing of these weapons. He participated in military actions in France, Belgium, Holland, and Germany. As was the case with other combat infantrymen in World War II, he had only vague recollections of geography or strategic considerations; he mainly was aware of the war in his immediate area. "Kirvey" was seriously wounded when his truck hit an antitank mine in March 1945. This injury took him out of the war, and he was on his way home when Germany surrendered. It is interesting to note that seven Hake brothers participated in combat during World War II, and five were wounded. After the war "Kirvey" operated a lumberyard in Wrightsville and later became an independent home builder. He continued to suffer the effects of his wounds for the rest of his life. "Kirvey" died on 25 September 2003, having spent his entire life in Wrightsville with the exception of his time in the military.[1]

"Kirvey's" youth in Wrightsville closely resembled that of most other young men and women of the Depression era:

"There were thirteen children in our family—six girls and seven boys—and we lived down on Lemon Street. The Great Depression was terrible for us—just terrible! We existed mostly on my mother's baked bread—she was always baking bread—and potatoes. Very rarely did we have meat. A lot of kids in the neighborhood were as economically deprived as we were, but they would come by, and my mother would give them molasses bread to eat. My father was a railroader at that time, and he did have steady work. But even with steady work I think he made something like $18 every two weeks. That was about his pay. We boys did a lot of hunting, fishing, and trapping along the Susquehanna River and the creeks that flowed into it. Then when I got a few dollars ahead, I'd give it to my mother to take care of some 'dues' [room and board].

"My schooling was very limited. I had to repeat first grade due to having scarlet fever, which ran through most of the family. I only got a month or two of schooling that first time around. Then in the seventh grade, I had a nasty teacher whom I couldn't please at all, so she failed me even though I had a grade average of seventy-five for the year. I repeated the seventh grade, and then I went into the eighth but quit school in 1938 before finishing the year.

With the coming of World War II, all seven Hake brothers were called into the military:

"My brother James had had previous military experience, so he was the first to go. The Army sent him to Officer Candidate School, and he came out as a second lieutenant. At about the same time, my brother Harry enlisted in the Army even though he was pretty well up in years. I think he was something like thirty-seven or thirty-eight. I think he was supposed to be discharged when he reached thirty-eight, but the same day he came home on leave, he got a telegram to report back. That was about the time the war broke out. My brothers Bill and Carl were the next to go, and then I went in on December 1, 1942. After I went in, then Raymond, then George, and then Kenneth, who was the last to go, went into the Army. This was terrible for our folks to have all their sons go into the service! I remember my mother crying on the day I left. Of course, my dad didn't say too much, but I knew it hurt him, too.

"I got my draft notice ordering me to report to Harrisburg for my physical and mental tests. There were quite a few of us from Wrightsville who went the same day. Anyway, I passed everything, and then they gave us two weeks to get our affairs in order. Then I was to report for induction on December 1, 1942.

"We went to Camp Kilmer, New Jersey, and then to Ft. Meade, Maryland. I stayed at Ft. Meade two days to get my shots and clothing. From there I went to Camp Adair, Oregon, for my basic training, and it was there that I joined the 104th Infantry Division. Afterwards, I was assigned to the artillery. After we got our ammunition, we started using the howitzers, and I worked my way up from cannoneer to first cannoneer. The first cannoneer would close the breech, elevate the piece, and pull the lanyard to fire the shell out there. I was very good at that because mathematics came easily to me. There at Camp Adair, I did well on all the tests, and my IQ was high enough that they sent me to Ft. Sill, Oklahoma, to the artillery school.

"I again did well at Ft. Sill. After I completed the artillery school, I became the artificer for Battery A, and my main job was to take care of all armaments—the howitzers, the machine guns, that type of thing. I'd repair them if they broke down, and I had a lot of other duties. If a man got killed, I would take over his position. So, I was like a 'jumper' in a factory, where you could do all the tasks.

"As we geared up to go overseas, we participated in the Oregon maneuvers of August and November 1944 and the California-Arizona maneuvers of November 1943 to March 1944. From March until August 1944, Camp Carson, Colorado, was our home, and we were getting our equipment ready there. We weren't sure whether we were going to the Atlantic or the Pacific. I personally didn't want to go anywhere, but if I had to make a choice, I'd rather go to Europe. I was prepared to die, but other than that, I knew that we had been trained well. Nothing, however, that you learned in training could prepare you for actual combat. You're not ready for those shells to come in and blow up all around you. Here in the States, you knew we were firing blanks, so you were not concerned, but over there it was the real stuff. That made a big difference.

From Camp Carson, the 104th Infantry Division, went to Camp Kilmer and then joined a convoy that left New York on 27 August 1944. By this time the casualties were mounting among the American infantry divisions already in combat in Northwestern Europe, so the 104th bypassed England and landed directly in France in an effort to get to the front lines as soon as possible:

"We went over as part of a convoy, and I was onboard the *George Washington*, which had been taken from Germany after World War I. Our convoy, we were told, was the first one to go from the United States to France without stopping in England. This ship pitched and yawed and made kids seasick. They were vomiting all around. The conditions inside the ship were muggy and stinky. I remember that I was sitting down in the hold playing poker when I started to feel woozy, like I was running out of air. I went up on the deck and found my way to the bow of the ship, and that's where I sacked down and slept. I stayed out there the whole way over and didn't mind it a bit after that.

"We arrived at Cherbourg, France, on September 7, 1944. Late that same afternoon, toward evening, we started to march. We marched for what seemed to be like three or four hours—maybe longer—through woods along this dirt road. We stopped near a place called Barneville, and then they brought our guns up to us after they were unloaded. At this time all I had was a carbine. I didn't have a sidearm. Since I was a sergeant, at first they sent me back to the rear with maybe two dozen men. It was my job to unpack the supplies that had been crated in the United States and then deliver them to our battalion and its batteries by truck. I also had to make sure that we had all the equipment that we were supposed to have. The stuff that they'd bring up from the docks was what we'd open and check to make sure that everything was there. We also worked closely with the Red Ball Express. For two or three weeks, we'd take supplies up to St. Lô, and then the Red Ball Express would take them to the American troops advancing across France. I guess these supplies were mainly going to Gen. George Patton's 3d Army. When the Red Ball Express stopped running, then we moved again.[2]

From this point forward, "Kirvey's" outfit was continuously on the move in the drive across France, Holland, and Belgium:

"By then we were on wheels. We had vehicles. Another one of my jobs was to drive the battery 'exec's' [executive officer] vehicle, which was a three-quarter-ton truck. We were in the lead truck for the battalion, leading the artillery. Our first action that I remember took place in Holland where we were hoping to clear out the German troops still remaining there. I think this was called the Battle of the Dikes [also known as the Battle of the Scheldt], and we were supporting the 1st Canadian Army as well as our own division. It was slow-going. The objective was to clear both banks of the Scheldt estuary so that the port of Antwerp could be used for Allied shipping.

"We were usually a mile or two to the rear of the front-line troops. When they'd call for support, we'd have to get our aiming point. Then when the fire commands came in, we knew the range, or the approximate range, and then we'd send out one shell to see where it hit. We also had forward observers out there to tell us how to adjust accordingly. There were four 105-millimeter howitzers in our battery, and we had all types or kinds of rounds. We had high-explosive; we had point-detonating and posit [proximity] fuses. A posit fuse round would explode so close to the ground. It was radio-controlled. There was a little radio receiver and a transmitter in the nose. That 105-howitzer was ideal for anything you wanted to kill. We could knock out tanks with it; we could knock down houses. With the exception of airplanes, we could hit anything. It was deadly against troops, especially those air-burst rounds. We caught the Germans out in the open and threw in a dozen or so rounds, and that would wipe them out. We did a lot of firing and used a lot of ammunition. We never had shortages of ammunition. Actually, the Battle of the Dikes didn't last too long. It didn't take too long to clear the Germans out of Holland.

"I do remember, however, that we did experience German counter-battery fire here in Holland. That was 'hairy' [scary]. I didn't believe in digging foxholes, but this one day I wish I had dug one. We received what they called 'marching' artillery fire. That's a string of artillery shells exploding maybe a half-mile away, and then it moves forward, and it keeps moving forward. The next one, I figured, would hit right where we were, but the next one never came, fortunately. The Germans were firing their '88s' [88-millimeter artillery pieces], and that was a mean weapon! Also, they could direct fire that gun at a greater range than we could our guns. There was no warning of incoming rounds when the '88' fired because they were coming in too fast. You didn't hear anything but the explosion. I was lucky—I mean, really lucky—because I should have been killed lots of times. I guess all we could do is pray. You were either going to get hit or you weren't.

After the campaign in Holland, "Kirvey" next remembered the plunge into Germany, particularly the Siegfried Line on Germany's western border and the Battle of Aachen:

"I remember what the Siegfried Line looked like. It was just a bunch of big, concrete anti-tank obstacles sticking up that we called 'dragon's teeth.' That's all it was. We had no problems getting over or around that.

"Then we were sent up to Aachen in late November 1944. We set up our guns in an old German position that time, one of their bunkers.

These bunkers were built out of logs and were pretty deep in the ground. They were open at the top so you could look out. For six days before the attack on Aachen began, we pounded the known German pillboxes that had been identified around the city, and then after the ground attack started, we switched to firing at German antiaircraft positions to the rear of the city. After the planes had bombed the German positions, we again began shelling the pillboxes and bunkers. Thank goodness for being in the artillery, because the fighting inside Aachen was house-to-house. By the time the Germans had been routed, the city was totally destroyed. We actually had Thanksgiving dinner at Aachen, and it consisted of gray turkey. Nobody could eat it. It was rotten, so we had a horrible dinner. We didn't stay around there too long after the battle, and then we moved on.

"I next remember that we crossed the Roer River, and that's where we came under a German air attack. I was on guard that night, and I observed a convoy of engineer trucks with pontoon boats on them. Later that same night, the Krauts came in with their Me-109s [Messerschmitt fighter planes], just blasting and bombing the hell out of everything. It looked like they were coming right at me! I was up against a big brick wall, and the bullets were hitting the wall around me. They were silver-white tracers—a greenish white. The hair stood up on my neck because there was no place for me to go. I wasn't going to run because I figured that at about the time you ran, you'd run into one of those tracers. I don't know how many engineers they killed, but we still crossed the Roer that night.

When the Germans initiated the Ardennes Offensive in late December 1944, the 104th Infantry Division was sent north into Belgium to reinforce the beleaguered American troops during the Battle of the Bulge. "Kirvey" offers a vivid account of panic stricken American troops in disorganized retreat during the early days of the enemy onslaught:

"At that time there was snow on the ground in our area, but not too much. We had a few warm days leading up to the Battle of the

Bulge. The snow was damned near all melted by the time the Bulge came. I don't even recall it being foggy or misty on our front. We were billeted in some old, half-destroyed buildings. We slept inside and had our artillery set up in back of these row houses. This was the only time I remember that we were short on ammunition. We supported the infantry as best we could after the Kraut attack started, but we had to stop because we were running low on ammunition. At that time we were, I believe, down to seventeen rounds of ammunition for the whole battery. We had expended all we had except for those seventeen, and we kept those in case we were in danger of being overrun. Then we could use those rounds for direct fire. Since we had no armor-piercing rounds we couldn't have stopped German tanks. What we had been firing and what we had left was high-explosive stuff for supporting infantry. Finally, a sergeant from the ammunition crew came up to me and said, 'Hake, let's go back and see if we can get some ammunition.' Well, we knew it would be risky, but we went anyway.

"We didn't get too far—maybe five, six, seven, eight miles—when we ran into all this stuff coming toward us. It was our own artillery and vehicles running away from the Germans. These American troops were completely disorganized! They were a rabble! So, we decided we'd better turn around and go with them, and that's what we did. We didn't go any farther because we'd have run into the Germans, who'd overrun our ammunition supply dump. Luckily, they missed us when they came through. So, we just turned around and went back to our outfit. I don't know what ever happened to these troops who were fleeing in panic.

The winter of 1944–1945 in Northwestern Europe one of the coldest on record, and it made life miserable for the American ground troops. In addition, as the Americans advanced into Germany, the casualties continued to mount. "Kirvey" described the travails in the life of a soldier during this period both in terms of dealing with the elements and the deaths of comrades:

"There wasn't any bathing and shaving. It was rare. We were on the line for about six months before we got a break to take a bath, and that was a tent set up with a diesel motor. We used hot water that ran through the diesel motor. At one place there was this butcher shop that had those big cast-iron kettles. I rounded up a bunch of guys' dirty clothes and threw them in this kettle. I filled it up with water and proceeded to cook them. Well, that was all right. Then I filled another one and rinsed the clothes. But holy hell! When I got them out and hung them up, they were only half as big as when I put them in! You don't wash wool in hot water, but I didn't know that.

"During the winter of 1944 and 1945, we usually tried to find shelter in a building that had been liberated. If we were out in a farming area, and if there was a barn nearby, we'd go into it. If there happened to be an abandoned German fortification, we'd use that. If we couldn't find a building, we'd sleep right on the ground.

"Sometimes, if we occupied a German building, we had to be on the lookout for booby traps, but I ran into only one booby trap. I was lucky. I went into this house that had been used by German troops to make these things. Scattered all over the floor and the table were different types of arming mechanisms, igniters, and other booby trap things. There was one gold-colored thing there with little bulbs on each end. It was about five inches long and maybe a half-inch thick. I picked it up and looked at it, but I couldn't see where it was put together. There were no markings on it. I thought, 'Well, that's funny! How would this thing work?' I took hold of it and pulled this switch. When I pulled it: `WHAM!' It blew my hand open, and it was singed black. But no metal got into my hand. I'll never forget that.

"I lost a good friend when we were assaulting Cologne sometime in February or March of 1945. We had moved forward to set up in this new position. It was late in the evening, about sunset, when we received some German counter-fire. I and another fellow were walking in the vestibule of this house when the shells came in. The shrapnel broke the glass all around us and went through the wall and into the house. It didn't hit either one of us, but a piece of shrapnel hit a young man who was carrying ammunition on his shoulder. The shrapnel went through the case of ammunition, through his helmet, and into his head. The shrapnel wasn't any bigger than a matchstick head, but it killed him instantly, right there. A couple other guys were wounded, but not too seriously. I and the kid who was killed were pretty good buddies, and I still have some emotions when I think about him. His last name was Randall. He was a couple years younger than I, and he was a gentle-type person. He wasn't a drunk; he didn't swear. He was just an ordinary, nice guy. Well, at the time you soon forget about things like this—you know, not completely, but you didn't dwell on it. You put it in the back of your mind, and that was it. It was the same way with replacements. We treated them gently and friendly, and we advised them as best we could. But when one got killed, you had to move on and not think about it too much.

"By this time we had the Germans trapped in the Ruhr Pocket. We moved every couple days, depending on how fast we could eliminate the Germans. Then we'd move forward again. Sometimes, if we hit a rough spot, we might set up for three or four days or even a week until we eradicated them. We'd get a fire mission for ten, fifteen, twenty rounds and then lay that on them. By this time I didn't have an attitude one way or the other about the Germans. Of course, I'd shoot them if I had to. I didn't necessarily hate them. We captured thousands of prisoners by this time. This was still wintertime, and it was cold. The Americans were hauling the Krauts back on cattle trailers, you know, with the boards around them. They'd load them up, and they'd start up the trucks and move forward maybe five or ten feet and then hit the brakes. That would pack the whole load in tight, and then they'd put some more on. They'd do that again and again, so those Krauts in the front must have been getting smashed. These prisoners were emotionless, expressionless, and I can see why, after being beaten around like they had been for almost a year.

Shortly after crossing the Rhine River, "Kirvey's" war came to an abrupt end in March 1945 when his vehicle hit an antitank mine severely wounding him:

"My getting blown up occurred on March 25—my one brother's birthday—right after we went across the Rhine River. At Remagen we had a pocket there about seven miles wide and maybe five miles deep. We were moving forward and were going down this road. There was a valley with hills to the right and the left, and we went down across this field. Then we turned left onto a dirt road. I was leading the convoy going down this road, and all at once I noticed that the road had been swept. I thought, 'Mines!' But before I hit the brakes, I hit an antitank mine. The explosion threw me out of the cab and over the back of the truck. There was an older man riding next to me, and later I saw that his torso was lying there, with his arms and legs torn off. Also later, I saw that the officer on my right side had lost part of one leg.

"When I hit this mine, there was an ungodly roar. I felt a sting in the lower part of my back, and then I went through what seemed to be this big, swirling tunnel and got spit out the other end. It was then like I was out among the stars, spinning through space. The strangest thing, which I cannot forget, is that I could view from all directions this tiny, green light. The next thing I knew, the light went out, and I heard this choking noise. I thought, 'It's my head lying here!'

"By that time, a guy riding in the back of the truck started calling, 'Hake! Are you all right? Are you all right?' He then reached in my mouth and was digging out crud [dirt], but I couldn't move. Then some officers came around, and one of them asked me where I was hurt. I told him I felt a sting down at my rectum, so they cut off my pants. I still couldn't move. I laid there for a couple more minutes, and after a while I had some feeling in my arms. I tried to look at my watch. I thought, 'If my watch is still running, I'm all right.' So, I picked up my arm, and I saw that my watch was running. I had a broken leg, and both my eyes were full of dirt or sand, whichever. I was all beaten up, but I obviously wasn't killed. I also had puncture wounds in my legs and stuff like that. Then they hauled me off to the hospital, and I was in the hospital for three months, I guess.

"Well, that's a weird story, too, after they got me to the hospital. I first lay out in that field all day by the road. Late in the evening, here came this ambulance, and it picked me up. In this ambulance, there were three other injured people, as I recall, in stretchers. Going down this bumpy road, they were moaning, and I was moaning. We got to this field hospital, which was nothing more than a bunch of tents. They took us in there, and they sat me up and the other three up. Nobody came around or did anything. I had to piss so badly, so I started hollering. A guy came over, and I said to him, 'I have to take a leak!' He said, 'Hey! This is a GI! He doesn't belong here!' What had happened is that they had me in with the German wounded. Anyway, they then got me out of there. They didn't do anything for me, though, at this field hospital. I guess there wasn't much they could do for me there. I wasn't conscious all the time.

"Eventually, I got to another hospital. It was, like, in a railroad building or a vacant factory. There were a lot of injured in there, moaning and groaning. My eyes hurt so bad that I started groaning, too. An old nurse, who looked like a bulldog, came over to me and said, 'What are you moaning about? There're guys in here worse off than you are! They have legs and arms gone!' I said, 'My eyes are full of sand. Can you wash them for me?' She said, 'No, but I'll give you some water and a basin.' I said, 'All right.' So, she brought me a basin of water and helped me to sit up. When I sat up, I got dizzier than hell. I started to rock back and forth, and she just walked away. I thought, 'Well, maybe I'd better lie back down. I then went black [lost consciousness]—just like that—and that was it, like all the lights went out.

"The next morning I woke up colder than hell. I was in this windowless building with a sheet over me, and there was a tag attached by a string to one of my toes. I started hollering, 'I'm cold! I'm cold!' A guy came over, and he said, 'Hell! He ain't dead!' They thought I had died in there!

Then they put some blankets on me and took me back in, but they didn't do anything except put grease on my legs and stuff like that. They still hadn't set my broken leg. They didn't do that for me until I got back to the 108th General Hospital in Paris two or three days later.

"They transported me to Paris on a C-47 [Douglas Dakota transport plane]. They strapped me in right above the wing. I could look out at that damned wing, and it was flopping like an old crow. I thought, 'Holy hell! The wings are liable to fall off!' In the meantime they were giving me morphine for my pain. They kept giving me shots of morphine, and I swelled up. My bottom part was swollen so badly that they couldn't get hospital clothes on me—the pants. They tried to put them on, but my legs had swollen so badly from the concussion of the mine explosion. I really think what kept me from getting blown apart was that I had on canvas coveralls. They kind of protected my legs and my bottom. I'm sure that that's what kept me from being blown apart.

"I got most of my treatment there at the 108th General Hospital. There they cleaned up my injuries—my legs and stuff. They helped me to the bathroom and ran hot water, and they helped me into the tub. I sat in there and played for an hour or more in that nice, warm water. Since I had a simple leg fracture, they didn't have to set it because there was no bone protruding. They didn't put a cast on it, but I had to stay in bed, though. I couldn't get up and run around. I actually left the hospital and was on my way back to the States before the war in Europe ended on May 7, 1945.

Even with his injuries, World War II was not necessarily over for "Kirvey," for the war in the Pacific was still going on. Although it was clear to the American high command that Japan was a defeated nation, there was no evidence to indicate that the militarists would consider surrender as an option. The kamikaze attacks increased in ferocity, and the Japanese garrisons on Iwo Jima and Okinawa inflicted heavy casualties on the invading American ground forces and ships at sea. There was almost total agreement among American military leaders that only a costly invasion of the Japanese home islands would bring the war to an end. If an invasion were to occur, troops that had fought in Europe were to be transferred to the Pacific after the defeat of Germany. Included in this operation was "Kirvey's" 104th Infantry Division. He did not look forward to fighting in the Pacific:

"I got a leave and came back to Wrightsville on leave for a while. Then I found out that the war was not necessarily over for me. I went back out to Camp San Luis Obispo in California, and there we were getting ready to take landing maneuvers for the anticipated invasion of Japan. When I heard about that, I decided that I wasn't going to go. I had made up my mind that I was not going! The day they put me on that ship to go to the Pacific, I was going to say, `To hell with it! Back off!' Hell, if that had come to pass, I'd probably still be in jail. After being through that mess in Europe, I thought that I had had enough, and I didn't want to be one of those poor bastards to fight in the Pacific. My battery commander was given a battery of artillery, and he went over, but he didn't get into any combat. He was lucky. As it turned out, though, the atomic bombs ended any thoughts of invading Japan.

"I also thought that the Hake family had sacrificed enough for this war. Seven of us went into the service, and five of us got wounded. Dick was wounded by bomb fragments. He had a chunk of metal in his stomach, and he had it removed after he came home. Bill had been hit by shrapnel, but it wasn't too serious. Ken had been hit by shrapnel and lost the tip of his finger. George had injuries to an eye. None of them were really serious except for Dick's and mine. Every one of us was in combat. Ken was a Seabee [a member of a Navy Construction Battalion (CB)]. They did demolition work, you know, with mines and stuff along the shores. George was on one of those landing craft, the LSTs [Landing Ship, Tank]. Carl was a radioman in the Philippines, and he spent quite a bit of time out in the mountains with the Filipino guerrillas. My brother Raymond's outfit was following along with us, but I never was able to make contact with him. To my knowledge—I certainly don't know for sure—no single family had had seven sons who were in the service and saw combat. My mother got a Sons in the Service banner from the governor of Pennsylvania one time. It had seven little blue stars set into a white rectangle.[3]

"Kirvey" returned to Wrightsville after the war, and he had some bitter feelings about the reception he received:

"I had a lot of bitter memories. I came home here, so proud of what we'd accomplished. I was patriotic. But I ran into a lot of ugly comments and scenes. On one occasion my brother Carl and I went to York for something. We got on the bus at the bottom of Hellam Street. It was full of people, and they were talking among themselves. They were saying, 'The war is over, but I wished it had lasted a little bit longer because I could have made a lot more money.'

"In Wrightsville I didn't see too much change in the way of prosperity, not as far as I could see. I know that I played around for a while before I went to work. Then I went to work for a contractor here in town by the name of 'Hops' Frey. He had a small business down here at the lower end of town, and a couple years later he wanted to sell it. I wanted it, so I went to the Veterans Administration in York because I wanted to borrow some money under the GI Bill to buy it from him. I only wanted $5,000 to start up a lumber business, but this man at the VA more or less laughed about it and said, 'Now, if you wanted $25,000 we might think about it.' Well, $25,000 scared the hell out of me, and I wanted nothing to do with that. So, I went to my brother-in-law. He mortgaged his house, and we got into the lumber business for a couple of years. We remained in the lumber business for eighteen years, but the Wolf Supply Company put us out of business. They moved in here and were a bigger outfit, so they could beat our prices. Then I built quite a few homes around town, including a development west of town.

"But I was in such sad shape physically. I had heart trouble, and my legs would swell. My back would also give out. My right leg, the one that I had broken, would come out of joint rather easily. It finally got to where I knew that I could not hold a job anywhere. Then I had a heart attack followed by a stroke, so I had to live on my Social Security check."

With the exception of his stint in the military, "Kirvey" lived all his life in Wrightsville. After his unsuccessful marriage, he moved into a manufactured home and personally built a pavilion where he and his cronies gathered for conversation and cards. "Kirvey" died on 25 September 2003.

Notes

1. Charles K. Hake, interview by the author, 9 August 2000, transcript, OH1361, Oral History Collection, University Archives, University of North Texas, Denton, TX.

2. Note: The Red Ball Express was a series of non-stop, around-the-clock truck convoys driven between the towns of St. Lô and Chartres to support the Allied drive to the Seine River. The name "Red Ball Express" comes from an old railroad term identifying a train that proceeded non-stop from its origination to its destination.

3. Note: The "Sons in Service" flag was used during World War II. Each family was entitled to hang such a flag in their window. There was a blue star in the center of a red-bordered white rectangle for each member in active service. The blue star was covered or replaced with a gold star if a family member died in action, hence the name of the organization "Gold Star Mothers" for women who had lost sons in the war. These flags were usually no larger than a foot long and were hung vertically from a hook in the front window of a home.

Figure 16. Pfc. William "Bill" Haugh

Chapter 15

Pfc. William "Bill" Haugh

H Co., 137th Inf. Reg., 35th Inf. Div.

Born in Hellam Township just outside Wrightsville on 21 August 1919, William Bill Haugh was a man of integrity and character. During World War II he could have avoided the draft. He had a vital, defense-related job at Riverside Foundry in Wrightsville, and his supervisor, who was a member of the York County Draft Board, offered to get him a deferment. In addition, Bill and his wife Grace had a young son and were expecting their second child at the time he received his draft notice on 16 June 1944. Because he had two brothers already in the service, however, Bill decided that he would have been shirking his duty to accept a deferment. Almost immediately after completing basic training, he was sent to Europe as a replacement troop. By the time he arrived, the Germans had initiated their Ardennes Offensive, and the Battle of the Bulge was already under way. Less than a week after arriving in France, Bill found himself on the front lines in Luxembourg as a machine gunner with the 35th Infantry Division. He later participated in the Rhineland Campaign and the drive across Central Europe. After the war Bill was reunited with his family, including the son whom he had seen just briefly before going overseas, and resumed his career at Riverside Foundry (later renamed Donsco) where he soon became the foundry supervisor for the owner,

Donald Smith. After retiring from Donsco in 1982, Bill and his sons developed their own foundry, H & H Castings, which is still an ongoing, prosperous enterprise. Bill Haugh died on 24 November 2003.[1]

Bill's upbringing on the Haugh farm in Hellam Township closely mirrored the accounts given by his sister Pauline ("Sis") and his brother Mervin ("Bo"), whose comments also appear in this book:

"It was a small farm of about fifty-six acres, and it wasn't what I would call a successful operation. At least it wasn't successful as far as I was concerned. It was pretty much a subsistence farm since we used most of what we grew and sold what was left to Wrightsville people. We always had plenty to eat, and we were clothed properly when we went through the Depression. That's where I started to work when I graduated from high school. I graduated from Wrightsville High School in 1937, and I farmed for a year or two there. I didn't necessarily want to go into farming, but there were few jobs any other place because of the Great Depression. There were four brothers and one sister in the family, and we all took our turns working on that farm.

After his brief stint on the family farm, Bill took a job at Riverside Foundry. He describes how he took an immediate liking to foundry work, which was to become his lifelong profession, and how Riverside began to prosper once again from government contracts during World War II:

"At the end of 1938, I went down and saw Donald Smith, and he got me a job at Riverside. I was first making twenty-five cents an hour, which amounted to $2.00 a day, but there were a lot of people working for only $1.50 a day. I was supposed to be learning a trade as a patternmaker, so I was getting that twenty-five cents to learn. Donald's father insisted that Donald learn the foundry business from the ground up, so Donald and I made patterns together.

"The only thing that brought us out of the Depression was World War II. In those couple of years between 1938 and 1941, they were working just three days a week. Years later, I read some of the Riverside literature, and I think it mentioned that they sold only $60,000 or $70,000 worth of castings a year before the war. Once we got into the war, we got busy. You got all the work you wanted, and you couldn't work enough. For the war effort we made hand grenade castings, and I think we could get six of them in a mold. So, they got this contract to make these grenades, and they machined them. They then painted them and shipped them to the arsenal in New Jersey where they put in the powder and armed them. We literally made millions of hand grenades. During the war we made hand grenades, rifle grenades, radar rings, and that type of stuff. So, that's where Riverside made a lot of its money. Due to the military draft, we lost a few molders, but not too many. Most of the molders were older, married men with children and were too old to go into the service.

By 1944, however, due to mounting casualties and fighting a war on several fronts, the US Army in particular needed more men. To fill the ranks, the military extended the draft age to where it was calling up older, married men with children. Bill Haugh was one who received a draft notice:

"When I got my draft notice, I was approached by Riverside's business manager, Reuben Strickler, who sat on the York County Draft Board. He didn't think I should go, and he offered to get me deferments. He thought I should stay in the foundry; that was his conviction But I never asked for any special favors. I didn't ask for a deferment. When he came to me, I said, 'I'll tell you, Reuben. If they think I should go, I'll go. I'm no better than the rest.' Two of my brothers were already in the service, and I thought I'd be letting them down if I took a deferment. I didn't want it to be said that I tried to stay out of the Army By this time I was twenty-five years old, was married, and had one son and another who was about to be born.

"So, I had decided to accept my draft notice, and I was inducted on June 16, 1944—right after D-Day. They loaded up a bunch of us and sent us to Camp Blanding, Florida. My basic training at Blanding lasted approximately seventeen weeks. Blanding was what they called an IRTC —Infantry Replacement Training Center. Then later they changed it to

'Reinforcement' instead of 'Replacement' because they thought the original designation didn't sound too good. At first they were going to send me to the armor artificer's school because of my mechanical aptitude, but then after six weeks they said, 'The war's winding down, and we have all of the artificers we need.' Little did they know that the Germans were planning the Ardennes Offensive. They still believed that the war would be over by Christmas, I guess. So, then they decided to put me into heavy weapons, and that's how I got to become a machine-gunner.

"By this time I was the father of two boys. When Kenny was born on September 9, 1944, they called me in and said, 'Hey! Your wife had a baby boy, but you can't go home because it's not an emergency.' That was part of life, I guess they figured. As it turned out, after the completion of basic training, I did come back home for a week, so I did get to see my second son before going overseas.

With the Army's mounting manpower needs in Europe, Bill departed for overseas duty almost immediately after his leave time had expired:

"After my leave had expired, the Army sent me to Ft. Meade, Maryland, and from there we went to Camp Kilmer, New Jersey. There we got on a train and rode to New York. We boarded the USAT *Thomas Barry*, AP-45, which was far from being a luxury liner. It had formerly been a combination passenger and cargo ship called the SS *Oriente*, but the Army had converted it into a troopship. We went from New York down to Florida and then headed east as part of a four-ship convoy. We went through the Strait of Gibraltar, then along the North African coast, and then we turned north and landed at Marseilles, France. I'm pretty sure we got there on December 4.

"At Marseilles, they loaded us immediately on a '40-and-8' train.[2] You could look out through the walls of the boxcars because they were shot full of bullet holes because it had been strafed many a time, the way it looked like. It was beat up. You had just enough room to lie down in there because it was filled to capacity with people. Night and day, they kept us moving until we got to Metz. It was there at Metz that we were divided up to where we would go. In my case, I was sent to the 35th Infantry Division as a replacement. More specifically, I was assigned to H Company of the 137th Infantry Regiment. H Company was heavy weapons, machine guns and mortars.

Four days after landing in France, Bill's 35th Infantry Division was sent into the front lines in Luxembourg to reinforce the beleaguered American troops engaged in the Battle of the Bulge. As a replacement, Bill received what can only be called on-the-job training for combat. In addition, he went into the line during one of the coldest recorded winters in European history:

"They dumped us somewhere down along the Moselle River, but when we got there, they took us up for the Battle of the Bulge right away. The 35th Division had already been through quite a bit of combat, and these veterans were tough.[3] They did their best to help replacements. They'd tell you about what would help you. Actually, though, they couldn't help you too much, but you learned real quickly or you were dead real quickly. Believe me, we were all scared. We had brave guys, but they were still scared. I learned to protect myself first because I'm no good as a dead soldier. Dead soldiers don't fight. So, first you look out for yourself. Don't sacrifice yourself for your buddy, but at least do your duty. But don't go out there and simply get yourself killed. That's foolish. You learned things to do for protection, basically 'get down' or 'get out.' I tried to be cautious and to take care of myself where I could and where it was applicable. I never would shirk my duty, but I wouldn't just go out there and get myself killed to be a hero. I had reasons to come back home—a wife and two children. You don't learn anything in basic training, really, that's going to prepare you for combat. You got there as a private, and then you made PFC. The higher ranks only opened if somebody in front of you got killed.

"From then on, I was with the Browning .30-caliber machine gun, and I carried the ammunition, about forty pounds of it. In going up to the front lines, other than clothing, you threw away almost everything you had been issued. You were not going to load up with things that you didn't really need. You had only the bare necessities with you. I always carried two 'pineapples' [hand grenades], one on each side of my chest, and I carried them clean across Europe. I always had them. I assumed that they had been made by Riverside Foundry in Wrightsville. Who else could have made them? Actually, I have no idea who made them, but I always carried a pair.

"As I said, we were coming up to the Bulge from the south in Jeeps along the Bastogne-Orleans highway. We came up at night, and it was blistering cold! Did you ever see it when it was so blistering cold that the snow sparkles? Well, that's the way it was. It was cold, cold! We drove without lights, and you couldn't see the road because it was covered with snow, so it was pretty tough going. You won't believe me if I told you what I wore after we got there, and I don't think anybody else will believe me. But I'll attempt to describe it. I wore one suit of summer underwear, and I wore two tops of heavy winter underwear and two bottoms of heavy underwear. I wore two pairs of OD [heavyweight olive drab woolen trousers] pants. I wore an OD shirt, and I wore a field jacket. I had one of those caps that go under the helmet. It comes down and goes under the shirt where you tie it. I wore three pairs of socks. I had a pair of regular socks; I had a pair that came just below my knees; and I had a pair that came up to my thighs. I picked up a pair of size 10D combat boots because a soldier who was in a foxhole with Sergeant Borcher got shot. My feet had been freezing when I had been wearing my size 9s. I guess somebody got his figures wrong when he measured my feet in the States for what I needed in Europe, so I ditched them. I wore those shoes all during the war, and I didn't get wet feet because the snow never melted at the Bulge. Believe it or not, I was able to move with all this gear on. But I was still cold! It was bitterly cold! And most times you slept on the ground regardless of what the weather was like.[4]

"I'll briefly describe my 'baptism to combat.' Actually, we were fighting in Luxembourg. That's where I started. As we were approaching the front, we heard our 155-millimeter cannons firing, and as we got still closer, we ran into our 105-millimeter howitzers, which had a shorter range. So, they took us up there by trucks, and we got to a place where they stopped. There were some buildings there, and a road ran down through. Then they told us to dig in. Well, some of the troops had already started to dig in when I had gotten there. I had an entrenchment tool, one of those that folded up and had a shovel at one end and a pick on the other end. I hadn't thrown it away since I figured that we were going to have to dig sometime or other. These guys grabbed my entrenchment tool right away. They needed a pick because the ground was frozen, and they needed to dig an emplacement for a gun. Well, that was the last time I ever saw that tool. So, I went to the top of an embankment that was in the corner of a field. There was a pile of tree roots and so on there, and I moved them away.

"That's where I was located when the firing started, and soon there were bullets flying everywhere. Our riflemen then went down the road where they found the Germans, and they started fighting down there. This activity went on most of the day, and we later moved into a heavy stone building. A tank had shot a hole in the side of it, and we went through the hole and into the building. Well, that building was a home, but over there animals live in the same building in a lot of places. There were a bunch of goats bawling because they weren't being fed. There was also an old man in there, and I reckon that when the tank shot at the house, he was killed. Anyway, that was the first person I saw that was actually killed in the war. Of course, I knew there were going to be dead people. There was no doubt about that; there was no other way it could be. I accepted it because there's not much you can do about it. He was there, and he should have left. I was never scared there—not at that time. That was the easy part of the day.

"It was getting dark by this time, and we were ordered to go to the top of this nearby ridge. We soon found out that the Germans had it zeroed in, and they started to bombard it with artillery. We then started to run and got off that ridge as fast as we could. After we came back down, we reassembled. We had a mortar sitting in back of that barn, shooting over at the Germans. Well, we had just gotten on the street when German mortar rounds started coming in on the group of us. They hollered, 'Get off the streets!' So, everybody ran for the houses. I ran over and went into a house and backed up against a wall. They were big stone walls about a foot-and-a-half deep. A piece of shrapnel hit a medic who was crouching behind me, and I never saw him after that. He was gone. That night the barn burned down because it had been hit by the German mortar rounds. Anyway, I learned one of my first combat lessons here. When artillery or mortar rounds come in, you hit the ground; you get down. You're going to be hit much quicker standing up than by being down. You get in back of anything—under, down under, anything. Woods aren't a good place because the artillery can cause tree bursts. But you have to learn to get down and protect yourself the best you can.

"It was here at the Bulge where I learned how they were going to use machine gun squads. When the American troops attacked, we were back of the riflemen with a hole dug in case they failed and had to come back. When night came during an advance, then the riflemen wanted us to stop the Germans, so we set up out in front while the riflemen were behind us. So, at nighttime we were out in front. So, when we sat out in front, we were just like the man [Francis Scott Key] who wrote the 'Star Spangled Banner.' We were looking out over the ramparts and out into 'no man's land.' Then if the infantry attacked the next day, we'd be behind them again. The foxholes that we dug in the Ardennes were about four feet deep or about belt-high. We'd then put logs across the top of them, and we also threw dirt around the whole thing. On many occasions we'd take over foxholes that had been used by somebody else, either by our own troops or even by the Germans. Usually, there were two men to a hole, and at night one would stand watch for an hour while the other tried to catch some sleep, and then we switched. Usually, we'd have a couple blankets lying at the bottom of the hole, so we could cover up while the other guy watched. I never had much trouble sleeping, and I never took off my clothes. You slept in them all the time. We even kept our shoes on all the time. You went to bed with your weapon close to you so that you were ready to move out at all times. I remember one time when a German 88-millimeter shell hit a pine tree that we had dug our hole under. It took the trunk off the tree, and it rolled down and came on top of me. Fortunately, I heard the shell coming, so I dropped down. If they were shooting high-angle fire, you could hear the shell coming down because it makes a whining noise. Now, with the mortars, you couldn't hear that whine. In fact, you normally don't hear the mortar round until it explodes. It's: 'SWISH! BOOM!' I sat there in my hole one night when the Germans threw in a whole barrage of mortar rounds. They all landed short of me, and there was only one that went off. Somebody on the other side apparently didn't set the fuses right.

"We got into the Battle of the Bulge right after Christmas 1944, but we couldn't move very far because they couldn't get the Air Force out to help us, and the Germans were trying to take advantage of that. They were trying to get us while they had an even chance because they knew they didn't have air cover and we did. We did have plenty of artillery, which made the battle more even, but once we got air support, that tilted things to our advantage. There was no doubt that the little fighter planes could come in there and help us.

"By the time the Battle of the Bulge was over, we were about three kilometers from Bastogne, and it looked to me like everything had been destroyed. With armies going through the same area three or four times, the forests were gone. They were shot to pieces. They destroyed everything. The Germans would pour on you everything they had. I think that every town in that area had been destroyed by artillery, tanks, bombs, or a combination of the three. There were also a lot of dead cows around. They'd be wandering around at night, and somebody would shoot them. Sometimes they'd step on land mines that blew them to pieces.

"Believe it or not, there were even some humorous things that happened around the time the Battle of the Bulge ended. After the battle, they finally brought up hot food, which we didn't see very often. Most of the time we had K-rations three times a day. Anyway, one time we were sitting down there at a place that was burned out, and there were a couple hundred dead Krauts lying there. They looked like cordwood piled up because they were frozen stiff as a board. We had a guy by the name of Gage, and he was standing there on top of this bunch of Germans who were frozen. He was eating a piece of a peach, and he turned and said to a corpse, 'Here, stiff, have a bite.' He stayed there eating his lunch on top of a bunch of dead people.

With the German defeat in the Ardennes, the US Army advanced into Germany at a rapid pace. Nevertheless, several months of hard fighting still remained, most of it taking place in small towns and cities:

"It took the Germans all night to retreat from the Ardennes. You could hear their horses going; you could hear their tanks going. There were all kinds of noise and so on, and then it just faded out. By this time it was no longer foggy and overcast, so now the Army Air Forces could get back into action. Boy! Those P-47 Thunderbolts were something else! They'd usually operate in groups of four, and they could easily destroy gun emplacements or tanks with their tremendous firepower. We saw very few bombers where we were, but we sure saw a lot of those P-47s. They were our friends!

"When we were clearing out a town, they warned us not to get out in the streets. Usually, though, the Germans would get out of the town once we got close. If we had a tank with us, somebody was going to come out pretty damned quick if you ordered them to do so. A lot of the cities were already destroyed when we entered them. I remember that we came through Aachen, and it looked like all the buildings had come down. I rode a Jeep that time, and they had taken bulldozers that pushed roads through the rubble.

"As we went through these German towns, the civilians didn't bother us too much, and most of them seemed to respect us. They had to respect that we were there, and there wasn't much they could do about it. What really happened there was that a lot of these towns still had people in them, and the local Nazis who were keeping them under control had fled. This made a difference. As we were getting near the Elbe River, the German civilians were trying to come over to us, to get away from the Russians, but we'd make them go back. We wouldn't even take them. Actually, I was kind of bitter at the Germans for years. I was prejudiced—sort of—because, look, Hitler didn't get to power without somebody backing him. He had to have the will of the people to do that, and they all clapped for him. I thought to myself, 'These people would have clapped their hands if I'd been lying in the gutter, dead.'

"By this time we were also taking literally thousands of prisoners of war. I saw rows of them that were four men abreast, and it looked like the line went on for miles. They were being marched west as we were advancing toward the east. They had given up, and they looked defeated. A lot of them were kids and old men, who were too old to be soldiers, really. They weren't physically fit, and I guess they were discouraged from constantly losing. They couldn't have had a good attitude toward fighting under those conditions because the Russians were beating them from one side and we were beating them from the other side. They looked almost helpless. You could say that's about what it amounted to. The towns and countryside were littered with abandoned weapons, I'm sure most of these guys had been drafted, just like me. Even during the Battle of the Bulge, I never saw anyone in my unit shoot a prisoner, although there were plenty of men who were bitter enough that they could have killed a German soldier, especially an SS trooper.

"On our way going up to the Elbe River, I can remember passing dead people for a couple of miles. They were shot. They were no more than prisoners who had on a uniform with a one-inch stripe of grey or some dark color on them. The Germans must have turned them loose and then practiced their marksmanship by shooting them, the way it looked to me. People were walking around among them. These were slave laborers, and half of them were starved and so on. I guess the Germans didn't want to give them up, or they didn't want anybody to talk to them. But the Germans did do that to these people. Whether people think so or not, the Germans did commit these atrocities. Today you have people who don't believe these things about the Holocaust, but, hell, they don't know any better. Ask somebody who was there. The Germans did kill people, and it was cruel the way they did it.

Finally, the war ended, and Bill's unit was pulled off the line. He then performed various occupation duties until the time had come for him to be rotated back to the States. Bill did not, however, participate in the raucous behavior carried on by many of the occupying American soldiers:

"They sent us into Hannover for a victory parade on May 8, 1945. We had a big parade, and the regiment paraded in the city. That was part of the celebration. They also flew over enough airplanes that you could hardly hear yourself talk. I think it took an hour for the planes to fly over. They must have flown them to show the Germans what strength we had. There were airplanes everywhere. Then the drinking began, and the guys started to fight back and forth amongst each other. Guys would get drunk, and there would be fights between men who had been on the line and those who were rear echelon troops. They were just stupid fights over stupid things brought on by alcohol. Well, the orders were that you were to carry weapon at all times, but as soon as the troops started that kind of carrying on, they said, 'Hey! Quit carrying weapons! If you're going down to a hotel, don't carry your gun!'

"I never went to those beer joints. I had a family back home, and I conducted myself properly while I was in Europe. I never bothered any women over there or did that kind of carrying on. I know that a lot of guys did, but I never got into that because I respected my family. I wasn't interested in running around and hunting for girls and that kind of stuff. A lot of guys in my company did it, and when it was time to come home, half of them were ashamed to come home. But I wasn't. I'm not saying that I was better than they were, but I didn't believe in that kind of stuff.

In fact, I went through the war, and I never drank any alcohol. I smoked no cigarettes. I got a pack of cigarettes every day that I was in Europe, but I gave them away to the other guys.

"One of my last duties before coming home was to stand guard at some of those slave labor camps. The slave laborers were still being housed in these camps. Originally, these camps had had double barbed wire around them, but it had been cut off by the time I was there. I remember seeing guard towers on each corner, and I'm sure the Germans would shoot the prisoners if they tried to get out. They were workers' camps, and probably after the workers got worn down, they'd kill them and burn them. I don't know for sure what the Germans did to them, but I do know that people were still there when I had guard duty. We were ordered to keep them in the camps, but we had almost no control over them. At night they would sneak out to raid German property in search of food, I guess. I used to shoot my carbine up in the air and bounce bullets around and so on. I saw one girl walk right in front of me one night to see what I was going to do. Well, I took my gun and: 'BANG!' I didn't shoot to hit her, but when I shot she turned right around and went back. My theory was this: 'Hell, you Germans brought 'em here! I didn't bring 'em here!" They'd go out and steal cattle, butcher them, and start to eat. I don't know what they got to eat before, if anything. Cabbage, probably, is what they had, if even that. I had no idea what nationality they were.

Since he had not accumulated enough points for rotation back to the States with the first contingents, Bill remained in the Army of Occupation, waiting impatiently for his turn to come home:

"There was only one thing that I wanted to be—I wanted to be a civilian. I said to myself: 'Man! I don't want to be in the Army any longer than I have to! It's not my life, and it's not what I'd like to do!' I missed my wife and children since my contact with them was very poor while I was in Europe. In letters I was restricted from saying anything about the weather, where I was, what country I was in, or anything like that. All I could ask my wife was: 'How are the kids doing? Is everybody all right?

How are my parents?' She sent me letters and some packages containing food and candy and so on, and they did get to me. They were real morale boosters.

"I didn't have enough points to go home immediately, since I had been in the Army for such a short time. I hadn't been wounded, so I didn't get any points for that, although I did get a few since I had two children. The next thing I knew, I was in the Army of Occupation and was sent to Brussels, Belgium. My time there had nothing to do with my military training. We were biding time, and it was boring duty.

"The only halfway exciting thing that happened there in Brussels occurred when they brought in all the 'brass'—President Truman, Gen. Patton, Gen. Hodges, and a bunch of other ones—going from Antwerp to Brussels. My unit and others had to go out and stand along the road with rifles as an honor guard. Truman was going to the Potsdam Conference [July 17-26, 1945]. He came down the road sitting in this open car and holding his hat to keep it from blowing away. Then he came down and inspected us.

For Bill the day finally came when he was designated to come back the States. He had mixed feelings about returning because the 35th Infantry Division was slated for duty in the Pacific since the Japanese has given no indication of surrendering short of the American conquest of the home islands:

"When I received word that I was to be shipped home, it was good news and bad news. I was picked to come home because I was in the 35th Division, which had been picked to make the landing on Japan. I got thirty days off and four days traveling time once I got back to this country. The Army said that we were picked because we were so good and had so much experience. Now, whether that was supposed to be a compliment or just to ease our getting thrown into another battle is altogether different. I'd probably be dead if we had gone to Japan. I don't know. You can't continue in combat forever because sooner or later you'd get killed. You had two ways of getting out of combat. One was death, and the other was the 'million-dollar wound.' You either got one or the other. Fortunately for us, as we were getting aboard the ship at Antwerp, the atom bomb was dropped, and the war was over.

"We boarded the *Cristobal* with 3,200 men on board, but the ship had been designed to haul just 2,000. The voyage was to last nine days but it took us eleven days to cross the North Atlantic because of storms. We finally landed in Boston and proceeded to Camp Miles Standish. Then I came home for thirty days, and I got word that I would be extended for another fifteen days, so that gave me forty-five days. Then the Army told me to take another fifteen days and then come back for my discharge. So, then I got my discharge on November 9, 1945, at Indiantown Gap, Pennsylvania.

After returning to Wrightsville, Bill wasted no time in fulfilling his wish to become a civilian as soon as possible and getting about the business of making a living:

"I had no problem adjusting to civilian life once again. I remember that I told a buddy back in Hannover, 'Hey! Just give me a chance to go back home and get a job. This is important to me. I don't want any kind of bonus for my service time. I want an opportunity to get ahead in this world.' So, I came back to Wrightsville with that idea, and I returned to Riverside Foundry right away. I didn't loaf. I actually worked at Riverside Foundry [later renamed Donsco] for forty-four years. Eventually Donald Smith picked me to be his foundry superintendent, and I developed an outstanding reputation in the foundry business. There wasn't much in that foundry that I didn't do. I helped modernize the foundry over the years, and, in fact, there wasn't much of that foundry that I didn't build. I went on to get several patents for my mechanical innovations. When I first went to Riverside, they were pouring three tons of iron a day; when I left as foundry superintendent, I poured seventy-five tons.

"Then I got to be sixty-two years old and I retired. Why? Because I wanted to build my own foundry with my two sons. Eventually, we expanded and established H & H Castings. We do make quality castings, and we're noted for it. I've made both my sons rich men.

"As I look back over my wartime experiences, I feel that we went in for the right cause. One thing it did do was that it made an era where my children at least didn't have to go through this carrying on. But will my great-great grandchildren have to do this again? I have a bunch of them, and that's my personal family, you know. I don't want to see anybody go to war."

As his story indicates, Bill returned to Wrightsville and had a highly successful career as a foundryman. He and Grace raised three sons and a daughter and lived in Wrightsville for the rest of their lives. Bill died on 24 November 2003. Bill Haugh was a great man.

Notes

1. William M. Haugh, interview by the author, 12 January 1999, transcript, OH1290, Oral History Collection, University Archives, University of North Texas, Denton, TX.

2. Note: The term "40-and-8" came from the World War I nickname for the cargo capacity of the standard European-style boxcars that were pressed into military service. They could carry forty men and eight horses.

3. Note: By the end of the war, the 35th Infantry Division had a 180.9 percent turnover in personnel. During 264 days of combat, it had 15,406 battle casualties and 10,082 noncombat casualties for a total of 25,408. See Stephen F. Ambrose, *Citizen Soldiers: The US Army from the Normandy Beaches to the Surrender of Germany, June 7, 1944-May 7, 1945* (New York: Simon & Schuster, 1997), 280. For a compact account of the Battle of the Bulge, see Peter R. Mansoor, *The GI Offensive in Europe: The Triumph of American Infantry Divisions, 1941-1945* (Lawrence: The Univ. Press of Kansas), 216-236. For individual experiences during the Battle of the Bulge, see Robert E. Humphrey, *Once Upon a Time in War: The 99th Division in World War II* (Norman: Univ. of Oklahoma Press, 2008), 81-134.

4. For excellent firsthand accounts of the Battle of the Bulge, see Michael Green and James D. Brown, *War Stories of the Battle of the Bulge* (Minneapolis: Zeneth Press, 2010) and Michael Collins and Martin King, *Voices of the Bulge: Untold Stories from Veterans of the Battle of the Bulge* (Minneapolis: Zenith Press, 2011).

Figure 17. Cpl. William "Bill" Smeltzer

Chapter 16

Cpl. William "Bill" Smeltzer

K Co., 179th Inf. Reg., 45th Inf. Div.

Born on a farm just outside Wrightsville on 5 May 1923, Bill hoped to avoid the draft by going to Pearl Harbor and working as a machinist at the naval base. After eighteen months of employment there, he returned to the mainland for thirty days of leave time. He expected to return to Pearl Harbor, but due to some glitches in paperwork, he received his notice of induction into the US Army in October 1944. The American infantry divisions fighting in Europe needed replacements for men killed or wounded in battle. Bill was shipped to Europe and spent a brief amount of time at a replacement depot (a "repple-depple" in GI parlance) before being assigned to the 45th Infantry Division, which had advanced into Germany by that time. He then participated in the Rhineland and Central European campaigns. Since he had been in Europe for less than a year when the war ended, he was among the last servicemen to be rotated back to the States because he had accumulated so few points. Shortly before being discharged, Bill returned to Wrightsville and married Corenna Young. He easily adjusted to civilian life once again. The Smeltzers raised two daughters, and after thirty-four years of federal employment, Bill retired in May 1978 at the age of fifty-five. Bill died on 17 September 2005.[1]

By mid-1944, the US Army needed replacements as casualties mounted during the drive across Northwestern Europe took its toll on the infantry divisions. Bill came back to the mainland after eighteen months on Oahu, fully intending to return and continue working at Pearl Harbor, but the military had other plans for him:

"After working at the Pearl Harbor Navy Base for eighteen months, I had a choice of three things. I could transfer to any base in the United States; I could take a straight discharge and get paid to come home; or I could take thirty days leave, come home, and then go back. I took the thirty days.

"When I came back to the West Coast, your local draft board had jurisdiction over you during the war if you were of draft age. I took my pre-induction examination in Harrisburg, and I got drafted into the Army and was sent down to Ft. McClellan, Alabama, to the infantry replacement training center. This occurred on October 10, 1944. Basic training was supposed to last seventeen weeks, but the Army was hard up for infantrymen, so they cut it back to fifteen weeks.

"Then I was sent to Ft. Shanks, New York, and got on a boat as part of a fifty-some-ship convoy. I want to tell you something. When you're going overseas as an infantry replacement, you've got a lot of thoughts. You know you've made some mistakes then, so you don't feel too good. There were thousands of people, it seemed like, on this ship, and I'd sit up on the deck at nighttime, and I thought, 'Man! I must have made a mistake someplace!' Most of these guys were younger than me. A lot of them were twenty-one or younger, and they used to call me 'Pop.'

As was the case with all replacements that landed in France, Bill and his comrades were initially herded into the infamous replacement depots, better known as "repple-depples" to the GIs. After the Battle of the Bulge, four out of five infantrymen up at the front were replacements, men who were inadequately trained and new to combat. The men in the "repple-depples" were just numbers, and most felt alone, helpless, and miserable.

His experiences closely resemble those of other GIs as described by historian Stephen Ambrose:[2]

"We went right into Le Havre, France, at night, and they sent us right to the railroad station there. Then we got on a train there in Le Havre—boxcars. No passenger cars, boxcars. In each car there were about forty guys with all their equipment, so you could hardly lie down. We were on that train for a couple days, and we never stopped until we hit the front lines.

"We ended up at the German border. Here they put us in this replacement depot, which was made up of guys going to the 3d, 36th, and 45th divisions. I happened to go to the 45th Division. I ended up with Company K, 179th Infantry Regiment. To tell you the truth, half the time you never know where you were at, really, but I was at that replacement depot when I went across the Rhine River on March 26. I believe it was at Mannheim, Germany.

"I joined the unit probably at the end of March 1945. Even though I came into the unit as a replacement and didn't know anybody already there, they were glad to see me. In fact, the guy they hooked me up with the first night on guard duty said to me, 'I'm really glad to see you because I'm expecting to go home as a result of your being here.' He was a married man with two or three kids, and he was about thirty-nine years old. I think that was how he was getting home, on account of his age. Now, the 'old pros' in the unit would give you some good advice. A lot of those old guys who were there, they were the ones who would save you. Otherwise, I never got to know any of the men very well because I wasn't with them too long. It wasn't like some of these outfits where they were all trained together in the United States for a year or two. Those guys got to know each other pretty well. But, if you got through the first couple of days of combat in the infantry, you had a good chance of making it, for a while, anyway.

Like most infantrymen, Bill remembered his combat experiences and how they affected him. It was also during this time that he saw German jet planes make their appearance:

"Well, the first dead German soldier I saw unnerved me, but after I saw my first dead GI, that really hurt. That hurt. You don't think too much about the dead German soldiers, even though there are more of them, because you're going past them so quickly. But when you see the first couple dead GIs, that really hurts.

"Combat is a rough business. You make up your mind that you're going to try to live, but you think about a lot of things. You wonder if you're ever going to see Wrightsville again and all that stuff. Combat is something you never get used to. See, when I got over there, they had the Germans on the run, so we were advancing rapidly. It wasn't like the guys over there in the winter at the Battle of the Bulge where they were dug into holes. We moved almost every day, and some days we moved thirty-five miles. We didn't have tanks with us. We had tank destroyers, and that was good because they had 90-millimenter guns that could knock out German tanks. That's the only thing that could stop those huge Tiger tanks. Anyway, one day they got us up at, like, 3:00 in the morning to get on top of these tank destroyers. When daylight came, we were thirty-five miles inside the German lines. These Germans didn't know where we came from. In our rapid advance, we encountered both their regular army guys like us and SS troopers. Their regular army guys were draftees like us and really didn't want to fight, but when we encountered those SS outfits, those guys were different. Them, you couldn't trust. See, they would mix the SS troops in with their regular army in order to maintain discipline. As we passed through German cities, the destruction and devastation was unbelievable. I don't know what the worst city I saw was. Maybe it was Nurnberg. But in some of those cities the only place you could walk was in the middle of the streets.

"I know that the 45th Division crossed the Danube River on April 27. In our case they had taken away our tank destroyers because there weren't any bridges where we went over. We had to go across in paddle boats. Holy hell! You have all those bandoliers of ammunition, and that Danube was so swift. If you'd ever fell overboard, you'd never come up. You'd have gone down like a chunk of lead. Well, we got out in the middle of the Danube, and there were seven of us in this paddle boat. What happened was that one of these German jets came over. Man! Was he ever traveling! We had antiaircraft guns on the back side of the river, and they shot at him but never hit anything. By this time it was about 10:00 in the morning when a formation of American medium bombers came over. There was about fifty of them, and I think they were heading for Munich. About that time two of these German jets flew into them and knocked eight bombers out of the air. I remember watching one of these medium bombers in particular because we were always looking for parachutes to open. This one bomber had an engine on fire, and it came straight down, and not a single man got out. We'd never seen anything go through the air that fast as those jets. All that morning we watched the P-47 Thunderbolts strafing the other side of the Danube, but they didn't fly nearly as fast as those jets.

"Anyway, we finally got across and went into this wooded area. Those P-47s were now strafing the German troops, and these planes were so close to us that you could see the spent shells coming out of those damned machine guns. They had caught a German outfit in there that was using horses to draw their equipment. Man! Those Germans who survived seemed to be half-crazy! There were dead horses lying all around, and they'd also hit a field kitchen, so the area was filled with pots and pans. By the time we got to this area, those P-47s had cut down saplings as thick as five or six inches in diameter. We could hardly walk through this area.

"So, it was just about getting dark, and we were sitting up there in these woods. I remember I was lying there on my back with my hands behind my head because we didn't dig any foxholes since we were on the move. Man! After a while, a couple rounds of artillery or mortar rounds started hitting the trees! Boy! That's really dangerous when they hit the trees above you there! You can't get away from them, and the tree bursts produce big splinters that can kill you. I don't know if these were short rounds from our own artillery or if the Germans had fired them. Anyway, that was scary.

During his stint in combat, Bill earned the Bronze Star, but he was not aware of anything meritorious he had done to receive this medal. It is true that Bronze Stars were awarded to infantrymen in large numbers during World War II as a morale booster. Army Chief of Staff George C. Marshall saw the Bronze Star as a way to recognize the ground troops for the heavy casualties they suffered and the miserable conditions that they endured. To be eligible the soldier had to have first received the Combat Infantryman Badge, which meant that he had participated in ground combat for an unspecified period of time:

"I eventually received the Bronze Star. To get it, you first had to earn the Combat Infantryman Badge, which you got for spending thirty days on the line, and I think I was on the line probably forty or forty-five days. I would say that almost anybody in the infantry could get the Bronze Star. You were really supposed to do something not expected of you —something outstanding. I'm not sure why I got it, really. It was for bravery beyond the call of duty or whatever you want to call it—something that was not really expected of you. In the infantry they expected a lot out of you, you know, so I'm not sure what particular thing that I did that warranted the Bronze Star. Actually, I guess you could have gotten one every day sometimes. In fact, I never got the Bronze Star until after the war was over.[3]

On 29 April 1945, the 45th Division liberated 32,000 captives at Dachau extermination camp and captured Munich during the next two days. Bill was in Munich when the war ended:

"My regiment didn't liberate Dachau; the other regiment took it. I had a chance to go over and see it, but I wouldn't go. Well, there was nothing good to see. Buddies of mine did go over, and they said how bad it was. I thought, 'That's a hell of a place to get some kind of disease or something.' I know there were two-and-a-half boxcars of bodies that they had to burn over there. I was as close as the smell, but I don't know how close I was to the actually burning. The smell alone was something that one never forgets. Oh, that was sickening! That was awful! You know, the amazing thing about it was that the people who lived ten or twelve miles away said they didn't know nothing about it. This was hard for us guys to understand. We couldn't understand that. Now, whether they did smell it or whether they didn't, I don't really know. I don't really know.

"We pulled into Munich about 10:00 in the morning, and our artillery came in with us. We were riding on tanks, and they had us divided off into what they called 'task forces.' I remember that we were supposed to be 'Task Force Riggs.' We were to take over the Dr. Alexander Welcher Chemical Office. We got up to this place, and it had big steel doors on it. They dumped seven of us there to take over that building. So, we finally got in, and we searched the place like we thought we should. Our instructions were that 'nothing comes in and nothing goes out.' We searched it thoroughly and found seventy rifles and two machine guns. The doggone Germans were changing into civilian clothes and running because they didn't want to go to prisoner-of-war camps.

"Well, anyway, somebody came in there and said, 'Hermann Goering's headquarters is right down the street from here,' so we went down the next day. His headquarters was nothing fancy. That's where I got a shoebox full of German military medals: Iron Crosses and all that jazz. I got a German Luger pistol and a camera there, too. We were always looking for stuff to loot, you know.

"When we first got word that the war was over, our first reaction was: 'Is the war really over or what?' We weren't really sure about anything. Most of us guys in the infantry were always skeptical because of all the false rumors we had heard throughout the war. We didn't know if it was the truth. Then when we were finally convinced that the war was really over, we all celebrated. We got all the drinks we could get hold of. During our thirty days there in Munich, we were pretty rowdy. We were doing a lot of drinking and womanizing. The Army had a non-fraternization program, but we walked up and down the streets with these German girls and talked to them and all that. I guess we had gotten out of hand because they sent us to a little farm town about sixty miles from Munich.

Like all GIs in the European Theater, Bill was eager to go home when the war ended, but he knew that he would be among the last to go because he had been overseas for just a short time. Since the Pacific War was still going on, Bill was aware of the probability of his being sent there because of his short time in the Army:

"Oh, everybody wanted to get home, but in my position there was no chance of leaving early because I had gotten into the Army so late and had gone over to Europe as a replacement. I didn't have the points to get top priority. Then, since I was still so new to the company, they decided to make me the BAR [Browning Automatic Rifle] man. Nobody wanted this assignment because we thought it was the sure ticket for being sent to the Pacific. You know, the rumors were flying around that we were going to Japan.

"As I said, we were sent up to this little town for a month or so, and then they loaded us up and took us to Camp Lucky Strike in France. All embarkation camps were named after cigarettes. Soon we got on a ship and went to Southampton, England, and we were there for a week while waiting for a ship. Since I had been overseas for only about six months, they told me I was headed for Japan. That didn't make me feel too good —not too good. I wasn't looking forward to that possibility because that would have been a tough deal over there.

"Well, we came back to the United States, and the Army sent me to Indiantown Gap, Pennsylvania. I mustered out on August 4, 1946.

Bill returned to Wrightsville and had no problems in adjusting to civilian life once again:

I was finally able to get into the Naval Ordnance Plant in York. In February 1948 I finally got a chance to become a machine operator, and I took it. I worked there until 1964 when the place was sold to AMF [American Machine and Foundry]. After a month with AMF, I had a chance to go to the Naval Supply Depot in Mechanicsburg, and I took it because I had the mindset that I wanted to retire from the government. So, I worked there for fourteen years and retired in 1978 with a total of thirty-four years of government service. I retired on my birthday on May 5, 1978, at age fifty-five. It was on payday, and then I left."

Bill married Corenna Young in 1946. They literally built their own home and resided in Wrightsville where they raised two daughters. Bill became very active in Boy Scouts and continued to hunt and fish almost up to the time of his death on 17 September 2005.

Notes

1. William Smeltzer, interview by the author, 3 August 1996, transcript, OH1131, Oral History Collection, University Archives, University of North Texas, Denton, TX.
2. Stephen E. Ambrose, *Citizen Soldiers: The US Army from the Normandy Beaches to the Bulge to the Surrender of Germany, June 7, 1944-May 7, 1945* (New York: Simon & Schuster, 1997), 276-279.
3. Note: In 1947 the policy was implemented that authorized the retroactive award of the Bronze Star to soldiers who had received the Combat Infantryman Badge during World War II.

PART IV

THE PACIFIC THEATER

THE PACIFIC THEATER

American strategy in the Pacific War called for a two-pronged offensive for defeating Japan. The Southwest Pacific Theater, under the command of Gen. Douglas MacArthur, had as its objective the retaking of the Philippine Islands. From bases in Australia, MacArthur sought to advance northward up the ladder of the Solomons and then drive Japanese forces from New Guinea before invading the Philippines. This strategy also called for the elimination or neutralization of Japanese installations on Guadalcanal and Bougainville in the Solomons, Rabaul on New Britain, as well as the capture of the Admiralties, New Ireland, and other enemy bastions. In addition to ground troops, he also had, in effect, his own naval forces and airpower to accomplish his mission. That accomplished, MacArthur then invaded and reconquered the Philippines. With the Philippines in American hands, the Japanese home islands were denied oil, tin, rubber, and other resources from Malaya, Burma [Myanmar], and the Dutch East Indies [Indonesia].[1]

The second prong of the American offensive was the Central Pacific Theater. Commanded by Adm. Chester Nimitz, this was almost strictly a Navy and Marine Corps undertaking with some help from US Army troops. It involved an island-hopping campaign across the Central Pacific to invade and destroy Japanese bases in the Gilbert, Marshall, and Mariana Islands. The capture of the Marianas (Guam, Tinian, and Saipan) set the stage for the long range bombing of the Japanese home islands. American Seabee units quickly constructed airfields on the Marianas for B-29s to begin a sustained strategic bombing campaign against Japanese cities. During the drive across the Central Pacific, Nimitz organized naval task forces built around a new generation of fast aircraft carriers that sought to engage and destroy the Imperial Japanese Navy. At the same time, Nimitz's submarine force waged a relentless campaign to destroy Japanese merchant shipping to block shipments of raw materials needed to feed the enemy population and run their war industries. In preparation for the invasion of the Japanese homeland, Nimitz decided that it was necessary to take the islands of Iwo Jima and Okinawa. Iwo Jima's radar easily detected flights of B-29s heading for Japanese cities and provided ample warning for the home islands' air defenses. In addition, Japanese aircraft operating from Iwo Jima could strike Tinian, Guam, and Saipan as well as harass B-29s en route to Japan. Perhaps most important, US airbases on Iwo Jima offered a safe haven where B-29s could refuel or make emergency landings. As for Okinawa, Navy and Marine planners saw it as the major staging area for the invasion of the Japanese home islands. The struggle for both Iwo Jima and Okinawa represented the bloodiest fighting of the island-hopping campaign.[2]

On a more personal level, the Pacific War, in historian John Dower's words, was a "war without mercy."[3] For the Americans in Europe, as mentioned on several occasions in this book, there were good Germans (Wehrmacht) and bad Germans (SS). In the Pacific War, there were no good "Japs." The fighting in the Pacific was much more savage than in the European Theater. The attitude on both sides was kill or be killed, take no prisoners, give no quarter, do not surrender, fight to the bitter end. Fierce racial hatred gripped virtually all participants, Japanese and American. Japanese fighting men died instead of surrendering not only due to adherence to the code of Bushido but also because of the disinterest of the Americans in taking prisoners. In the various island-hopping campaigns, Japanese garrisons were wiped out almost to the last man. After the initial series of humiliating defeats and mass surrenders in the Philippines, Wake Island, and Guam, and the subsequent mistreatment of prisoners on both sides, American fighting men also almost never surrendered voluntarily. When the desperate Japanese initiated the *kamikaze* attacks, known as *tokubetsu kōgekitai* in Japan, beginning with the invasion of the Philippines and continuing them through the Okinawa Campaign, American servicemen viewed such tactics with a combination of disbelief and disgust. These American attitudes toward the Japanese are reflected in the following interviews.

Notes

1. See Stephen R. Taafe, *MacArthur's Jungle War: The 1944 New Guinea Campaign* (Lawrence: Univ. Press of Kansas, 1998).
2. See Ronald H. Spector, *Eagle against the Sun: The American War with Japan* (New York: The Free Press, 1985) and Alan Schom, *The Eagle and the Rising Sun: The Japanese-American War, 1941-1943* (New York: W.W. Norton & Co., 2004).
3. John W. Dower, *War without Mercy: Race and Power in the Pacific War* (New York: Pantheon Books, 1986).

Chapter 17

Cpl. Jacob W. "Jakie" Snyder

8th Antiaircraft Artillery Btn., USMC

Born on 30 March 1923, in the rural community of Broadback in York County, Pennsylvania, Jacob "Jakie" Snyder was one of twelve children born to John and Nellie Snyder. A victim of the Great Depression as were many youngsters of his generation, "Jakie" left school at an early age and enrolled in the Civilian Conservation Corps (CCC) where he learned the machinist trade. With the coming of war, he enlisted in the Marine Corps in February 1943. After the usual Marine boot camp training, he was eventually assigned to the 8th Antiaircraft Artillery Battalion, which saw duty in the Pacific at Apamama Atoll in the northern Gilbert Islands and on Okinawa. Being in an antiaircraft artillery battalion, "Jakie" did not experience front line combat as an infantryman. His unit did, however, play an active role in the defense of American ships under attack by *kamikazes* during the Battle of Okinawa. He had the same hatred for the Japanese that was characteristic of his fellow Marines in the Pacific War. After the war, "Jakie" settled in Wrightsville where he worked as a cabinetmaker. He married and raised a son. During the postwar years, he was active in veterans' organizations, particularly the local American Legion post in Wrightsville. "Jakie" died on 17 February 2004.[1]

Growing up during the late 1920s and 1930s, "Jakie" was caught in the throes of the Great Depression, but he coped by enrolling in the Civilian Conservation Corps, a work relief program for single young men established by President Franklin D. Roosevelt's New Deal:

"I had five brothers and six sisters, and I fell in the middle. My education wasn't too good. I went as far as the eighth grade, and that was it. From there I went into the CCC because we were in the middle of the Great Depression. I don't know exactly when I went in, but I stayed for my six-month enlistment. In some ways the CCC prepared me for the military because we had inspections, reveille, leave time, and things like that. In fact, we were under the control of the Army from 4:00 PM until 8:00 AM. I learned the machinist trade in the CCC because we took classes in that trade at William Penn High School in York. That's where I learned the trade and how to read blueprints.

"When I left the CCC, I got a job as a laborer for a railroad up in Mechanicsburg, Pennsylvania, and then I went to Miami, Florida, and went to work in a machine shop. Since I was young and free, I decided, 'I'm going down to Miami,' because everybody was talking about Miami at that time. So, I went. The war was already on, so I must have been there in 1941 and 1942. I got a job in a small machine shop with only about twelve workers, but the owners got into a squabble, so they closed down the shop.

"In the meantime, though, I had decided to enlist in the Marine Corps and was waiting for the call. So, two months later I got my notice to report for my physical examination.

"Jakie's" career with the Marine Corps started on 22 February 1943, when he was sworn in at Harrisburg:

"I joined the Marines because I thought they were 'the man's outfit.' I had tried to get into the Marines when I had become of age and before the draft started, but I was too short. That's what kept me out. By this time, however, they had dropped some of the earlier requirements because they needed warm bodies. From Harrisburg they sent me to Parris Island, South Carolina, for boot training, which lasted for eight weeks. Since every Marine is a rifleman, we went up to the rifle range after the routine drilling was done. If he's good, he becomes a marksman or an expert.

"After boot camp they loaded us up and took us to New River, North Carolina, and slapped us in this antiaircraft school. The reason they were forcing this schooling down our throats was that the Marine Corps had never manned 40-millimeter guns before the war, so they wanted to put a crew through here pretty quickly and then break us up to teach the fellows out in the islands. We went out to the oceanfront for firing and learning the gun, so our class was designated as being qualified to do this teaching. Since I wasn't tall enough to be a gun director or the rangefinder, I was assigned as the generator operator because they needed power for this gun. Later on, I was the mechanic for a 40-millimeter gun.

"Then after we learned all about the 40-millimeter, they sent us to Camp Pendleton, California. From there we were assigned to the 8th Antiaircraft Artillery Battalion and were shipped out to Wallis Island. No fighting ever took place there. The old Marines that were there, we taught them to use the guns, and then we had to sit back and take orders from them. We didn't do any training or anything. We were standing by to ship out, and after they figured these guys were trained well enough, we did get our orders to ship out.

After completing its assignment on Wallis Island, the 8th Antiaircraft Artillery Battalion was slated for duty on Apamama Atoll in the northern Gilbert Islands to defend an American airbase there from Japanese aerial attack. In the meantime the Battle of Tarawa had begun on 20 November 1943, and for the first time Marines faced stubborn Japanese opposition in an amphibious landing. Casualties were so heavy that the Marine command considered diverting "Jakie's" unit to Tarawa to reinforce the beleaguered invaders. The Marines finally established a beachhead, however, making it unnecessary to deploy the 8th Antiaircraft Artillery Battalion.[2]

"From Wallis Island we were to go to an island called Apamama, which is about seventy-five miles from Tarawa. Before getting there, though, our course was changed, and we were slated to go into Tarawa as infantry because the first two waves of Marines had suffered so many casualties. I don't care if you're a musician or a cook or whatever; you're still a Marine rifleman. So, they had issued us ammunition and had diverted our course because we were going to Tarawa. Five LSTs [Landing Ship, Tank] left from Wallis Island. We were five days out on the sea, and there was nobody in sight except our five ships. I'm telling you, on the sixth day I came up on the topside, and I never knew that the United States had so many ships. Wherever you looked—I don't care how far your eyes went—all you saw were ships, ships, ships! As it turned out, though, before we got there, the Marines had finally gotten ashore, and they didn't need us. So, they brought us back on course for Apamama. Before we got to Apamama, an American submarine crew went in there and secured the island. They claimed there were only about twenty-five Japs on the island when the submarine crew went in.[3]

"When we got ashore, we set up our antiaircraft guns. We had 90-millimeters, 40-millimeters, 20-millimeters, and .50-calibers. They wanted to put an airstrip on Apamama to begin bombing Truk, the main base in that area for the Japs. Truk was so well-fortified that it couldn't be attacked by warships, so they wanted to get a B-25 base built quickly to keep Truk busy. So, we finally got ashore, and the Seabees [CBs, or Navy Construction Battalions] built the B-25 strip. The bombers came aboard, and every day they'd go out and bomb Truk.[4]

With the American B-24 heavy bombers and B-24 medium bombers pounding the Marshall Islands and Truk on an almost daily basis, the Japanese retaliated by bombing the installations on Apamama:

"We were in Jap bombing raids. The first raid killed one of our fellows in Fox Battery. Since the island was at sea level, we couldn't dig trenches, so we built up our gun pits with sandbags and then put mounds of sand up against the bags. Anyway, the Japs tried to bomb us pretty nearly every night. At nighttime one Jap plane would first come over, and we called him 'Washing Machine Charlie.' Then when the bombers came over, you could always tell that they were Jap planes because they had a miss in the revolution of their engines. Only bombers came over. The Japs didn't send any fighter planes because we had no fighters of our own, and the Japs probably knew that. We never had to throw the searchlights on them because we could identify them by the sounds of their engines. Our 90-millimeter guns were sighted in with radar, but our 40-millimeters were visually directed. So, when the Japs made their run the first night, we found out the next morning that they had dropped tin foil [radar-jamming aluminum strips called 'chaff'], and that interrupted the radar on the 90-millimeters. Oh, they shot every Goddamned place! In fact, we had so many duds that night. They'd go up and come down and explode—bad ammunition from our country. When General Quarters would sound, first the 90-millimeter men would go out and man their guns, but we wouldn't go out to our 40-millimeters because we had to wait until the Japs had come down to a certain altitude. Then we'd go out and man our guns. Anyway, the Japs would always come over every evening, right at dusk, and try to bomb us, until our B-25s destroyed their planes on the ground. The Jap raids went on for about two weeks, I guess. Every morning, and pretty near all day long, the B-25s would fly over to Truk and bomb. I don't know how many B-25s were on Apamama, but there were an awful lot of them. That island was only five miles long and two miles wide, so it was almost man standing against man because that's how many people were on this damned island. The truth be known, the Jap bombers did very little damage. Almost every bomb missed the island because it's only about two miles wide, and they were way up in the air. Pretty nearly every bomb went out in the ocean. We did shoot down a few Jap planes because we could see our tracers going through them, and the planes would come down.

Being stationed on this desolate island meant that "Jakie" and his young buddies had to make their own entertainment:

"Our living quarters there were nothing more than grass huts. They had grass roofs on them. The floors were nothing more than sand. The bamboo walls went up about four or five feet from the ground, and then they were open up to the roof. We had platforms that we slept on. The food wasn't too bad, except that we had to eat damned K-rations for the first week until our kitchen got set up. Then we had good food. The merchant marine handled the ships that brought in our food, and about every two weeks a ship would pull in, and we'd unload it. They built a coral ramp out so far, and barges would bring the stuff to the edge of the ramp. To prevent theft of the medicinal alcohol and beer and the officers' liquor rations, there would be an officer on each corner for guard duty.

"Our main form of recreation was drinking. We made our own alcoholic beverages. In fact, we had a 'Rebel' [southerner] corporal who was raised on the banks of the Mississippi River, and he had been a moonshiner. We'd make our booze out of fig bars or anything we could find. Anything we could get, he'd make into whiskey. Brother! We always had booze. We had the still hidden, and at first I didn't know where it was. One time our colonel came through and made an unannounced inspection. I thought they had buried the still in one of our gun pits because he made the guys tear up their gun pits. Later, I said to our sergeant, 'Where's our booze hidden?' He said, 'Under your bunk!' I could have fainted! Christ! If the colonel had found it, I'd have been sent to Ft. Leavenworth! That stuff you could pour on a rock and light it with a match. You couldn't even see the flame. That's how strong it was. And every time you'd drink it, tears would come to your eyes. But we still drank it. That's what we did—anything to kill time.

"That island, like I said, was so crowded that we had no place to go. It had been a beautiful island before they started cutting it up with bombs and such. The natives were beautiful, and they all wore grass skirts. Their breasts were exposed, so our chaplain started issuing them T-shirts to cover their breasts. So, then they'd take the T-shirts and cut holes for their titties to come out. Every one of them did it!

"While we were on Apamama, we were subjected to broadcasts from 'Tokyo Rose.' Boy! How she ever got her information, I don't know, but she'd identify each outfit right to a 'T.' She didn't know it, but we loved her. Music-wise, she was heaven! As soon as she came on, they put her broadcast on the loudspeaker, and everyone on the island would hear her. We wouldn't turn her off.[5]

After several months on Apamama, the 8th Antiaircraft Artillery Battalion was sent back Kauai in the Hawaiian Islands to prepare for the invasion of Okinawa. A heavily fortified Japanese stronghold, Okinawa was intended for use as the staging area for the assault on the Japanese home islands:

"In April 1944, the Army came in and relieved us, and we were shipped back to Kauai. There we went on training missions seven days a week. We didn't know it at the time, but we were training for the invasion of Okinawa. In our case we were shooting at airplane-towed sleeves with our 40-millimeters. Every day we would shoot. Our gun still didn't have the use of radar or proximity fuses. We still had the pointer, the trainer, the range-finder, and all that stuff. We took that gun to Okinawa.

"After we left Kauai for Okinawa, we were aboard a Liberty ship, I believe, for close to thirty days. On the ship we did nothing but chip paint for the Navy. At about the halfway mark, we stopped at Eniwetok, and there we got off the ship and went through a lot of calisthenics. After we left Eniwetok, we might have been at sea for another six days. It wasn't until two days after we left Eniwetok that we found out that our ultimate objective was Okinawa.

"On the way back to the ship at Eniwetok, the captain got on the bullhorn and said that Roosevelt had died [on 12 April 1945]. The whisper going around on the ship was: 'We're gonna lose the war!' They thought we were going to lose the war because Roosevelt had died. It was on my lips when we got aboard, and I was ready to say: 'It's a good thing the son-of-a-bitch is dead!' If I had said that out loud, I would have probably been killed, I'll tell you that! I would have never made it home, so I kept my mouth shut. For one thing, I didn't think the man deserved three terms. The second thing, I think he sold us out at Pearl Harbor. If he had lived, he would have been the most disgraced President we ever had.[6]

"Jakie's" unit was part of the sixteenth wave to go ashore at Okinawa, so he did not witness the size of the original task force lying offshore when the invasion commenced on 1 April 1945. This task force was larger in terms of men and ships than the one that took part in the Normandy invasion:[7]

"We were in the sixteenth wave to go into Okinawa, so we never really saw the size of this great task force. We were still sitting aboard ship at that time. When we got there, I couldn't see much of the fleet because of all the smoke coming from the antiaircraft guns that were firing at the damned suicide planes coming in. I remember seeing a big hospital ship getting hit, and a couple of cruisers. In addition, all we could see was the flashes and the big explosions of the Navy's shells when they hit on land. When I saw those 16-inch guns blasting away, I thought, 'How can those Japs withstand those explosions?'

It was at Okinawa where the Japanese unleashed the full fury of the suicide planes in an effort to destroy the American capital ships, especially the aircraft carriers. Like most of the Americans who experienced this phenomenon, "Jakie" reacted with both astonishment and disgust that they were fighting an enemy who wished to die rather than live:

"Like I said, we were sitting aboard ship for about four days after we arrived. The bombardment was still going on when we got there, and it was still going on when we went in on the sixteenth wave on April 16. We were still aboard when the *kamikazes* were coming in, and it was our primary duty at that time to guard against them. We had our guns set up aboard ship. These were temporary emplacements, of course. It was like an arsenal all around. Christ! When all those *kamikazes* came in, all that you were seeing was almost solid tracers. They almost lit up the sky. The *kamikazes* could come in at anytime, and they did a lot of damage even though very few of them got through. There's no question about that. When they did come in, a lot of them came in at the same time. Seeing these Jap suicide planes makes you think of one thing—you're going to have to get him before he comes down into a ship. The only thing you were praying for was that you could get them before they got down close because after they got hit, if the pilot wasn't dead, his plane was damned sure going to hit a ship. That's the reason you wanted to blow them up while they were up in the air really high. They could come in any way. It may have looked like the skimmers would come in low to the surface of the water to draw fire away from the guys coming in from high altitudes. It almost looked like that, but I don't know if that was the plan or not. It was hard to imagine that these bastards didn't care if they died doing this. In fact, most of them wanted to die! We couldn't understand that kind of thinking. Even when we went ashore on April 16, the *kamikazes* were still coming in and giving us a hard time. At that time I really hated the Japs. I hated them for what they did to our fellows at Pearl Harbor.[8]

With the constant waves of suicide planes coming in, "Jakie" and his buddies were eager to get off the ship and establish positions ashore on Okinawa:

"We wanted to get off that ship. We went over the side on landing nets, and then they lowered our guns with cranes onto barges because we couldn't take them in ourselves. We weren't on a LST [Landing Ship, Tank], and with a LST you can run up to the shoreline and pull the guns off. As soon as we got ashore, we found out where we were supposed to be stationed, and we were assigned to a cemetery. They were trying to get us ashore because they needed us to protect the airfield, which they were already building. We then set up our gun right away and started shooting. The *kamikazes* were still coming in, so we'd just shoot away. You could see the tracers going through the planes, even in the daytime. To guard against Jap infiltrators, we'd post guards on an outer circle. A guard stood every so far apart. We had to stand guard every night, and each gun crew had a man standing guard on his gun. That's the way we got through the nights there. I had my M1 rifle and a .45-caliber pistol that my dad had sent me.

"By this time I was a corporal and a generator mechanic. I had a Jeep, a reconnaissance vehicle, and a 'six-by-six' [a six-wheel vehicle with all six wheels capable of transmitting power from the engine] signed out to me. The captain used the Jeep all the time, so I volunteered to haul stuff up to the front in the 'six-by-six.' I wasn't on the front lines at all, so I volunteered to use the truck to haul stuff up to Sugar Loaf Hill.[9] The Marine Corps made a push for Sugar Loaf Hill, and they claimed they lost 1,000 men, just like that, in the initial push because the Japs were up on top and were just dropping fire down. The Marines had to withdraw. They didn't retreat; they just withdrew. Then orders came out to take the hill at all costs, so they finally took it. Once they got up the hill, then it was getting the Japs out of the tunnels in the mountain. They used flamethrowers there, and a lot of the tunnels were blasted shut.

"Well, I got within a half-mile of Sugar Loaf, and then I'd unload my supplies. I was hauling mostly ammunition. All I heard was shooting and cracking, like the Fourth of July. That's all I heard during the fighting. I remember that Sugar Loaf was sloped. It went up a little, and then it turned right into a mountain. Up on top, like I said, the Japs could just stand up there and drop stuff down on the Marines. All you saw were bodies laying there. That's all. I saw them come back with the dead Marines in the 'six-by-sixes'—a layer of bodies, a layer of sheets, and a layer of bodies. I know it broke my heart. I remember smelling it—the dried blood. They hauled the bodies back to a certain place and buried them temporarily. They lay them in a little ditch, covered them up, and then they set crosses around. It was just a Goddamned shame! That's all I can say. The Marines who came off the hill after it had been taken were mad—damned mad. There's another thing that pissed me off. When the US Government turned the island over to the Japs years later, we had one of the prettiest cemeteries over there for the Marine Corps that you'd ever want to see—nothing but crosses—and the damned Japs have it all now.[10]

After Okinawa had been secured, the 8th Marine Antiaircraft Artillery Battalion moved up to a location known as Bolo Point. The men were slated to become infantrymen for the upcoming invasion of the Japanese home islands, a prospect none relished:

"After the battle, we moved up to Bolo Point. There we turned in all our antiaircraft guns to what they called the 7th Base Depot. We were then going back into the infantry, and according to our commanding officer, we were slated to go in as infantry to Tokyo Bay. A lot of us knew what was going to happen. Although they didn't tell us in so many words, we knew we were going to Japan. We didn't feel good at all about that prospect. Boy! I'm telling you, I was hoping that we would never have to do it because we were artillerymen—antiaircraft—and when they made us turn in our guns, we knew what the hell was up. We were going into the infantry. They had everything set up for the invasion of Japan, but then the atomic bombs were dropped, and the war was soon over. Those two bombs saved thousands of American lives, and I'm glad they were dropped. So, we were on Bolo Point when the war ended. Oh, we carried on and on when we got the news! People were crazy!

With the war over, most of the men in "Jakie's" outfit left Okinawa in November 1945:

"They started flying out a lot of the older fellows. I only had thirty-two months in, so they were taking out the thirty-six-month men first. Then I guess they must have run out of planes because they starting shipping out men. As the ships became available, why, you went home. I came home by ship, and we landed in Oakland, the same port from which we had left to go overseas. From Oakland they sent me to the Great Lakes Naval Training Station, and that's where I got discharged. Four of us had a hell of a good time there before we came back home. In my case I got on a train from Great Lakes to Harrisburg [Pennsylvania].

"I had wanted to reenlist, but they wouldn't give me a rank. I said, 'If you give me sergeant, I'll stay in.' The scuttlebutt was—it showed it on our promotions, which were temporary—that they were going to break everybody back one rank and give them a permanent rating. So, if I had been a sergeant and they broke me back to corporal, I wouldn't have given a damn, and I could have stayed a corporal for the rest of my life. But this 'ninety-day wonder' said, 'No ranks handed out!' I said, 'All right. You tell Uncle Sam to kiss my ass, and I'll kiss his!' That's just what I said, and then I left. So, I came out of the Marines as a corporal.

"Jakie's" experiences in World War II and the Marine Corps changed his life. For the rest of his years, he remained active in veteran's organizations:

"I'll tell you what—World War II and the Marines made a man out of me. It made me look at things a lot differently than I probably would have if I had stayed here and there wouldn't have been a war. I have never regretted going into the service. Uncle Sam gave me some experience that money can't buy. The only thing I regret was the killing. That's all. The memories are still with me, and they'll never take them away. Never! Whenever a plane comes over, it seems like I always have to look at it. It was a long time before I ever got the memories of bombing out of my head. Even after I was married, I could hear the bombs come down. That's the fortunes of war.

"Ever since the end of the war, I've been active in veteran's organizations, especially the American Legion here in Wrightsville. My one really big accomplishment that I'm really proud of is the war memorial at Fairview Cemetery. I wanted it done, so I kept on it, pushing, pushing, until it got done. The monument was officially dedicated on Memorial Day 1999. The reason I wanted to do this is because I wanted to continue to respect the comrades who are lying out in cemeteries around the world. I wanted it not for me; I wanted nothing of that for myself."

After the war, "Jakie" married and made his home in Wrightsville where he worked as a cabinetmaker. He and his wife were the parents of a son. "Jakie" died on 17 February 2004.

Notes

1. Jacob W. Snyder, interview by the author, 8 August 1999, transcript, OH1310, Oral History Collection, University Archives, University of North Texas, Denton, TX.

2. The American Joint Chiefs determined that the strategic prize to be taken were the Japanese-held Marshall Islands with their eight airfields but that first the Gilberts had to be occupied. The Gilberts consisted of sixteen atolls scattered along the equator. Among these atolls, Tarawa and Apamama had military significance because of their potential use as sites for airfields. In Japanese hands, the airstrips threatened the American sea lanes of communication between Pearl Harbor and Australia, and New Zealand as well as approaches to the Marshall Islands. Once in American hands, the same airfields could be used to support reconnaissance missions and bomber strikes against the Marshalls. The Japanese recognized Tarawa's strategic importance and supplied their garrison with generous amounts of troops, weapons, and fortification materials. On Tarawa, the Marines were to encounter the most sophisticated series of defensive positions until the invasion of Iwo Jima in 1945. See Joseph H Alexander, *Utmost Savagery: The Three Days of Tarawa* (Annapolis, MD: Naval Institute Press, 1995).

3. Note: Apamama Atoll, with a population of about 3,000 local inhabitants, is approximately twelve miles long and five miles wide. In August 1942 a Japanese naval landing force occupied the island, and shortly thereafter Japanese engineers constructed on Apamama the best airfield in the Gilberts. Apamama became the only atoll in World War II to be captured by a submarine landing party when the American submarine USS *Nautilus* landed a force of seventy-eight Marine Amphibious Scouts to seize the atoll from a small Japanese garrison on 21 November 1943. Naval Construction Battalions (Seabees) immediately began improving and enlarging the airfield after Apamama's seizure, and then medium and heavy bombers of the 7th Air Force, escorted by fighters, began hitting Japanese installations throughout

the Caroline and Marshall islands. See Alexander, *Utmost Savagery*, 29, 68-69, 218-224, 237.

4. Note: Truk in the Carolinas was long considered impregnable against attack by warships. During World War II Truk with its magnificent lagoon was one of the Empire of Japan's main bases in the South Pacific Theater, being the principal anchorage for the Combined Fleet. It was then used extensively for operations against Allied forces in New Guinea and the Solomon Islands. See Ronald H. Spector, *Eagle against the Sun: The American War with Japan* (New York: The Free Press, 1985), 271.

5. Note: "Tokyo Rose" was the GI pseudonym for Iva Ikuo d'Aquino, who broadcast English programming and popular music to Allied troops in the Pacific as part of Japanese propaganda to undermine American morale.

6. Note: Snyder's chronology may be a bit hazy. The invasion of Okinawa began 1 April 1945, and Roosevelt died 12 April 1945. It is unclear, however, when Snyder's ship left Eniwetok, since he did not go ashore at Okinawa until the sixteenth wave landed.

7. Note: For an excellent account of the Battle of Okinawa from the perspectives of both the Americans and the Japanese, see George Feifer, *Tennozan: The Battle of Okinawa and the Atomic Bomb* (New York: Ticknor and Fields, 1992.

8. Note: For a detailed description of the *kamikaze* campaign, see Feifer, *Tennozan*, 195-229.

9. Note: In May 1945 the Japanese fortified a series of hills east and north of Naha on Okinawa. The capture of these positions was essential, and it fell to the 6th Marine Division to capture this area in order to outflank the Japanese and bring the campaign to a successful conclusion. One of the fortified hills was Sugar Loaf. In a ferocious battle lasting until 18 May 1945, the Marines eliminated all Japanese resistance on Sugar Loaf. The intense fighting cost the Marines 2,662 casualties and opened the way to victory in this costly

battle of the war in the Pacific. See James and William Belote, *Typhoon of Steel: The Battle for Okinawa* (New York: Harper and Row, 1970), 259-271.

10. Note: For a detailed account of the fighting for Sugar Loaf, see Feifer, *Tennozan*, 251-354.

Figure 18. Electrician's Mate 2d Class Leonard "Son" Bock

Chapter 18

Electrician's Mate 2d Class Leonard "Son" Bock

PC-1135 and PC-1138

Born on 14 September 1925, in Wrightsville, Leonard "Son" Bock joined the Navy at the age of seventeen while still in high school. He was the middle child of Victor J. "Jerry" and Katherine "Cass" Bock. He had an older sister, Elmira Jane, and a younger sister, Rose Marie. Usually called "Son" or "Red" (because of his red hair), he was an outstanding athlete in both basketball and baseball. His naval career in World War II was filled with adventure. "Son's" first ship participated in the destruction of a Japanese submarine off the Marshall Islands; he witnessed Japanese civilians and soldiers committing suicide by jumping off the cliffs of Saipan; his second ship served picket duty during the *kamikaze* attacks off Okinawa; and he was one of the few survivors when his ship went down during a typhoon off Okinawa in October 1945. After the war, "Son" received enough credits through the United States Armed Forces Institute to graduate from Wrightsville High School in 1947. He attended what was then York Junior College with help from the GI Bill of Rights, and he later played four years of minor league baseball in the farm system of the Philadelphia Athletics. "Son" had two children by his first marriage and three children by his second marriage. With the exception of his service time and his career in the minor leagues, he lived in Wrightsville all his life. "Son" died on 14 November 2002.[1]

Filled with patriotic fervor and eager for adventure, "Son" quit high school at the age of seventeen and enlisted in the US Navy on 14 September 1943:

"I was in school when we heard about Pearl Harbor, and I wanted to get into the service right away, like every other kid. I couldn't get in until my seventeenth birthday, which is September 14, so that would have been not quite a year after Pearl Harbor. One hundred percent, I wanted to get into the war. Being a young kid, I guess I loved the action, I thought that what the Japs had done was a dastardly thing, and so I wanted to get into the service because I felt it was something I had to do. I wanted to go into the Regular Navy, which eventually I did, but I wanted to go in for six years. Well, I had to go in under the so-called 'kiddy cruise,' because I was only seventeen years old.[2] That's the only way they would accept me. I was surprised that my parents allowed me to join, but I pestered them so much that they consented. Besides, my grades weren't all that great in high school at that time. Anyway, within about seven or eight days, I was on a train to Philadelphia to get sworn in on October 22, 1942.

"I took my Navy boot training at the Naval Training Center at Bainbridge, Maryland. For me boot camp lasted for a total of about four-and-a-half months. Then I took some aptitude tests, and I apparently did pretty well, so the Navy sent me to electrician's school at Newport, Rhode Island. I was at Newport for four months, and when I got out I went from second class to first class seaman as an electrician 'striker' [trainee].

After completing the electrician's school at Newport, "Son" was assigned to his first ship, PC-1135:

"From Newport I was assigned to PC-1135, which had been built way up on the Mississippi River. I think it was built by the Defoe Shipbuilding Company in Bay City, Michigan. It was a small combat ship and sometimes was classified as a submarine chaser. PC stood for 'patrol craft.' It was a new ship, and we picked it up in New Orleans for the shakedown cruise in the Gulf of Mexico. I'm guessing that about 75 percent of the crew were brand new seamen. We did have some old hands. Our machinist's mates were old hands; our coxswain's and boatswain's mates were old hands. As far as armament, we had a 3-inch/.50- caliber on the forecastle; amidships we had a single 40-millimeter in a tub; and then up on the flying bridge we had three 20-millimeters, and down on the main deck we had four 20-millimeters. Then we also had depth charges and 'mousetraps.'[3] As a 'striker' I stood electrical watches while we were under way, and at General Quarters I was a gunner on a 20-millimeter up on the flying bridge. I continued to study, and I took the test for electrician 3d class and passed. Being wartime, I'd say that promotion was probably a lot faster than it would have been in peacetime.

PC-1135 was temporarily sent to Panama prior to permanent deployment to the Pacific Theater. The ship's first taste of actual combat would occur in the Marshall Islands Campaign where it received partial credit for the sinking of the Japanese submarine I-32 on 23 March 1944:

"We went into Panama and operated with this sea-going tug. It was to tow around ten harbor tugs to Pearl Harbor, and we were to be the escort. After we got to Pearl Harbor, they kept us there for I don't know how long, getting us seaworthy and putting on additional guns, and refueling. Pearl Harbor was like Panama City.

"By the time we left Pearl Harbor, the invasion of the Marshall Islands was already going on. In fact, it had started quite a long time before.[4] I'll tell you, I was as 'gung-ho' as a cowboy when we pulled out. I thought I was indestructible, and I was! Well, when we got to the Marshalls, Kwajalein had been secured. Most of the time I was down below in the electrician's room on the main switchboard, and at General Quarters I was a gunner on a 20-millimeter topside. For the most part we were running picket duty out around Kwajalein where all the bigger ships were located. We had great sonar and radar gear. This went on for about two weeks.

"Then we headed back down to Majuro because that's where Task Force 58 was located at that time. Well, we got word that this Jap submarine was prowling around. It turns out that the US Navy was reading Jap codes, so we knew exactly what they said and where their submarines were operating. The Navy knew that this sub was one of the biggest submarines that the Japanese had. It was a transport submarine with a seaplane mounted on its bow, and it was trying to feed these Jap troops on the islands that had been bypassed by our troops. This island, Wotje, apparently still had a whole bunch of Jap soldiers on there, and our intelligence knew that about 1:00 in the morning the Japs were going to be at a certain destination. Our Navy knew everything because the subs would have to come to the surface to transmit their messages back to Japan, and we could pick them up right away back at Pearl Harbor. Of course, we lower-ranking personnel didn't know anything about this at the time. So, they sent two 'tin cans' [destroyers] and a DE [destroyer escort] and us to try to destroy the submarine. I guess that's all they apparently could free, and I guess they thought that that was enough to do the job.

"We might have been halfway between Majuro and Wotje when we picked up this Jap sub on our sonar. I was a 3d class electrician's mate by this time because my General Quarters station was now down in the main electrician's room where the main switchboard and the two generators were housed. To my knowledge the destroyers and the DE made two runs depth-charging the sub because I could feel the vibrations on our ship. I don't know how far away they were, but I had my earphones on because we were at General Quarters, so I could hear the inter-ship communications for everything being said.

"Well, these ships didn't get the sub, but the DE picked him up again before daybreak. So, they started rolling off more depth charges. About this time, I remember hearing a guy up on the quartermaster's deck shouting, 'Son-of-a-bitch! Son-of-a-bitch! I don't think they got him!' I could hear him talking like that because he was pushing the button on his headphones. I don't know whether or not he knew he was talking to everybody on the ship. Then, all of a sudden, he shouted, 'Here we go! Here we go!' So, they apparently picked up the submarine again, so now we were going after him. I said to myself, 'Oh, man!' I crossed my fingers for good luck because one of my daily jobs was to check those 'mousetraps' to make sure that saltwater didn't electrically short them out, because they're battery-operated. They'd sure as hell blame me if they didn't work because I had to sign a paper saying that I had inspected them and had taken the readings with my ohmmeter and my ammeter and my voltmeter and got good readings. I had to fill out this form every time I did it, which was at least once a day.

"So, anyhow, I heard this 'PFFTTT! PFFTTT!' That's about what it sounded like, only it rattled the whole ship when each bank of 'mousetraps' would take off. Then everything was quiet. I remember that this was right around daybreak by this time, and we were still at General Quarters. Then, all of a sudden: 'PFWHOOM!' I mean, the whole ship vibrated, and I thought we had been hit by a torpedo! Then everybody started screaming. This guy up there manning the phones on the quartermaster deck went crazy. He was a 1st class quartermaster, I think, at that time. Now he shouted, 'We got the son-of-a-bitch! We got the son-of-a-bitch!' They didn't really know if they had gotten the sub, but it was a good indication because the 'mousetraps' only explode on contact with metal. Then daybreak came, and the flotsam started coming up. The decking on the sub was all wood, and then that came floating up. Then body pieces were all over the place, and you could tell where they were because the sharks started feeding on them after a while. Then there was a great, big oil slick—I mean, a monstrous thing. Well, the DE and we kept running circles around this slick for about that whole day, from daybreak on, just to make sure we'd gotten it. They had to verify the kill, which they eventually did. They verified it. There was no doubt that that

Jap sub had been sunk, and then we got an 'atta boy' from our skipper. That was real big shit for me, you know, as a seventeen-year-old kid.

"Anyhow, it took us about a half-day to get back to Majuro because we were pretty far south. We had this broom displayed up on there like submarines would do to signify that they had had a successful war patrol. The big foghorns were going 'WHOOP! WHOOP!' Even this big aircraft carrier joined in.[5]

Between battles every Navy ship and its crew had to perform routine duties, including watches, reprovisioning, and shipboard maintenance. Many of these activities became routine for the crews, but they had to be done:

"Shipboard routine became monotonous between battles. You stand watch; you stand watch. You have four hours on watch and four hours off. Otherwise, you'd sleep, or you'd write 'lies' in letters to your family and your girlfriends. You'd go down below and throw dice, which I did quite a bit of. There were no movies because we were such a small ship. The bigger ships had movies, but we didn't. There were always things to do in the electrical department. Saltwater always tears the hell out of wiring, especially when you're in a convoy and bad weather and everything, and there are always other things that go wrong and have to be repaired. Every four hours I'd have to change generators. We had DC current there, and it's a little tricky to switch from one generator to another, but after a while you can do it with your eyes closed. You get into a routine.

"We got R & R [rest and recreation] when we were near some atolls. There was nothing but sand and coral there, maybe a couple palm trees, and there might be a half-dozen ships there. We didn't wear any clothes. Nobody wore any clothes. We were stripped bone-naked. It was no big deal being naked. You know, all you've got is a bunch of naked men who are uglier than hell. We'd get this 3.2 beer, and there were beer drinking parties most of the time. The cooks would give us hot dogs and hamburgers. We played volleyball, and they had pick-up softball on the sand. I did mostly eating. There were virtually no restrictions on our activities, because you don't realize how tight you are until you get to a place like that. You really don't. But I never, never got scared until we got to Okinawa. I was young enough, but then I was getting pretty much experienced, too.

After R & R, reprovisioning, and making repairs and upgrading equipment, "Son" and the PC-1135 crew took part in the Marianas Campaign in June-July 1944 when American forces invaded the islands of Saipan, Tinian, and Guam to establish bases for the strategic bombing of the Japanese home islands by American B-29s. It was here that young Bock looked on in horror as he watched Japanese and Korean civilians committing mass suicide by jumping off the cliffs at Marpi Point on Saipan:

"When the initial shore bombardment took place at Saipan, I was down below in the electrician's room. They had several battleships there, and you could hear these things firing. You'd hear that rumble, and then you'd hear 'SWOOSH! SWOOSH! SWOOSH! SWOOSH!' It sounded like a freight train going right over the top of you because we were underneath all that firing. You'd grit your teeth, but after a while you'd get used to it. You see, the battleships were about twenty miles off shore, and we were right next to the shore. That was before we were on picket duty.

"After the landings, we went on picket duty up and down around Tinian and then out around Marpi Point. This is when we started popping bodies. The Japanese civilians were jumping off the cliffs—these men, women, and children. The bodies would bloat up, and the sharks were feeding on them. But we couldn't stop. We'd just keep going, and we'd pop them. They'd go 'SPEEEEW!' You know, the air would come out of the bodies, and then down they'd go. The sharks were all over the place there. And they stunk! It stunk like hell, especially when we squished a couple of these bodies. But we had to go straight through them. We'd be up on the bow when we weren't on duty or something, and we'd just be looking. That's when we saw these big, bloated bodies, and our bow would cut right through them. We did that for, I guess, about three or four days. We were on picket duty at that time, watching for anything, particularly submarines.

"We didn't have to watch the suicides taking place with binoculars. It was plain to see. I'm guessing that it wasn't ten miles between Saipan and Tinian—that channel there. I saw a woman holding a kid by the hand when she jumped. Now, she jumped down on the rocks below the cliff. Most of them hit the rocks, but some went clear out on the point, and they went down into the water. You could hear the guys on our ship saying, 'Jesus Christ! There goes another one!' We could see the Marines up there, and they had loudspeakers and everything else, trying to get them to stop. These civilians were told by the Jap troops that they were going to be raped and then killed, period. It was a terrible sight to see these suicides. When I saw all this happening, I was scared. It scared me because I hadn't seen people die before. You know, I was just over seventeen years old, and I didn't want to cry. But I was scared. Most of them jumped into the rocks, but some of them went up at the far end there, and they'd hit the rocks and bounce into the water. That scared me! I just was never used to seeing people die, although we did know that all the Jap sailors in that submarine had been killed. It's a funny feeling, I'll tell you. It's just the damnedest feeling deep in your stomach when you see somebody dying like that, especially women and young kids, babies even. I thought to myself: 'What in the hell kind of an enemy are we dealing with here?'[6]

At the conclusion of the Marianas Campaign, PC-1135 did some convoy duty and then headed for Brisbane, Australia, to have a bent propeller repaired, and the crew had an opportunity for a bit of shore leave. At Brisbane, "Son" transferred from PC-1135 to PC-1128:

"Well, in 1944 I must have gotten the word that I was going to be transferred. You see, I had passed the test for 2d class electrician's mate, but in order to get the rating and the pay raise, there had to be a slot on the ship for me. Since there was no opening on PC-1135, I had to transfer over to PC-1128. Before that, however, we had run a convoy down to Guadalcanal, and we ran aground down there and bent one of our screws. They then sent us to Brisbane, Australia, and put us in dry dock. While the repairs were being made, they turned us loose in Brisbane for eleven days.

"After we got a new screw or got the other one straightened out, we were sent to the big anchorage at Ulithi. It was a big atoll shaped something like a horseshoe. When we got there Ulithi was nothing but ships. There were attack aircraft carriers, battleships, and heavy cruisers in there as well as hundreds of other ships. Although we didn't know it at the time, they were getting us ready for the next big campaign, which was Okinawa. It was here at Ulithi that I transferred to PC-1128. This ship was built by the same company that built PC-1135, and the two ships were exactly the same. I do think, however, that it was less 'GI' [less formal] than the first ship.

The invasion of Okinawa started on 1 April 1945. Since the Japanese evidently had given no indications of surrendering, American planners believed that nothing short of the occupation of the home islands would bring an end to the war because the atomic bombs were not generally known even in the upper echelons of the command staff, and they viewed Okinawa as the logical staging base for the invasion of the southernmost Japanese home island of Kyushu as an opening to Operation Downfall. During the Okinawa campaign, PC-1128 mainly performed picket duty against incoming kamikaze *attacks*:

"We left Ulithi without a convoy. We just ran! We started out a couple ships at a time. Our first job was to assist the destroyers and minesweepers to clear mines. We knew where the Jap minefields were located. These were mostly contact mines anchored by cables. We got up in the vicinity of Okinawa about ten days before the invasion fleet arrived, so we were supposed to have the area cleared of mines for these ships. Oh, I'd guess we probably blew up maybe a couple dozen mines ourselves. The minesweepers would cut them loose, and then we'd destroy them with rifles and .30-caliber machine guns. To do this, we had to hit the spiked detonator points. During this operation, we did not take any fire from Jap shore batteries. The *kamikazes* were not yet a factor, although we knew about them because they had hit our sister ship off Mindoro [Philippines] and sank her.

"Apparently, we cleared the mines pretty quickly because it was a little over ten days later that the invasion started. When dawn came, there was nothing—no ships in sight. Then at daybreak, it was just solid—solid with ships from one end to as far as you could see. It was solid with big ships, little ships, troop transports—everything. But there was still no Jap fire from shore. Then our battleships started letting go. Of course, the Japs were all ready for them because they had moved back to tunnels, underground tombs, and everything else. But the battleships kept pounding away until the troops hit land. They kept firing and firing, and we could actually see the 16-inch shells flying through the air on their way toward onshore targets.

"A couple days later, they sent us on picket duty up north of the island. Then the shit started to hit the fan. The Jap aircraft started coming over in groups. As it turned out, these *kamikazes* were looking for big stuff because they kept going over us. They didn't bother us at that time. Then maybe a couple days later, they assigned us to this island called Kerama-retto. COMSOPAC [Commander South Pacific] was there on a command ship. They assigned us the duty of laying down a smoke screen early every morning all the way around the inside of this island. We had these smoke pumps that generated smoke, and it was real heavy and thick. This smoke would lay there right on into the darkness, so that's the way we had it timed.

"The favorite time for the *kamikazes* to come over was in the early evening, and I'm going to talk about one episode that indicates that point. We were always on alert status during that time. Well, one night we didn't anchor because it was about time for us to do our turn around the island and lay down more smoke. I was up on the flying bridge with this other fellow, leaning on the guns. We were talking. All of a sudden, he said, 'Jesus Christ! Look here coming!' Here came this *kamikaze.* He must have flown the whole way from Kyushu right over the water. There were some small mountains there at this Kerama-retto, and he came over them and then came down. He went right over our ship. Honest to God! I remember this as plain as anything! He might have been 200 feet above us at the most. I could see his leather hat, and he had this scarf whipping out over the cockpit canopy. He looked like he was just driving to the park, you know. He'd look over, and I just knew he was looking at me. I looked up at him, and I could have shit. By this time, the guy I was talking with hopped into the gun tub, and he shouted, 'Strap! Strap!' So, I strapped him into the gun mount, and he started firing at this guy with our 20-millimeter. But this plane just banked ever so gently over the top of us. The only time that I felt like he was going into action was when he made his turn to go down, and he was bent forward like he was trying to line himself up or was aiming or something. He had two bombs under his wings—one under each wing. It was a single-engine plane, but it wasn't a Zero. We were maybe fifty yards away from the COMSOPAC command ship, which was a big transport, and this plane went in right at the waterline. Nothing happened, however, because nothing exploded. So, he just completely ignored us and went on by. Totally! Totally! But I was still scared as hell then because he came so near to us. I can still see him in my sleep. Honest to God!

"We didn't call the *kamikazes* crazy, because they were not crazy. This is the way they were brought up and taught. They felt that, if they were dying for the emperor, they would have a better life once they got to where they were going. I'm sure that at one time or another I said, 'They've got a lot more guts than I do. I wouldn't do it.' But what they did was awesome! It was absolutely awesome. I still don't understand how they could get that way, but what the hell.

"Somebody else took over our job at Kerama-retto, and we went back out on picket duty. After leaving we did shoot down a *kamikaze.* Like I said, when we went to General Quarters, I was down in the electrician's room, but I could hear our antiaircraft guns pumping away. Of course, I had on my earphones, so I could hear what was going on. I heard this: 'Well, we got him! We got that son-of-a-bitch!' Then I heard over the earphones: 'There goes a second one! We got him! We got him!' But I think they only gave us credit for the first one because they apparently blew him up. In fact, that was the only way you could stop them, was to blow them up, because they'd keep coming—even though they might be dead—once they got their sights on you. The first guns on our ship to fire at them were the 40-millimeters and the 3-inch/.50-caliber. Then the 20-millimeters would kick in as the *kamikaze* got closer, and then when you heard the .50-calibers firing, you knew that sucker was getting in real close. That would scare the shit out of you, too! We only slept intermittently because when we were out on the picket line we never knew when we'd see them. Often they'd come as one or two together, and they'd come in right above the waves. You'd never spot them. I mean, they're in and they're out, and it's all done before you even realized that they were there.

"Out off Okinawa, where we now were on picket duty, we saw what the *kamikazes* could do. I saw them hitting ships when I had a chance to go topside, when I wasn't on duty and when we weren't at General Quarters. We never started shooting at them until the Navy combat air patrols had their whack at them. See, the carriers had them spotted fifty miles away, and they'd send up their fighters. Then once they got past the planes, the picket ships started firing, and so did our carriers, all of whom were under way. The Navy planes probably shot down a greater percentage of the Jap planes coming over because the Jap planes were not fighting at all. All they were doing was coming through, so for the Navy planes it was a turkey shoot.

"Son" and his shipmates were still on picket duty off the coast of Okinawa when they heard the news of Japan's surrender. They assumed that they would be going home shortly, but their worst nightmare was soon to occur

when PC-1128 got caught with a large number of other Navy ships in a violent typhoon in October 1945. What follows are "Son's" harrowing experiences during that storm:

"When we heard that the war was over, we all went crazy. Everybody got up and fired their weapons into the air. I was scared to go outside because the shrapnel was falling all over the place. Then we were all getting a little homesick because we had seen enough of this crap, and we figured we'd be seeing no more *kamikazes* or anything else. By this time we were anchored maybe 150 yards off the stern of the battleship USS *Pennsylvania*. All of a sudden, I saw this Jap plane coming in with a torpedo underneath it, and I thought, 'Jesus Christ! Here comes another *kamikaze*!' He came right over us and went right for the *Pennsylvania*. He was up pretty high before he started flattening out. Nobody was ready for this, so all our guns were put away, so to speak. He came in flat and laid his torpedo down, and it hit the *Pennsylvania* on the side, oh, probably a quarter of the way from the stern. Then he kept on going. Well, they managed to save the *Pennsylvania*. This was a little bit 'hairy' [scary] to us because we were going to start running a convoy of ships with Marines aboard for the occupation of Japan. Well, our convoy was assigned to a city that, I think, had a population of about 200,000 called Wakayama on Honshu. Nothing ever happened, though. We stayed there just one day, and the landings were made without any problem.

"After this, the shit really hit the fan. We had already gone through a couple small typhoons, but then we heard that this big typhoon was coming. It had first hit the Philippines, but we heard that the worst part of it was to come toward us. All the ships that were in the anchorage there were to go out to sea to ride out this storm. So, we raised our anchor and headed out west of Okinawa. We were hardly the type of ship to withstand a huge typhoon, since PC-1128 was only175 feet long and twenty-three feet wide at the beam.[7]

"It was about October 9 when the typhoon really hit us. I was in the flying bridge, so I can verify that I saw what was happening on the barometer. You've got a nail at 27 barometric pressure. That's as low as she'll go, and that barometer was right down on top of that nail. It was flat on that nail at 27 even. That is what, I think, actually sunk our ship. The barometric pressure was so great that once we got under way we went to General Quarters as the storm got worse and worse and worse. All of a sudden, our two banks of V-16 diesel engines stopped running. They say that we were probably forty miles west of Okinawa—in that general area—trying to ride out the storm when these main engines quit. The engines probably burned up because the barometric pressure was so great that the air pressure stopped the seawater from being pulled into the ship to cool these engines. Then we started rolling, first one way and then the other. Our ship could really take a big roll. We could take a thirty-five to thirty-eight-degree roll and still come back up. But it kept getting worse, and then we were probably, I guess, hit broadside by a wave that took us down. That's what I think.

"I felt the ship rolling over. We all had our life jackets on—that's automatic. Right beside the main switchboard was this ladder, a metal ladder. When I felt us going over and over, I thought, 'The son-of-a-bitch ain't coming back!' So, I started scooting up that ladder. The hatch was 'dogged,' you know, locked, and I started to panic then. But I got the 'dogs' open, and I walked right into the water because the ship was going down.[8] I know that the waves by this time were as high as the steeple of the Lutheran church here in Wrightsville—about 200 feet high. But I was comfortable. I was loose as a goose because I came to the sense that: 'What the hell. If I'm dead, I am; if I'm not, I'm not.' Being raised along the Susquehanna River, I never had a fear of water. I just had that attitude. So, what I basically tried to do was tread water, but I was always in motion with these damned waves **way, way** down and way, way up. I swallowed a lot of saltwater, and a couple times I didn't think I was going to be able to breathe. In the meantime, the ship was down. It was gone.

"I'd say that around noontime—I'm guessing because I have no idea with respect to time, but it was sometime late in the afternoon or early evening—I saw this raft, and I got to it. I have no idea how I did it because you can't swim in water like that. I think there were ten to twelve guys on there—all from our ship, including the skipper. There was not much conversation aboard the raft. You're saying things, but you're talking scared, and probably half the conversations didn't make any sense.

"Sometime early the next morning, we must have hit the eye of the storm because, all of a sudden, it was just like total silence. We still had tremendous waves, but nothing like the original ones. By that time we had lost two or three kids. We had these lines attached to their life jackets, and we tied them together and tied them on the back of the life raft. Now, the life raft was a great, big balsa thing with ropes that enabled you to lie on the inside. Well, there was nothing left of the balsa by this time, and the only thing holding it together was the ropes. So, we were just hanging on the sides and holding on to these ropes until early the next morning.

"Apparently, the skipper had been bitten on his leg by a shark, and it took his calf off. It was probably a small shark that had bitten him. So, we put him up on the ropes. That way he could be out of the water without any problems although he didn't seem to be suffering too much. By that time, three or four or five guys tied to the life raft were dead. I remember the last kid who died. I was trying to hold him up because I was pretty strong then. The kid looked over at me, and, all of a sudden, he vomited. The vomit hit me in the face. I think it was then that he died.

"Anyhow, the next day the storm started tapering off. There was still a storm, but the winds had moderated probably to less than a hundred miles per hour. So, we were talking, and I don't know what the hell we were talking about. I guess we were talking about what we were going to do next because we had no idea where we were at or whether or not we were close to Okinawa. I couldn't tell what was north or east or south or west because it was murky, a gray sky, because the storm was still hanging around although the worst of it had passed over. Incidentally, I didn't have a stitch of clothes on because the big waves tore off all my clothes—my dungarees, my shirt, undershorts. I had nothing on, but I did have my identification tags. They stayed on, but otherwise I was stark naked. Others were naked, too, because the waves tore everything off of us.

"Sometime late in the afternoon—I don't know for sure—a big fleet minesweeper was out there looking for survivors. They were headed right toward us, and, of course, those who still had on clothing took off their shirts and dungarees and flagged it. But apparently they had us spotted pretty early. It came up almost right parallel to us. The minesweeper had one of these rope ladders—debarkation ropes—and the last thing I remembered was three or four guys coming down the ropes. They couldn't put a boat out over the side because the seas were still too rough. I had had it about then because exhaustion had set in. I'd guess that I had been in the water for anywhere from twenty-five to forty-five hours. I really don't know for sure. I vaguely remember somebody grabbing me underneath my arms and holding me up. They got everybody up on deck, and I passed out about that time. It was about two or two-and-a-half days before I woke up and found out that they had put me in a bunk. During this time, it seemed to me like everything was floating. They said they fed me soup sometimes, but I don't remember any of it because I was in a daze. We later found out that we probably went down —I'm guessing—thirty-five or forty miles west of Okinawa. When the minesweeper found us, we were sixty to eighty miles south in the South China Sea. That's how far apparently the current and the storm took us, I guess. It was in the South China Sea where they found us, so we did a hell of a lot of floating during those hours. There were about fifteen of us on that raft at first, but I'd say that five at most survived—at the most.

"All of us, including me, had life jacket burns, so we were all rubbed raw. Then after about two days in the bunk, I started getting carbuncles. I had forty or fifty carbuncles—from the saltwater—that came up.

Anywhere you looked on my body, I had these carbuncles. They really, really hurt. The corpsmen couldn't do anything for me until the carbuncles came to a head. Then they'd take a sharp razor and slit them and popped them. Afterwards, I bet I had scars on me for two or three years after I got out of the Navy—just from the slitting—but they have since disappeared.

"Anyway, they took me off the ship and put me in the hospital. When I got in the hospital, the nurses started rubbing me with all this lotion and everything for my raw skin. Obviously, they gave me underwear and a T-shirt and all that sort of thing because I had lost everything when the ship went down. I also had a lot of money in the ship's safe, and I lost that, too. I had nothing—my wallet, photographs, souvenirs, clothing. I was tall and muscular, but I had lost a lot of weight because I could hardly eat anything for a long time. I couldn't get food down, and if I could, then I'd vomit.[9]

"From Okinawa they brought us back to Treasure Island in San Francisco Bay, and they put all us survivors from the ship together. Of that whole ship's crew, there were only seventeen survivors out of a complement of 135 or 140 men. On Treasure Island they gave us a total physical examination, and they fed us and gave us all new uniforms and everything. Then they shipped us by Pullman cars to Great Lakes Naval Training Center at Waukegan, Illinois, for reenlistment or discharge. Then I reported to the Philadelphia Navy Yard.

"Son's" homecoming was one probably repeated in thousands of homes throughout the United States as the veterans returned to their families and loved ones:

"I sent a telegram home: 'I'll be in Lancaster tomorrow around 7:00.' So, lo and behold, there was Jerry Bock crying, and my younger sister Rose Marie came running up. She had grown so much since I had been away. Mom was very stoic when I went in the house. About four or five hours later, Jane came back from Washington, and she banged through the door, bawling and hugging. But it was a pleasure to see them again. I had missed them—I really did—because I went into the Navy as just a kid. Of course, when you go into the service like that, you've got to grow up and become a man in a matter of months, you know, change from a kid to a man.

Like so many other veterans, "Son" took a great deal of pride in his having contributed to the winning of the war, but he had some problems adjusting to civilian life once again:

"As I said before, the war made a man out of me, and it taught me a hell of a lot about responsibility—how to give orders and take orders. The service does that to you. I grew up very quickly in the Navy because before I went in I was just a big, overgrown kid. I had a great deal of pride in having served during that period. When the veterans returned to Wrightsville, we were absolutely 'the men' like all other veterans were. The people in town had pride in you, and you had pride in the people of Wrightsville for appreciating what you had done.

"On the other hand, I did have problems in adjusting after leaving the Navy. It took two years. I never liked to talk about my wartime experiences. I didn't want to talk about it because I had lost a lot of good friends when our ship went down in the typhoon. My experience when the ship was sunk was without a doubt the worst thing that happened to me. I didn't want to be around anybody when I first came home. So, it took me a good two years to acclimate—it really did.

With the exception of his service time and a four-year career in the minor leagues, "Son" lived in Wrightsville. He married, divorced, and remarried, having two children by his first wife and three with his second wife. "Son" died on 14 November 2002.

Notes

1. Leonard Bock, interview by the author, 7 August 1997, transcript, OH1193, Oral History Collection, University Archives, University of North Texas, Denton, TX.
2. Note: Under the minority or "kiddy cruise," a person could enlist at age seventeen and serve until age twenty-one. Normal Navy enlistments were for six years.
3. Note: A "mousetrap" is a forward-launched ASW [antisubmarine warfare] weapon similar to, but smaller than, the "hedgehog."
4. Note: The Marshall Islands Campaign took place during January-February 1944 with the goal of penetrating the eastern defensive ring protecting the Japanese Empire. The principal American objectives were the capture of Kwajalein and Eniwetok. Other islands taken with little cost by American forces were Wotje and Majuro. See Samuel Eliot Morison, *The Two-Ocean War: A Short History of the United States Navy in the Second World War* (Boston: Little, Brown and Company, 1963), 312-317.
5. Note: For the record, on 23 March 1944, Fleet Radio Pearl picked up a signal message from the Japanese submarine I-32 to headquarters. At that time I-32, a supply submarine, was transporting provisions to Japanese troops on Wotje. A hunter-killer group composed of the USS *Halsey Powell* [DD-686], USS *Hull* [DD-350], USS *Manlove* [DE 36], and USS PC-1135 was ordered to intercept and destroy the sub. The following morning at 4:22, some fifty miles south of Wotje, the *Manlove* picked up I-32 on radar after it dove on sonar. The *Halsey Powell* initiated the attack and expended all her depth charges in the hunt. The *Manlove* and PC-1135 then took up the attack using "hedgehogs" and "mousetraps" respectively. Their attack was successful. Deep underwater explosions along with an oil spread shortly confirmed the death of I-32, which went to the bottom with all 106 hands. See Navy Department, Office of Chief of Naval Operations, Naval History Division, *Dictionary of American Naval Fighting Ships* (Washington, DC: Government Printing Office, 1968), 3:219; and *Dictionary of American Naval Fighting Ships* (Washington, DC: Government Printing Office, 1969), 4:221.

6. Note: For another description of the civilian suicides, see Harold J. Goldberg, *D-Day in the Pacific: The Battle of Saipan* (Bloomington: Indiana Univ. Press, 2007), 199-204.
7. Note: According to the official US Navy records, on 9 October 1945, Typhoon Louise shifted from a predicted path 150 miles west of Okinawa to an actual path that brought the center of the storm less than fifteen miles east of Okinawa's southwest coast. By noon visibility was zero, and the wind was 60 knots from east to northeast, with tremendous seas breaking over the ships. At 2:00 the wind had risen to 80 knots, with gusts of far greater intensity, and the rain that drove in horizontally was more saltwater than freshwater. Even the larger ships in Buckner Bay were dragging anchor under the pounding of 30- to 35-foot waves. By 4:00 the typhoon reached its peak, with steady winds of 100 knots and frequent gusts of 120 knots. At this time the barometer dipped to 968.5 millibars. This was the lowest reading that the barometers recorded, and was probably the point of passage of the center of the typhoon, but the maximum winds continued unabated for another two hours with the gusts becoming fiercer. Under such conditions, it is understandable that some of Bock's comments about the storm differ from the official record. See "Commander in Chief, US Pacific Fleet and Pacific Ocean Areas Report," Serial 0395, 11 February 1946, World War II Command File, Operational Archives Branch, Naval Historical Center, Washington, DC.
8. Note: In naval parlance a "dog" is a lever used for securing a watertight door aboard ship.
9. Note: According to US Navy records, PC-1128 grounded 9 October 1945, at Buckner Bay, Okinawa, and was found to be beyond repair. It was destroyed in 1946. The *Dictionary of American Naval Fighting Ships* has no history available for PC-1128.

PART V

STATESIDE MILITARY SERVICE

STATESIDE MILITARY SERVICE

During World War II, thousands of military men and women saw duty in the United States. Although they never served in combat zones, their contributions to the war effort cannot be overlooked. Stateside soldiers served as coast artillerymen, drill instructors, flight instructors, aircraft mechanics, drivers, ferry pilots, weather forecasters, mapmakers, supply clerks, corpsmen, medical doctors, psychologists, chaplains, and finance officers. In some cases, men being trained for overseas duty never left the States because the war was over before they could be sent to combat zones. More than 400,000 American military women served at home and overseas, almost always in noncombatant roles. More than 60,000 Army nurses and 14,000 Navy nurses served stateside and overseas during the war. In 1942 the Navy established the Women Accepted for Voluntary Emergency Service [WAVES], and a year later the Army organized the Women's Army Auxiliary Corps [WAC]. In 1943 the Marine Corps created the Marine Corps Women's Reserve, and the Coast Guard soon followed with the formation of the SPARs [after the motto *Semper Paratus*]. Women in the various military branches filled jobs in communications, intelligence, supply, medicine, and administration. Others served as storekeepers, clerks, photographers, drivers, and records keepers. The Women Airforce Service Pilots [WASPs] flew stateside missions as aircraft ferriers, test pilots, and antiaircraft artillery trainers. In 1943 the Cadet Nurse Corps was formed, and by the end of the war it had trained 125,000 women for possible military service.[1]

Notes

1. Note: See Sally Van Wagenen Keil, *Those Wonderful Women in Their Flying Machines: The Unknown Heroines of World War II* (New York: Rawson, Wade Publishers, 1979); Bettie J. Morden, *The Women's Army Corps, 1945-1978* (Washington, DC: Government Publication Office, 1992; Paula Nassen Poulous, ed., *A Woman's War, Too: Women in the Military in World War II* (Washington, DC: National Archives and Records Administration, 1966); June A. Willenz, *Women Veterans: America's Forgotten Heroines* (New York: Continuum,1983); and Allan M. Winkler, *Home Front USA: America during World War II* (Arlington Heights, IL: Harlan Davidson, 1986).

Figure 19. CPO Elmira "Jane" Bock

Chapter 19

CPO Elmira "Jane" Bock

Anacostia Receiving Station, Washington, DC

Born on 31 October 1923, in Baltimore, Maryland, Jane Bock spent her youth and early adult years in Wrightsville before joining the WAVES (Women Accepted for Voluntary Emergency Service) during World War II. She was the oldest of three children born to Victor J. and Katherine Drenning Bock. The Bock family moved to Wrightsville when she was approximately two years old after her father, a professional baseball player, was offered a job at the American Chain and Cable Company in York on the condition that he pitch for the firm in a local industrial league. After graduating from Wrightsville High School in 1940 and working in several secretarial positions, she joined the Navy on 18 November 1943. Her decision to enlist was based on patriotism and a desire to experience the world beyond Wrightsville. After the usual Navy training for women, she was assigned to an administrative position in the Fire Control School at Anacostia Receiving Station, Washington, DC. By the end of the war, she had worked her way up through the enlisted ranks and mustered out as a chief petty officer. Shortly after returning to Wrightsville, she married Edward Silar. Jane and Ed raised four children, and they currently live in Allentown, Pennsylvania. [1]

The Bock family suffered through some of the worst effects of the Great Depression, and her experiences during that time may have subconsciously determined her later decision to join the Navy:

"I went to school in Wrightsville where we had what I consider today as the absolutely perfect academic system. We had nothing but academic courses and none of the special things—two years of Latin, two years of French, four years of history, four years of English and literature, and four years of science and math. I graduated from Wrightsville High School in 1940, but I could find no job, and I certainly was unable to afford to go to college.

"It was a very, very poor time during the Depression. Our family was 'poor to hungry.' I wanted so much to go to college, but back then we didn't have ways to go if you didn't have the money. I wanted to major in physical education. Obviously, I now needed a job, but there were few choices available. Around the time I finished high school, Dad got a job, so there was a little bit of income coming in, so I finally ended up going to Prowell's Business School in York. At Prowell's, I had English, typing, shorthand, and training in general office procedures.

"The first job I took was with the Lancaster Red Roses baseball team, which was a farm club for the Philadelphia Athletics. Actually, my father got me that job. It was a very, very hard job for someone who had never worked before. I typed up all the contracts; I did all the correspondence; I had to account for all the money that came in from the gate receipts. I did all of that, and I had to stay late at night. I was working ten, twelve hours a day. For all this work, I got paid $12 a week. I stayed there until the season ended, and then I went to work for the PP&L [Pennsylvania Power and Light Company]. At PP&L, I made $12 a week, but I was working fewer hours than I was with the baseball club. In addition, PP&L gave me money for transportation expenses. I was working there when I decided to join the Navy.

Like many Americans, Jane was swept up in the surge of patriotism that engulfed the country following the Japanese attack at Pearl Harbor and American entry into World War II. Like her brother "Son," she decided to join the Navy:

"I had just come home from church when I heard about Pearl Harbor, and that's all I remember. I must have heard about it at home. I guess that when I came home, the news was on the radio. Pearl Harbor was so remote for most people, but I'm sure we were all horrified. The next thing I remember is that within a short period of time, Walnut Street seemed to have been emptied of draft-age young men, and you must remember that there were a lot of families with a lot of kids living on that street.

"By November 1943 I was working up to going into the service because it was the ultimate, patriotic thing to do. I thought to myself, 'This is what I have to do.' Absolutely! I was motivated for patriotic reasons. It was the times. People had attacked us. I don't think that anyone went into the service for anything other than patriotism. That was one of the most outstanding things about the war. The whole thing was that people felt like this was something they had to do. Everybody was contributing, and this was an opportunity for me. In the meantime, my brother 'Son' had quit school and went into the Navy.

"Believe it or not, my mother really encouraged me. She always wanted me to 'spread my wings,' so to speak, even in those days. She wanted me to do something that, if she had been able, she would have done. That's the only way I can put it. She didn't give it a second thought; she just thought it was absolutely wonderful that I wanted to take advantage of this opportunity. The Navy needed women in the worst way. They absolutely needed us. The Navy had to have storekeepers; they had to have yeomen. And women would be freeing up men for sea duty and combat. That was the essence of setting up a women's branch.

"But I had to wait until I was twenty because you could not go in until you were twenty. Well, my dad knew the recruiter, so all the paperwork was actually done before I had actually enlisted. My birthday is October 31, so I went in and had all the papers completed before I was twenty. I was sworn in at the Navy recruiting station in York on November 18, 1943. I chose the Navy because 'Son' was in the Navy, and I liked the water, having been raised up along the Susquehanna River. At that time women, of course, could not go aboard warships.

After being sworn into the Navy, Jane went through the usual boot camp for women and eventually was sent to a specialized school where she received a yeoman rating:

"All in all, I was absolutely excited because it was the beginning of an adventure. And I've always liked adventures all my life. We went to Hunter College in New York City, and that's where we had our boot camp. This was the farthest I had ever been from home. We were housed in apartments that the Navy had confiscated around campus for women who were in boot camp at that time. They had been individual homes, I guess, at one time. There were maybe two or three women to a room, maybe even four. Each room had bunk beds. We were on the fifth floor, the top floor, and when you went to take a shower, there were maybe two drops of water coming out. There was only one shower for the whole apartment, so the people on the first floor had the benefits because they could get the most water.

"This was before I was aware of much about lesbians or gays of any sort, so I didn't think of anyone doing anything untoward toward me. As I recall, I didn't run across any lesbians in boot camp. But, anyway, two or three of us would have to take a shower at a time, or else you would never get any water. That was the way we had to do it. I didn't have a lot of inhibitions, ever, so I had no problems. But for some of those poor girls, it was very sad to have to undress in front of the rest of us. So, there were some who had difficulty undressing that way, but I didn't. There was a bathtub, too, and if you chose to use it, you could. But who had time to take a bath?

"We took specific classes at the college. Almost all our classes were taught by women. Some classes dealt with Navy customs. Since I had played around the Susquehanna River all my life, I had no trouble at all with the lifesaving requirements. I can't remember all that we studied, but we went to class pretty long every day. Otherwise, we had to parade; we had to march. We were in platoons, and we had to march back and forth from the barracks to the classrooms. We did everything as a platoon. We had all kinds of inspections. It was white gloves stuff. We were taught how to make a bed, and they'd better be taut. They checked by bouncing a coin on the bed. Most of us had never made beds Navy-style, but we learned in a hurry. The Navy had strong rules in those days. Man! You just didn't deviate! There were certain rules and regulations, and you had better adhere to them, or you'd have problems.

"As I indicated concerning group showers, all of us had to make adjustments to military life and how to get along with others. I can remember having a variety of roommates. I was with an older girl, and like me she wanted to have new experiences. She was neat. Then I had a girl who was wealthy, and she had never washed a dish. It was really a cross-section of people, but there were no black girls. There might have been some in our building, but I just don't remember them. If there were any, I'm sure that they would have been segregated. Overall, though, I don't remember any serious problems. I think we all did reasonably well.

At the end of boot training, Jane and her comrades were eventually assigned to another base for training in a specialty.

"At the end of boot camp, we had a big parade, and we received the rank of apprentice seaman. Then we waited around until they found specialized schools for us. We had no choice of where we would go or what advanced school we would attend. I did have a skill even before I enlisted in the Navy. Since I had been a secretary, I was pretty sure that after boot camp I was going to go eventually for specialized training as a yeoman. They had all these tests that they gave us. These were more or less intelligence tests. Well, my guess was correct, for I was assigned to the yeoman school at Oklahoma A & M College at Stillwater. Almost immediately, we got on a train sometime in January 1944 in New York and left for Oklahoma.

"Well, let me tell you about the train trip. Anyway, as always, we were billeted, and because of my name, Bock, which started with 'B,' I was lucky enough to get assigned to a room instead of one of the sleepers. Two other girls and I were in this room together, and they picked one of these girls to be in charge of that car. Then every night she had to check beds by pulling back the curtains to make sure that everyone was in. The second or third night, she came tearing back into our room, and she was hysterical. She couldn't even really tell us what she saw. She said, 'I pulled back the curtain, and there were two girls being intimate! I really can't tell you what they were doing! I can't even tell you!' She asked, 'What am I going to do? I feel like I have to tell somebody!' I said, 'Yeah, I guess.' So, she did tell somebody, and they took these girls off the train at the next station. Now, we really 'buzzed' about that for some time. It was hysterical! Being from Wrightsville, I don't ever remember anything like that happening there, so this affair did make me aware of people who had different sexual proclivities. That was really the only time I ever experienced anything like that—and it didn't happen to me.

At Oklahoma A & M College, Jane underwent advanced training as a yeoman "striker":[2]

"We got there, and we were billeted once again, and we went to classes. I took classes with all the college students. We took English, which was always my favorite subject, and other academic courses, and I made an 'A' in all the courses that I took. We always had studying to do at night and things like that. In addition, I remember that we had training in naval correspondence, learning about all the forms and so forth used by the Navy. I can't remember how long we were at Oklahoma A & M, but we learned a lot while we were there.

"When I had completed my training here, I was then a seaman second class. I was still a yeoman 'striker.' At the end I found out that I was to be assigned to the Advanced Fire Control School at the Anacostia Receiving Station in Washington, DC. After I got there, I was thrilled to death that I didn't have to go downtown to the Navy Department. Anacostia was at the Navy Yard on the other side of the Anacostia River.

At Anacostia, Jane diligently applied herself to all assigned duties, took advantage of all opportunities open to women for promotion, and eventually rose to the rank of chief petty officer by the end of the war.

"All the Navy's advanced schools were located at Anacostia. There was the Advanced Music School; Advanced Gunnery School; Advanced Fire Control School. I was assigned to the Advanced Fire Control School, which involved training for the firing of naval guns. It was the beginning of newer radar as well as new methods for firing the gun mechanisms. I can't remember where I started out, but there were maybe ten clerical workers in our office. We did a lot of curriculum typing for the school and for the teachers. In those days they didn't have ways to do these things other than somebody sitting down and typing it. Then we would reproduce our work on Rand ditto machines.

"I made petty officer 3d class almost right away after I got there. That process involved taking tests, and I passed the first time. There were a lot of openings for women in the offices. I eventually started assigning men to go back out with the fleet. They came into the Advanced Fire Control School as rated men, and then I was reassigning them. Most of these men had seen a lot of action—had their ships sunk and all that kinds of stuff. Then they were sent back to our school to learn new things that were coming along. Anyway, we would get our listing of how many men would go to certain ships, and then I would pick them by ratings. Many of them would come in and try to get their assignment changed, and if there was a way to do something different, we'd try to help them. And there were ways. At the height of the war, we were working night and day because the schools went night and day. Our day started early.

We'd start the new day at 7:00 AM, and we'd normally work to 7:00 PM —twelve-hour days. We would work so many straight days before we got time off. They'd usually give us two days off in a row.

"I continued to get promotions. I went to petty officer 2d class and then to petty officer 1st class while I was there. Openings were readily available for those who qualified, so there was no discrimination between men and women for promotions. There were a lot of openings for women in the offices. To show you how fast promotion could be, I was not even in for a full three years, and I made every grade. You could move up if there were openings and you passed the examinations. So, I made 3d class, 2d class, and 1st class ratings, and then I decided to give it a whirl to study for chief petty officer. I had to take more intensified tests. I had to type faster; I had to take shorthand faster. But more than that, it concentrated on naval correspondence—fourteen copies of everything—and all the material you had to know that was in the book I had to study to make chief. And I did it!

"I was requested to work on a secret project while I was at Anacostia. There were several officers who were also assigned to this project, which had to do with secret-type fire control systems. These systems were brand-new and unknown to the enemy. Before I was officially assigned, I was investigated in Wrightsville; I was investigated everywhere. And I didn't even know this until I got out of the service. I went into this project, and my job was to take shorthand notes, and then I had to transcribe them. I would go in in the morning, and they would lock the doors. Then I had to listen to these men sitting there and talking. I was locked up in a room with them, and before I was permitted to leave, I had to type up that information. I then gave them what I had typed, and then I shredded all my notes. They had the final copy of what I did, and if they had corrections for me, I had to redo it. That was an interesting project. Most of this was technical stuff, and all I knew was that it had to do with fire control. They were discussing new fire control systems, and what they were talking about was highly technical. I would just take as many notes that would make sense. I did so much every day, and I think I was involved in that project for maybe three, four, or five weeks.

Jane's account of her work experiences at Anacostia presents a view of World War II Navy customs concerning service etiquette as well as official attitudes toward gays and pregnant women:

"At Anacostia we had a lenient, less formal atmosphere in our office than those who worked at the Navy Department. They were not sticklers for anything in our office. We could work with open collars when it was hot, but my friends at the Navy Department could not do this. Getting the job done was the most important thing at our base. Of my supervisors there, we had one woman who was head of the WAVES contingent in the office. Her name was Dutton, and she was a very nice lady, very generous, and eventually married one of the officers there. We really worked hard, so she did not ride us hard like they did in a lot of Navy places. We had a lot of material that we had to get out in a day's time. In addition, we never really had any problems in our work relations with male colleagues. There was no condescension on their part. We were there to do a job; they were there to do a job.

"We had one boy working for us, and he got discharged because he was gay. That was a shame. He was a neat kid, but somehow or the other they found out about him. It was crazy. I always thought he was effeminate, but I didn't think he was gay. He had come in, and he worked hard and everything, but he eventually had to go. From then on, there were nothing but women in our office.

"The Navy did have policies concerning women who got pregnant. And it was happening. In those days, they could not stay in if they were pregnant. They had to go; they were discharged. No case like this appeared in my office, but I know it happened in some of the other schools. I swear, a lot of girls did it just to get out of the service. Well, I shouldn't say that, but I think that maybe some of them did get pregnant for that reason.

"The Navy had no policies discriminating against married women coming into the WAVES. I think that sometimes married women joined because they were having marital problems. I found that to be true in several cases. Maybe they weren't divorced yet, but they were having problems. On the other hand, single women could get married and still stay in the WAVES. They didn't discharge them.

As she advanced in rank, Jane received the privileges that accompanied her promotions to petty officer status:

"In the meantime, I had moved off-base to southeast Washington, DC. At first I lived in regular barracks on the base. Each of us had a bed and a chest. I don't think we had separate rooms, but I can't remember for sure. Living in the barracks was not great, so at the first opportunity I got to move off-base because everybody else was doing it. Then, too, they gave us extra money to live off-base. I don't know of anybody that I worked with who stayed on-base. They just didn't. Once I made petty officer 3d class, I could move right off, and I moved in with two other girls. One was a civilian who owned the apartment, and she rented to my friend Mary and me. Mary and I shared a bedroom because in Washington in those days housing of all kinds was in short supply. There was no place to get a private room. We stayed there with her in all the heat of Washington without air-conditioning, and Washington had to have been at that time the hottest place on God's earth! Absolutely! We used to go out at night and sit on the park benches because we couldn't stand to be in the bedroom.

"I stayed there for a while, and then when Mary got married, I moved into a bigger apartment in southeast Washington with two other girls. I stayed there until I got out of the service. We took the bus to work every day, and now that we had a subsistence and housing allowance, we had to pay for our meals on the base. It wasn't much money, but the rent was cheap, and the food was cheap, although none of us were great cooks. So, we ate out a lot.

While at Anacostia, Jane witnessed the aftermath of President Franklin D. Roosevelt's death on 12 April 1945, and the end of the war in the Pacific:

"We had a service for the President at the base, and I walked in the funeral procession. They took so many women to march behind the caisson, and we walked with a whole lot of people. I was a Democrat, and still am, so what can I say? I think everyone knew he was ill, and I'm certain that everyone was in a sad state of mind. Since I was born in 1923 and he came into office in 1933, he was the only President I really ever knew up to that time. We listened at our house to the Fireside Chats. They were usually on Sunday nights, and we always listened to them because he certainly had a commanding voice. His voice was impressive. Since Mom had been given a job with the WPA, President Roosevelt was certainly a favorite of hers.

"I was working on V-J Day [Victory over Japan Day] when we received the announcement that the war was over. When Germany had surrendered, there wasn't much celebrating because there was still so much going on in the Pacific. When Japan surrendered, though, we all cheered and hollered and did what everybody else was doing, but we still had to go to work. On V-J Day, I couldn't get home because there were no buses running. My friends were out celebrating, but I was still on the job. I remember that I walked home. I walked into our apartment, and I couldn't find anybody. I stayed inside because I was afraid to go out since they were wild out in the streets. There were some wild shenanigans going on, and I thought, 'I'll just say in the apartment until somebody comes in.' I can't remember the details, but all I know is that I felt so lonely because everybody else was celebrating and I was not with them. I stayed there until, finally, toward morning, somebody else came in. But it was a joyous time.

While at Anacostia, Jane had another traumatic experience when she learned that her younger brother's ship had gone down in a typhoon off the coast of Okinawa on 8 October 1945: [3]

"As I mentioned, I took the tests and finally made chief petty officer about six or eight months before I was discharged. I could have been discharged within a few days of the end of the war, but they asked me to stay. I stayed for an additional six months so that I could train four men to take our jobs. I went up into the Fire Control School where they gave me rooms, typewriters, and books. These men gave me no trouble because they were only too glad that they didn't have to go back to sea. They were tough guys who had seen a lot of combat, but they were always respectful of me. As a chief petty officer, I commanded respect, and I got it from them.

"I had a friend who worked down in that part of the Navy Department that kept track of the whereabouts of ships, so I knew there was a typhoon. I gave her the number of my brother's ship. I didn't know exactly where his ship was located, but I did know that it was somewhere around Okinawa. So, I called and asked her to let me know if anything happened. And she did. She said, 'The ship was sunk, and we don't know yet how many are safe.'

"I almost died! I mean, I was absolutely uncontrollable! I was so upset! Then my biggest problem was: 'Dare I tell Mom and Dad? Should I tell Mom and Dad?' Finally, I decided that I would call them. I said, 'I don't know yet what the story is on him.' Mom said that after hearing from me, she and Dad walked back and forth across the bridge, I think, two or three times that night. I'm talking about the mile-long bridge across the Susquehanna between Wrightsville and Columbia.

"My friend had 'Son's' name and knew everything about him. It must have been a few more days when she called me and said, 'I have good news! He was saved! He's safe!' Well, I called my parents with the good news. He was in a hospital on an island for some time, so then we waited for him to come home. But it was so wonderful in retrospect that this person in the Navy Department was able to provide me with this information. This was a very traumatic and trying period for me, but my roommates were wonderful. I went to work as usual because things like this were happening to everybody. There were so many people who went through similar trauma with their husbands and boyfriends and so on. But, thank God, 'Son' had nine lives, you know.

"I got leave to be there in Wrightsville when 'Son' came home on survivor's leave, and that was exciting, too. I saw him walking down the street, and I almost tore him up. He has always said, 'You almost choked me to death!' We did a lot of weeping because he and I were very close. It was a really, really wonderful thing. He had a lot of psychological problems—I know he did—when he came home because he had had an unbearable experience. It was just a miracle that he survived.

When Jane mustered out of the Navy on 19 August 1946, she was unsure of what she wanted to do in the future:

"After the war I was having some problems deciding what I wanted to do, but I knew I had to get on with my life. At first I was going to stay in Washington and get a job because I had gotten used to the big city life. I really saw no future in returning to Wrightsville, and I knew I didn't want to stay there. I had a wonderful time growing up there along the Susquehanna River and all that, but getting a permanent job and using my skills was almost non-existent. I would have had to find employment in either York or Lancaster. Then I decided, 'Okay, I'm not going to stay in Washington. I'm going to apply for college. I'm going to do what I originally wanted to do.' I decided that I was going to go to a school that had a major in physical education, so I enrolled at Grove City College in western Pennsylvania. When I got to Grove City College, I found out that the dean of women was an ex-WAVES officer, and I'll never forget that. So, I got all the information, and she was thrilled to have me there. But then I saw all these young kids around. I came home, and I said, 'I can't do that. I don't think I can go and be a young kid anymore.' So, I never did go to college, and this is something I still regret. Of course, the GI Bill would have paid for every bit of my schooling. So, anyway, I came back to Wrightsville. Then the War Assets Administration in Marietta hired me because I had all these points. I was made the secretary to the head of the whole War Assets Administration, which was responsible for selling off government war material.[4] The pay was excellent, so I made a lot of money there.

"Then I started dating Ed Silar. He had come home from school while I was still working for the War Assets Administration, and I wasn't really dating anybody in particular at the time. His folks lived on Walnut Street, too, so we started dating. Well, we married in January 1948, and then we left Wrightsville when Ed attended law school at Vanderbilt University in Nashville, Tennessee. From that time on, except to see family, we really haven't been back to Wrightsville very often.

"Ed and I have four grown children: Theodore, Priscilla, Frederick, and Polly. My time in the Navy had been an interesting, wonderful experience, and I have nothing bad to say about it at all. That experience of being away from home and making a contribution to the war effort changed me for the better, and I have used that experience to encourage my daughters and make them strong women. And I think they are strong women today."

Ed eventually took a permanent job with Allstate as a claims adjustor in Allentown, Pennsylvania. They raised their four children there, and Ed and Jane still reside in Allentown.

Notes

1. Elmira Jane Silar, interview by the author, 12 August 2000, transcript, OH1359, Oral History Collection, University Archives, University of North Texas, Denton, TX.

2. Note: A "striker" is an enlisted person in training for a specialized technical rating.

3. Note: See the previous selection from the interview with Leonard "Son" Bock, whose ship, PC-1128, sank during a typhoon off the coast of Okinawa on 8 October 1945.

4. Note: Established in January 1946, the War Assets Administration, part of the Office of Emergency Management, disposed of surplus consumer and producer goods, industrial and maritime real property, and airports and aircraft located in the United States and its territories.

Figure 20. Sgt. Charles "Pete" Yeager

Chapter 20

Sgt. Charles "Pete" Yeager

222d Combat Crew Training School
US Army Air Forces

Born on15 June 1918, in Baltimore, Maryland, Charles "Pete" Yeager's family moved to Wrightsville in 1925. He was the oldest of eight children, four boys and four girls, born to William and Anna May (née Dietz) Yeager. A victim of the Great Depression "Pete" quit school to find employment and held several jobs before enlisting in US Army Air Forces in October 1942. During World War II, all his duty was stateside, including stints at Amarillo, Texas, Chanute, Illinois, and Ephrata, Washington. "Pete's" permanent station was at Ardmore Army Air Field in Oklahoma where he eventually served as a crew chief responsible for the maintenance of B-17 heavy bombers. The base at Ardmore was part of the 4th Air Force and was used for the training of bomber aircrews. His career during World War II, while not glamorous, is another example of the vital role played by those involved in the training of crews for combat duty in the European and the Pacific theaters. Following World War II, "Pete" enlisted in the Army and saw combat in the Korean War as a forward air observer. After his discharge, he returned to Wrightsville where he lived for the rest of his life. He had married before initiating his military career, and he and his wife raised a daughter. "Pete" died on 11 February 2007. [1]

"Pete" was working at Lancaster Malleable when the war started. As a married man with no children at the time, he believed that it was just a matter of time before he was drafted, so he decided to enlist in order to pick his desired branch of the military:

"In the meantime, I had joined the CMTC, Civilian Military Training Camps, as it was called. It was something like the National Guard. You'd go for training thirty days out of a year, and I attended that in 1936, 1937, and 1938. I went first to Ft. Meade, Maryland, for infantry training, and then I was transferred to Ft. Hoyle, Maryland, for artillery training. You received military training, and in your fourth year, if you passed the tests that you had to take, then you could apply for a commission in the US Army. I was already planning to join the Army, and I had the big idea that if I could get a commission, I'd go in. But I wasn't recommended to go back for a fourth year because I hadn't completed my education, and you had to have a high school diploma or its equivalent to qualify. Anyway, that's where I got my early military training.[2]

"So, when the war started in December of 1941, I was working at Lancaster Malleable, and I had a Triple-A [AAA] draft deferment. In 1942 I went in to see the boss and said, 'I'm going to enlist in the service.' Well, he couldn't figure that out. He said, 'We've got the deferment for you. We've got government contracts. Why do you want to go in?' I said, 'I've got the feeling that, having been attached to the military, one of these days when the supply of people gets low, they're going to grab me because I don't have any children. I'm going to get caught in the draft.' When I went into the service, I wanted to have my choice of branches, not what they were going to push me into. So, I worked at Lancaster Malleable until October of 1942, and then I decided that I was going to enlist.

"I talked it over with my wife, but she never said very much to me about my decision to join. Having been from a military family, she never said anything, and her father never discouraged me. I said to her, 'If I can go in the service and keep a guy who has a family from having to go in, I think this is why I'd like to do it.' Also, I wanted to serve the country, but I was not going to wait to be drafted and have the government push me around the way they did with draftees. So, I went to York and enlisted in the Air Corps [US Army Air Forces]. I think they took me because when the recruiter asked if I'd ever worked on air-cooled engines, I told him that I certainly had. I had a motorcycle for years and did all the repair work on it. At that time in Wrightsville, most of the guys who were eligible had already been drafted.

"I was sworn in at Harrisburg on October 2, 1942. Then we went to the New Cumberland Army Depot and got our uniforms there. While at New Cumberland, I ran into my brother. He enlisted in the Regular Army and had been sworn into the Army on October 6, 1942. That was the last time I ever saw him because his landing craft hit a mine during the invasion at Anzio, and his body was never found.

Shortly after he joined, the US Army Air Forces decided that "Pete" had the aptitude and skills for assignment to aircraft maintenance training. It is interesting that all his training was accelerated due to the massive aerial buildup under way at this time:

"Hell, I never took basic training, and I guess that happened because of my training with the CMTC. I had been discharged from the CMTC, and that information was part of my records. So, they sent me by train to Miami, Florida, to take a bunch of tests. There we took tests concerning our IQ and all this stuff. I'll never forget. I wanted to be a pilot. I was going to be a hot shot fighter pilot. Well, when I got through with these tests, the lieutenant looked at me, and he said, 'Yeager, you'll never find your Goddamned way home!' I had never taken geometry and that stuff, so he said, 'We'll recommend you to go for training at the B-17 school out in Amarillo, Texas.'

"Of course, we went to school there, and the schooling was intensive. At that time the Air Force was building up their bomber commands, their fighter commands, and they were needing maintenance people—people to service the planes and keep them flying. They were trying to rush them through. Our specialty was the B-17 bomber, so naturally we didn't study anything but B-17 bombers. We went through intensive training on oxygen systems, engines, propellers, electrical systems, and control systems. We had certain classes for all those categories. The B-17s that we worked on were old ones that didn't even have the tail gunner position in them yet.

"After I graduated at Amarillo—I think it was March 11, 1943—I got assigned to Chanute Field, Illinois, for a six-week course. When I got there, they told me that I was going to be specializing in aircraft instruments, so that's what I studied up there. We went through classes to learn the different instruments—how to calibrate a compass, how to calibrate airspeed indicators, the electrical systems, and so forth. All the instruments that they used in planes, we had courses on them. They rushed us through pretty fast because they needed maintenance people. For the guys who already had training, they were pushing them overseas. They were going to the South Pacific, England, and so forth.

"Then they set up the 2d Air Force Training Command, and I was sent to Ephrata, Washington, where I was assigned in April 1943 to the 395th Bomb Group as an instruments specialist. They were flying patrols off the West Coast. That's when those Jap submarines came in and threw a couple shells into California, so the bombers were flying patrols out there.[3] I had no further training other than my regular duties. If they needed work done on the instruments in the bombers, I went out and worked on instruments. That's where I met a master sergeant and flight line chief by the name of 'Pop' McLawrence, who took a liking to me. He saw that I was interested in the aircraft and learning about them, so he let me work on other things on the planes like maintenance on the engines and stuff like that. So, I worked around with different crew chiefs. I'd change the spark plugs and work on the electrical systems. I learned quite a bit from him after I got out of school. I knew some of it, but I learned a lot more by actually working on it out there.

"When I was there at Ephrata, the 395th got orders to move, and the rumors were that we were going to the South Pacific. We packed up and got on a train for Seattle, and all the bombers flew to Boeing Field. When we arrived, however, they said, 'Don't unpack anything. They've just changed our orders.' So, we got back on a train and headed for Ardmore Army Air Field in Oklahoma. My first question was, 'Where the hell is Ardmore?' I didn't know where the hell Ardmore was.

"Pete" spent the rest of his World War II career at Ardmore where he eventually was promoted to sergeant and designated as a crew chief for a B-17. His description of the work done here at Ardmore again underscores that the stateside military made significant contributions to the war effort:

"I was disappointed at first because I really did want overseas duty in a combat zone. To this day I think that my prior training, plus the schooling that I got, kept me from being assigned to a crew and going overseas to a combat area. But at the time, I couldn't figure out why they kept pushing me around by sending me here and there and denying me a combat assignment.

"We went to Ardmore as the 395th Bomb Group, but after a short time —a month or two—they changed it to the 222d Combat Crew Training School. From then on we trained combat crews, and most of these crews went to England. I stayed with the 222d Combat Crew Training School from the time I arrived in the fall of 1943—October or November—until the end of the war. After I got to Ardmore, we were losing a lot of specialists. We were losing propeller specialists, engine specialists, and radio specialists because they were sending them overseas as replacements. So, we wound up with just a cadre who had those specialties.

"As an instruments specialist, my job was to calibrate, repair, and replace instruments. If I got a report from a pilot that an airspeed indicator wasn't working right, I would replace it. We often didn't have time to take it down to the maintenance depot there to repair it, so I'd draw a new one out of Supply, and I'd replace the defective one. Later on, we'd send back the defective instruments, and the civilian workers would repair them. So, I was dealing with all the instruments on the panel in the cockpit of the airplane.

"Then I got assigned as a crew chief on a B-17 bomber—575 was the number of the bomber—and I worked with that airplane the whole time I was there. Before that, I worked on whatever aircraft that needed my expertise. When I came out of the school at Amarillo, I was promoted to Pfc, and after I completed the school at Chanute, I was promoted to corporal. Then, when I got assigned as crew chief, I got another stripe, which made me a buck sergeant. A buck sergeant was simply a newly minted sergeant. So, I had a maintenance crew and the specialists working with me because I was in charge. I had to keep all the records and everything, the flight records and stuff that they had, and I'd determine when the aircraft was ready to fly or was not ready to fly. If it wasn't ready to fly, I'd assign it to the repair line. Sometimes they put a lot of pressure on me because they needed so many training flights at a time when my plane wasn't ready to fly. In fact, I almost got court-martialed one time because I wouldn't certify a plane as ready to fly.

"Let me tell you about a typical day in the life of a crew chief. First, it depended on what flight your plane was assigned to. They flew around-the-clock training missions. If you were assigned to a morning flight, and they were going to Galveston, Texas, or Havana, Cuba, you'd have twelve planes going down there. I had eight other specialists besides myself—propeller specialists, electrical specialists, engine specialists, and so forth. Then we had just plain mechanics that changed the oil and stuff like that. So, we'd get up at 2:00. 2:30, 3:00 in the morning, and we'd check the plane, make sure it was all gassed up. Then we'd slowly advance the idle speed of the engines to full power, check the superchargers, and make sure that everything was working okay—that the engines weren't missing, weren't cutting out, and stuff like that. We'd make sure that the oxygen gear was all in order and that everything was up to par and make sure that all the guns were stowed. Now, the armorers took care of the ammunition, but we had to make sure that that stuff was all on the plane when they were ready to fly. The crews would take high-altitude gunnery practice going down, and sometimes the B-26s would tow these target sleeves [cloth material used as aircraft-towed targets], and the gunners would fire at them. As crew chief I often flew with the bomber as far as Galveston if it was going to Havana. Then we'd stay in Galveston, and they'd go on the Havana; and when they returned, we'd check the plane and make sure that everything was all right. Then we'd fly on back to Ardmore.

"For every bomber, we had a 25-hour inspection, 50-hour inspection, 75-hour inspection, and 100-hour inspection. This means that after twenty-five hours of flight, the 25-hour inspection kicked in. The 25-hour inspection was just mainly changing the oil and checking to make sure the spark plugs were okay and making sure the engines were running all right. We'd rev up the engines and check the superchargers, check the controls to make sure that the elevators and ailerons were working properly. You'd crawl through the length of the fuselage and make sure that the cables weren't frayed or anything like that. Most of what I just described was a visual check. When you got to the 50-hour inspection, then you pulled the cowling off the engines, and you checked the engines thoroughly. You checked the wiring on the spark plugs, and you checked the glycol tanks to make sure that they had glycol in them because the crew used glycol heaters at high altitude. So, it was a constant checking of everything.

"As crew chief, I had to sign off that everything was working properly or not working properly. In other words, they had the record of aircraft maintenance broken down in your flight record, your flight data, and that stayed with the plane. It didn't matter where that plane went, that flight data stayed there from the day the airplane came out of the factory.

If there was a minor thing wrong, you indicated the problem with a red diagonal line. There was a little block that you marked. If you put down a red diagonal, then across from it where it said 'Remarks,' you'd write down what the problem was or the prospects for a potential problem. When the pilot came in, he always checked over that information so that he knew that there was something that he should keep his eye on. If there was nothing wrong, then you simply put down your initials to indicate that that part was operating properly. Now, minor problems you could get by with because the plane was still flyable. If there was something that was absolutely inoperable, then I'd put down a red 'X.' Then if the pilot was willing to sign it, fine. He then had to put his initials on there to release the plane for flying. Otherwise, that plane was staying on the ground. When we had new guys, I'd check behind them because I had a little bit more experience than some of those guys had. I always felt that when that plane was in the air, I wanted it to be in the best condition that I could possibly make it. I know that we had some crew chiefs there who would sign off on a plane when they weren't in safe flying condition, and as a result we lost some crews.

"The B-17 was a great airplane. In my experience, it was a most stable airplane. I flew in other airplanes, but that was the most stable one I ever flew in. They were a lot more stable than the B-24. I also heard the guys returning from combat in Europe talk about the B-17. The planes had engines shot off of them; they had ailerons shot off them. And they'd come back with all that damage! They landed! They brought their crews back! Those guys who went through flak and flying missions unescorted against German fighters **worshipped** that airplane! I talked to quite a few pilots and crewmen who had been overseas. They also described it as a 'forgiving' airplane because there could be pilot error and it would compensate, and I think that's one of the reasons why we used them for training. For the ground crews, the B-17 was not a hard plane to work on. I mean, once you pulled the cowling off an engine, everything was right out there in front of you. These B-17s had Wright-Cyclone engines, and the mounting on them was great. To work on them was fairly easy. I can't recall anything that might have been a frequent problem. Occasionally, we had a problem with the landing gear, which was electrically operated, but then the plane had a back-up, manually operated crank. So, you'd just crank it down and make sure it was then locked.

"We always had spare parts, so when we needed them we had them available. If we didn't have them, we'd take them out of another plane. A lot of times, when a plane would go in for a 150-hour inspection, then we would scavenge them for old parts when they were going to put in new parts, like, the altimeter or compass or something like that. As I mentioned earlier, I had a motorcycle for years, and I was always searching for used parts, and so were many of the troops who had had hotrods and used cars before the war. As civilians we'd go out and hunt for the cheapest parts we could find. When these guys went into the service, and got in a tight spot when needing parts, they could always figure a way to solve the problem.

"I flew as the flight engineer a couple times. We had new pilots coming in, and I had some frightening experiences with them on training flights. With these new guys coming out of two-engine transition and then coming to four-engine planes, I'd go out with them sometimes on what were called 'transition flights.' They would shoot landings [practice approaches] and come up and go around to shoot another landing. These were touch-and-go landings. They did that for three or four hours at a time. Sometimes they'd let the airspeed start getting up, and I'd have to whack them on the back of the head and say, 'Hey! Bring the airspeed up!' The co-pilot would then throttle it up because the pilot had plenty to do just bringing the plane in and landing it. Sometimes they'd fail to come in level, or else they'd hit the runway: 'WHUMP! WHUMP! WHUMP!' They weren't used to handling four-engine planes. I was still in my original airplane, but we changed transition crews quite often. Almost every day a new crew would be assigned to my airplane for training in bombing, gunnery, or whatever. It depended what phase of training they were in. In 1943 and 1944, we had a tough schedule in that we were really running new crews through as fast as possible. In fact, sometimes, in my opinion, I thought they were running them through a little too fast. I didn't think that these guys were getting the training that they should have had in gunnery and stuff like that. But they were losing so many of them over there in Europe that they needed replacements as fast as we could send them to England. In fact, we were training new pilots and crews right up until the war ended.[4]

At Ardmore, "Pete" observed the use of WACs [Women's Army Corps] as mechanics. According to him, they were accepted for their skills and experienced no backlash from the men:

"In fact, we had WACs working on the B-17s. When I was there at Ardmore, the Air Force finally brought in WACs as instruments specialists. After I made crew chief, we had WAC instrument specialists, propeller specialists, and electrical specialists. We never had any WACs in gunnery that I know of. As I remember one time, I called for a specialist to look at an oil gauge, and this dude is up there with fatigues on, you know. I grabbed him by the leg and said, 'Hey! How soon are you going to be done with what you're doing?' Here was a woman!

"We never gave it much thought to having women work on the airplanes. We never thought anything of it. The ones that I had experience with knew their business. They knew their job; they knew their business. They were great! Oh, the guys would kid them and stuff like that, but no nasty remarks were made to them or anything like that. They were dedicated to their job. The WACs really helped in the war effort because they released guys for combat crews needed in Europe and the Pacific.

Almost all of the training cadre at Ardmore were veterans of the air war in Europe and had completed their required number of missions before returning to the States. "Pete" held these men in high esteem:

"I had a lot of rapport with these veterans who had come back from Europe and were training these new crews. They'd talk to you and ask if the airplane was ready to go. In my opinion they were heroes because they had seen quite a bit of action. But they were subdued, and they just figured that they had simply done their job. It was the same way with the enlisted crewmen who had flown in the air war. They weren't cocky; they weren't arrogant. They never wallowed in self-pity for what they had to go through by being sent into combat. Their attitude seemed to be that they had been given a job to do, and they did it to the best of their ability in order to get this war over with as soon as possible. I never heard one of them say he was sorry for having been sent into combat. I was lucky, but, hell, a lot of those airmen weren't so lucky. The Air Force lost a lot of men in those daylight raids over Germany.

The casualties of war hit home for "Pete" when he learned that his brother, Bob Yeager, was listed as missing-in-action during the invasion at Anzio, Italy, in October 1944:

"I got the news from my wife in March 1944 because my parents had gotten a telegram saying that Bob was missing-in-action. All I knew was that he had gone through the North African Campaign. Bob had gotten wounded in the shoulder in Sicily, but after he recuperated, they sent him back to duty with his old unit. See, he wasn't declared killed-in-action until 1948. Nineteen forty-eight! My mother and dad wouldn't even talk about it. I'd ask them, and they'd only say that they'd gotten telegram that he was missing in action. They never found his body; they never found anything. Bob was on a 'Limey' [British] craft, and I never could figure that out. Why the hell was he on a 'Limey' craft? Most of the information that I got about Bob came from Donald W. Peters, who was on the same landing craft. He said he was below decks when the ship hit a mine and that there was a tremendous explosion. Wilfred was wounded in the blast and ended up in a military hospital for a while.[5]

With the end of the war, "Pete" had to decide whether to take his discharge and get out of the service or to make the military a career:

"When the war in Europe was over, there was a big celebration on the base. We never got off the base. They confined us to the base, but we still had a big celebration. Everybody was shouting, 'The war's over! What's now going to happen to us?' Since most of us had never been overseas, we thought that maybe they would send us to the Pacific because the war against Japan was still going on. Anyway, gradually so many guys were sent to other places, and some guys got discharged. Soon it seemed like only we old guys were the only ones left at Ardmore. Then we got orders to go up Muskogee, Oklahoma, and we were supposed to go with a liaison squadron to Karachi, India [now Pakistan].

"Then it so happened that the Air Force needed men for occupation duty in Europe, so a friend and I reenlisted for a year because we didn't want to go to India. At that time you could reenlist for one year because all the guys who had been in Europe were coming home and they needed men for the Army of Occupation. We were still in the Air force, though. This reenlistment occurred on October 22, 1945. They gave us a sixty-day leave, and I came home to Wrightsville. Then we reported to Ft. Meade, Maryland, and they sent us to Goldsboro, North Carolina. Then the next thing you know, they told us we were going to Europe. So, I spent the next nine or ten months at Landsberg, Germany.

At the end of his enlistment, "Pete" returned to Wrightsville. To him the war had not changed the town very much. At the time of his return, the economy was not good, and he had trouble finding a decent job. As a consequence, he joined the US Army for a three-year hitch:

"My enlistment was up in December 1946 and I got home right before Christmas. I landed at New York City and then went down to Ft. Dix, New Jersey, where I got my discharge on December 22, 1946. When I returned to Wrightsville, I could see very few changes in the town. It did seem to be, however, more prosperous. Because of the war the elderly people in particular were making good money. They had not gone into the service, and they were working long hours and bringing home good money. That was the biggest difference that I saw.

"When the veterans came home, the citizens of Wrightsville greeted us and treated us well. I thought I would kind of be shunned because of the fact that I hadn't been overseas during the war, but the guys who had been overseas and had seen action never had a negative word for me. At first I feared that they'd think, 'Well, he just tried to get out of going overseas.' But, hell, I was in the service during World War II, and if they didn't send me overseas, it wasn't my fault.

"By the time that I got home, however, times had gotten tough, and I couldn't find a decent job. The economy had gone downhill around here. Now, I could have had jobs, but they didn't pay decent money. I had made up my mind that I was not going back into a foundry—if I didn't have to. That was damned hard work! I had worked at it from the time I had been a teenager, so I knew how hard that work was. Even so, I did mold for a short time down at Riverside Foundry after I returned to Wrightsville.

"In the meantime, to supplement my income, I had joined the National Guard, the 103rd Medical Battalion, in Lancaster. That was in 1947, I guess it was. Then in 1949 I got discharged from the National Guard, and I reenlisted again, this time in the Regular Army. Work had gotten slow again, so I said, 'Hell, I can make more money in the Army with my pay and spousal allotments. By this time my daughter had been born, and I had my wife. Eventually, I was sent to Japan and ended up in the Korean War where I served as a light mechanic in a light aviation section, but that's another story."

"Pete" did not make the service a career. After his Army hitch had been completed, he chose to return to Wrightsville and find steady employment. He eventually bought the same house that his parents had owned, and he raised his family there. "Pete" died on 11 February 2007

Notes

1. Charles W. Yeager, interview by the author, 4 August 1998, transcript, OH1254, Oral History Collection, University Archives, University of North Texas, Denton, TX.
2. The Citizens' Military Training Camps (CMTC) was established by the War Department to form a Citizens' Reserve of 10,000 men between the ages of sixteen and thirty-five, providing they could meet certain physical requirements and present proof of good character. A full term of military training was planned at permanent camps in various parts of the country. Training involved tanks, field and coast artillery, infantry, cavalry, and Signal Corps. A young man who successfully completed the advanced courses was qualified for appointment as a non-commissioned officer in the Organized Reserves. Upon passing a special examination, a person was eligible for receiving a commission as a second lieutenant in the organized Reserves.
3. Note: On 23 February 1942, a Japanese submarine fired on an oil refinery in Santa Barbara, California; on 21 June 1942, a Japanese submarine surfaced at the mouth of the Columbia River and fired eight shells at a coastal battery at Ft. Stevens, Oregon.
4. Note: During World War II, approximately 6,000 heavy bombers (B-17s and B-24s) were lost during operational sorties, and another 2,000 were written off as a result of crashes or extreme damage. In addition to the 6,000 heavy bombers, there were 500 medium bombers and 2,500 fighters lost. Over 30,000 airmen were killed or missing in action, and another 30,000 became prisoners of war. Only one in three airmen survived the air battle over Europe during World War II and the casualties suffered by the 8th Air Force exceeded those of the US Marine Corps and the US Navy combined. See Roger A. Freeman, *The Mighty Eighth: A History of the Units, Men, and Machines of the US 8th Air Force* (London: Cassell & Co., 1970)
5. Note: See the interview with Donald Wilfred Peters earlier in this volume for more details about the sinking this ship.

PART VI

ARMY OF OCCUPATION: GERMANY

On V-E Day, Gen. Dwight D. Eisenhower, Commander of the Supreme Headquarters Allied Expeditionary Force [SHAEF], had sixty-one American divisions with 1.6 million men in Germany. When the shooting ended, these divisions in the field became occupation troops, charged with maintaining law and order and establishing an Allied military presence in this conquered country. The first objective was to control the German population and discourage resistance from Nazi diehards by stationing troops in every part of the country. Divisions were spread out across the countryside as well as occupying German cities. Frequently, units as small as squads and platoons deployed at distances far removed from their company headquarters. The occupation troops manned border stations, operated checkpoints at road junctions, guarded bridges, and sent out patrols to apprehend curfew violators. They also placed guards at US Army installations, DP [Displaced Persons] camps, jails, telephone exchanges, factories, and banks. The purpose of this policy was to demonstrate to the German people that they were defeated and their country fully occupied. In addition, the Army of Occupation combated disease, hunger, and crime; preserved cultural artifacts, reestablished industry and utilities, and resolved potentially serious problems involving currency, housing, education, newspapers, and elections.

For the occupying GIs, the Army's policy of non-fraternization with German civilians, issued in May 1945, proved most onerous and was widely violated. Exactly how widespread fraternization was no one in authority seemed to know or wanted to know. Without combat to motivate and occupy the troops' minds, gender issues came to the fore because there were twice as many German women as men in the 25-30 age brackets. With food being so scarce for German civilians, many women traded sex for Army rations and cigarettes. Finally, due to pressure from individual congressmen and the State Department, this policy was lifted in stages, and by September 1945 the entire policy was completely dropped. As one historian noted, "There was [now] a new Watch on the Rhine—by handholding American GIs and German girls taking advantage of the relaxed restrictions on fraternization." Marriages between white US soldiers and German women were not permitted, however, until 1946. In the two interviews that follow, one is essentially the story of how one couple, an American GI and a young German woman, dealt with Army policies toward fraternization. The other describes in detail the activities a member of the Army of Occupation at the local level. [1]

Notes

1. Note: See Earl F. Ziemke, *The US Army in the Occupation of Germany, 1944-1946* (Washington: US Dept. of Defense, Dept of the Army, Center of Military History, 1975), 1, 320-325; quote on p. 325. See also John Willoughby, *Remaking the Conquering Heroes: The Postwar American Occupation of Germany* (New York: Palgrave-St. Martin's Press, 2001); and Petra Goedde, *GIs and Germans: Culture, Gender, and Foreign Relations, 1945-1949* (New Haven: Yale Univ. Press, 2003).

Figure 21. TSgt. Gerald "Jerry" Johns

Figure 22. Irmgard "Jackie" Stieger

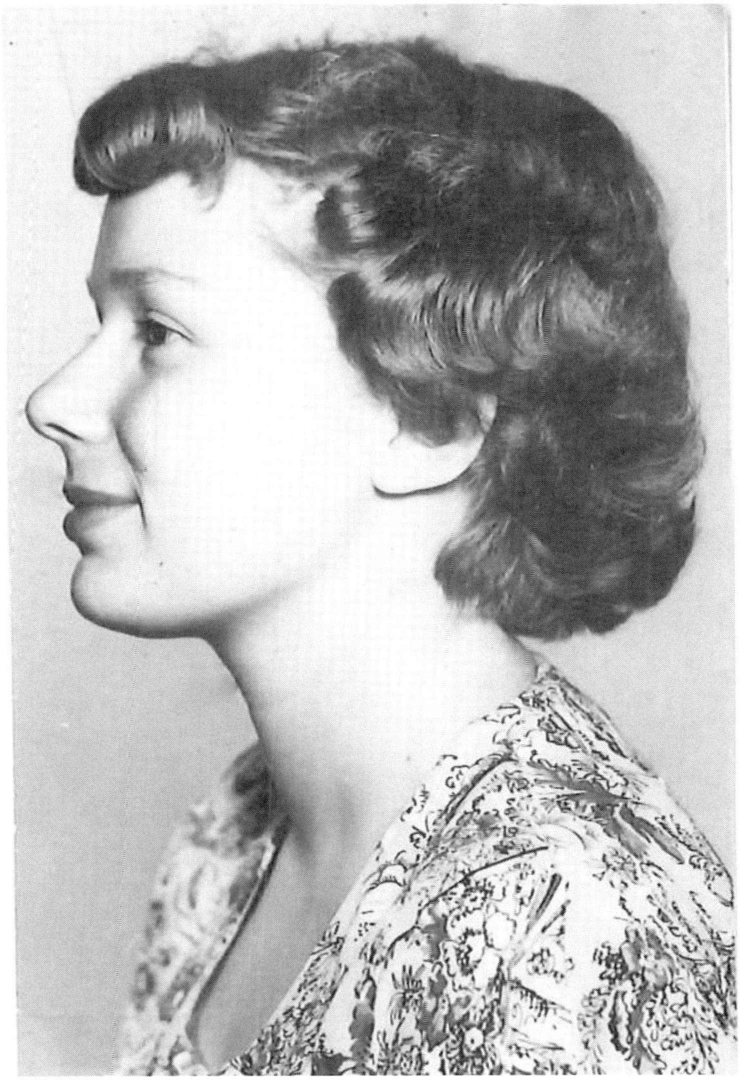

Chapter 21

TSgt. Gerald "Jerry" Johns and Irmgard "Jackie" Stieger-Johns

Supreme Headquarters Allied Expeditionary Force (SHAEF) US Forces European Theater (USFET)

Born on 20 March 1925, Gerald Jerry Johns was drafted just a few days following his high school graduation in 1943. He spent most of his military career in Europe as head of the officers' mess for SHAEF and later, after the conclusion of the war, in the same position for USFET (US Forces European Theater). When the officers' mess moved from Frankfurt to Kronberg Castle, in Hesse, Germany, Jerry met the sixteen-year-old Irmgard Steiger, who came from the nearby farming village of Schönberg-in-Taunus. Kronberg Castle had formerly been the residence of the German imperial family. At the time they met, she was a civilian waitress at the castle. They courted during the remainder of Jerry's stay in Germany. Before leaving for the United States, he proposed to Irmgard ("Jackie") and after receiving her parents' consent, he was able to wade his way through the Army's red tape concerning war brides and get permission to bring her to the States. On 2 September 1947, she and Jerry married. He worked for the US Postal Service for thirty-one years, retiring in 1982, while she was employed by the John Wright Company, a subsidiary of the Riverside Foundry, in Wrightsville for forty-six years. They made their home in the town and had two children. Jerry died on 9 September 2007, while "Jackie" still lives at their family residence in Wrightsville.[1]

With the build-up for D-Day already under way, the US Army needed manpower to fill the new divisions then being formed. As a member of the Wrightsville High School Class of 1943, Jerry was drafted almost immediately after graduation:

"I graduated from Wrightsville High on May 28, 1943, and on June 6, 1943, I was sitting down at Ft. Meade, Maryland. It took me just that long to get out of school and into the Army. I had about a week off, I think, and then I went into the service. I took infantry basic training at Camp Croft, South Carolina, and was there until November 2, 1943. Basic training was thirteen weeks, but we had extended maneuvers up in the Tennessee Valley and then at Myrtle Beach, South Carolina, on LCI [Landing Craft, Infantry] training. Obviously, we were in training for the cross-channel invasion of France.

"From Myrtle Beach, I reported to Camp Shanks, New York. At this time I was assigned to K Company, 116th Infantry, 29th Division. On December 26, 1943, I left for overseas on the *Isle de France*, which had been one of the premier luxury liners of that day. There were 26,000 troops aboard that ship, so it was crowded. This was a fast ship, and we went without any escort. By this time, they had cleared out most of the German submarines. It took us just four days to cross the Atlantic, and we landed at the Firth of Clyde in Scotland on December 31.

After his arrival in Scotland, for no particular reason, Jerry was pulled out of the ranks and put in charge of an officers' mess. From that time forward, he was no longer an infantryman:

"By the time we got to Scotland, they were already building up for the invasion of France. Shortly after our arrival, they lined up our company one morning, and they pulled out some guys: 'You, you, you, and you! Fall out! Pack up! You're leaving!' We left there and went to Phoebe Farms in England. That was the location of Gen. Eisenhower's headquarters for SHAEF [Supreme Headquarters Allied Expeditionary Force]. From there we went into London, Kingston, Bushy Park. That was to be the permanent headquarters for SHAEF. Bushy Park was outside Kingston, which was a suburb of London. When I arrived, I was put in charge of the officers' mess, D Mess. Really, the only experience that I had had with messes was soda-jerking while I was going to high school. They said, 'You take care of this.' I was eighteen years old, and I was given that responsibility. We fed 630 officers a day, three meals a day. My primary job was to see that the food was there, to see that they were served, to see that everything ran smoothly. I supervised about eighteen men, all of the GIs, and I was just a Pfc at that time. Initially, all this took place at Bushy Park. But then we left there. We closed that mess, and I went down to Portsmouth prior to the invasion. This was in the middle of or late April 1944.

In supervising the officers' mess at Portsmouth, Jerry had first-hand observations of some of the leading military figures as well as some big-name entertainers who came through with the USO troupes:

"Oh, my! We served all of them! We served just about all the main officers of SHAEF. We served 'Ike' [Eisenhower], Gen. George Patton, Gen. Omar Bradley, Air Mshl. Sir Arthur Tedder. They had various troupes coming through, and they all ate at our mess. I met Jack Benny and Paulette Goddard. I met Glenn Miller. He came three or four times to our mess. Glenn Miller was an aloof person. He always seemed to have things on his mind, but he was still congenial. He was not outgoing, but he was nice.

"For the first three months I was there, I didn't have any time off at all. We were running the mess from 4:00 in the morning until 11:00 at night, seven days a week. Then I finally got an assistant and got some time off. My worst problem in running this mess was dealing with the personnel under me. I had sergeants and staff sergeants under me, and they balked at everything I did because I was just an eighteen-year-old. I had more problems with this than with anything else. Then after a while, it smoothed out and ran smoothly.

While at Portsmouth, which was one of the major ports for the build-up for D-Day, Jerry observed the preparations under way for that historic event:

"When we went down to Portsmouth, the build-up in that area for the Normandy invasion was **tremendous. Everywhere** you looked, **anywhere** you went, men and material were all ready to go. You couldn't even walk across the street without seeing a vehicle or something else stacked up there, supplies ready to go. This occurred all over the place. Every little nook and corner cranny was jam-packed full, plus they had camouflage nets over the tops of the supplies and equipment. Down to the south, around the bend from Portsmouth, they had a falsified area built up to allow the Germans to think we were going to Pas de Calais. That was all out there.

"They had a dummy area all fixed up, and that wasn't camouflaged. That was out in the open, but there wasn't anything in there other than dummy equipment.[2]

"The troops that I met there were anxious to get on with the invasion and get it started. Some of them had reservations, of course, but for the most part they were anxious to get out of Portsmouth and go. They were tired of training and tired of just hanging around. They wanted to go and get it done. Fortunately for me I wasn't in the 29th Division anymore. When I went to Phoebe Farms, I left the 29th Division because I was assigned to SHAEF at that time. I was in Headquarters Command in SHAEF. The 29th along with the 1st Infantry Division was to lead the assault on Utah Beach. [3]

After the establishment of the Normandy beachhead and the push inland, Jerry closed down the officers' mess in England and crossed over into France to establish another officers' mess for SHEAF:

"At the end of July 1944, we went across the English Channel. SHAEF had moved across to Jullouville, France, and that's where they set up their first headquarters. I left Portsmouth and went back to London to close out the mess there. I was responsible for everything in that mess being closed. I signed it over to the British, got on a Piper Cub, and flew across the English Channel to Jullouville. From there, when Paris fell in late August, we went into Versailles. SHAEF set up headquarters in Versailles in late August. I was in Versailles maybe a month or five or six weeks at the most, and in early September we moved into Paris. Then I was in Paris maybe four or five months. I was given the Scribe Hotel, which was right across from the Lido Club. The Scribe Hotel was three-quarters of a block long, and big, and I had the whole hotel. Now, I not only had it for the officers' mess, but I also had a hotel to run. There wasn't anything touched in Paris by the war. It had been declared an open city, and nothing was touched.[4] This was a forward area, however, and we were so busy that we didn't have time to enjoy it. We got up, went to work, came home, went to bed; got up, came home, went to bed. This was the routine seven days a week. There were no days off, and that didn't ease up until we got well into Germany.

At the conclusion of the war in Europe, Jerry remained as part of the US Army of Occupation where he was now assigned to USFET [US Forces European Theater]. Upon entering Germany, Jerry was struck by all the devastation he saw, especially in Frankfurt, and the suffering of the German people, who were on the brink of starvation:

"What I did notice in Frankfurt was all the damage from the Allied bombing. It was really devastated. Down near the train station, everything in that area was leveled. The docks and Rhein-Main [now Frankfurt] Airport were also destroyed. In fact, the Army was working twenty-four hours a day on the Rhein-Main Airport to get it open and functioning again. At first the trains didn't run, but they finally got them back into service. Most of this work was done by German civilians under American supervision.

"There were, of course, a portion of the civilian population that was bitter because of the war damage, but for the most part I truly believe that most of the civilians were glad it was over. They were still under stringent orders and rules, but now they didn't have to be worried about being killed from a bomb or a bullet. The Germans had no food, no nothing, until we came in. The Americans set up a program so that nobody would go hungry, but this took time. That's one thing that helped to turn around the attitudes of the German people: 'Well, the Americans are not so bad after all.' But in the beginning of the occupation, it was bad. They didn't have potatoes; they didn't have anything. They were eating the seed potatoes that were supposed to be put in the fields, when they could get them. The longer the Americans were there, the more pleasant our relationship with the Germans became, but both sides were still very distant and proper.

"During this time the black market was booming! It was booming! When we were in downtown Frankfurt, we were right next door to the CID [US Army Criminal Investigation Division], and they'd come out and bust up one black market setup after another. As soon as they would close one, though—'ZIP'—another one would open up again. It was terrible! The most prized items were food, cigarettes, and clothing. Food was first, clothing was second, and then cigarettes. We came in, and when they finally got food distribution set up, we gave them cornmeal. Corn to Germans is maize, and these people had never eaten any of that.

They had wheat, barley, oats and so forth, but they never ate corn, which they considered animal food. At first they wouldn't touch corn.

"When we first went into Germany, German POWs, who had been captured locally, worked for us, but later they pulled out all the POWs. Then they screened and brought in German civilians. When they closed the mess at the Annex in Frankfurt, I went down to the Park Hotel, which was catty-cornered from the Bahnhof, the train station. All German civilians who sought employment with us were first interviewed by a nonpartisan board, which later on, before I moved from Frankfurt, I became a part of. They came in, and you took their papers. Basically, it was a matter of determining if they had an affiliation with the Nazi party. They were party members if they had a party card. A lot of Germans did not belong to the Nazi party, but they had supported it. They did not belong because you had to pay dues to get into it, just like our clubs around here. When they came in, the first thing you asked was: 'Where is your card?' We had a list—lists from courthouses, from captured Nazi documents, and so forth. Of course the Germans kept **very** good records on every little thing—every little thing—and you looked down to see if their name was on that list. If we hired them, they were given food ration stamps and so forth. Every meal that they ate with us, you peeled off the ration stamp. There was no stealing because they were searched coming and going so that no food would be missing. These people were willing and able and were very hard workers because these were highly sought positions. At the Park Hotel, I had a full staff of German civilians—beautiful people. I had Karl Fischer, who had been the chef for Hermann Goering. Karl had been a staff sergeant in the *Luftwaffe*, but had been discharged when he came to us. He was a chef, a beautiful person and a beautiful man. I let him handle the kitchen, and I handled the rest of the hotel. As a result, we had a smooth-running operation.

Jerry's last and most eventful assignment was his move to establish an officers' mess at Kronberg Castle. It was there that he met his future wife, Irmgard Stieger.

"I left the Park Hotel in Frankfurt 'under duress' and eventually ended up at Kronberg Castle. My mess officer was Lt. Virginia Sue Speidel, and she and I had been together most of the time in Europe. She was assigned to establish an officers' mess at Kronberg Castle. Lt. Speidel left first, and then she called me to join her. She said, 'Get ready to come out!' I said, 'I'm not leaving Frankfurt because I like Frankfurt!' I had a suite of rooms on the fifth story of the Park Hotel. I had my own private bath; I had everything. I did not want to leave this setup. She responded, 'I'm not asking you! I'm telling you! Get ready to get out!' Well, two weeks went by, and I didn't join her. Finally, two MPs pulled up with a Jeep and a trailer, and they said, 'Get your ass in this vehicle!' I said, 'I've got to get my stuff!' They said, 'We'll get it for you!' God! Did they ever clear my rooms!

"All right, fine, I'm now out at Kronberg Castle, which at that time was occupied by the Headquarters Command, USFET. It was a showplace located in the foothills about six miles outside Frankfurt. The estate consisted of about 250 acres, and the castle, which was built around 1888 or 1892, was formerly the summer home of the widow of Emperor Frederick III of Germany. The castle and the surrounding grounds were beautiful. By the time I got there, Kronberg Castle had become an exclusive country club for Allied officers.

"I had a bad attitude at first. Inside, I was angry, mad, because I didn't want to be there, but I couldn't do anything about it. I had to be there. Anyway, since I was the supervisor of the mess, the first night I was on duty, I lined up the waitresses right before they undertook their responsibilities. I always did this with the waitresses. So, I lined them up and checked them out to see if their uniforms were proper and so forth. Then we went in and opened the meal. When I walked in, there she was [Irmgard "Jackie" Stieger], ladling the soup. One person carried the tureen, and another one had the ladle. She looked up and saw me, and I must have frightened her because she spilled chicken noodle soup all over this poor captain's tunic. He jumped up and screamed. I wasn't even looking at her, but when I saw what happened, I said 'Oh, my God!'

Irmgard then gave her version of what happened and her first impressions of Jerry:

"When I looked up, he stood there, and he looked so mean that he made me nervous. Gerald scared me so badly! He could look very mean, so I got nervous. Instead of putting the soup in this officer's bowl, I missed the bowl and poured the soup all over him. He had noodles hanging everywhere! Right after I spilled the soup on the officer's uniform, Gerald called me into his office. He gave me a warning and put me on kitchen duty. I had to wash dishes and polish things. Then I went back to work, and shortly afterwards I tripped over a big, thick rug when I was carrying a tray, and peas spilled all over the dining room. So, I was put in the kitchen again. I was never meant to be a waitress. Anyway, I didn't like Gerald at that time.

Irmgard Stieger's story before her initial encounter with Jerry provides a glimpse of life inside Germany during the Nazi era:

"I was born in Schönberg, Germany, in 1928. It was a small village near other little villages. All these little villages are now incorporated into Kronberg. It was a little village with farmers, surrounded by farms. It had a school that only went to the eighth grade. When I finished, my parents sent me to business school in Frankfurt, which was about twenty miles away. Going to business school didn't mean you had to go to high school first. So, after eighth grade, I went to business school in Frankfurt. That was when the war was going on.

"Being born in 1928, I was about five years old when Hitler came to power. I was very young. Although I was just a little girl, I remember being taken into the BDM, which is like the Brownies—*Bund Deutscher Mädel [League of German Girls].* This is what is sometimes called the Hitler Youth. This was not a voluntary thing. I had to do this. When you were ten years old, you had to join. I should mention, though, that you could not join this organization if you had any other kind of blood except German. They researched your background, and you had to be 100 percent German or you could not join. I was taken in on Adolf Hitler's fiftieth birthday. I've never forgotten that. He was fifty when I became a member. We had to do things for soldiers at the front. They taught us how to knit, to make stockings, and to sort clothing that was going to the front. We also had to learn all about Hitler—from his birth and what all he did. We always had a lot of parades—a lot of parades. We had to learn how to march and how to sing the songs and make sure we all marched in step. My father was in favor of my joining, but he never joined the Nazi party.

"My father was an insurance agent. Although he never joined the Nazi party, he seemed to favor the Nazis. He may have felt that to do so was good for his business. When they had torchlight parades and marched through town, my father would stand out there, and he'd yell, '*Heil Hitler!*' The Nazis thought he was a **wonderful** man because he was cheering and '*heiling.*' But he was a very 'tight' [parsimonious] man, so he didn't want to pay the dues. On the other hand, my mother was very much against the Nazis.

"I remember that one time Adolf Hitler was coming to Frankfurt. I was ten years old, and we little ones had to stand in front of the crowd. We were given baskets with flower petals, and whenever he got out of his vehicle and walked along the line of people, we had to throw these petals. Then he would come along and shake our hand. When he shook my hand, I thought, 'I will never wash that hand again!' I thought that was so wonderful. Ha! My God! I was right there! For the youth, Hitler had a great deal of charisma.

"There was a Nazi apparatus in our village because there were fanatics there, like our *burgermeister*. He had to be a Nazi in order to be our *burgermeister*. In our village we had two Jewish families. One had a shoe store, and they were very nice people. Then there came a time when something happened, when they started to go after the Jews. The SS came.

They forced these people out of their homes, and then they ransacked their homes and then burned them. We thought that was terrible, but they still did it. Since our village was surrounded by woods, the Jews fled to the woods. The SS hunted those people everywhere, but I don't think they ever caught them. These Jews were nice people, and they had friends. They must have found shelter with somebody, and to our knowledge they did escape, at least at that time. What they did to Jews, we never knew. That was strictly a secret. We knew there were concentration camps, and even German people would be incarcerated there. But what they did in there, we never knew.

"During the war, Frankfurt was bombed big time by the Allies, but our little village was spared because it was in a valley between mountains. We could see the waves and waves and waves of airplanes coming across. In the daytime it was the Americans, and at nighttime it was the English. Our windows would rattle in my village when the planes came over the top of it because there were so many planes. We could look out our windows and watch the antiaircraft guns shooting. I remember my father and me standing at the window and watching. First, they had these searchlights go up in the sky, and when plane got in the middle of the beam, the guns would shoot. We would be cheering for them to shoot that thing down: 'Fire a little closer! Fire a little closer!' Sometimes a stray piece of shrapnel would hit a roof.

"While I was at business school in Frankfurt, the sirens would go off, and right away we had to go down into the basement. In the beginning it wasn't too bad, but when the Americans really started bombing, then they built air raid bunkers. We then had to leave school and go in this bunker with all the other civilians. The whole neighborhood had to go in there because these bunkers were supposed to be bombproof. However, one time, my last day of school, we had to go in the bunker, and it took a direct hit. The fact that I was down in the basement of that thing probably saved my life, but I was trapped there for three days and two nights.

Like most families in postwar Germany, the Stiegers had to cope with deprivations of all kinds, especially food:

"We listened to the war news on the radio. We knew that the Allied forces were in France, but we were always told lies. They said that the Americans would never cross the Rhine River, but then one night as we lay in bed, we heard the Germans blow up those bridges to prevent the Americans from coming across. Before we knew it, the Americans were rolling in with tanks. Then we knew the war was over. We were glad, though, that it was the Americans who were coming and not the Russians. Oh, my gosh! Not the Russians!

"I remember my first contact with the Americans. My mother had sent me to the next village because we didn't have a butcher shop in our village. She said, 'You'd better go and get us our meat and bread ration because the Americans might cross the Rhine.' I took my bicycle and went to Oberherstadt, which was the next little town, and the tanks were rolling in. I turned around on my bike and went home. I never peddled so fast! I yelled, 'The Americans are coming! The Americans are coming! Get in the cellar!'

"At this time there was panic in our house. You see, I had a German military-type helmet because I had been taken into the fire company. All the men were gone, so anybody who could take their place got a regular German military-type helmet. My mother also cut up and buried my Hitler Youth uniform. When the American soldiers rolled into our village, they went house to house with bayonets fixed. They even searched down in the cellars. My mother tried to destroy the helmet by hitting it with an ax, but she was only able to dent it. Then one of the soldiers found it and asked my mother where the soldier was who belonged to that helmet. My mother pointed to me! They still thought there was a soldier in the house, so they took their bayonets and went through our feather beds and everything.

"This was my first contact with American soldiers, and I was scared to death! Otherwise, we remained inside and tried to stay out of sight as best we could. Then the Americans took over the town hall, and all citizens had to go there for an interview to see who was a Nazi and who wasn't a Nazi. We had to get new identification cards. Everybody had to have one. I did have to tell them about my membership in the Hitler Youth when I got my new identification card. Then they knew that I had belonged to it, but it wasn't held against me. That wasn't being a Nazi; that was just like the Girl Scouts. We didn't have anything to do with political stuff. They took my picture and put it on the new card.

"We lost the war, and order had to be reestablished. At first when the soldiers came, it was chaos. Then we were at the mercy of the local farmers. They would give you food only for something in return. I would go to a farm and milk cows so that I would get a quart of milk in return. I worked in the fields picking strawberries. My father was disabled, so he couldn't do anything. My mother took care of him, so I was the one who worked.

"After the war was over, the food situation got even worse. That was when we almost starved because the Americans gave us the impression that we had to suffer a little bit. At first the Americans seemed to be interested only in who the good guys were and who the bad guys were. Then we received new ration cards, and although the food ration wasn't much, we could live on it. One thing the Americans did was to send us corn, something that we had never eaten before. Corn in German means wheat, barley, anything to make bread. For us, corn was animal food, so I had never, ever had corn to eat before. The rationing of food was strictly enforced. We didn't get a whole lot of food, but it was enough to survive on.

In order to establish a better life for her parents and herself, Irmgard decided to apply for a job in the officers' mess at nearby Kronberg Castle:

"I couldn't go back to school because all the books had to be changed and purged of Nazi propaganda. They were all Nazi books. Everything in them had to do with Hitler, so there had to be new books printed. In the meantime, they gave us a choice. Since we weren't going to school, we had to either work on a farm or go to work for the Americans. Well, I volunteered to work for the Americans because I thought, 'I can get some food.' My mother and father were reluctant at first to give their consent because I was only sixteen years old. I had heard that they were hiring waitresses over at Kronberg Castle, but because of my age I could only work in the afternoon, serving coffee and tea and stuff like that. That was when my parents agreed to let me go there. I also think that they believed that if I worked for the Americans I could bring some food home. It was just a small walk—about fifteen minutes—from our village. I used to love to ride horses, so I had gone over there to ride because they had a stable. So, I was very, very familiar with the castle.

"So, I went to see the caretaker, who was also the royal family's lawyer. He was an old gentleman who was engaged by the Americans to be in charge of the castle. I said to him, 'I want to go back to school, but in the meantime I must find a job.' He asked, 'Do you have your family's permission? At your age you can only serve at breakfast and at tea time.' So, I went back to my parents and got them to sign a permission slip, and then I went back to the castle to see him. He said, 'You can start tomorrow.' They needed people to work at the castle, and they particularly needed people from the surrounding area, people they could trust.

"After I started working there, I took things home although we were not allowed to take anything. When guests would leave, we'd clean the tables. If there were butter balls and things left, I would take them home. Sometimes I'd smuggle my mother in and give her coffee because my parents could not get any coffee. I'd give her coffee and pastries. The Americans would throw away food, anyway, and I couldn't understand that, so I smuggled things out. If we were caught, the penalty was severe. We would be automatically suspended from work, and all our ration and identity cards would be taken. Nothing was worse than to lose your identity card and your ration card.

Being among the first of the locals to be hired, Irmgard worked at Kronberg Castle for almost a year before Jerry was assigned there. During that year she had first-hand knowledge of the theft of jewelry and other ancestral property hidden there by Prince Wolfgang von Hesse-Kassel, the owner of the castle:[5]

"The Americans sent out Capt. Kathleen Nash to operate the castle as an officers' club, and she is the person who stole the crown jewels. She had made me her private maid, and then I had to lay out her uniform in the morning. I had to serve her personally. If she wanted something in her room, I would bring it up to her. I saw these jewels in Capt. Nash's room, but I didn't pay much attention to them. I thought they were costume jewelry, or I would have wondered where she got all that stuff. It was all there. She had a boyfriend then, Col. Jack Durant. Capt. Nash was transferred to Cogen Haus, which was an officers' club for colonels and up, and she took me with her. I didn't like it there, so I quit her and went back to the castle. Shortly afterwards, she went back to the United States. Then I was in my room much later when all hell broke loose. There were MPs everywhere, and they even searched my room. I was a prime suspect, I guess, since I was her maid.

By the time Jerry arrived at Kronberg Castle, the theft of the Hesse property had been discovered, and what follows are his remembrances of what then occurred:

"Lt. Sue Speidel and I were at Kronberg Castle when the theft was uncovered. What happened was that Sophie, one of the daughters of the Landgräfin von Hessen, was going to be married to the king of Greece. She sent a letter—I was there when this letter arrived—to Sue, the commanding officer of Kronberg Castle, requesting that she be allowed to come in and get a string of pearls to wear for her wedding. They were her grandmother's, who was the former Princess Royal of England,

Queen Victoria's daughter. Sue gave permission, but when they went and looked for the box, they saw nothing but a hole. Then all hell broke loose. Every room in the place was searched. **Everybody's** quarters were searched. They couldn't find the jewels, so they then deducted that they had been stolen by Capt. Nash. She was back in the States and completely out of the service by the time all this got started. Nash was arrested, tried, and sentenced to prison. So were Durant and Watson.

Strange things seemed to happen to young Irmgard while working at Kronberg Castle besides the theft of the crown jewels and spilling soup and peas. On one occasion while horseback riding, she almost ran over Gen. Eisenhower:

"During the war the SS occupied Kronberg Castle, and they had a stable there. They occupied the stable, and I took riding lessons from them. I was still going to school at the time. My instructor was a SS officer. Boy! There was no socializing with him! He was strictly all-business, so you **never** socialized or talked about anything other than business. The officers in the *Wehrmacht* and the SS observed class distinctions. I was amazed by the Americans because they were down to earth. They were congenial, where the German officers were not. This is all my way of telling about my encounter with Gen. Eisenhower.

"Poor Eisenhower! He might never have been President! At the castle we had fifty-two riding horses, and Eisenhower would usually take a daily ride. Because I was a good rider, I used to take officers' children out riding. We were close to lots of woods, and we would ride through the woods. When we were ready to come back, the horses would sense the stables and go faster. The girl I was with was ready to ride faster, so I said, 'Let's race home!' There was a big gate to go through, and to go into the stable there is an archway into the courtyard of the stable.

"We were coming in, and I was in front of her. There was an officer standing there, just watching. Then MPs came running from everywhere, yelling, 'Stop! Stop! Stop!' It was Eisenhower, who was standing there, and I almost rode him down. But he didn't make any effort to get out of the way. The MPs were going to punish me in some way, but Eisenhower said, 'That's all right. That's okay. She did no harm. No one can stop a horse when its mind is set on getting home fast.' He was so friendly, not like our German officers. He made a big impression by walking and grooming his own horse.

At Kronberg Castle, Jerry also had occasional contacts with Gen. Eisenhower, but never as traumatic as Irmgard's:

"At the time that I arrived at the castle, the pressure was off for Eisenhower, and he had his deputies do most of the legwork. He was an avid rider, so he would ride daily. Then he'd come in, have tea, and then go back to whatever he was doing. This was an almost daily ritual. The contacts I had with Eisenhower were very nice—very, very nice. All the pressure was off of him, so he was amiable all the way through.

After Jerry adjusted to his new position at Kronberg Castle, his anger subsided, and he began to take notice of Irmgard. Here they describe their courtship and the events leading up to their marriage:

"As I mentioned before, my attitude, when I went out there, was that I did not want to go because I had everything I wanted in Frankfurt. I came out to the castle, and inside I was angry. But I couldn't do anything about it because I was ordered there, so I made the best of it. That attitude lasted for about a month, but then it started to change. I got to know more German civilians out there at the castle than I had at Frankfurt. At that time in Frankfurt, the Army still had that non-fraternization ban going, so you could not be seen anywhere with civilians. We could not be seen together on the streets. Then out at the castle regulations were lax because they didn't have anybody patrolling the streets like they did in Frankfurt. At Kronberg I got to know the German people. When you'd go into town, you'd see that they were just ordinary people like we were.[6]

"Gerald would arrange parties in the castle for the people who worked there, with music and dancing and everything. When they had these personnel parties, Gerald and I would dance together. He was a **great** dancer, and I **loved** to dance. We were denied so much during all those years that I was growing up, because of the war, so it was wonderful to hear this Glenn Miller music. Gerald brought in American records. Then there was a local place where the personnel from the castle went, and we'd dance there, too. So, that's how we got together. Gerald was a wonderful dancer, and that's how we fell in love. It was through music and dancing that we got together.

During their courtship, the couple occasionally ran into uncomfortable situations due to the US Army's ban on fraternization with German civilians. Jerry remembered on such occasion at an officers' club in Frankfurt:

"I had taken her out one night to an officers' nightclub in Frankfurt. To do this, I had to ditch my Army uniform with the sergeant's stripes and get another jacket. So, I had on a civilian jacket. She and I walked in and sat down facing one another at a table, and we got up and danced once. I came back, and I felt a tap on my shoulder. I looked around, and here is Col. Woodward. He said, 'Sergeant, I don't know what you're doing here, but you take that German and mosey out of here.' I said, 'Yes, Sir.' Obviously, 'Jackie' was not supposed to be in there, and neither was I since this was an officers' nightclub. We got in only because I knew the sergeant who was running the club. Anyway, we walked out and went back of the stage and looked around. Col. Woodward got up and left the club, so we came right back out and started dancing again. We spent the night there dancing in that nightclub. That affair brought us closer together. We were both young and devilish. But that was just one incident.

Jerry's military duty in Germany was winding down when he decided to propose to Irmgard. His first hurdle was receiving her parents' permission, and the second was getting around the Army's ban on such marriages in Germany. What follows is Irmgard's account of the engagement:

"We couldn't get married in Germany before he left for the States in 1946, but before leaving he came to my family's home and made his proposal to my mother and father. They couldn't believe it at first that I was even dating an American serviceman, but he came down and wanted to propose. Gerald didn't speak very good German. My father spoke some English, but my mother didn't speak any English, none at all. At this point we had been dating for about eight months.

"Well, he comes in, and he brings two bottles of champagne. Gerald had been to their home before, and my father liked him. He used to drop me off in the Jeep when I was done working. But my mother was very much worried about this whole situation. Anyway, Gerald came in, and we sat around the dining room table. He poured us a drink of champagne, and then he started proposing. He said it in broken German, and what he said was totally wrong. But he said, 'I am going home, and I want to marry your daughter in the near future.' My father exclaimed, 'Ha! How will you do this?' There was no air mail, and there was a lot of paperwork involved. Gerald said that he would take good care of me, but my mother said to my father, 'Just wait until he is where the pepper grows. She'll forget all about him.' Gerald didn't understand, so he said, '*Ja! Ja*!' Pepper doesn't grow in Germany, and what she meant was that it grows far, far away. She meant, 'Wait until he is far, far away. She'll forget all about him.' That's what she was wishing for. So, my family didn't take his proposal with a whole lot of enthusiasm, but my father finally said, 'All right.' That's when my mother jumped in with her comments about the peppers, but my father's consent was all we really needed.

After returning to Wrightsville, Jerry broke the news to his parents, who voiced no objections to him marrying a German girl:

"I did not tell my parents that I hoped to marry a German girl until I came back to Wrightsville. My paternal grandfather came from Baden-Baden, Germany, and all my aunts and uncles spoke German, which 'Jackie' found out later when she attended a family reunion. Actually, I had hinted about getting married in letters before I came home. When I did come home, I showed my mother pictures and said, 'Now, there she is. She's coming over here.' My mother was wonderful. So, neither of my parents objected to my marrying 'Jackie.'

Irmgard also remembered the positive reception she received from Jerry's parents:

"His mother wrote a wonderful letter to my parents. She told them not to worry, that I would be coming to a nice community and that they would do everything in their power to make the transition from one country to another easy for me. She told my parents that the culture here was very similar to German culture, which was certainly true in Gerald's family. As I said, my father could read enough English to translate, so this letter was the turning point for my parents.

"Even if my parents had not given their approval, I would have signed the papers myself. I would have come to Wrightsville no matter what. I told them, 'Don't worry about me. As long as I am healthy, I can work. If it doesn't work out, I can come back to Germany.' But I was never worried about that. I still have those papers I had to sign.

The next hurdle for the young couple was to obtain permission from the US government for Irmgard to enter this country. On 29 June 1946, Congress passed the GI Fiancées Act, sometimes dubbed the "Sweethearts Law." It amended the War Brides Act of 2 December 1945 to facilitate the admission to the US of fiancées of members of the American armed services. At first the "Sweethearts Law" did not include German fiancées, but that restriction was changed in January 1947. Jerry remembered the bureaucratic red tape that had to be completed before Irmgard's admission to this country:[7]

"You cannot imagine the red tape! We couldn't get married in Germany because of the Army's restrictions. They didn't allow it. After she came here, we had to go through a lot to satisfy the US government. That was the first hurdle. Then there was the judicial district to be dealt with. Then there were consenting letters from my parents, from her parents, from the preacher who was going to marry us—**everything**—

and they had all those papers to be completed. We had originally planned to be married in the Locust Street Methodist Church in Wrightsville. At the last minute, they came in and said, 'Hold it! You can't! You don't have any documents from York County!' I called up and said, 'What does the County of York have to do with this, if it satisfied the state and the United States Government?' They said, 'It must be on the record.' She was only eighteen at the time, and she had just two days left on her thirty-day visa. So, we packed up and went down to Maryland and got married on September 2, 1947.

After marrying Jerry, "Jackie" encountered few problems in adapting to her new country as the residents of Wrightsville welcomed and accepted her. Jerry and "Jackie" (the nickname she is known by in Wrightsville) made their permanent residence in Wrightsville and raised a son and a daughter there. He retired in 1982 after thirty-one years with the US Postal Service, and she retired in 1995 having worked forty-six years as a decorator for the John Wright Company, a subsidiary of Riverside Foundry (later Donsco). Jerry died on 9 September 2007. Jackie still resides in the original home that she and Jerry bought.

Notes

1. Gerald and Irmgard Johns, interview by the author, transcript, OH1200, 11 August 1997, Oral History Collection, University Archives, University of North Texas, Denton, TX.

2. Note: To deceive the Germans, an entirely fictitious 1st US Army Group (FUSAG) under the command of Gen. Leslie J. McNair and Gen. George S. Patton was positioned in southeastern England. It was organized to create in the minds of German agents the idea that the main invasion was to occur at Pas de Calais. The attempts at deception included fake radio traffic, partially camouflaged dummy landing craft in the ports of Ramsgate, Dover, and Hastings, fields full of papier-mâché and rubber tanks, and increased train traffic in the area. See Stephen E. Ambrose, *D-Day June 6, 1944: The Climatic Battle of World War II*(New York: Simon & Schuster, 1994), 82.

3. Note: Johns's original regiment, the 116th Infantry, was to be the first assault wave to land at Utah Beach at 6:13 AM on 6 June 1944. See Ibid., 156-157.

4. Note: Actually, Adolph Hitler had ordered that Paris be burned, but the German military commander of the city refused to heed the order.

5. During the Allied air raids on Frankfurt in October 1944, the Hesse family, led by Prince Wolfgang of Hesse-Kassel, decided to hide ancestral and personal property at Kronberg Castle, the family residence. He created an inventory for all this property, which belonged to Prince Richard and his wife, Prince Christoph and his wife, Prince Wolfgang and his wife, as well as the jewels and other property belonging to Princess Margarethe, the dowager of Landgrave of Hesse. The jewels of the House of Hesse were placed in a large box and buried in the basement of the castle. The hole was then covered with concrete.

In April 1945 American forces occupied Kronberg Castle and requisitioned it for use as an officers' club. Then the castle was turned over to the Mess Section, Headquarters Command, USFET. Capt. Kathleen Nash was appointed Mess Section representative, so she was essentially in charge of the castle from June 1945 until 1 February 1946. In November 1945, while exploring the castle, Capt. Nash, Maj. David Watson, and Col. Jack Durant, Nash's lover, discovered the patch of fresh concrete in the cellar. They broke through the concrete and found zinc-lined boxes full of jewels. Nash then secreted the gems to her suite where she laid them out on the floor. The plunder included loose gemstones, pieces of jewelry, silver, tableware, and books, later appraised at a total value of $2.5 million. Nash and Durant next removed the gems from their original settings and smuggled them and the other loose gems back to the United States.

Meanwhile, members of the Hesse family were informed of the discovery of the hiding place, but when the family and their representatives contacted Capt. Nash on several occasions to seek the return of their property, she informed them that the items would be returned once the castle was vacated. In late 1945, Nash, Durant, and Watson smuggled the gems into the United States, but when they tried to fence them, military authorities arrested them. In the meantime, Nash and Durant had married in an attempt to prevent her from testifying against her husband. Nevertheless, the three were tried and sentenced to prison. See Kenneth D. Alford, *Nazi Plunder: The Great Treasure Stories of World War II*(New York: Da Capo Press, 1991), 147-155.

6. For an excellent description of the breakdown of the American non-fraternization policy, see Petra Goedde, *GIs and Germans: Culture, Gender, and Foreign Relations, 1945-1949*(New Haven: Yale Univ. Press, 2003), 42-79.

7. See Jane Mersky Leder, *Thanks for the Memories: Love, Sex, and World War II* (Westport, CT: Praeger Publishers, 2006), 125.

Figure 23. Pvt. William "Bill" Crumbling

CHAPTER 22

PVT. WILLIAM "BILL" CRUMBLING

A TROOP, 25TH MECHANIZED CAVALRY, CONSTABULARY

Born in Wrightsville on 23 September 1927, William Bill Crumbling was the youngest of William and Grace Crumbling's eight children. There were seven boys and one girl in the family. While working at Susquehanna Casting, he joined the US Army on 1 December 1945. After an abbreviated basic training, he shipped out for Germany as part of the Army of Occupation. Most of Bill's time in Germany was spent around Regensburg and the surrounding rural communities in the state of Bavaria. The basic assignment of his unit was to send out patrols for extended periods show an American presence to the German civilian population and to demonstrate who was in charge of the occupation. His story covers several examples of the American occupation as seen through the eyes of an eighteen-year-old at the time. After being mustered out of the Army, Bill returned to civilian life where he worked as a long distance truck driver for many years. He currently lives with his wife in rural York County just a few miles outside Wrightsville.[1]

Bill's decision to join the Army was based on his dislike of foundry work and a thirst for adventure as a soldier.

"I was the youngest of the eight children. I quit school in the ninth grade and went to work at Susquehanna Casting in Wrightsville. To my knowledge this foundry didn't have any war contracts. It continued to make what I'd call trinkets, little things you'd put in your house. After tending to that cupola, I soon knew that I had no desire to make foundry work a career. No way! No, sir!

"Before I joined the service, I had three brothers who were in the Army. Lloyd ['Lem'] was in Europe and was wounded; Charles ['Chise'] was in the combat engineers, and, although he never talked about it, I guess he saw combat; and Warren ['Wazzy'] put thirty years in the service but was never in combat. I don't remember my parents ever talking about the fact that they had three sons in the Army. I know they were proud of it because in the window my mother hung the flag with the three stars on it.

"It was in the middle of October 1945 when I got my draft classification. Even though the war was over, I guess they were still drafting men for the Army of Occupation. Anyway, instead of waiting to be drafted, I decided to join the Regular Army for an eighteen-month hitch because my understanding was that if you waited to be drafted, you could be in for six months to six years before you'd get out. I couldn't wait to go in! Something just told me I needed to get in. Maybe it was because I already had had three brothers who served. There was no pressure on me to join —nowhere, no way. But I was sort of excited. The service offered me a new life because I'd be farther away from home than ever before. Up to the time I joined, I don't think I'd been any further from home than York or Lancaster.

"I signed up in York and was processed in Harrisburg. From there I went briefly to Ft. Meade, Maryland, and then I took my basic training at Ft. McClellan, Alabama. We took infantry basic training, and it was very short. It only lasted about six or seven weeks.

From Ft. McClellan, Bill went to Ft. Dix, New Jersey, for transit to Germany in December 1945 as part of the US Army of Occupation. For him at the time, it was the beginning of a new adventure:

"Even though I didn't know what to expect, it was thrilling to say, 'I'm going over to Germany!' We got on board what they called a Liberty ship, and it was small and slow. We landed at Le Havre in France and stayed just a short time there. This is where I saw my first starving children. I said to myself, 'What in the world is going on here?' There were kids trying to get food out of these cans. I had never before seen anything like that. Around Wrightsville everybody had plenty of food, so to see these kids digging around in cans was disheartening.

Bill stayed in Le Havre for just a brief time. On 11 January 1946, he was assigned to A Troop, 25th Mechanized Cavalry, and received his permanent assignment at Regensburg, Germany. His unit's primary duty was to make extended forays into the various towns outside the city in an effort to show an American presence among the civilian population. Bill's comments on the conduct of the German civilians indicate a certain compliance and resignation to the American occupation of their country:

"When we got there, Regensburg was just a shell. There was nothing there but walls of buildings, maybe a chimney sticking up here or there. Everything was gutted out. There were windows with no panes or frames. Everything was gone. All that you'd see of buildings was whatever was made of mortar and cement blocks. The inner city was just gutted; there was nothing there. There was nowhere for us to go in town. Everybody had sort of moved to the outskirts of town, so those areas were pretty heavily populated. Anywhere they could find a room was taken by them, so that's where they would mostly live. I don't know whether or not they had electricity and running water. In Regensburg we never had any trouble. I personally never had a bad word said to me or any instance where anybody tried to give me trouble—nowhere. Not one person ever gave me a rough time. They were nice to us; they were good to us. Some of our guys weren't nice to them, but I always was. I've never been one of these rough-and-tumble guys.

"Our barrack was right on the outskirts of the town. This barrack that we occupied had formerly been occupied by the German army. They called it the Regensburg *Kaserne*, which I believe is the German word for barrack. It was built in a circle. In the center was a parade ground, and then the buildings were halfway or three-quarters of the way around. Inside a barrack there were big rooms with maybe eight to ten bunks in each one. In fact, these German military barracks were nicer than the ones we had back in the States. On one side of the American area was a Polish outfit, and on the other side of us was a black outfit. There wasn't much contact between the black troops and our unit, and what contact there was wasn't too friendly. We just stayed away from each other. They didn't bother us, and we didn't bother them. I don't remember any blacks ever coming into our club. I'm sure they had their own club. The Polish outfit hated the Germans, but we personally never had any trouble with them. They mostly guarded prison camps in the area, and these camps held a lot of SS troopers.

"We were actually put into what was called the 25th Constabulary, and I was an armored car driver. Although we were stationed in Regensburg, every couple months we would go to a town maybe fifty or sixty miles from there—anywhere around the perimeter. We would take our armored cars and Jeeps, and we'd just take over a town and perform our duties. The local population knew that we were there, and we didn't have trouble with anybody. We were supposed to put on a show of force. We'd patrol these towns, and whoever was in charge of our group—there were no officers, so it might it might have been a sergeant—had to find the *burgermeister* of every town that we occupied. We then had to get his signature to acknowledge that we had visited this town. They weren't so sure of what they were signing. Some thought they were admitting to being a Nazi by signing this paper. Of course, nobody in these towns ever admitted to being a Nazi. We'd usually patrol a town for thirty days, and we'd stay in that town the whole time. Every town had a little building of some kind, such as a hotel, where an Army post would be established. Anywhere we could find a place to house maybe a platoon of men, we would take it over and stay there. The purpose of these patrols was just to let the Germans know that we were there and in charge: 'You are still under occupation, which you will be for years to come. Who knows? Maybe we'll be here indefinitely.' We had our sidearms, mostly .45-caliber Colt semiautomatics, or carbines. Some guys, maybe the guys driving the Jeeps, carried their rifles. So, we had to go in these towns and check them out. Most of these towns, if they had 3,000, 4,000, or 5,000 people, had their own little brewery, and most had started brewing again. I loved that German beer. That beer was good! It was the best! So, all in all, these patrols were fun. We had a good time.

"The Germans were all good to us; they were all nice. In these little towns they caused us no trouble. They just went their way and did their thing. They did a little agricultural work because most of these were farming communities. They would take their wagons and go through one end of town to get to their fields. We never had any trouble with anybody. Nobody tried to give us a rough time or thought the war was still going on. I guess they thought, 'Get this damned thing [military occupation] over and let us get back to our normal lives.' They certainly didn't want any more war. They didn't want to fight you and raise a fuss or anything. They just wanted to get back to their farming and back to their factories. We never found any weapons. I guess they knew to get rid of the guns because if we did find them it would mean big trouble. We really never had any trouble with Germans on these patrols. It probably helped us that for the most part these towns were located in the boondocks and had mainly been untouched by the war. Maybe some GIs had gone through some of these towns to get to Berlin, but there was no damage in these towns. All in all we had a good relationship with them.

"In general, I think the Army of Occupation treated the German civilians well. We didn't bother them, and they didn't bother us.

Some German civilians worked on the post at Regensburg. They were employed as maintenance people, and a lot of them worked in our kitchens. They also painted buildings and kept them in repair. They liked the kitchen positions because they got their meals that way, and they got paid a few dollars. I don't think our cooks bothered them too much. The cooks knew that some of the food was being smuggled out—a couple cans of this, a couple cans of that—but they didn't care.

"I have another interesting story that occurred on one of these patrols to a small town about fifty or sixty miles out from Regensburg. There was a little police station there, and out in front on the side, in about a six-by-six feet circular field, was a big concrete swastika. It was a big swastika. It was maybe about six inches thick, and it was around four or five feet in circumference. Our commanding officer said, 'Crumbling, get that swastika out of here.' So, somehow, I found a sledgehammer and a wheelbarrow. I brought up the sledgehammer and the wheelbarrow, and when a German came down the street, I'd motion to them with the sledgehammer and say, 'Hey! Break up that thing!' So, he'd stand there and break a little bit of the cement off it. This cement swastika did not have any steel reinforcement rods embedded in it, so that made it easier to break it apart. I could detect that they didn't like to break up this swastika, I guess in case there were still some die-hard Nazis around. But they'd break up a little, and I'd then say, 'Okay! Go!' He'd go and then another German would come around, and I'd make him put the broken pieces in the wheelbarrow. He'd load up the wheelbarrow, and then I'd have another one take the rubble to the designated place, which was an open lot out a block-and-a-half down, and dump it at the end of town. He'd bring back the wheelbarrow, and I'd have them repeat this process all afternoon. This took all day, so I had to do no work. They beat this swastika to bits. I'd have one to break it up, one to load it, one to carry it, and one to empty it. So, it took me three or four hours to get the job done. Nobody said a word. That was the only symbol of Nazism that I ever saw on these patrols, and for some reason, no one ever bothered to destroy it before we appeared.

When Bill was not out on patrols to nearby villages with his unit, he was assigned various work details where he supervised SS troops:

"We guarded a lot of SS troopers, whose prison camp wasn't too far from Regensburg. It was just like any other POW camp. It was a big area with barbed wire all around it. The SS troops had things organized and more or less ran their own game inside the camp. They continued to wear their own uniforms because we weren't going to dress them in GI clothes. From time to time the Allied authorities would release a bunch of twenty or thirty privates and corporals, but they detained indefinitely the really bad guys. My unit was like policemen or patrolmen, and the higher-ups would use us for whatever needed to be done.

Despite Army regulations to the contrary, American troops fraternized with German women and engaged in black market activities in postwar Germany:

"Well, we weren't supposed to fraternize, but that was like telling you not to drink water when you're thirsty. We certainly fraternized, but the Army authorities never bothered us. We had a club in downtown Regensburg, so there were German girls coming and going. The girls were there in town for you. That club was a source for them to get their candy and cigarettes. Maybe you'd have a little food for them. So, you had a date when you went into town, and we would dance with them. Everybody was sort of tight-lipped about what they did when they dated. Whether anybody had sex with them, nobody would comment too much about that. I guess some guys had steady girlfriends, but it wasn't always possible because we were on the move most of the time.

"You had a lot of people from all over Europe coming in. I knew one girl from Latvia, and she was hunting for a place to live, to work, to make a living, and have enough for food and clothing. Since there wasn't anything for them at home, they would come to an area where they thought the GIs were so they could get food, money, and clothing. That's what they were after.

"I don't think that venereal disease was too much of a problem in Regensburg. I knew of only one guy who had syphilis, but with penicillin you could get four or five—maybe ten or fifteen—shots, and then you'd be cured. All you had to do was go to the first sergeant's office or to the officer of the day and get some condoms. You'd go in there, and they'd urge you to take them because they always had plenty of condoms around. In fact, we used to use condoms to 'blouse' our trousers. You'd put your pants up and then roll them down, so you'd look like a paratrooper. They'd raise hell: 'They're not for blousin'! They're for usin'!' So, we'd get hell for that.

"I never got into much of the black market. Like I said, we had a Polish outfit on one side of us in Regensburg. One day this American soldier came down and said, 'Do you have any cigarettes that you want to sell?' I said, 'Not necessarily. Why do you want them?' He said, "Do you want to make some money? This Polish outfit next door will give you $100 for a carton of cigarettes.' So, I took a carton down there where they were standing along their fence. I said, 'Do you want to buy?' They said, 'Yeah! Yeah!' So, I got $100 for this carton of cigarettes. Now, if you had maybe somebody in the States send you, say, ten cartons of cigarettes a month, that's $1,000 a month that you could have made, but then we were only allowed to send a certain amount of money back home at that time. That was the only time I ever sold anything on the black market. I really didn't have much opportunity to do it because we were in and out of Regensburg so much.

"Cigarettes were for bartering because this was like money for the Germans. They would sell you something for a carton of cigarettes, and then they'd sell the cigarettes to some other guy. We'd also bargain with them in exchange for chocolate or food that we had. The Germans really loved chocolate. If you could get some extra coffee, that, too, was like gold because they couldn't get any coffee in town. Our mess sergeant had a girlfriend at the end of town, and every night we'd see him going there with a little bagful of stuff. I guess he was keeping somebody in town, his girlfriend or maybe her whole family. Soap was also a good bartering tool. It was a big thing to the Germans. Like, they'd do your wash for a couple bars of soap. That was a good deal to them, and they loved that. As you know, Germans are a clean people. Boy! As soon as they could get soap, that was better than money. It often took the place of money.

"I do remember a guy from Wrightsville who evidently participated heavily in the black market. We were in Bremerhaven about a day before we were to ship out, and I was standing in line for dinner. So, I'm standing there, and I'm thinking, 'Damn! I know that guy standing there!' This guy was a master sergeant or something, and I said to myself, 'Oh, hell! That's 'Snake' [Edwin] Blessing!' He might have been about twenty of twenty-five feet from me, so I yelled, 'Hey, 'Snake!' Nobody looked around, so I yelled again: 'Hey, 'Snake' Blessing!' Then he looked around, and I said, 'Hi, 'Snake.' How're you doing? Come over here!' So, we sat down to eat after we got our food. 'Snake' was Regular Army. He was a twenty-five-year man. 'Snake' told me he was on a black market mission. He actually told me that. This was his second time over to Germany. He had been over for combat, went home, and then came back for the occupation. He said, 'I'm over here to make money. I'm over here on a black market mission. I'm going to get into the black market.' So, he went back over just to buy and sell stuff. In the occupation you had a chance to make some money if you had stuff there or had somebody back in the States send it to you.

As part of his German adventure, Bill also had occasion to observe first-hand the Nazi extermination camp at Dachau:

"One time they gave me a colonel to take from Regensburg to Dachau, which was near Munich. He was a full colonel, and I think he was in the SS. I don't know why they were taking him to Dachau. They just gave me a folder with his papers in it and said, 'Take him to Dachau, drop him off, and then come back.' Another guy was driving this 'six-by-six' [six-wheel-drive truck], and I was armed with a .45 and had this colonel sitting where I could see him.

"So, we took him to Dachau and pulled inside. All I had was his paperwork in a brown, sealed envelope. When we pulled over, I gave him some cigarettes to smoke, and he moved from the front to the back of the truck. The people at Dachau knew he was coming; I'm sure of that. So, we went in and gave this guy the paperwork, and then these GIs just grabbed the colonel and threw him off the back of the truck. Man! He hit the ground, and I thought, 'What the hell is this?' I didn't say that out loud, of course. He bounced when he hit the ground, and I was thinking, 'These guys must be combat guys!' Here I was, giving him cigarettes and treating him like an officer, but they just grabbed him, threw him off, and shoved him through a doorway and into a building there.

"I knew a little about Dachau, so I asked a guy if I could look around a little bit. He pointed and said, 'Go in there.' All the ovens were in this building. They were all cleaned, but they were all open in a room about twice the size of double-wide manufactured home. There were maybe fifteen, twenty, twenty-five of these ovens in a line and around in like a circle. It looked like each oven was big enough to shove body inside. How deep they were, I don't know, but I'd guess they were seven or eight feet deep. So, I walked around the whole thing and viewed it, but I didn't go around to any of the other places. There was no stench of death, but then this was seven or eight months after Dachau was liberated. But it made me think. I knew that there were people who died in there. Were they dead when they threw them in? Was anybody just unconscious when they threw them in? Were they burned alive? You don't know this. It made me think, a crematorium like that. How could people do something like that to another human being—just throwing them in?

By the time his enlistment was about to end, Bill was ready to get out of the Army and return to Wrightsville:

"As my time was wearing down, I was ready to come home. I was twenty-and-a-half when I came home. I wanted to get back to where I could cock my leg up at a bar and have a drink instead of sitting at a table as we had to do in Germany. I had signed up for a year-and-a-half.

"The day before we came home, three or four of us went down to the PX and bought some Aqua Velva shaving lotion to drink on the way to the train station. Then we bought two bottles of Four Roses whiskey. Drinking that Aqua Velva will give you a quick drunk. We got on that train, and I never did see anymore Aqua Velva because I was 'loaded [drunk].' I never saw any of the Four Roses, either. So, I didn't remember anything until we got to Bremerhaven. I was still drunk or hung over, and I was dragging my duffel bag. It took maybe a couple or three blocks to get from the train station to our ship, and, all of a sudden, I had a hole in my bag. When I got to the ship, half my clothes were laying all over the dock. All I had was a couple pairs of shorts, a pair of pants, and a shirt. I had nothing else to bring home. So, I went over with nothing, and I almost came back with nothing. Coming home, I was on KP duty again."

After returning to civilian life, Bill eventually married and spent a career as a long-distance truck driver. Since retirement he has become an active member of the Locust Street Methodist Church in Wrightsville. He and his wife live a few miles outside Wrightsville.

Notes

1. William Crumbling, Interview with the author, 7 August 1998, transcript, OH1260, Oral History Collection, University Archives, University of North Texas, Denton, TX.

CONCLUSIONS

"HOME"

For Wrightsville's veterans, whether they served overseas or stateside, home is what they all thought about during their time in the military. In a sense, "home" became a kind of refuge after the initial shock of induction into an unfamiliar military as its alien culture enveloped them. Home was what they used as a kind of yardstick to measure the rigors of military life. Their first shock probably came in the pre-dawn hours of basic training or boot camp as drill instructors yelled at them to awaken. Soon every feature of their civilian lives—birthdays, clothing, family meals, recreation—disappeared into a system deliberately designed to produce the GI. Now, close-order drill, group punishment, and military etiquette became part of their daily routine. All that these young men and women had absorbed during a lifetime at home disappeared as the military trained and prepared them for combat.

Then combat left its own indelible mark on the GI's vision of home. Throughout Europe and the Pacific, American service personnel were exposed to the horrors of modern warfare, and human suffering placed home in a completely different perspective. As the war dragged on, and as casualties and exhaustion decimated the ranks, home was seen as a sanctuary from war's carnage. In this context, home meant clean sheets, home-cooked meals, comfort, and a real sense of gratitude from people for a job well done.

With the coming of victory, the troops overseas and stateside celebrated with gusto. Once the festivities ended, however, happiness was replaced by a sense of impatience. "When do we go home?" "How soon will we leave this pesthole and go home?" Thus began the clamor for redeployment home. In barracks and tent cities as well as aboard ships at sea, servicemen waited impatiently for their names to appear on lists tacked onto central bulletin boards that would set their homecoming in motion. The return for most homeward bound men depended on their position in the military's point system.

So, what was "home" like for the veterans as they returned to Wrightsville? Unlike many other towns and cities throughout the United States, the physical structure of Wrightsville did not change very much as a result of the war. There was no marked influx of persons seeking defense-related jobs, for the workforce in the foundries was already in place since it was made up of older, married men with families, men not therefore subject to the draft. With no increase in population, there were no strains placed on the existing school system and infrastructure, nor were there shortages in housing as was the case for numerous boomtowns during World War II. Even with the return of the veterans, Wrightsville's population in 1950 was about the same as it had been in 1940, and it remained an overwhelmingly white Anglo-Saxon Protestant town. The war had no effect on the numbers of African Americans residing in town. What few remained were almost all elderly couples, and the school system had no black children enrolled in the postwar years. As before the war, the very small African-American minority remained almost invisible.

The one distinct change that the returning veterans did discover in Wrightsville was a new-found sense of prosperity on the part of those civilians who had had steady work and made good wages due to the war effort. During the Great Depression, most residents of Wrightsville had very little money to spend, and during the war their purchasing power was restricted due to the rationing of civilian goods. With the end of the war, American industry resumed the production of civilian goods, and the pent-up demand for these items led to the widespread purchase of new houses, automobiles, and household appliances. Many veterans were astonished by the large number of people who owned automobiles in Wrightsville after the war as opposed to the few who owned them before the war.

The attitudes of local women toward work changed as a result of their experiences during the war. Historians of the home front during World War II argue that the conflict provided a stimulant for the later women's movement beginning the 1960s and 1970s, but it would be an exaggeration to apply that observation to the women of Wrightsville. For some who had worked in the defense industry or who had served in the military, World War II did create a thin wedge that they expected to pry open for additional opportunities and a change in status once peace came. It was after the war when the women of Wrightsville sought employment avenues beyond the sewing and cigar factories and silk mills, although some did return to those jobs. Homemaking was no longer considered a necessarily acceptable option for them. During the postwar years, for example, many more women obtained employment in non-molding positions in the local foundries.[1] After dismissal from their defense-related jobs as the war wound down, others looked for similar work with industries in Columbia, York, and Lancaster. Whether they sought new avenues of employment or returned to the traditional jobs open to women in Wrightsville, they encouraged their daughters to aspire to higher goals and new careers.

For the veterans themselves, they returned as changed men. They entered the service as immature young boys, but the war forced them to grow up fast. During their time in the military, they matured as they learned what real toughness was. They came back to Wrightsville with a feeling of pride in what they had contributed toward winning the war, and they appreciated the welcome they received from the town's citizens. Their experiences during the war gave them a new sense of self-worth after being battered about by the Great Depression. Most saw service in World War II as an unpleasant interruption, and they were now ready to return to civilian life and get on with the job of making a fulltime living for perhaps the first time in their lives. The images of combat quickly faded. Most did not dwell very long on their battlefield experiences, and very few had problems adjusting again to life in Wrightsville. To the contrary, they went about the business of securing the American Dream: job security, marriage, buying a home, raising a family, and having a pension. If they did not find satisfactory work in Wrightsville, they commuted to jobs in Columbia, Lancaster, or York. Surprisingly, few veterans took advantage of the educational opportunities offered by the GI Bill of Rights. This omission occurred because, after so many years of unemployment or partial employment during the Depression, they were eager to get about the business of making a living as soon as possible during the good economic times after the war.

Events of the late 1960s and 1970s, not World War II, transformed Wrightsville. By that time the cigar and garment factories as well as the silk mills had disappeared. Due to a combination of mismanagement, failure to produce new products, slowness in adopting current technology, and an inability to compete, Wrightsville Hardware and Susquehanna Casting barely limped along. Eventually, Susquehanna Casting went out of business, while Wrightsville Hardware was bought by Electro Platers of York. Riverside Foundry, on the other hand, was much more nimble. It employed the latest foundry technology, produced new products according to market conditions, and continued sound management practices. Riverside Foundry today is known as Donsco ["Don's Company"], a name derived from its longtime proprietor Donald Smith. During the postwar years, Donsco expanded to the point where its ongoing operations in Wrightsville and other nearby communities had created an entity that was bigger than all three of the old foundries combined.

By the end of the 1970s, Wrightsville had become a bedroom town as people found better paying jobs in Lancaster and York. Wrightsville was no longer a self-contained community. In addition to the demise of the old industries, most retail businesses also disappeared because they could not compete with the "big box" stores located in York and Lancaster. No longer were there hardware stores, clothing shops, lumberyards, and meat markets. Due to public school consolidation in the late 1950s, Wrightsville lost its local high school. Trains no longer passed through Wrightsville, and in March 1963 the Pennsylvania Railroad Company dismantled the iron bridge, which had been built in 1897. With the coming of the Interstate Highway System, much vehicular traffic bypassed Wrightsville. Although the old Lancaster-York Intercounty Bridge (now known as Veterans Memorial Bridge) is still in service and used heavily by local residents, a new four-lane, steel and concrete bridge was built farther north in 1969 with money from the National Highway Trust Fund. This bridge routed vehicles around Wrightsville to connect with the Interstate System. Today the population of Wrightsville numbers around 2,200, which is about what it was in 1940.

Wrightsville still remains very much a river town. The two bridges provide conduits across the Susquehanna for motor vehicles, and many residents continue to use the sidewalk on Veterans Memorial Bridge for exercise. People still use the river for hunting, fishing, boating, and other forms of recreation. Particularly during the spring and summer months, the river is a magnet drawing tourists to admire the beauty of the Susquehanna Valley, and numerous festivals, celebrations, and fun runs are held in connection with the river. To promote tourism Wrightsville has joined two nearby river towns, Columbia and Marietta, to form Rivertownes PA. With the demise of much of the Pennsylvania steel and coal industries and the modernization of waste water and sewage treatment plants, old-timers contend that the Susquehanna today is cleaner than at any time during their memories. On the other hand, runoff from commercial fertilizers (phosphates and nitrates) coming into the river from agricultural land still presents an environmental problem for the Susquehanna as well as the Chesapeake Bay. As has been the case since the coming of the earliest inhabitants, the Susquehanna continues to influence the lives of all who have lived along its banks, including the river town of Wrightsville.

Notes

1. During the war two Wrightsville women took jobs as riveters assembling Corsair fuselages at the Armstrong Cork and Rubber Company in Lancaster, Pennsylvania. After the war they both found employment at local foundries. See Mary Jane Dellinger, interview by the author, 26 May 2000, transcript, OH1345, Oral History Collection, University Archives, University of North Texas, Denton, TX; and Corenna Smeltzer (née Young), interview by the author, 11 August 1999, transcript, OH1308, Oral History Collection, University Archives, University of North Texas, Denton, TX. Corenna Smeltzer's interview was not included in this book.

BIBLIOGRAPHY

Primary Sources

PUBLISHED DOCUMENTS

"Commander in Chief, US Pacific Fleet and Pacific Ocean Areas Report," Serial 0395, 11 February 1946, World War Command File, Operational Archives Branch, Naval Historical Center, Washington, DC.

Navy Department, Office of Chief of Naval Operations, Naval History Division. *Dictionary of American Naval Fighting Ships.* 8 vols. Washington, DC: GPO, 1968-1991.

US Department of Commerce. Bureau of the Census. *Total Population of Ten Congested Population Areas: 1944.* Series CA-1, no. 11. Washington, DC: GPO, 1944.

———. *15th Census of the US, 1930.* Washington, DC: GPO, 1930.

Wrightsville Borough Municipal Authority. *Wrightsville Borough Council Minutes, 1942-1944.*

NEWSPAPER CLIPPINGS

York Dispatch and *York Gazette and Daily* (PA), 1941-1945. Personal scrapbook of Geraldine Forry (née Keller).

ORAL HISTORY INTERVIEWS

University Archives, University of North Texas, Denton, TX

Blouse, Glenn. Interview by Ronald E. Marcello, 3 August 1998. Transcript, OH1262.

Bock, Leonard. Interview by Ronald E. Marcello, 7 August 1997. Transcript, OH1193.

Crumbling, Lloyd. Interview by Ronald E. Marcello, 9 August 1997. Transcript, OH1187.

Crumbling, William. Interview by Ronald E. Marcello, 7 August 1998. Transcript, OH1260.

Dellinger, Mary Jane. Interview by Ronald E. Marcello, 26 May 2000. Transcript, OH1345.

Forry, Alfred. Interview by Ronald E. Marcello, 12 August 1998. Transcript, OH1261.

Garver, Mervin. Interview by Ronald E. Marcello, 6 August 1999. Transcript, OH1309.

Hake, Charles, K. Interview by Ronald E. Marcello, 9 August 2000. Transcript, OH1361.

Haugh, Mervin. Interview by Ronald E. Marcello, 31 May 1999. Transcript, OH1298.

Haugh, William M. Interview by Ronald E. Marcello, 12 January 1999. Transcript, OH1290.

Johns, Gerald and Irmgard Johns (née Stieger). Interview by Ronald E. Marcello, 11 August 1997. Transcript, OH1200.

Leber, Pauline. Interview by Ronald E. Marcello, 9 October 1998. Transcript, OH1266.

Marcello, Alfred J., Jr. Interview by Ronald E. Marcello, 7 August 2000. Transcript, OH1356.

McCune (née Myers), Evelyn. Interview by Ronald E. Marcello, 4 August 1996. Transcript, OH1148.

Peters, Donald W. Interview by Ronald E. Marcello, 6 August 1998. Transcript, OH1273.

Reisinger, Edward L. Interview by Ronald E. Marcello, 5 August 1999. Transcript, OH1312.

Siler, Elmira Jane (née Bock). Interview by Ronald E. Marcello, 12 August 2000. Transcript, OH1359.

Smeltzer, Corenna (née Young). Interview by Ronald E. Marcello, 11 August 1999. Transcript, OH1308.

Smith, Donald M. Interview by Ronald E. Marcello, 12 August 1996. Transcript, OH1147.

Snyder, Jacob W. Interview by Ronald E. Marcello, 8 August 1999. Transcript, OH1310.

Yeager, Charles W. Interview by Ronald E. Marcello, 4 August 1998. Transcript, OH1254.

Secondary Sources

BOOKS

Alexander, Joseph H. *Utmost Savagery: The Three Days of Tarawa.* Annapolis, MD: Naval Institute Press, 1995.

Alford, Kenneth D. *Nazi Plunder: The Great Treasure Stories of World War II.* New York: Da Capo Press, 1991.

Ambrose, Stephen. *Citizen Soldiers: The US Army from the Beaches of Normandy to the Bulge to the Surrender of Germany, June 7, 1944-May 7, 1945.* New York: Simon & Schuster, 1997.

———. *D-Day June 6, 1944: The Climactic Battle of World War II.* New York: Simon & Schuster, 1994.

Atkinson, Rick. *An Army at Dawn: The War in North Africa, 1942-1943.* New York: Henry Holt & Company, 2002.

———. *The Day of Battle: The War in Sicily and Italy, 1943-1944.* New York: Henry Holt & Company, 2007.

______. *The Guns at Last Light: The War in Western Europe, 1944-1945.* New York: Henry Holt & Co., 2013.

Belote, James, and William Belote. *Typhoon of Steel: The Battle for Okinawa.* New York: Harper and Row, 1970.

Blum, John M. *V Was for Victory: Politics and American Culture during World War II.* New York: Harcourt-Brace, 1970.

Bordewich, Fergus M. *Bound for Canaan: The Underground Railroad and the War for the Soul of America.* New York: HarperCollins Publishers, 2005.

Brands, H. W. *Traitor to His Class: The Privileged Life and Radical Presidency of Franklin Delano Roosevelt.* New York: Doubleday, 2008.

Breuer, William. *The Invasion of Southern France.* Novato, CA: Presidio Press, 1988.

Brinkley, David. *Washington Goes to War.* New York: Alfred A. Knopf, 1988.

Burns, James MacGregor. *Roosevelt: The Soldier of Freedom.* New York: Harcourt-Brace, 1970.

Chandler, Lester V. *America's Greatest Depression, 1929-1941.* New York: Harper & Row, Publishers, 1970.

Collins, Michael and Martin King. *Voices of the Bulge: Untold Stories from Veterans of the Battle of the Bulge.* Minneapolis: Zenith Press, 2011.

Delaney, John P. *The Blue Devils in Italy, a History of the 88th Infantry Division.* Nashville, TN: Battery Press, 1988.

D'Este, Carlo. *Fatal Decision: Anzio and the Battle for Rome.* New York: HarperCollins Publishers, 1991.

———. *World War II in the Mediterranean, 1942-1945.* Chapel Hill, NC: Algonquin Books of Chapel Hill, 1990.

———. *Decision in Normandy.* New York: HarperPerennial, 1994.

Doubler, Michael B. *Closing with the Enemy: How GIs Fought the War in Europe, 1944-1945.* Lawrence: Univ. Press of Kansas, 1994.

———. "The Travails of the American Combat Soldier in Europe." In *Major Problems in the History of World War II: Documents and Essays,* edited by Mark A. Stoler and Melanie S. Gustafson. New York: Houghton Mifflin Company, 2003.

Dower, John W. *War without Mercy: Race and Power in the Pacific War.* New York: Pantheon Books, 1986.

Edsforth, Ronald. *The New Deal: America's Response to the Great Depression.* Malden, MA: Blackwell Publishers, 2000.

Fairchild, Louis. *They Called It the War Effort: Oral Histories from World War II Orange, Texas.* Austin, TX: Eakin Press, 1993.

Feifer, George. *Tennozan: The Battle of Okinawa and the Atomic Bomb.* New York: Ticknor and Fields, 1992.

Freeman, Roger A. *The Mighty Eighth: A History of the Units, Men, and Machines of the US 8th Air Force.* London: Cassell & Co., 1970.

Fussell, Paul. *Wartime: Understanding and Behavior in the Second World War.* New York: Oxford Univ. Press, 1989.

Goedde, Petra. *GIs and Germans: Culture, Gender, and Foreign Relations, 1945-1949.* New Haven: Yale Univ. Press, 2003.

Goldberg, Harold J. *D-Day in the Pacific: The Battle of Saipan.* Bloomington: Indiana Univ. Press, 2007.

Green, Michael and James D. Brown. *War Stories of the Battle of the Bulge.* Minneapolis: Zeneth Press, 2010.

Grew, Joseph C. *Turbulent Era: A Diplomatic Record of Forty Years, 1904-1945.* Boston: Houghton Mifflin, 1952.

Hapgood, David and David Richardson. *Monte Cassino.* New York: Congdon & Weed, Inc., 1984.

Herman, Arthur. *Freedom's Forge: How American Business Produced Victory in World War II.* New York: Random House, 2012.

Hess, Gary R. *The United States at War, 1941-1945.* Arlington Heights, IL: Harlan Davidson, 2000.

Hibbert, Christopher. *Il Duce: The Life of Benito Mussolini.* Boston: Little, Brown and Company, 1962.

Holm, Jeanne M. *In Defense of a Nation: Servicewomen in World War II.* Arlington, VA: Military Women's Press, 1997.

Humphrey, Robert E. *Once Upon a Time in War: The 99th Division in World War II.* Norman: Univ. of Oklahoma Press, 2008.

Keil, Sally Van Wagenen. *Those Wonderful Women in Their Flying Machines: The Unknown Heroines of World War II.* New York: Rawson, Wade Publishers, 1979.

Kennedy, David. *Freedom from Fear: The American People in Depression and War, 1929-1945.* New York: Oxford Univ. Press, 1999.

Kindsvatter, Peter S. *American Soldiers: Ground Combat in the World Wars, Korea, and Vietnam.* Lawrence: Univ. Press of Kansas, 2003.

Kirkpatrick, Ivone. *Mussolini: A Study in Power.* New York: Hawthorne Books, 1964.

Kleber, Brooks E. and Dale Birdsell. "The Chemical Warfare Service in World War II." In *The US Army in World War II.* Washington, DC: Office of the Chief of Military History, 1966.

Klein, Philip S. and Ari Hoogenboom. *A History of Pennsylvania.* University Park: The Pennsylvania State Univ. Press, 1980.

Leck, Greg. *Captives of Empire: The Japanese Internment of Allied Civilians in China and Hong Kong, 1941-1945.* Bangor, PA: Shandy Press, 2006.

Leder, Jane Mersky. *Thanks for the Memories: Love, Sex, and World War II.* Westport, CT: Praeger Publishers, 2006.

Linderman, Gerald F. *The World within War: America's Combat Experience in World War II.* New York: The Free Press, 1997.

Lingeman, Richard R. *Don't you Know There's a War Going On: The American Home Front, 1941-1945.* New York: G.P. Putnam's Sons, 1970.

Mansoor, Peter R. *The GI Offensive in Europe: The Triumph of American Infantry Divisions, 1941-1945.* Lawrence: Univ. Press of Kansas, 1999.

McManus, John C. *The Deadly Brotherhood: The American Combat Soldier in World War II.* Novato, CA: Presidio Press, 1998.

———. *The Americans at Normandy: The Summer of 1944—The American War from the Normandy Beaches to Falaise.* New York: Forge Books, 2004.

Miller, Marc. *The Irony of Victory: World War II and Lowell, Massachusetts.* Champagne: Univ. of Illinois Press, 1988.

Morison, Samuel Eliot. *The Two-Ocean War: A Short History of the United States Navy in the Second World War.* Boston: Little, Brown and Company, Inc., 1963.

O'Neill, Paul. *A Democracy at War: America's Fight at Home and Abroad in World War II.* New York: The Free Press, 1993.

Overy, Richard. *Why the Allies Won.* New York W.W. Norton & Co., 1996.

Pate, J'Nell. *Arsenal of Defense: Fort Worth's Military Legacy.* Denton, TX: Texas State Historical Association, 2011.

Perrett, Geoffrey. *Days of Sadness, Years of Triumph: The American People, 1939-1945.* New York: Coward, McCann, Geoghegan, Inc., 1973.

Polenburg, Richard. *War and Society: The United States, 1941-1945.* Philadelphia: J. B. Lippincott Company, 1972.

Poor, Henry V. *History of the Railroads and Canals of the U.S.A.* New York: John H. Schultz & Company, 1860.

Poulous, Paula Nassen, ed. *A Woman's War, Too: Women in the Military in World War II.* Washington, DC: National Archives and Records Administration, 1966.

Saylor, Roger B. *The Railroads of Pennsylvania.* University Park: The Pennsylvania State Univ. Press, 1964.

Schom, Alan. *The Eagle and the Rising Sun: The Japanese-American War, 1941-1943.* New York: W. W. Norton & Co , 2004.

Shaw, Ronald E. *Canals for a Nation: The Canal Era in the United States, 1790-1860.* Lexington: The Univ. of Kentucky Press, 1990.

Spector, Ronald H. *Eagle against the Sun: The American War with Japan.* New York: The Free Press, 1985.

Spinney, Robert G. *World War II in Nashville: Transformation of the Homefront.* Knoxville: Univ. of Tennessee Press, 1998.

Stoler, Mark A. and Melanie S. Gustafson, eds. *Major Problems in the History of World War II: Documents and Essays.* New York: Houghton Mifflin Company, 2003.

Taafe, Stephen R. *MacArthur's Jungle War: The 1944 New Guinea Campaign.* Lawrence, KS: Univ. Press of Kansas, 1998

Tomblin, Barbara B. *With Utmost Spirit: Allied Naval Operations in the Mediterranean, 1942-1945.* Lexington, KY: Univ. of Kentucky Press, 2004.

Willenz, June A. *Women Veterans: America's Forgotten Heroines.* New York: Continuum, 1983.

Willoughby, John. *Remaking the Conquering Heroes: The Post War Occupation of Germany.* New York: Palgrave-St. Martin's Press, 2001.

Winkler, Allan M. *Home Front U.S.A.: America during World War II.* Arlington Heights, IL: Harlan Davidson, Inc., 1986.

Ziemke, Earle F. *The U.S. Army in the Occupation of Germany, 1944-1946.* Washington, DC: US Department of Defense, Department of the Army, Center of Military History, 1975.

PAMPHLETS AND BOOKLETS

Historic Wrightsville Association, Inc. "Historic Lime Kilns of Wrightsville, PA." Wrightsville, PA: Historic Wrightsville, Inc., n.d.

Historical Committee. *Wrightsville's Book of Facts.* York, PA: H. O. Birnstock, Trimmer Printing Company, 1923.

Lehman, Donald. *Wrightsville, 1736-1976: Gateway to the West.* Wrightsville, PA: Historic Wrightsville Association, Inc., 1976.

Shank, William H. *Historic Bridges of Pennsylvania.* York, PA: Buchart-Horn, 1966.

———. *The Amazing Pennsylvania Canals.* York, PA: The Historical Society of York County, 1965.

Wrightsville High School Alumni 100th Anniversary, 1895-1995.

MISCELLANEOUS

Able, Poff, Leitheiser American Legion Post 469, Wrightsville, PA. Cemetery Records.

Index